VARIETIES OF MARXISM

THE VAN LEER JERUSALEM FOUNDATION SERIES

VARIETIES OF MARXISM

edited by

SHLOMO AVINERI

MARTINUS NIJHOFF / THE HAGUE / 1977

SET IN ISRAEL BY ISRATYPESET, JERUSALEM

PRINTED IN THE NETHERLANDS

CONTENTS

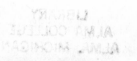

PREFACE

The essays included in this volume are based on papers delivered at the International Symposium on Varieties of Marxism, held at the Van Leer Jerusalem Foundation on June 16–19, 1974, and dedicated to the memory of George Lichtheim. When the idea of such a symposium was first raised, the organizers planned to have George Lichtheim as one of the main speakers at the event. In our last and brief meeting in London, I suggested this to him and Lichtheim gave his consent to attend the symposium, though at that time no date was yet fixed. His tragic death a few months later left a gap not only in the program of the symposium but in Marxist studies generally; it was felt that perhaps one way of paying tribute to his contribution to the study of a subject so near to his mind would be to name the symposium in his memory and devote an introductory paper to an attempt at an intellectual portrait of George Lichtheim as an historian of ideas.

The volume as published includes all papers delivered at the symposium, with the exception of the papers of J.L. Talmon (Jerusalem) on 'Marxism and Nationalism' and Gajo Petrović (Zagreb) on 'Yugoslav Marxism'. Appended is also a short obituary written by me on Lichtheim for the journal *Political Science* published by the American Political Science Association.

Contemporary history caught up with us at least on two instances during the planning and execution stages of the symposium. The Yom Kippur War of October 1973 almost caused us to postpone, if not cancel, the whole event: it broke out when most of our contributors were about to send in their papers, and the disruption in academic life in Israel (universities were closed for a whole trimester), made it doubtful whether we would be able to hold the symposium as originally scheduled. But after many deliberations and in line with the general atmosphere of bringing university life back to normal as soon as possible, we decided to go ahead as planned. Consequently, some of the papers presented by Israeli contributors were written while their authors were still on active reserve duty in the Israel Defence Forces – and

the list of our Israeli participants includes, among others, a tank officer, a paratrooper, a military correspondent, two intelligence officers,
a field educational officer. Few countries, one would have to admit,
have Marxian scholars who engage in such activities.

Our second brush with current events was slightly more comical.
When the date of the symposium approached, we learned that it
would coincide with the visit to the Middle East of then President
Richard Nixon. To our consternation and amusement, we found out
almost at the last moment that our opening session would occur
exactly at the time at which President Nixon was scheduled to pay an
official visit to the residence of the President of Israel, Professor
Ephraim Katzir. It so happens that the Presidential Residence in Jerusalem is immediately adjacent to the Van Leer Jerusalem Foundation
where the symposium was to take place, and the whole area was to be
cordoned-off and closed to traffic for security reasons for the whole
evening. We found ourselves at the risk of being unable to reach the
Van Leer building, and it took all the resilience of the organizers as
well as the good-natured cooperation of the Jerusalem Police Head-
quarters to find a way to make it possible for the participants to enter
the Van Leer Jerusalem Foundation more or less at the time when the
Presidential motorcade would pass by, with some of the security men
stationed on top of the Van Leer building which overlooks the Presidential Residence, slightly below it down Talbiyeh Hill. Some of the
participants may still keep as souvenirs the special permits issued most
incongruously by me, on Van Leer stationary and with the authority
of the Jerusalem Police, which permitted them to cross the police
barriers. Trivial as this incident may seem I am sure George Lichtheim
would have relished the irony of Marxian scholars cooperating with
the police so that President Nixon's peregrinations would not interfere
with their scholarly activities.

* * *

Our aim in this symposium as well as in the volume based on it, was
mainly that of confronting not only varities of Marxism but also
approaches and methods. Following Lichtheim's own methodology of
viewing Marxism in its double role as a historical phenomenon as well
as a theoretical problem, we tried to be as careful as possible in our
selection of subjects. While the papers of O'Malley, Kamenka, Rotenstreich, Jay and Yovel attempt to delineate a number of the philosophical parameters of Marxism, Knei-Paz, Fetscher, Spence, Schapiro,
Hellman, Kolatt, Shamir, Sivan, Golan, Pelczynski, Sprinzak and
Thomas try to deal, in different ways, with individual thinkers or with

Marxist movements or parties in a concrete historical and geographical context. Rubel raises a question of historical interpretation within the realm of the history of ideas, while Marian Sawer traces the ramifications of the problem of non-European models of development within various Marxist schools.

It is the scope of the issues and problems discussed here that attests both to the impact Marx and Marxism have had on world affairs and to the variety and diversity of the influences that went into the formation of Marxism as well as flowed out of it and have moulded the configurations of our present world. The obsolescence just as the vitality and richness of many aspects of Marxism clearly stand out in the pluralism of the ideas and issues discussed in this volume.

*   *   *

The idea of holding this symposium would have never materialised were it not for the assistance and imagination of Professor Yehuda Elkana, Director of the Van Leer Jerusalem Foundation, and I would like to thank him and his staff for their relentless effort on our behalf and for the facilities put at our disposal both for the symposium itself and for the consequent publication of its proceedings. The extremely generous contribution of the Van Leer Jerusalem Foundation was supplemented by grants from the Hebrew University of Jerusalem and the Israel Universities Study Group, and I would like to thank them on behalf of all concerned. Many thanks go to Mickey Blumberg for her resourcefulness and efficiency in smoothing out the many organizational problems involved in the planning and coordinating work connected with the symposium, and to Esther Shashar for her patient and invaluable editorial help. Last but not least, Shlomit Finkler of the American Friends of the Hebrew University was of especial help in many more ways than she probably imagined at the time.

S.A.

Jerusalem, May 30, 1977

GEORGE LICHTHEIM:
SKETCH FOR AN INTELLECTUAL PORTRAIT

GEORGE L. MOSSE
University of Wisconsin, Madison/The Hebrew University of Jerusalem

Why is this conference dedicated to George Lichtheim? Not, I think, because of his early journalistic work in Jerusalem, important as it was at the time, and not even because of the great impact of his personality upon all who knew him, but rather because of his contribution to Marxist scholarship. In all that has been written about George Lichtheim since his death, no intellectual portrait has emerged based upon his contribution to Marxist studies. But only such a portrait would do justice to his memory. I cannot write such a portrait here, but before a scholarly conference called in his name I must attempt to assemble some of the pieces which should go into such a portrait, and indicate what I believe were the main themes which informed his mind and his approach to Marxism. This is how George Lichtheim would liked to have been remembered, and this is the way he should live on in history.

What confused many of those who wrote about him since his death was the fact that Lichtheim refused to become a system builder, that much of his originality came in asides which were never properly followed up. Here he resembled his friend Franz Borkenau, but differed from many of his fellow scholars who could not quite grasp how the great historian of Marxism could fail to follow the example of the men and movements he analyzed so brilliantly. But Lichtheim believed that with the close of the 19th century the age of intellectual system-building had passed, and he might well have said with Hegel that "all unifying power had disappeared from the life of man."

Yet this attitude seems inconsistent with the fact that Lichtheim was a devoted Hegelian, and that his constant emphasis upon Hegel's method and system may well prove to be one of his most important legacies to modern scholarship. For he stood squarely in the tradition of those thinkers who after 1918 wanted to join Marxism and Philosophy once more: Karl Korsch whom he rather admired, and George

Lukács whom he came to despise. But unlike these men Lichtheim came from Marx to Hegel and not from Hegel to Marx. This fact is important, for it meant that he saw Hegel in the proper perspective, and this in turn led to his conviction that Hegelianism contained truths much beyond its Marxist interpretation, truths which must be accepted by the historian if he was to get history right. Lichtheim's attitude towards Hegel is perhaps best summed up through his condemnation of George Lukács: once the Hegelianism of *History and Class Consciousness* had been abandoned, Lukács exchanged analysis for apologetics. Lichtheim repeated often that while Hegel's system was the most important since Aristotle, it was, at the same time, the final synthesis of which Europe was capable. Small wonder that system-building was no longer possible after this final accomplishment.

Hegel was the last great European system-builder: for Lichtheim as for so many of his generation philosophising was confined to Europe. He never shared the widespread admiration for Mao's thought (which he called a medieval Hegelianism), nor the longing for the vigour of the United States. That country with its wealth and bustle seemed to him to have produced proportionately very little in the way of important thought and scholarship. To be sure, he really knew only New York and San Francisco, and was apt to confuse the New York Jewish intelligentsia with American intellectuality, but more fundamental attitudes were also involved.

Lichtheim believed that tradition mattered, indeed was vital for the progress of philosophy, and, after all, as he used to remark, it was Europe which had provided the laboratory for human thought. All else, in a sense, was commentary or imitation.

Europe formed and circumscribed his intellectual orientation, and yet it would be wrong to classify Lichtheim as a "central European intellectual," whatever that may mean. Unfortunately many of his obituaries did just this, especially in the Anglo-Saxon world. To be sure, there is Lichtheim's often polemical style, his refusal to be frivolous and clever, but there was also apart from Hegel a second decisive influence upon his mind which must not be forgotten: the French Enlightenment. Indeed his preference for France over Germany lay in his admiration for the Enlightenment which provided that unified view of life which he found lacking not only in his own time but in the German past as well where Lutheranism had torn it assunder. Moreover, the Enlightenment had made Hegel possible in the first place. Lichtheim took great delight in emphasizing that Marx received his true education in France rather than in Germany. Socialism for him was a projection into the 19th and 20th centuries of the 18th

century "party of humanity," whose dynamic came from the application of dialectical, critical thought to the fundamental principles of
rationality and justice. Such critical thought was of necessity individualistic. When he castigated Foundation grants which resulted in little,
he was in reality contrasting the creativity of the individual scholar to
the aridity of group research; reaffirming that individualism which (as
we shall see later) was close to the core of his faith. His stress upon the
Enlightenment base of Marx's thought, meant that he had no use for
those who transformed Marx into a romantic, an Old Testament prophet or The Red Prussian. Here in itself he made a major contribution
to our understanding of Marx, freeing him from the barnacles of a
liberalism which was apt to criticize all that departed from its norms
as irrational and romantic. France was George Lichtheim's reference
point, and only in the last years of his life did he discover in Jürgen
Habermas, and through him, in Theodor Adorno, contemporary
German thinkers with whom he could identify.

Here his pessimism about the modern world proved crucial. Lichtheim did depart from his models of Hegel and the Enlightenment
through his sense of the tragic in history. For example, socialism had
succeeded in nations where it was doomed to failure, and had failed in
nations where it might have succeeded. At times he did see the cunning of reason at work and the dialectic of victory and defeat. He
shared his pessimism with the Frankfurt School and this as well as
their Hegelianism seemed congenial. However, in the last resort, his
increasing sympathy for that School rested upon very narrow foundations: Lichtheim had no love for the integration of psychoanalysis
with philosophy, and was not interested in the culture criticism which
constituted one of the School's main activities. Instead, Lichtheim saw
rays of hope in world historical figures, especially in General de Gaulle
whom he fitted into this category for, in Hegelian fashion, the General presided over the modernization of France under an archaic arma-
ture. But above all, men like de Gaulle and Churchill opposed the two
forces which Lichtheim saw as the villains of the nineteenth and
twentieth centuries: positivism and populism.

Guided by the Enlightenment he shared the disdain of the crowd
with the Frankfurt School. He was the heir of Voltaire rather than
Rousseau. Solely the individual counted, and the very concept of "the
people" typified a process of de-humanization. Lichtheim had no use
for George Lukács's argument that the intellectual must join himself
to the working class if he is to avoid isolation, even if this means
engaging in polemics rather than analysis. I can still see his derogatory
smile when he faced a similar argument by the New Left on the

campus of the University of Wisconsin. Compromise with any such
reality destroyed the one force without which Lichtheim believed no
change was ever possible: the concept ideology which signified transformation, and which provided the essential foundation for the exercise of a critical mind. The problem of the isolation of the intellectual
was therefore a pseudo-problem which he refused to take seriously at
all. This attitude also confirmed his disinterestedness in popular culture. Perhaps here he was nearer to some of the *philosophies* than to
Hegel who did take popular myths and symbols seriously.

Lichtheim's hostility to positivism once more grew out of his dual
heritage of Hegelianism and the Enlightenment. Indeed, positivism and
the irrationality of populism were the two poles within which, for
him, most of the twentieth century moved; for example, he refused to
discuss what he called the nonsense of "positivisitic" Soviet philosophy on the one hand or the "rubbish" of fascist irrationalism on the
other. Here he was close to that liberalism which he thought was
finished: after all, they shared common sources of inspiration. Lichtheim rejected the outdated, classical economics and was skeptical of
the working of parliamentary government, but looked upon the world
with a humanism tempered by a rigid belief in intellectual integrity
and the rational mind.

Lichtheim's *Marxism* (1961) established his name, though some of
its themes can be traced back as far as 1950. The book represented a
new departure in Marxism as a historical and critical study. Up to that
time books on Karl Marx had, with few exceptions, been either expositions of his thought or had presupposed that Marx stood outside
historical time, presenting dynamic relationships valid as long as capitalism continues to exist. Lichtheim broke sharply with both of these
traditions. His discussion of Marx's thought was at one and the same
time an exposition, a critique and a history. He simultaneously stood
both inside and outside Marx, true to the Hegelian praxis. The Marx
who emerged was imprisoned within the flow of time, a child of
Hegelianism and the Enlightenment, however much he might conceal
this later under a mantle of positivism. Marx was rivetted to his age
by, among other things, his archaic economics and his outdated model
of the French Revolution. In Lichtheim's analysis Marx became a man
for one and not for all seasons.

The Hegelian progression of history stopped for no one. Engels
began to erode the original dynamic and humanist impulse through his
positivism, and Lenin completed the job by applying the ideology to
an underdeveloped country for which it was never designed. We are
back with the tragic element of history. Yet this tragedy was part of

the historical progress, and it would have been directly counter to all Lichtheim stood for if he had wanted to recapture for our own times the historical Marx, a 19th-century figure.

These main themes were also carried through in his other book on the early socialists. It is well to recall these themes, for here Lichtheim emphasized the historical and dialectical dimension in our way of looking at Marx, and thus restored not only the historical Marx, but also our own perspective. If he is to be compared with any of his predecessors, it should not be Karl Korsch whose works are too fragmented and, towards the end, positivistic, but rather to Arthur Rosenberg who introduced a similar historical perspective into his *History of Bolshevism*. Lichtheim respected both these men, though neither unravelled the mind of Marx to the depth of his own study on *Marxism*.

For George Lichtheim the historical perspective and the emphasis upon the dialectical, critical mind was always joined to the ideal of wholeness, of seeing the totality of any problem in its historical setting. It was the concept of ideology which provided that unity for which he always longed and which must be added to Hegelianism and the Enlightenment as forming his mind. It was the great ambition of his last years to write a history of the concept of ideology; after his book on Marxism he saw this as his most important task. He finished only one essay on the subject, but for him this was one of his most important writings. Indeed, it exemplified the elements of his mind which we have indicated: the historicism — showing how Napoleon invented the term — and praise for the critical mind of the ideologues who took their philosophy seriously and were unconcerned with daily politics. Napoleon cursed them, but it was they who made the more lasting contribution to the European attitude of mind, transcending national boundaries and conquests. This is, in fact, how George Lichtheim saw himself, precisely in the image of these ideologues whose history he so badly wanted to write.

The fate of a freelance writer is a difficult one in our society. Lichtheim had to write to make a living and had to judge what was in demand. Perhaps wrongly he believed that no one would want to read a study on the ideologists. Yet it is a high tribute to the consistency in his life, that he never compromised his integrity for the market place and never became a feuilletonist, even during the dying days of this genre. When he wrongly thought he had become popular and unscholarly he used a pseudonym (George Arnold), especially when he felt that he had to indulge in prophecy about the future. But, above all, he was a scholar living by his pen, a unique position in our day whose strain no doubt told with the passage of time. He could have been a good teacher, and I saw him at work in discussion groups as well as lectures, but he lacked the taste for it. Lichtheim taught through his writing and by the example he set through a life of devoted scholarship and sterling integrity. A disciplined mind confronted the world based upon some of the best philosophical insights France and Germany had to offer. Here again he differed from most of the Weimar left-wing intellectuals with whom he has once more been often wrongly identified. He did not believe in a world of brothers or in the inherent goodness of man; neo-Kantianism left him cold and he gave it short shrift in his writings. His was a tough-mindedness which deplored wishy-washiness, unproven and unhistorical assertions, theology without dogma. Through his kind of confrontation with the world he became one of the foremost scholars of his generation. For, and I return to the point I tried to make at the beginning, it is as a historical scholar that he wanted to be remembered and that he will be remembered, and that is why it is so fitting to dedicate this conference to his memory. But his importance as a scholar cannot be divorced from the way his mind worked, from the kind of tough-mindedness and quest for intellectual unity he himself exemplified and which, quite rightly, he found missing in his own lifetime.

George Lichtheim defies classification as either a Central European intellectual, a left-wing intellectual or even a social democrat. Instead he exemplified those great European traditions he thought were finished, but which instead he helped to transmit: the Enlightenment, Hegelianism and the core of the liberal faith. To be sure, these traditions have been and are always besieged by positivism, populism, and irrationality. But scholars must swim against the tide. Lichtheim was primarily a superb historian, and it is as such that he himself understood his task and judged the result of his work. George Lichtheim was a great scholar: not only because of his writings and his nearness to historical truth, but also because he stood like a rock for the very ideals which make scholarship possible.

MARX, MARXISM AND METHOD

JOSEPH J. O'MALLEY
Marquette University, Milwaukee

There will be little by way of original interpretation in this paper. It was written with an eye to the recent development in the United States of interest in Marx's method. This interest, so far as I can tell, is especially evident in economics and political science, among a small but growing minority of younger academicians who are curious about the possibility that Marx might provide a methodological alternative to the perspectives and principles long in vogue and presently dominating work in their fields. Insofar as this interest is more in Marx's method than in specific points of economic doctrine, and looks more to its possible adoption and application to the contemporary world than to simply an historical understanding, it would seem to be guided by what Engels, near the end of his life, wrote to Werner Sombart: 'Marx's whole manner of conceiving things is not a doctrine, but a method. It offers no finished dogmas, but rather points of reference for further research, and the method of that research . . . ' [1] It remains to be seen if Engels's words, apparently long-since forgotten in the camp of official 'Marxist-Leninist' orthodoxy, will be heeded elsewhere, and whether Marx's method, faithfully applied, will bear practical fruit in the form of the better human society which both Marx and Engels sought.

This paper was also written in the suspicion, wrong perhaps, that this interest in Marx's method is not accompanied by an adequate appreciation on the part of many of the academicians mentioned, of the influence of Hegel on Marx's 'manner of conceiving things'. For that reason I will be reviewing matter quite familiar to you who are gathered here to honor the memory of George Lichtheim. And I hope that this review will serve in our seminar at least to stimulate and advance discussion of one of the varieties of Marxism: philosophical Marxism at the heart of which is the question of the Hegelian elements in Marx's thought.

I

In Marx's mature writings there are two texts that deal explicitly and at some length with the question of scientific method. The first is Marx's posthumously published 'Introduction' to *A Contribution to the Critique of Political Economy*;[2] the second is his 'Author's Preface' (or 'Afterword') to the 2nd German edition of *Capital* I.[3] In both of these texts Marx also compares himself with Hegel on the subject of method, and identifies what he takes to be the basic error in Hegel's thought. Though written over fifteen years apart, these texts not only agree in all essential points regarding scientific method and Hegel's thought, but in fact complement one another so as to constitute together a more adequate expression of Marx's views on both subjects than does either text alone. Moreover, the views they express on both subjects repeat positions taken by Marx in his earliest theoretical writing, his *Critique of Hegel's Philosophy of Right* of 1843.[4] A review of the doctrine on method and the criticism of Hegel given in the later texts, with reference to what is found in the *Critique* of 1843, will allow us to see some of the principal features of Marx's methodology and some of the important Hegelian elements of his thought.

In the text from *Capital* (1873) Marx quotes at length from a Russian review article on the subject of his own method in *Capital* I. He approves the reviewer's remarks, calls them a 'striking and generous' account of his method, and adds some comments of his own. The main points of the text are these: A critical inquiry into human society must view the subject-matter as organic and evolutionary, i.e. as a totality or unity of functional correlates in process of evolving through successive forms. Science *(Wissenschaft)* aims to grasp through investigation *(Untersuchung)* and then express through exposition *(Darstellung)* the organic connections of the elements that constitute a given form, and the variation of the connections that occurs in the transition *(Übergang)* of one form into another. The aim of the scientific enterprise is to disclose 'the special laws that regulate the origin, existence, development and death of a given social organism and its replacement by another'; and the method that governs the scientific enterprise is the 'dialectical method'. Yet, the method of inquiry *(Forschungsmethode; Forschungsweise)* must be distinguished from the method of development or exposition *(Darstellungsmethode)*. The two differ formally. The method of inquiry is 'severely realistic', that of exposition is 'dialectical'.[5] Inquiry begins with the matter *(Stoff)* under study, and submits this to observation and inves-

tigation; the matter must be appropriated in empirical detail by confronting and comparing 'facts' *(Tatsachen)* in their historical setting
and connection. This done, exposition will adequately describe the
organic connections and their evolutionary movement so as to 'mirror'
in conceptual (ideal) terms the 'life of the subject-matter'. The exposi-
tory scheme will express a conceptual scheme which is the scientific
counterpart-in-thought of the real world of historical social production.[6]

In this text Marx leaves unclarified the details of the two-fold
method of 'realistic' investigation and 'dialectical' exposition, though
he clearly implies that investigation involves empirical, including historical, research, and that both investigation and exposition involve
'abstraction' or abstract conceptualization.[7] Furthermore, he says nothing about the character of the concepts that are employed, beyond
the general assertion of their objective validity which he implies when
he speaks of the exposition as being an 'adequate description' and
'ideal reflection' of the subject matter.[8] In his 'Introduction' of
1857, Marx deals at some length with both of these questions.

In the 'Introduction' Marx distinguishes two procedures or methods applicable to the subject-matter of political economy: analysis and
synthesis. The starting point of study, of 'observation and conceptualization' *(Anschauung und Vorstellung)*, is an objectively existing 'concrete whole' or 'unity of diverse elements' *(Zusammenfassung vieler
Bestimmungen . . ., also Einheit des Mannigfaltigen)*: it is that concrete totality which goes by the name of 'modern bourgeois society'.[9]
Inquiry begins with a 'chaotic conception' *(chaotische Vorstellung)* of
this whole. Analysis refines this conception by breaking it down into
its proper constitutive elements; these are, relative to the original conception, 'simpler concepts' *(einfacher Begriffe)*, less and less complex
abstractions *(immer dünnere Abstracta)*. Each of these simpler concepts is the counterpart-in-thought of a constituent element of the
existing concrete whole. Since that whole is an organic totality of
mutually related elements, the concepts that correspond to its elements are relational in their conceptual content. Further, since each
element of the organic totality relates ultimately to all the others,
each corresponding concept has its meaning, ultimately, in reference
to all the other concepts. Finally, since any element, within its overall
relationship to all the others, relates more immediately to some than
to others, analysis establishes an order of relationships among the
conceptual counterparts of those real elements.[10]

Once analysis arrives at the 'simplest determinate conceptions'
(einfachsten Bestimmungen), which are the thought-counterparts of

the basic constituent elements (and relations) of the existing concrete whole, a 'scientifically correct' *(wissenschaftlich richtige)* theoretical treatment of the subject-matter can begin. This treatment will be synthetic in form. It begins with the simplest, most abstract concepts, retraces the path of analysis in proceeding from more to less abstract concepts, and concludes with a concept of the 'living' and 'integral whole' now grasped in the fullness of its organic detail; it concludes i.e. with a concrete concept, a 'rich conceptual totality of many specific conceptions and relations'. [11] Throughout this text what is unmistakably implied is that the concept of the whole which results from synthesis, and *a fortiori* the concatenated simpler concepts which are its constitutive notes, have valid objective reference: in the words of *Capital,* they 'mirror' the real.[12] What the text of the 'Introduction' adds to the text of *Capital* is the notion that the empirical observation and research mentioned in *Capital* carry with them on the part of the researcher a process of conceptual analysis, and that the dialectical exposition mentioned in *Capital* expresses a process of conceptual synthesis.

Taken together, then, the texts of *Capital* and the 'Introduction' assert a doctrine on scientific method which has the following essential points:

1) Science begins with a subject-matter, a concrete object, whose existence as a complex whole independent of the thinker is presupposed, but whose nature and makeup are only vaguely understood;

2) in order to achieve and communicate a full and clear grasp of that subject-matter, science uses two distinct procedures – inquiry and exposition, to which correspond respectively two formally distinct cognitive methods – conceptual analysis and conceptual synthesis;

3) conceptual analysis is a cognitive movement from the chaotic *Vorstellung* of the whole to abstract concepts *(Begriffe)* of its parts, and this movement is nourished and governed by empirical observation and research;

4) conceptual synthesis is a 'dialectical' cognitive movement from the abstract concepts of the parts to a concrete concept *(Begriff)* of the whole, and this movement is expressed in the theoretical exposition;

5) accordingly, the overall movement of scientific thinking is from chaotic *Vorstellung* to concrete *Begriff* of the concrete object, via two moments – conceptual analysis governed by empirical study, and conceptual synthesis expressed in 'dialectical' exposition;

6) finally, empirical realism and 'dialectics' are thus distinct but

complementary aspects of scientific theory, and the dialectically elaborated theory has full objective reference insofar as it is governed by empirical data, is merely a theoretical expression of them.[13]

Taken together, these texts also assert an appraisal of Hegel that is at once critical and laudatory. By way of criticism, Marx charges Hegel with the error of having 'mystified the dialectic.' The error is twofold: first, Hegel hypostatizes human thinking into an absolute subject, called the 'Idea'; second, he identifies this absolute subject as that which generates the real. The two aspects of this error are pointed out in both texts. Thus in *Capital:*

> For Hegel, the process of thinking, which under the name of the 'Idea' he even transforms into an independent subject, is the demiurge of the real, with the real constructed as merely the external appearance of the Idea.[14]

And in the 'Introduction':

> Hegel fell into the error . . . of considering the real to be the product of self-synthesizing thought *(sich zusammenfassenden Denkens)*, of thought probing and unfolding itself out of and by itself; whereas the method of advancing from the abstract to the concrete . . . is by no means . . . the process by which the concrete (real) itself comes into being. . . . Philosophical consciousness . . . mistakes the movement of categories for the real act of production . . . whose product is the world.[15]

Thus, the 'Introduction' also clarifies what is meant in *Capital* by 'the process of thinking' which Hegel mystified: it is precisely that synthetic movement of scientific thinking which is distinct from and presupposes investigation and analysis, and which is expressed in the 'scientifically correct' method of treatment and exposition. This point cannot be missed for Marx goes on immediately in the 'Introduction' to assert that taking the 'movement of categories' to be an act of production 'is correct' so long as one is speaking about the synthetic production (in thought, and correlatively in the theoretical exposition) of the concrete concept, which is 'in fact a product of thought, of comprehension', the end result of a 'working up *(Verarbeitung)* of observation and conceptual representation *(Vorstellung)* into concepts *(Begriffe)*' Hegel confuses the concrete concept and the concrete real, and, accordingly, takes the real to be 'a product of a self-generating concept *(sich selbst gebärenden Begriffs)* whose thought is beyond or above observation and representation'.[16]

Now, this criticism of Hegel, as it is stated in the passage from *Capital*, was expressed 'almost thirty years' earlier by Marx, in the

opening pages of his *Critique of Hegel's Philosophy of Right,* where it
was summarized in the charge that Hegel's philosophy is marred by
'logical, pantheistic mysticism':[17] in *The Philosophy of Right,* for
example, Hegel's theoretical treatment of modern society and polity
presents itself as a history of the life-movement of the Idea proceeding
self-generatively from abstract to progressively more concrete stages in
the phenomenal guise of empirical institutions.[18] Moreover, in the
Critique one also finds the same charge made in the 'Introduction'
which specifies and clarifies the criticism voiced in *Capital:* what Hegel
has 'mystified' is the synthetic movement of thought from abstract to
concrete concept, i.e. he has mystified the 'correct' method of scien-
tific-theoretical presentation. This is the sense of Marx's claim in the
Critique that Hegel makes 'what is most simple . . . most complex and
vice versa. What should be the point of departure (of empirical investigation) becomes the mystical result, and what should be the rational
result becomes the mystical point of departure'; here Hegel turns
the 'true method upside down', 'stands it on its head'.[19] This is
exactly the same charge, and in the same words, repeated thirty years
later in *Capital*:

> The mystification which dialectic suffers in Hegel's hands, by no means
> prevents him from being the first to present its general form of working in a
> comprehensive and conscious manner. With him it is standing on its head. It
> must be turned right side up again, if you would discover the rational kernel
> within the mystical shell.[20]

What is to be found in Hegel's texts, therefore, 'within the mystical
shell', is the 'scientifically correct' method of theoretical treatment
and exposition. Hegel has 'discovered' this method;[21] and 'its general form of working' is to be found, presented 'in a comprehensive
and conscious manner', in his texts. One does not, therefore, find the
'rational' form of dialectic, the 'scientifically correct' method of theoretical exposition, by rejecting Hegel, but on the contrary by accepting him, by becoming (or remaining) his pupil; by accepting him, that
is, with a single qualification which comes down to this: ignoring his
'pantheistic' and 'mystical' talk about 'the Idea' and its world-creative
movement; or rather recognizing his talk as simply Hegel's bizarre,
'idealist' way of carrying through and describing the method he discovered, the 'scientifically correct' method of moving from an abstract
to a concrete grasp and exposition of a subject-matter.[22] Marx's criticism of Hegel thus carries with it both praise of Hegel and an acknowledgment: it was Hegel who provided him the method of his own
theoretical work, his scientific treatise on the modern world.[23]

But there is a further acknowledgment made in this text from *Capital*:

> In its mystified form, the dialectic became the fashion in Germany, because it seemed to transfigure and to glorify the existing state of things. In its rational form (however) it is a scandal and abomination to bourgeoisdom ... because it includes in its comprehension and affirmative recognition of the existing state of things, at the same time also, the recognition of the negation of that state (of things) ... because it is ... in its essence critical and revolutionary.[24]

If the 'rational' form of the dialectic, the correct method of theoretical science, is found in Hegel, so too are the things that follow upon it: the 'comprehension and affirmative recognition of the existing state of things', including 'the recognition of the negation of that state'. In short, a theoretical grasp of the world which is 'critical and revolutionary' is also found in Hegel. How is this so? Part of the answer is given in this text from *Capital*, and part in the *Critique* of 1843.

First, as Marx notes in *Capital*, both the mystified and the rational forms of dialectic have an identical subject-matter: 'the existing state of things'. Though it is presented *(dargestellt)* differently within each − seemingly 'transfigured and glorified' by the one, in a 'critical and revolutionary' way by the other − that subject matter remains one and the same. A distinction is implied between the dialectic as method of theoretical treatment, and the empirical subject-matter which is treated. The sense and the implications of this distinction are seen by glancing again at Marx's *Critique* of 1843. There he explicitly distinguishes not only between the two forms (in the *Critique* called 'mystical' and 'proper') of dialectical exposition, as in *Capital*, but also between the method of exposition − whether rationally (properly) or mystically applied − and the empirical content of the exposition, a content comprised of the data of observation and research. Now, this content, Marx notes, remains the same whether the method is rationally or mystically applied. In fact, the only thing Hegel's mystification of the method brings to the content, i.e. to the empirical data about 'the existing state of things', is a difference in 'the way of considering it or the manner of speaking' about it.[25] But if this is so, then one may get from Hegel more than the correct method of theoretical science; one may also get a certain empirical content, certain empirical data about 'the existing state of things'.[26]

Now since the seeming 'transfiguration and glorification' of that state of things derives from the mystified dialectic; since, in other words, it is the effect of hypostatizing the achievement of a concrete *Begriff* of the totality of real things into a God-like being which is manifested in those things; then demystifying the dialectic[27] and recapturing its rational form *eo ipso* divests the empirical data of its mystical disguise. Their transfigured and glorified appearance vanishes; reality appears 'in its own terms'; and it appears, moreover, within that scientifically correct mode of treatment which allows a concrete grasp of the 'life' of the subject-matter, of the existing state of things, of its elements and relations — and of those tendencies within it that explain its 'origin, existence, development and death' as a transient form already bearing within it the harbingers of its successor.

What Marx recognized, therefore, was that, whether Hegel knew it or not, his mystified view of things merely disguised what is really a 'scientifically correct', 'comprehensive and affirmative', but also a 'critical and revolutionary' grasp of the existing state of things. He recognized, and acknowledged, that his demystification of Hegelian 'science' did not remove him from the field of Hegelian science; that his criticism of Hegel actually opened up to him a field of scientific inquiry and exposition whose methodological principles, overall subject-matter and (at least some) specific empirical data comprised his Hegelian legacy. That is why he called Hegel 'that eminent thinker', why he called himself Hegel's pupil, and why he called Hegel his 'master'.

I would like now, briefly, to exemplify elements of this Hegelian legacy as it is found, first in the content, and second in the form of Marx's theory of the modern world.

II

'The reform of consciousness . . . through analysis of mystical consciousness, whether religious or political, which fails to understand itself' — This programmatic statement, written by Marx to Ruge in the fall of 1843[28] and subsequently used as the motto of the *Deutsch-Französische Jahrbücher,* summarizes what Marx had already done for himself in his *Critique of Hegel's Philosophy of Right.* This work was an 'analysis of mystical consciousness', in fact of the paradigm case of mystical political consciousness. Moreover, the analysis uncovered something that Hegel had, apparently, failed to understand was present in his own thought: a critical and revolutionary view of the existing social-political state of things.[29]

Recent commentary has highlighted some of the critical views and revolutionary conclusions which, though explicitly stated for the most part only in later texts of Marx, derived originally from his analysis of *The Philosophy of Right* and remained thereafter integral features of his social and political doctrine. These include the concepts of the proletariat as 'universal class', the 'abolition of private property', and 'true democracy' (featuring universal suffrage); these concepts are said to be Marx's critical counterparts, respectively, to Hegel's bureaucracy, entailed landed property, and Estates Assembly as means of transcending the civil-political duality of modern life. Insofar as the origin of these 'classical' Marxian concepts may be traced back to Marx's demystification or 'transformative criticism' of *The Philosophy of Right,* they are taken to represent Hegel's legacy to the content of Marx's social and political theory.[30] Marx's notion of a 'classless society' is another case of this; its origin, too, may be traced back to Marx's *Critique of The Philosophy of Right.*

In the part of the *Critique* devoted to Hegel's doctrine on the legislature, there is a lengthy and obscure passage in which Marx pinpoints the mystified character of Hegel's doctrine, prescribes a corrective reading of Hegel to cure the 'illusion' created by the mystification, but then moves on without himself applying the prescription and drawing the conclusions he evidently believes it would yield. At issue is the question of whether or not a legislature constituted so as to reflect the estate-divisions of civil society can mediate the opposition between particular and general (or universal) interests. I shall summarize the passage in question, then carry out Marx's prescription and draw the conclusions implied.[31]

Hegel attempts to justify an estate-constitution on the grounds that the estate-divisions of modern society, which have as their 'civil' meaning the pursuit of particular interests, acquire when carried over into the legislature a different meaning, a 'political' meaning, which is of concern for the universal interest. Accordingly, Hegel's 'subject' is the estate (or estate-divisions), and the two 'predicates' he attaches to the subject are the two 'essentially different' characters or 'determinations' referred to as 'civil' and 'political meaning'. Though valid as a characterization of the estates in their mediaeval existence, [32] the two meanings cannot be simultaneously predicated of modern estates because, as Hegel himself acknowledges, the essential feature of modern life is a sharp duality between the civil and political spheres.[33] His estate-constitution, therefore, is an attempt to deal with modern reality by wholly inappropriate use of a mediaeval model (. . . 'the estate-constitution purports to resolve through a reminiscence . . .'). Hegel foists onto his subject two distinct and opposed 'meanings', thereby 'artificially' maintaining the 'identity' of his subject. This identity is 'illusory' ('There is an apparent identity here: the *same subject*, but in *essentially different* determinations, and thus in fact a *double* subject.'), and it derives from mystification.[34]

The mystification involves two things. First, although man is the real subject whose social-political actualization is at stake Hegel makes the estate, instead of man, his social-political 'subject'; and second, Hegel makes civil and political 'meanings' the predicates of the estate rather than vice versa. Accordingly, Marx's prescription for 'curing the illusion' created by this mystification is also two-fold, though only the first part of it is explicitly given: reverse Hegel's subject and predicate, then ask whether the new predicate (civil estate, or estate divisions) really represents the 'essence' and constitutes the 'true actualization' of the new subjects (civil 'meaning' and political 'meaning', or concern for particular interests and concern for the universal interest). Now, the answer to this question is clear: on the basis of Hegel's own empirically accurate understanding of modern society, the civil estate (and estate-divisions) expresses the essence and constitutes the actualization of concern for particular interests only. From this, the conclusion follows that an estate-constitution will not do, for it merely carries the struggle of particular interests over into the legislative power of the political state, making the political sphere an illusory rather than real pursuit of the universal, making the state a mere extension and disguised version of civil society, which Hegel himself acknowledges to be a *bellum omnium contra omnes.*[35]

But the second part of Marx's prescription, though only implicitly stated, should also be applied, and its appropriate conclusion drawn: reintroduce the real social-political 'subject', man, then predicate the civil and political 'meanings' of him, and ask whether Hegel's original 'subject' (estate or estate-divisions) expresses the 'essence' and constitutes the 'true actualization' of man's civil and political character; i.e. ask whether, or which of, man's social-political characteristics are expressed and actualized in his existence within the estate and estate-divisions of modern life. Again, on Hegel's own view of modern life, the answer is clear: man's existence within these divisions is restricted to concern for and pursuit of particular interests; this is to say that in the present estate-'determinations of his being' he is an 'exempted and restricted thing'. This conclusion, derived from Hegel himself, is but the 'affirmative' side of a coin whose other side is a 'critical and revolutionary' conclusion and demand: the actualization of man's social-political 'essence' requires the elimination of all divisions within society which constrain man's consciousness and concern to particular interests and their pursuit. In sum, Hegel's vague and dimorphic

mystification of modern civil divisions not only seemingly 'transfig-
ures and glorifies' the modern, 'preeminently the estates-'constitution, but it also masks the fact that the existence of social-economic
divisions precludes man's fulfillment as a social and political being. It
precludes, that is, what Hegel himself rightly demands of a rational
social-political order, namely, that it constitute a synthesis of particular and universal.[36] Therefore Hegel's own doctrine carries an implicit
demand for an elimination of those divisions; a demand for what Marx
will soon come to call 'the classless society'.[37]

We can trace the development of this demand to explicit formulation through some of Marx's texts that follow the *Critique*. In "The
Jewish Question" Marx notes that man within the constitution of
'political democracy' (referred to in the *Critique* as the 'Republic' or
'abstract state-form of democracy') remains

> man in his uncivilized and unsocial aspect, in his fortuitous existence and
> just as he is, corrupted by the entire organization of our society, lost and
> alienated from himself, oppressed by inhuman relations and elements – in a
> word, man who is not yet an *actual* species-being.[38]

Because of the organization of society, with its oppressive relations
and elements (no doubt meant to include its socio-economic divisions), man 'is active as a *private individual*, treats other men as
means, reduces himself to a means, and becomes the plaything of alien
powers'.[39] Therefore:

> Only when the actual, individual man has taken back into himself the ab-
> stract citizen and in his everyday life, his individual work, and his individual
> relationships has become a *species-being*, only when he has recognized and
> organized his own powers as *social* powers so that social force is no longer
> separated from him as *political* power, only then is human emancipation
> complete.[40]

Then, after having identified the 'proletariat' as the 'universal class'
which will effect this emancipation,[41] Marx, in *The German Ideology*
(1845–1846), explicitly ties this emancipation to the establishment of a
classless society'

> ... the communist revolution ... abolishes the rule of all classes with the
> classes themselves, because it is carried through by the class which no longer
> counts as a class in society, is not recognized as a class, and is in itself the
> expression of the dissolution of all classes, nationalities etc., within present
> society.[42]

And finally, at the conclusion of *The Poverty of Philosophy* (1847):

> The working class, in the course of its development, will substitute for the old civil society an association that will exclude classes and their antagonism, and there will no longer be political power properly so-called, because political power is precisely the official *résumé* of the antagonism within civil society . . . In an order where classes and class antagonism no longer exist . . . *social evolutions* will cease to be *political revolutions.*[43]

Thus what begins in 1843 in the demystification of an Hegelian text becomes in 1846–1847 an integral and explicitly stated tenet of Marx's critical theory of modern society. But this tenet is already there in the text of 1843; and it is there because and in so far as it was already in Hegel's *Philosophy of Right*, 'hidden within the mystical shell'.

III

Marx failed to complete his full scientific treatise on the modern world, his 'Economics'. Yet he said enough about it to allow us to discern its essential methodological and structural features. It was to have embodied the 'materialist' conception of society and polity; it was to have been elaborated in accordance with the 'scientifically correct' method of theoretical treatment and exposition; and it was to have been, in appearance at least, a critical counterpart to Hegel's treatise on 'ethical life' in *The Philosophy of Right*. I shall briefly discuss each of these features, for they allow us to see the Hegelian elements, and therefore the legacy of Hegel, in the form as well as the content of Marx's theoretical view of things.

On Marx's own word, his 'materialist' conception of the relationship between society and polity took shape in the period 1843–1846, beginning with his *Critique of Hegel's Philosophy of Right* and culminating in *The German Ideology*. Troubled by questions about the relationship between economic interests and politics, and about the socialist and communist doctrines that had come to his attention, he had evidently judged that the key to his questions was to be found in Hegel:

> The first work I undertook to resolve the questions that troubled me was a critical review of Hegel's philosophy of right . . . My studies led me to conclude that legal relations as well as forms of the state are not to be understood by themselves nor explained by reference to the so-called general development of the human mind, but rather that they have their roots in

the material conditions of life, which Hegel, following the example of the
English and French of the eighteenth century, summed up under the name
of 'civil society'; and that, moreover, the anatomy of civil society is to be
sought in political economy.

. . . .

[Friedrich Engels and I] resolved to work out in common the opposition
of our view to the ideological view of German philosophy . . . This resolve
was carried out in the form of a criticism of post-Hegelian philosophy'. [44] . . .

The first statements of that 'materialist' conception are to be found
in the *Critique* of 1843, where Marx unmasks Hegel's mystification,
first of the relationship between civil society and state, and second of
the relationship between private property and the political constitution. In the first instance, the empirical fact is expressed, though
mystified, in Hegel: relative to the state, civil society is the more basic
sphere of human activity. Hegel's order of scientific (philosophical)
treatment respects this fact; in *The Philosophy of Right* civil society is
treated prior to the state. And though when treating the state Hegel
makes civil society appear to be the product of the mystified state-
Idea, the empirical fact remains: the state issues from *(hervorgehe
aus)*, is a product of, civil society.[45] This fact receives further specifi-
cation in the demystification of Hegel's view of the relationship between private property, specifically entailed landed property, and the
constitution. In the Middle Ages the political constitution and the
arrangements of private property were one and the same.[46] In modern
times, too, the political constitution remains in a real sense 'the constitution of private property'; private property is in fact the 'support' of
the modern political constitution; the modern state is a disguised form
of the property arrangements in civil society, a disguised form of the
power of private property:

What, then, is the power of the political state over private property? *Private
property's own power,* its essence brought to existence. What remains to the
political state in opposition to this essence? The *illusion* that it determines
when it is rather determined.[47]

Demystification of *The Philosophy of Right* has, therefore, yielded
the view that legal relations and the state are rooted in civil society,
specifically in the relations of private property. This conclusion, which
was also supported by the research in political history and theory that
Marx carried out while doing the *Critique,*[48] established a program of
further research — namely, into the 'anatomy of civil society' — whose

data would still be treated in accordance with the theoretical method derived from Hegel.

These points of the materialist view which derive originally from the *Critique,* and the methodological points related to them, reappear in *The German Ideology* stated explicitly as part of a criticism of 'post-hegelian philosophy'. Against the 'young Hegelian's' pseudo-scientific treatment of history, society and state as actualization of abstract 'Man', 'Criticism' etc., there is the insistence – to be repeated, as we have seen, years later in the 'Introduction' of 1857 and *Capital* – that the presupposition of science is an existing subject-matter whose constituent elements and relations must first be uncovered by a large work of empirical study and observation:

> The premises from which we begin are not arbitrary ones, not dogmas, but real premises from which abstraction can only be made in the imagination. They are the real individuals, their activity and the material conditions under which they live, both those which they find already existing and those produced by their activity. These premises can thus be verified in a purely empirical way.[49]

This empirical study, which provides the data for scientific theory and which is not to be distorted by mystical interpretation, will bring to light in detail the actual connections between the productive activity and organization of civil society, and the political constitution, or state, which, in the words of the earlier *Critique,* 'issues from the mass of men' in their empirical actuality:

> The fact is, therefore, that definite individuals who are productively active in a definite way enter into definite social and political relations. Empirical observation must in each separate instance bring out empirically, and without any mystification and speculation, the connection of the social and political structure with production. The social structure and the state are continually evolving (or 'issuing': *hervorgehen*) out of the life process of definite individuals . . . as they *really* are . . . [50]

Given this empirical observation and research, the 'active life-process' of human society can be 'described', not as the activity of 'imagined subjects' (such as 'the Idea'), which bring themselves to phenomenal form in historical human activity and institutions, but as the 'practical activity' of men themselves. The theoretical description ('depiction' or presentation) of that activity will be in terms of the relations, groupings and institutions within which that activity is carried out and into which it issues; and the description will clarify by the use of 'abstractions' the sequence of separate but related 'strata' which empirical study has shown to obtain in the totality that is animated by that activity. 'Real, positive science' thus has its starting point in what speculative (Hegelian) philosophy takes to be the end result of the workings of its mystical subject, namely 'real life'. This life is the common subject-matter of both science and speculative philosophy. The latter, however, mystifies the method of science, and so too the empirical data, about which, as a consequence, it engages in 'empty talk'; whereas 'real science', on the other hand, applies the demystified, the 'rational', form of the method to the empirical data, and thus constitutes 'real knowledge'.[51]

When Marx then proceeds, in *The German Ideology*, to give a brief account of his 'abstractions' and an example of his method in application, he begins with a basic (and abstract) view of man satisfying his basic needs; then he proceeds to concretize this view into a concept of 'production' as comprised of four elements or moments, in the context of which consciousness and language are introduced.[52] He then proceeds to the 'division of labor', classes, the origin and nature of the state, exchange among nations and, finally, the 'world market', which represents not only the transformation of history into 'world history' but also the matrix for the revolution which will usher in a new historical epoch and form of social production.[53] This order of doctrinal development in these pages of *The German Ideology* coincides with what Marx was to announce eleven years later as the plan of his 'Economics'; and immediately following this first sketch, which proceeds from man as subject of production and concludes with the all-embracing concept of the world market, Marx summarizes his materialist view of history, society and polity, and the order of theoretical treatment which is proper to it:

> This conception of history depends on our ability to expound *(entwickeln)* the real process of production, starting out from the material production of life itself, and to comprehend the form of intercourse connected with this and created by this mode of production (i.e. civil society in its various stages), as the basis of all history; and to show *(darzustellen)* it in its action as state (etc.) . . . by which means, of course, the whole thing can be depicted *(dargestellt)* in its totality (and therefore, too, the reciprocal action of these various sides on one another).[54]

The main points of this passage (and of what follows it regarding productive forces and relations, and revolutions therein) are repeated thirteen years later, in the *Preface* of 1859, from which we quoted at the beginning of this section.[55] That *Preface* opened with one of

Marx's statements of his plan for his 'Economics'. As we turn to a closer consideration of that plan, we should note once more that the 'materialist' doctrine of *The German Ideology,* which clearly points ahead to Marx's work on the Economics and to its governing plan, also had its origins, as Marx himself noted, in his 'studies' of 1843 and his 'critical revision' of *The Philosophy of Right.*[56] We should not be surprised, therefore, to find a relationship between that work of Hegel and Marx's projected 'Economics'.

In Marx's writings there are at least seven statements of his plan for the 'Economics'.[57] The first of these, in Marx's 'Introduction' of 1857, comes at the conclusion of the discussion on method. After identifying the 'scientifically correct' method of political-economic theory as one which proceeds synthetically from an abstract to a concrete grasp of the subject-matter, Marx concludes that

> The arrangement obviously has to be 1) the general, abstract determinations which obtain in more or less all forms of society, but in the sense explained above. 2) The categories that make up the inner structure *(innere Gliederung)* of civil society and on which the fundamental classes rest. Capital, wage labor, landed property. Their interrelation. Town and country. The three great social classes. Exchange between them. Circulation. Credit system (private). 3) Synthesis *(Zusammenfassung)* of civil society in the form of the state. Taken in relation to itself. The 'unproductive' classes. Taxes. State debt. Public credit. The population. Colonies. Emigration. 4) International relation of production. International division of labor. International Exchange. Export and import. Rate of exchange. 5) The world market and crises.[58]

The relationship between this and what Marx earlier sketched out in *The German Ideology* is not hard to see.

Marx subsequently introduced three modifications into the plan, none of which alters its basic structure: first, rubric 1 ('the general, abstract determinations . . .') drops out; second, rubric 2 is expanded into three rubrics, each of which is devoted to one of the 'categories that make up the inner structure of bourgeois society', or one of its 'fundamental classes'; and third, the order of treatment of 'wage labor' and 'landed property' is reversed. Marx communicated the plan with these modifications for the first time to Lassalle, emphasizing its scientific character:

> The work . . . is a *critique of the economic categories* or, if you like, the system of bourgeois economy critically treated *(dargestellt)*. It is at once a treatment *(Darstellung)* and, through that treatment, a criticism of the system . . .

> The treatment, I mean the style *(Manier)*, is completely scientific. . . . The whole is divided into 6 Books: 1. On Capital (including some preliminary chapters). 2. On Landed Property. 3. On Wage Labor. 4. On the State. 5. International Commerce. 6. World Market.[59]

Shortly after, in announcing the plan to Engels, Marx clarifies the reversal of 'wage labor' and 'landed property': treating capital, then landed property, then wage labor is in keeping with the 'dialectical' as well as the 'historical' relationship of these categories and their corresponding social classes within the totality of modern social production.[60] The plan as expressed to Lassalle and Engels appears subsequently in the opening lines of the *Preface* of 1859:

> I consider the system of bourgeois economy in the following order: *capital, landed property, wage labor; state, foreign commerce, world market.* Under the first three rubrics I examine the conditions of existence of the three great classes that comprise modern bourgeois society; the connection of the three remaining rubrics is self-evident.[61]

What is self-evident is that the order of the plan, with its division into two groups of three rubrics, is governed by both the 'materialist' view and the 'scientifically correct' method of theoretical elaboration. In keeping with the former, 'civil society' (the first three rubrics) is treated prior to the 'state' which issues from it; in keeping with the latter, the entire treatment begins with the most 'abstract determinations',[62] and it ends with the most concrete concept of that totality whose existence is presupposed by the entire scientific effort, but which is apprehended at the beginning only vaguely and chaotically: the modern world of social production.

Both of these aspects of the plan appear most clearly in Marx's statements of it in Notebook II of the *Grundrisse*. The first of these, which retains the divisions of the plan as set down in the 'Introduction' of 1857, is especially striking:

> In this first section, where exchange value, money, prices are looked at, commodities always appear as already present. The determination of forms is simple. We know that they express aspects of social production but the latter itself is the presupposition. However, they are *not posited* in this character (i.e. as aspects of social production). And so, in fact, the first exchange . . . does not lay hold of and specify the whole of production. It is the *available* overflow of an overall production. . . . But by itself, it points beyond itself toward the economic relations which are posited as relations of production. The inner structure *(innere Gliederung)* of production therefore forms the second section, the synthesis in (form of) the state *(Zusam-*

menfassung im Staat) the third, the international relation the fourth, the world market the conclusion, in which production is posited as a totality together with all its moments, but within which, at the same time, all contradictions come into play. The world market, then constitutes both the presupposition of the whole as well as that which underlies it. Crises are then the general intimation which points beyond the presupposition, and the urge which presses toward the adoption of a new historical form.[63]

The rubric on the 'world market' thus represents the final stage of a six-stage synthesis which yields a concrete concept of the existing world of social production.

If the 'Economics' was indeed to have been such a work of theoretical synthesis (or, if one prefers, of the 'dialectical' development of a concrete concept),[64] then a relationship may be seen to obtain between the 'Economics' and Hegel's *Philosophy of Right.* The relationship is one of structural and thematic parallel, a first glimpse of which may be had by examining Marx's rubric on the 'world market'. That rubric, as spelled out in the *Grundrisse,* intends the concrete world-totality of production which is shot through with contradictions and driven by an impulsion — manifested in crises but embodied in the proletariat — toward the establishment of a new form of society in which the state is destined to be abolished. Now, this view of the world market repeats what is said earlier in *The German Ideology,* where, moreover, Marx identifies the world market as that empirical reality which Hegel has mystified as the 'world spirit' in its most concrete socio-political guise, 'world history'. Against this mystification of world history, Marx asserts:

> ... [The] transormation of history into world history is not indeed a mere abstract act on the part of 'self-consciousness', the world spirit, or any other metaphysical spectre, but a quite material, empirically verifiable act. . . .
> In history up to the present it is certainly an empirical fact that separate individuals have, with the broadening of their activity into world-historical activity, become more and more enslaved under a power alien to them (a pressure which they have conceived of as a dirty trick on the part of the so-called world spirit, etc.), a power which has become more and more enormous and, in the last instance, turns out to be the *world market.* But it is just as empirically established that, by the overthrow of the existing state of society by the communist revolution . . . and the abolition of private property which is identical with it, this power, which so baffles the German theoreticians, will be dissolved; and that then the liberation of each single individual will be accomplished in the measure in which history becomes transformed into world history.[65]

It appears therefore, that Marx's final rubric of the 'Economics' is his materialist counterpart to the Hegelian notion of *Geist* as 'world history' – which, as a matter of fact, is also the final rubric of *The Philosophy of Right.*

Pressing this relationship between Marx's projected masterwork and the political masterwork of Hegel yields the following parallel:

Marx's 'Economics'   Hegel's *Philosophy of Right*
                                            Part III: 'Ethical Life'

1) Capital,
2) Landed Property, ... 1) Civil Society (as composed of the
3) Wage Labor;   agricultural, business, and
                                                 bureaucratic 'estates').
4) State . . . . 2) State (in its internal constitution).
5) Foreign(or international)
      Commerce . . . . 3) International Law.
6) World Market, ... 4) World History.[66]

In sum, then, it appears that Marx's 'Economics' was to have been his critical and 'materialist' counterpart to Hegel's idealist treatise on 'ethical life'. This is not surprising in view of the fact that the project and plan of the 'Economics' developed out of methodological and socio-political positions which, formulated in *The German Ideology,* actually originated in *The Critique of the Philosophy of Right*; and not surprising also in light of Marx's acknowledgement in 1873 that his debt to Hegel touched not only on method but on content as well, and that that debt went back to the same *Critique*. Marx's plan of the 'Economics' shows as clearly as anything the nature and extent of his connection with and debt to Hegel. His 'demystification' of Hegel was a correction of the 'master'; and that is something quite different than a break, either permanent or temporary.[67]

* * *

Marx failed to complete his 'Economics'; in fact he saw into print only the smaller part of his material for the first rubric, 'On Capital'. The reason for his failure may be found in the harsh circumstances of his life together with the fact that the work as a whole demanded more than could be done by one man. But there may be an additional reason, one which derives from the character of the work as projected on the model of Hegelian 'science'. The 'world' of economy, society and polity, Hegel wrote, cannot be grasped in a fully scientific way until it has already reached a kind of nodal point in its world-historical development, a point at which its shape has 'grown old'.[68] Now, Marx's correspondence through the last thirty years of his life is studded with references to 'new' discoveries, materials and documents that required renewed study and reflection on his part. It was a case of scientific synthesis awaiting a further gathering and analysis of empirical data. But there are also references to new crises and new developments requiring new works of observation, and to phenomena entering new phases and not yet ripe to the point where their significance was clear.[69] Here, too, it was a case of science awaiting new data, but beyond that a case also of changes *in the world* that prevented, or delayed, the work of scientific synthesis. Do not Marx's letters, especially near the end of his life, betray a growing awareness that the world which he was seeking to grasp and to depict in its totality and in a scientific way had not yet grown old enough for him to do so? To pose the question is not to deny the genius of Marx, nor the validity of his fundamental insights and criticisms in his own day, nor the timeliness and revolutionary potential of his writings in our day. This much at least is clear: the task of applying Marx's thought and method to our own world cannot help but be a difficult one; perhaps, too, it remains doomed to only modest success — unless, that is, amidst the din and turmoil around us there are to be detected the soft wing beats of the Owl of Minerva.

NOTES

1. Engels to Sombart (11 March 1895), in Karl Marx/Friedrich Engels, *Werke*, vol. 39 (Dietz Verlag, Berlin, 1959 ff.), pp. 428–9. This edition cited hereafter as *MEW*. An example of current interest in Marx's method in the United States may be seen in Bertell Ollman's 'Marxism and Political Science' (with comments by Isaac Balbus and this writer), *Politics and Society*, Winter 1973–4, 491–521.

2. Written August–September 1857; cited hereafter as 'Introduction', with references to the German original in Karl Marx, *Grundrisse der Kritik der politischen Oekonomie. Rohentwurf (1857–58)* (Dietz Verlag, Berlin, 1953), pp. 3–29. Marx's discussion of method is on pp. 21 ff.

3. Dated 24 January 1873; cited in Karl Marx, *Capital*, vol. I, translated by Edward Aveling and Samuel Moore, edited by Frederick Engels, revised by Ernest Untermann (C.H. Kerr and Co., Chicago, 1932), pp. 16–26; esp. 21–26 (with references also to the German in *MEW*, vol 23).

4. Written Spring–Summer 1843; cited hereafter as *Critique*, with references to the English version of Annette Jolin and Joseph O'Malley (Cambridge University Press, 1972); and the German in Karl Marx, *Frühe Schriften* I, edited by Hans-Joachim Lieber and Peter Furth. (Cotta Verlag, Stuttgart, 1971), pp. 258–425.

5. *Capital* I, pp. 22–24; *MEW*, vol. 23, pp. 25–7.

6. *Ibid.*, pp. 23–5; *MEW*, vol. 23, pp. 26–7.

7. Cf. in the Preface to the 1st German edition: 'In the analysis of economic forms . . . neither microscopes nor chemical reagents are of use. The force of abstraction must replace both'. *Ibid.*, p. 12; *MEW*, vol. 23, p. 12.

8. 'Only after this work (of investigation) is done, can the actual movement be adequately described. If this is done successfully, if the life of the subject-matter is ideally reflected as in a mirror . . .' (Erst nachdem diese Arbeit vollbracht, kann die wirkliche Bewegung entsprechend dargestellt werden. Gelingt dies und spiegelt sich nun das Leben des Stoffs ideel wider . . .). *Ibid.*, p. 25; *MEW*, vol. 23, p. 27.

9. *Grundrisse*, pp. 21–2, 26.

10. *Ibid.*, p. 21. This view of the relationships among the real elements, and so too among their conceptual (and categorial) counterparts, is expressed throughout the 'Introduction'.

11. ' . . . bis ich bei den einfachsten Bestimmungen angelangt wäre. Von da wäre nun die Reise wieder ruckwärts anzutreten, bis ich endlich wieder bei (den Ganzen) anlangte, diesmal aber nicht als bei einer chaotischen Vorstellung eines Ganzen, sondern als einer reichen Totalität von vielen Bestimmungen und Beziehungen'. *Grundrisse*, p. 21. This describes the 'wissenschaftlich richtige Methode'.

12. E.g.: 'The method of advancing from the abstract to the concrete is simply the way in which thought appropriates that concrete (object) and reproduces it concretely in the mind. . . . The real subject continues to lead an independent existence after it has been grasped as it did before, outside the mind, so long as it is grasped in a purely speculative or theoretical way. Hence . . . the subject, society, must always be kept in mind as the presupposition'. (. . . die Methode vom Abstrakten zum Konkreten aufzusteigen, nur die Art für das Denken ist, sich das Konkrete anzueignen, es als ein geistig Konkretes zu reproduzieren. . . . Das reale Subjekt bleibt nach wie vor ausserhalb des Kopfes in seiner Selbständigkeit bestehen; solange sich der Kopf nämlich nur spekulativ verhält, nur theoretisch. Auch . . . muss das Subjekt, die Gesellschaft, als Voraussetzung stets der Vorstellung vorschweben.) *Grundrisse*, p. 22.

13. Because the dialectical synthesis is governed by the conceptual analysis (the

synthetic transitions being the reverse of the analytic transitions), and the analysis by empirical investigation (whose data suggest and support the analytic transitions), the dialectical structure of the exposition is governed by the empirical data, by the subject-matter, the objectively existing concrete totality. In short, the dialectic is determined by the subject-matter. Only if this is so can it, and the concrete concept it yields 'mirror' the subject-matter and constitute a true scientific grasp of it. Accordingly, though the dialectical exposition may appear to be 'a mere a priori construction', it is not (*Capital* I, p. 25): the order of arrangement of categories in the exposition is determined not by the order of appearance, in the historical evolution of production, of the real elements they name, nor by the order of their own appearance in the history of political-economic thought, but by 'the organic connection' of the real elements they name within modern society; this is the reason e.g. why 'capital' must be treated before 'landed property' ('Introduction', *Grundrisse*, p. 28). This dependence of dialectically elaborated science, for its truth, on a massive work of empirical observation and research cannot be overstressed (*Capital* I, pp. 24–5). Marx's clear recognition and scrupulous respect of that dependence, and what it implies by way of research, was one of the chief reasons why his own theoretical masterwork went largely unwritten. More concerning this below.

14. *Capital* I, p. 25; *MEW*, vol. 23, p. 27.

15. *Grundrisse*, p. 22.

16. *Ibid.*, p. 22.

17. *Critique*, p. 7; *Frühe Schriften* I, p. 262.

18. To cite the main topics of *The Philosophy of Right*: will, abstract right, morality and ethical life, the latter including family, civil society and state, with 'state' further treated as constitutional law, international law and world history. Though Marx's manuscript contains a critical commentary only of the section on 'constitutional law', and indeed not all of that, his criticism touches on *The Philosophy of Right,* and the entire edifice of Hegel's philosophy, as a whole: its overall form is 'mystified' dialectic. Cf. *Critique*, esp. pp. 7–11, 12–15, 17–18, 23–4, 39–40, 83–4; *Frühe Schriften* I, pp. 261–7, 268–73, 275–8, 284–5, 305–7, 365–6.

19. *Critique*, p. 40; *Frühe Schriften* I, p. 307: 'Und es versteht sich von selbst. Der wahre Weg wird auf den Kopf gestellt. Das einfachste ist das Verwickeltste und das Verwickeltste das Einfachste. Was Ausgang sein sollte, wird zum mystischen Resultat, und was rationelles Resultat sein sollte, wird zum mystischen Ausgangspunkt'. Also *Critique*, pp. 8–9; *Frühe Schriften* I, pp. 263–4, which concludes: 'The fact, which is the starting point, is not conceived to be such but rather to be the mystical result.'

20. *Capital* I, p. 25; *MEW*, vol. 23, pp. 27–28.

21. Marx to Engels (16 January 1858); *MEW*, vol. 29, p. 260 (cf. note 23 below).

22. Cf. *Capital* I, p. 25; *MEW*, vol. 23, p. 27. 'What Hegel calls 'the Idea . . . is for me nothing else than the [subject-matter] transposed and translated into the form of thought in the human mind'. Hence, in the *Critique* Marx often prefaces his comments on a Hegel passage with statements like: 'Let us translate [Hegel's passage] into prose [or common language] as follows . . .' 'Taken rationally, Hegel's sentences mean only the following . . .' ; etc.; cf. *Critique*, pp. 7, 8, 16, 23; *Frühe Schriften* I, pp. 261, 263, 274, 284. Throughout the *Critique* Marx implicitly affirms the validity of the theoretical method which is 'hidden within the mystical shell' of the *Philosophy of Right*. Hegel is correct, for example, to treat 'family' and 'civil society' prior to 'state', which is the more concrete concept; but he errs in treating them as particular moments of the Idea and products of its activity as it 'sunders itself into the two . . . in order to . . . become explicit as infinite actual mind'; *Critique*, pp. 7–9; *Frühe Schriften* I, pp. 261–5 (concluding with: 'The entire mystery of the *Philosophy of Right* and of Hegelian philosophy in general is contained in these paragraphs'.); also Marx's analysis of Hegel's Par. 270, *Critique*, pp. 15–17; *Frühe Schriften* I, pp. 272–5. In the 'Introduction' of 1857, Marx also cites Hegel in support of his own point that the scientifically correct theoretical ordering of categories (abstract to concrete) need not, though it may, reflect the historical order of existence of the elements and relations of production: 'Hegel, for example, correctly begins the *Philosophy of Right* with possession *(Besitz)* as the simplest *(einfachsten)* juridical relation of the subject. But there is no possession preceding the family or master-servant relations, which are far more concrete relations . . . The concrete substratum of which possession is a relation is always presupposed. It is incorrect that possession develops historically into the family. Possession, rather, always presupposes this 'more concrete juridical category'. In cases, however, where the simpler relation historically preceded and developed into the more complex relation: 'the path of abstract thought, rising from the simple to the combined [which Marx has already called the 'scientifically correct' method – J.O.], would correspond to the real historic process'. *Grundrisse*, pp. 22–3.

23. This acknowledgement is found especially in Marx's correspondence, for example:
  Marx to Kugelmann (6 March 1868): '[Duhring] knows very well that my method of development [*Entwicklungsmethode* (i.e. as applied in *Capital I* – J.O.)] is *not* Hegelian, since I am a materialist and Hegel is an idealist. Hegel's dialectic is the basic form of all dialectic, but only after it has been stripped of its mystical form, and it is precisely this which distinguishes *my* method'. *MEW*, vol. 32, p. 538.
  Marx to Kugelmann (27 June 1870): 'What Lange says about the Hegelian method and my application of it [again, in *Capital* I – J.O.] is really childish. First

of all, he understands nothing about Hegel's method, and secondly, as a consequence, even less about my critical use of it . . . Lange is so naive as to say that I
'move with rare freedom in the empirical matter (*empirischen Stoff*)'. He hasn't
the least idea that this 'free movement in the (empirical) matter' is nothing but a
paraphrase for the *method* of treating *(behandeln)* the [empirical] matter —
namely, the *dialectical method*'. *MEW*, vol. 32, p. 686.

In the text destined for *Capital* II, but left unpublished, Marx writes: 'In a
review of the first volume of *Capital*, Herr Duhring remarks that, in my zealous
devotion to the scheme of Hegelian logic, I even discover the Hegelian figures of
the syllogism in the form of circulation. My relations with Hegel are quite simple.
I am a disciple of Hegel, and the presumptuous chattering of the epigoni who
believe they have buried that eminent thinker strikes me as frankly ridiculous.
Still, I have taken the liberty of adopting toward my master a critical attitude, of
freeing his dialectic of its mysticism, and of thus subjecting it to a profound
change'. Karl Marx, *Oeuvres, Economie II*. Edition établie par Maximilien Rubel,
(Gallimard, Bibliothèque de la Pléiade, Paris, 1968), p. 528; see also Rubel's note
on pp. 1688–9. Cf. *Capital* I, p. 25; *MEW*, vol. 23, p. 27.

Marx to Engels (16 January 1858): 'By the way, I am getting some nice
developments *(Entwicklungen)*. For example, I have thrown out the whole doctrine on profit as it stood up to now. In the *method* of treatment *(Bearbeitens)*
the fact that by sheer chance I again skimmed through Hegel's "Logic" has been of
great service to me. If some day I have the time for such work I would like very
much to make accessible to common sense, in two or three printers sheets, what is
rational in the method which Hegel discovered but at the same time mystified'.
MEW, vol. 29, p. 260. It is generally assumed that Marx never got to this project. A
notebook of Marx containing material gathered in 1860–61 (I.I.S.H. Amsterdam,
#B96) includes the beginnings of a summary of the *Logic* (4 ms. pp.); the sum-
mary includes Hegel's doctrine on 'Being', and it breaks off after a few lines on
the doctrine on 'Essence'. Cf. the *Critique*, p. 89; *Frühe Schriften* I, p. 373, where
Marx also projects a critique of Hegel's *Logic*.

The letter to Engels just cited is taken by some commentators to mark Marx's
'return' to Hegel after a long period of anti-Hegelianism which purportedly began
around 1844–45 and is especially evident in Part One of *The German Ideology*
(1845–46); cf. J.E. Seigel's review of B. Ollman's *Alienation*, in *History and
Theory*, vol. 12(3), 1973, esp. 341–2. I will return to this question later.

In the texts quoted, Marx, in addition to acknowledging his debt to Hegel
regarding his own theoretical method, affirms the distinction between the two
moments of science — empirical investigation and theoretical development/exposi-
tion — with their respective and 'formally distinct' cognitive methods of conceptual 'analysis' and 'synthesis'; and he also indicates that the term 'dialectic' most
properly applies to the second moment. I believe translators and commentators
should be more careful to respect Marx's distinction, and e.g. be wary of rendering
Marx's '*Entwicklung*' as 'analysis,' which confuses the distinction. Hegel appears
to have made a similar distinction between empirical investigation and theoretical
(i.e. philosophical-scientific) elaboration of a subject-matter; cf. e.g. *Die Vernunft*

in der Geschichte, edited by J. Hoffmeister (Felix Meiner Verlag, Hamburg, 1955), pp. 25–30 (in Hartmann's abridged English version – *Reason in History* – pp. 10–12).

24. *Capital* I, pp. 25–6; *MEW*, vol. 23, pp. 27–8.

25. *Critique*, pp. 8–9; *Frühe Schriften* I, pp. 262–3: 'Der Unterschied ruht nicht im Inhalt, sondern in der Betrachtungsweise oder in der *Sprechweise*'. (Emphasis in the original.) Also, *Critique*, p. 9; *Frühe Schriften* I, p. 264: 'Thus empirical actuality is admitted just as it is . . . but the empirical fact in its empirical existence has [due to the mystified method of treatment] a significance which is other than itself'. This is to say, in the words of *Capital*, that the mystified dialectic seems 'to transfigure and to glorify the existing state of things'. Cf. *Critique*, e.g. pp. 24, 39–40, 116; *Frühe Schriften* I, pp. 285, 306, 410.

26. Precisely because the theoretical content of *The Philosophy of Right* has a good measure of empirical accuracy, Marx can carry out a simultaneous criticism of Hegel's theoretical treatment of socio-political institutions, and of the existing institutions themselves; and acknowledgments of that accuracy are found throughout Marx's *Critique*, e.g. pp. 8, 36–7, 44, 51, 55, 64, 72; *Frühe Schriften* I, pp. 262, 301–02, 313, 321, 326, 338–9, 350; also Marx's 'Introduction to . . . the Critique . . .', published in the *Deutsch-französische Jahrbücher* (February 1844); in the *Critique*, pp. 135–7; *Frühe Schriften* I, pp. 495–6. Cf. the remarks of Eric Weil, in *Hegel et l'Etat* (J. Vrin, Paris, 1966), esp. pp. 113–15. Weil suggests that Marx's shift from an almost exclusively political focus in the *Critique* to a more social- and political-economic focus in the 'Introduction' of 1844 stemmed more from his critical examination of Hegel's treatment of 'civil society' (projected in the *Critique*, but apparently never written) than from his Parisian encounter with the working class. Marx's first draft, at least, of this published 'Introduction' (as well as 'The Jewish Question', also published in the 1844 *Jahrbücher*) predated his move from Kreuznach to Paris. This seems to lend weight to Weil's thesis. Unfortunately, however, the first draft of the 'Introduction' is lost. Still, there is the possibility that a textual comparison of the 'Introduction' with Hegel's treatment of 'civil society' will tend to show that Hegel, as well as Stein and others, was a first source of Marx's empirical information about the social- and political-economic 'state of things'. Cf. Marx's comments on 'civil society' in the *Critique*, pp. 80–82; *Frühe Schriften* I, pp. 361–4. On the dating of the 'Introduction' (1844) in relation to the *Critique* and 'The Jewish Question', see Bert Andréas, 'Marx et Engels et la gauche hégélienne', *Annali*, Instituto Giangiacomo Feltrinelli (Milan) 1964/65, vol. 7, 1965, esp. 355–6, 358, 377.

27. Or whatever the procedure of correcting Hegel's dialectic be called, e.g. 'standing it on its feet', 'stripping away its mystical shell' etc. – or as characterized in recent commentary (Avineri et al.), subjecting it to Feuerbachian 'transformative criticism'; all of these reduce to the same thing, the crux of which is

recognizing that Hegel's demiurge-Idea is simply a hypostatization of the method (or mode) of human thinking required for a 'scientifically correct' theoretical treatment and exposition of empirical subject-matter.

28. *Frühe Schriften* I, p. 450.

29. Cf. 'Introduction to ... The Critique ...': 'The criticism of the *German philosophy of right and of the state,* which was given its most logical, profound and complete expression by *Hegel,* is at once the critical analysis of the modern state and of the reality connected with it, and the definite negation of all the past *forms* of *consciousness in German jurisprudence and politics,* whose most distinguished and most general expression, raised to the level of a science, is precisely the *speculative philsophy of right.* ... This abstract and extravagant *thought* about the modern state ... the *German* thought-version of the modern state ... which abstracts from *actual man,* was possible because and in so far as the modern state itself abstracts from *actual man,* or satisfies the *whole* man only in an imaginary way'. *Critique,* pp. 136–7; *Frühe Schriften* I, p. 496 (emphases in original). The *Critique* was a first step in the process of 'discovering the new world by ... *ruthless criticism of the existing order*'; *Frühe Schriften* I, p. 447.

30. Esp. Shlomo Avineri, *The Social and Political Thought of Karl Marx* (The University Press, Cambridge, 1968); also 'The Hegelian Origins of Marx's Political Thought', *The Review of Metaphysics,* vol. 21(1), September 1967, 35–50.

31. The text: 'The [modern] dualism of civil society and political state, which the *Estate*-constitution purports to resolve through a *reminiscence,* appears in that constitution itself, in that the *difference of estates* (the differentiation within civil society) acquires in the *political* sphere a meaning different than in the civil sphere. There is apparent identity here: the same subject, but in an *essentially different* determination, thus in fact a *double* subject; and this *illusory identity* (it is surely illusory, because the *actual subject,* man, remains constantly himself, does not lose his identity, in the various determinations of his being; but here man is not the subject, rather man is identified with a predicate – the estate, and at the same time it is asserted that he exists in this *definite determination* and in *another* determination, that he is, as this definite, exempted and restricted thing, something *other* than this restricted thing) is artificially maintained by at one time having civil estate-division as such assume a character that should accrue to it only in the political sphere, and at another time reversing things so that estate-division assumes in the political sphere a character that does not issue from the political sphere but from the subject of the civil sphere. In order to present the one limited subject, the definite estate (the estate-division), as the essential subject of both predicates, or to prove the identity of both predicates, both are mystified and treated in an illusory and vague dimorphism *(Doppelgestalt).*

'Here the same subject is taken in different *meanings,* but the meaning is not one determined by the subject itself *(ist nicht die Selbstbestimmung)*, but is rather an *allegorical* determination foisted on the subject. . . . The meaning that civil estate-division assumes in the political sphere does not come from it, but from the political sphere. . . . The reverse is also true. This is the *uncritical,* the *mystical* way of *interpreting* an *old world-view* in terms of a new one, through which it becomes nothing but an unhappy hybrid. . . . This lack of *criticism,* this *mysticism* is the enigma of the modern constitutions (preeminently the Estate-constitutions) as well as the mystery of Hegelian philosophy, especially of the *Philosophy of Right* and *Philosophy of Religion.*

'The best way to rid oneself of this illusion is to take the meaning as what it is, as the *proper determination* [or actual character], then make it as such the subject, and consider whether its *ostensibly* proper subject is its *actual predicate,* i.e. whether this expresses its essence and true actualization'. *Critique,* pp. 83–4; *Frühe Schriften* I, pp. 364–6.

32. E.g., *Critique,* p. 72; *Frühe Schriften* I, p. 350: '[In the Middle Ages] the *estates of civil society* in general and the Estates, or *estates given political significance,* were identical. The spirit of the Middle Ages can be expressed thus: The estates of civil society and the political estates were identical because civil society was political society, because the organic principle of civil society was the principle of the state'.

33. *Ibid.*: 'But Hegel proceeds from the separation of "civil society" and the "political state" as two essentially different spheres, firmly opposed to one another. And indeed this separation *does actually exist* in the *modern* state. The identity of the civil and political estates in the Middle Ages was the *expression* of the *identity* of civil and political society. This identity has disappeared; and Hegel presupposes it as having disappeared'.

34. Cf. Avineri, *The Social and Political Thought of Karl Marx,* p. 22.

35. *Critique,* pp. 41–2; *Frühe Schriften* I, p. 309. This conclusion has an obvious relation, as Avineri points out, to Marx's call for 'true democracy' and universal suffrage; cf. *Critique,* pp. 29–31, 121; *Frühe Schriften* I, pp. 292–4, 417; Avineri, *The Social and Political Thought of Karl Marx,* esp. pp. 202–20.

36. E.g. *Critique,* pp. 71–2, 76 ff.; *Frühe Schriften* I, pp. 348–9, 355 ff. Here Hegel aims to establish 'a genuine link between the particular which is effective in the state and the universal'. His estates-constitution, however, fails in all respects to do so.

37. Cf. 'Introduction to . . . The Critique': '. . . . the *German* thought-version of the modern state . . ., which abstracts from *actual man,* was possible because and insofar as the modern state itself abstracts from *actual man,* or satisfies the *whole* man only in an imaginary way'. *Critique,* p. 137; *Frühe Schriften* I, p. 496.

Though the discussion in the *Critique* centers on 'estates' not 'classes,' Marx is already moving into an analysis of class in these very pages of his manuscript; cf. e.g. *Critique*, pp. 80–81; *Frühe Schriften* I, pp. 361–3; and M. Rubel, Introduction to Karl Marx, *Oeuvres*, *Economie* II, xxix–xxx. We should note other texts in the *Critique* which bear especially close relationship to this demand. For example, within the modern state as depicted in Hegel's *Philosophy of Right*, if man is to achieve political actualization he must 'abandon his civil actuality, abstract from it, and retire from this entire organization into his individuality . . . for as a state-idealist he is a being *who is completely other, distinct*, different from and opposed to his own [civil] actuality'. Accordingly, to function as a political being he 'must renounce his estate, civil society, the *unofficial* [i.e. nonpolitical] *estate*, in order to achieve political significance and efficacy; for it is precisely this *estate*, which stands between the *individual* and the *political state*'. *Critique*, p. 78; *Frühe Schriften* I, pp. 358–9.

In another place, Marx notes that the bureaucracy emerged historically as a feature of the gradual separation of civil society and state, 'of the particular interests and the absolutely universal'; and it is supposedly a particular estate whose interests as such coincide with the universal interest. It is however, merely the 'imaginary identity' of particular and universal interests, an imaginary identity which actually gives the opposition between them 'a legal and fixed form'; and so the bureaucracy must be abolished in the achievement of a real identity of those interests. But 'the abolition of the bureaucracy can consist only in the universal interest becoming *really* – and not, as with Hegel, becoming purely in thought, in *abstraction* – a particular interest; and this is possible only through the *particular* interest really becoming *universal*'. *Critique*, pp. 45–6, 48; *Frühe Schriften* I, pp. 314–5, 318. Within a few months Marx identifies the 'proletariat' (mentioned in the *Critique* only as *'der Stand der unmittelbaren Arbeit'*) as the 'estate', 'class' and 'sphere' in which particular and universal interest really coincide, and which, significantly, embodies the demand for *'die Auflösung aller Stände'*. With this, the 'proletariat' becomes explictly Marx's 'critical and revolutionary' counterpart to the bureaucracy as *'allgemeine Stand'* in Hegel's *Philosophy of Right*, and *eo ipso* those to whom it falls to effect what will be called the 'classless society'. Cf. *Critique*, pp. 81, 141–2; *Frühe Schriften* I, pp. 362, 503–4; and Avineri, *The Social and Political Thought of Karl Marx*, pp. 37–8, 57 ff.

38. *Writings of the Young Marx on Philosophy and Society,* edited by Loyd D. Easton and Kurt H. Guddat (Doubleday, Garden City, 1967), p. 231; *Frühe Schriften* I, p. 468.

39. *Ibid.*, p. 225; *Frühe Schriften* I, p. 461. Cf. the *Critique*, p. 81–2; *Frühe Schriften* I, p. 363: 'Present civil society is the accomplished principle of *individualism:* individual existence is the final end, while activity, labor, content, etc., are *merely* means . . . The *actual man* is the *private man* of the present-day political constitution. . . . The estate . . . separates man from his universal nature. . . .'

40. *Ibid.*, p. 241; *Frühe Schriften* I, p. 479.

41. In the 'Introduction to ... the Critique ...': '... a class in civil society that is not of civil society, an estate that is the dissolution of all estates, ... a sphere of society ... that cannot emancipate itself without emancipating ... all the other spheres of society....'; *Critique*, p. 141; *Frühe Schriften* I, p. 503; cf. *Critique*, p. 81; *Frühe Schriften* I, p. 362. This 'dissolution of the existing order of things' includes 'the negation of private property'; *Critique*, p. 142; *Frühe Schriften* I, p. 504.

42. *Feuerbach: Opposition of the Materialist and Idealist Outlooks* (The first Part of 'The German Ideology' published in accordance with the text and arrangement of the original manuscript) (Lawrence and Wishart, London, 1973) (hereafter: *Feuerbach*), p. 43; the corresponding German edition, *Die deutsche Ideologie* 1. Band. Kapitel 1, in *Karl Marx/Friedrich Engels/Gesamtausgabe (MEGA)*, *Editionsgrundsätze und Probestücke* (Dietz Verlag, Berlin, 1972) (hereafter *Probeband*), p. 64. Cf. also *Feuerbach*, pp. 53, 72–3; *Probeband*, pp. 76, 97–8.

43. *Misère de la Philosophie*, in Karl Marx, *Oeuvres, Economie* I. Edition établie par Maximilien Rubel (Gallimard, Bibliothèque de la Pléiade, Paris, 1963), p. 136.

44. *Preface to A Contribution to the Critique of Political Economy* (dated January 1859; hereafter *Preface* of 1859); *MEW*, vol. 13, pp. 8–10.

45. *Critique*, pp. 8–9; *Frühe Schriften* I, pp. 262, 263–5: 'The Idea is given the status of a subject, and the *actual* relationship of family and civil society to the state is conceived to be its *inner imaginary* activity. Family and civil society are the presuppositions of the state; they are the really active things; but in speculative philosophy it is reversed'.
    ... 'Family and civil society make *themselves* into the state. They are the active force. According to Hegel they are, on the contrary, *made* by the actual Idea. It is not their own life's course which unites them into the state, but rather the life's course of the Idea.... The political state cannot exist without the natural basis of the family and the artifical basis of civil society; they are its *conditio sine qua non;* but the conditions are established as the conditioned, the determining as the determined, the producing (or producer) as the product of its product. ... The fact is that the state issues from the mass of men existing as members of families and of civil society; but speculative philosophy expresses this fact as an achievement of the Idea.... Thus empirical actuality is admitted just as it is and is also said to be rational; but not rational because of its own reason, but because the empirical fact in its empirical existence has a significance which is other than it itself. The fact, which is the starting point, is not conceived to be such but rather to be the mystical result'.

46. *Critique*, p. 32; *Frühe Schriften* I, p. 296.

47. *Critique*, p. 100; *Frühe Schriften* I, p. 388. Also: 'Thus, at its highest point
the political constitution is the *constitution of private property*. The highest
political inclination is the *inclination of private property* ...'; *Critique*, p. 99;
Frühe Schriften I, pp. 386–7.

'. . .What Hegel presents as the end, the determining factor, the *prima causa*, of
primogeniture is, instead, an effect of it, a consequence, the power of *abstract
private property* over *the political state*, while Hegel presents primogeniture as the
power of the political state over private property. He makes the cause the effect
and the effect the cause, . . . ' etc.; *Critique*, p. 100; *Frühe Schriften* I, p. 338.

'The highest political construction is the construction of abstract private property'. *Critique*, p. 100; *Frühe Schriften* I, p. 389.

'*Independence, autonomy*, in the political state whose construction we have
followed so far, is *private property*, which at its peak appears as inalienable *landed
property*. Political independence thus flows not *ex proprio sinu* of the political
state; it is not a gift of the political state to its members, nor is it the animating
spirit [of the political state]. Rather, the members of the political state receive
their independence from a being which is not the being of the political state, from
a being of abstract private right, namely from abstract *private property*. Political
independence is an accident of private property and not the substance of the
political state. . . .The significance that *private property* has in the political state is
its *essential*, its true significance. . . .

'Thus, if independent private property in the political state, in the legislature,
has the *significance of political independence*, then it *is* the *political independence*
of the state. Independent private property, or *actual* private property is then not
only the support of the constitution but the *constitution itself*. And isn't the
support of the constitution nothing other than the constitution of constitutions,
the primary, the actual constitution?' *Critique*, pp. 107–8; *Frühe Schriften* I,
pp. 398–9.

48. Marx was no doubt referring to this research, which is recorded in his five
Kreuznach Notebooks from the summer of 1843, as well as the *Critique* when he
spoke of the 'studies' that led him to the 'materialist' view of society and the
state. When read in the light of his Kreuznach excerpts, Marx's statements in the
Critique – 'property is the support of the constitution' etc. – assume a significance beyond what they appear to have when encountered in the *Critique* alone.
The excerpts show him to have been, already in the summer of 1843, much closer
to (I think in fact already at) the materialist view of the state, as summarized in
the *Preface* of 1859, than is often supposed. Still unpublished, these notebooks
have been generally ignored by commentators – D. Rjazanov and M. Rubel being
the notable exceptions. Cf. also Günther Herre, *Verelendung und Proletariat bei
Karl Marx* (Droste Verlag, Düsseldorf, 1973), pp. 35–44.

49. *Feuerbach*, p. 18; *Probeband*, p. 37. Cf. *ibid.*, p. 25; *Probeband*, pp. 45–6:
'This method of approach *(Betrachtungsweise)* is not devoid of premises. It starts
out from the real premises (or presuppositions – *Voraussetzungen*) and does not

abandon them for a moment. Its premises are men, not in any fantastic isolation and rigidity, but in their actual, empirically perceptible process of development under definite conditions'.

50. *Ibid.*, p. 23; *Probeband*, pp. 43–4; cf. note 45 above.

51. *Feuerbach*, pp. 25–6; *Probeband*, pp. 45–6: 'As soon as this active life-process is described, history ceases to be a collection of dead facts as it is with the empiricists . . . , or an imagined activity of imagined subjects, as it is with the idealists.

'Where speculation ends – in real life – there real, positive science begins: the representation *(Darstellung)* of the practical activity, of the practical process of development of men. Empty talk about consciousness ceases, and real knowledge has to take its place. When reality is depicted *(. . . mit der Darstellung der Wirklichkeit . . .)* philosophy as an independent branch of knowledge loses its medium of existence. At the best its place can only be taken by a summing up *(Zusammenfassung)* of the most general results derived through abstraction from the observation of men's historical development *(Resultate . . . die sich aus der Betrachtung der historischen Entwicklung der Menschen abstrahieren lassen).* These abstractions have in themselves, i.e. if considered apart from real history, no value whatever. They can only serve to facilitate the arrangement *(Ordnung)* of the historical material, to indicate the sequence *(Reihenfolge)* of its separate strata *(Schichten).* . . . Our difficulties begin only when we set about the observation *(Betrachtung)* and the arrangement, the real depiction *(die wirkliche Darstellung),* of our historical material, whether of a past epoch or of the present'. Cf. the text from *Capital* I given in note 8 above.

Speculative philosophy thus 'loses its medium of existence' precisely because 'true positive science' preempts both its method and subject matter, leaving 'empty talk' as the only thing proper to it. In *The German Ideology,* the methodological discussion bears directly on a 'science' of history; but the principles asserted apply *mutatis mutandis* to a 'science' of existing society, as the end of the text just quoted, and those to follow, suggest.

The fact that Marx does not go on to state in detail the 'premises' *(Voraussetzungen)* that govern the 'removal of [the]difficulties' involved in the observation and arrangement of the historical material is not crucial. These premises, he notes, will be made evident only 'by the study of the actual life-process and the activity of the individuals of each epoch' *(Ibid.,* p. 26; *Probeband,* p. 46); by which I take him to mean that the particular 'abstractions' and the order of their sequence in the depiction of a particular epoch will be determined only by the empirical study of that epoch: i.e., once again, the 'dialectic' is determined by the subject-matter; cf. note 13 above.

52. *Ibid.*, pp. 31–3; *Probeband*, pp. 51–5.

53. *Ibid.*, pp. 36–42; *Probeband*, pp. 56–65.

54. *Ibid.*, p. 44; *Probeband,* p. 65.

55. Cf. note 44 above.

56. I do not believe, therefore, at least with respect to the questions treated here, that *The German Ideology* represents in Marx's intellectual development either a final *coupure* or a temporary departure from Hegel.

57. In chronological order:
1)   'Introduction' of 1857 (late August—mid-September 1857); *Grundrisse,* pp. 28—9.
2) ⎱ *Grundrisse* (October 1857—end of February 1858), Notebook II (November
3) ⎰ 1857); *Ibid.,* pp. 138—9, 175. (Cf. also *Ibid.*, pp. 186—92.)
4)   Marx to Ferdinand Lassalle (22 February 1858); *MEW,* vol. 29, p. 551.
5)   Marx to Engels (2 April 1858); *MEW,* vol. 29, p. 312.
6)   *'Preface'* of 1859 (January 1859); *MEW,* vol. 13, p. 7.
7)   Marx to Joseph Weydemeyer (1 February 1859); *MEW,* vol. 29, p. 573.
    On the genesis and significance of the plants for the 'Economics', see Maximilien Rubel's Introduction to Karl Marx, *Oeuvres. Economie* II (Gallimard, Paris, 1968), xvii—cxxvii, the help of which I gratefully acknowledge here.

58. *Grundrisse,* pp. 28—9. On rubric 1, cf. *Ibid.,* pp. 7—10, 22—8.

59. Letter of 22 February 1858; *MEW,* vol. 29, p. 551. The preliminary chapters of *Capital* eventually appeared as *A Contribution to the Critique of Political Economy* (1859).

60. Marx to Engels (2 April 1858); *MEW,* vol. 29, p. 312: 'The whole mess *(Scheisse)* should break down into 6 Books: 1. On Capital. 2. Landed Property. 3. Wage labor. 4. State. 5. International Commerce. 6. World Market.
    '1. *Capital* breaks down into 4 sections. a) Capital in general... b) *Competition... c) Credit,* where capital appears in contrast to individual capitals as the universal element. d) *Share-capital* as the most consummate form (passing over [*überschlagend*] into communism), together with all of its contradictions. The transition *(Übergang)* from capital to landed property is at the same time historical, because the modern form of landed property is a product of the working of capital on the feudal-etc. landed property. So too, the transition of landed property into wage labor is not only dialectical but historical, because the final product of modern landed property is the general establishment of wage labor, which then appears as the basis of the entire mess'.

61. *MEW,* vol. 13, p. 7. The letter of February 1, 1859 to J. Weydemeyer (*MEW,* vol. 29, p. 572) has it thus: 'I divide the whole of political economy into 6 Books: Capital; Landed Property; Wage Labor; State; Foreign Commerce; World Market. Book I on Capital breaks down into 4 divisions: *Division I: Capital in general*

breaks down into 3 chapters: 1. Commodity; 2. Money or simple circulation; 3. Capital'.

Marx then goes on to say that the first two of the three chapters of *Capital* make up the contents of *A Contribution to the Critique of Political Economy*, and he lists those contents in a detailed breakdown. The first chapter is an historical account of the analysis of the commodity; the second is on 'money or simple circulation'. Marx subsequently notes 'that the analysis *(Analyse)* of the simple money-forms is the most difficult, because it is the most abstract, part of political Economy' *(MEW*, vol. 29, p. 573).

It appears then, that the 'scientifically correct' method of treatment/exposition – moving from 'abstract' to 'concrete' – obtains overall, though not necessarily within particular parts and subparts of the 'scientific' exposition: there are parts in which Marx's treatment is indeed conceptual analysis; e.g. he begins *Capital* I with 'the commodity,' then quickly analyzes it into its relatively more 'abstract' components, use- and exchange-value etc. Overall, however, his plans for the whole of *Capital* and for the 'Economics', of which 'Capital' was to be but the first rubric, clearly show his intention to proceed so as to achieve and convey a progressively more concrete concept of the modern ('bourgeois') world.

62. Hence Marx's references to his 'preliminary chapters' of the treatise 'On Capital' as 'the most abstract part of political economy'; Marx to Lassalle (12 November 1858), to Weydemeyer (1 February 1859); *MEW*, vol. 29, pp. 567, 573; cf. Marx to Engels (2 April 1858); *MEW*, vol. 29, pp. 312–18; and *Grundrisse*, p. 162.

63. *Grundrisse*, pp. 138–9. The second statement follows an elaborate outline of the rubric on 'capital,' and it is closer in form to what was subsequently communicated in the letters and published in the *Preface* of 1859: 'After capital, landed property, then wage labor, would have to be treated. Given these three categories [i.e. capital, landed property, wage labor], there would be movement of price, that is to say circulation now determined in its internal totality. Moreover, the three classes as three fundamental forms of production and as the presuppositions of circulation. Then the *state*. (State and civil society. – Taxes, or the existence of the unproductive classes. – Public debt. – Population. – The state and its external tendencies: colonies. External commerce. [. . .] – Finally, the world market. Encroachment of bourgeois society on the state. Crises. Dissolution of the mode of production and type of society based on exchange value. Real organization of individual labor as social labor and vice versa.)' *Grundrisse*, p. 175.

64. That this was Marx's intention can hardly be doubted. As he struggled to complete the first rubric, 'on capital,' with a growing awareness that he would get no farther than that, he made clear to Engels that his treatment of that rubric was to be an 'artistic' and 'dialectically organized' whole. Marx to Engels (31 July 1865); *MEW*, vol. 31, p. 132.

65. *Feuerbach,* pp. 41–2; *Probeband,* pp. 62–3. The 'world market' is thus another instance of 'demystifying' Hegel. Cf. also *Ibid.,* pp. 38–40, 75–6; *Probeband,* pp. 58–60, 101, where this 'world-historical' liberation entails the 'overthrow' not only of individual states but of the state as such.

66. The parallel becomes more striking when one recalls the relationship between Marx's 'proletariat' (Rubric 3) and Hegel's bureaucracy as 'universal estate'; and when one reexamines the versions of the plan of the 'Economics' given in the 'Introduction' of 1857 and in Notebook II of the *Grundrisse:* rubrics 1–3 comprise altogether the 'inner structure of civil society', and rubric 4 is the 'synthesis of civil society in the form of the state . . . in relation to itself'. Cf. also, in the same versions, Marx's indication of the relationship between his rubrics 4–6 above, and Hegel's view of his final three points in the *Rechtsphilosophie:* 'The state is (a) its inner structure as a self-relating development – *inner state law or the constitution;* it is (b) a particular individual, and thus in connection with other particular individuals – *international law;* (c) but these particular spirits are only moments in the development of the universal idea of spirit in its actuality – *world history'. Enzyklopädie* (1830), edited by F. Nicolin and O. Pöggeler (Felix Meiner Verlag, Hamburg, 1969), para. 536, p. 413. In *The Philosophy of Right,* Hegel has it thus (para. 259): 'The Idea of the state (a) has immediate actuality and is the individual state as a self-dependent organism – the *Constitution* . . .; (b) passes over the relation of one state to other states – *International Law;* (c) is the universal Idea as a genus and as an absolute power over individual states – the mind which gives itself its actuality in the process of *World-History.' Ibid.,* translated by T.M. Knox (The Clarendon Press, Oxford, 1962), p. 160; in Hoffmeister's German edition (Felix Meiner Verlag, Hamburg, 1967), pp. 212–13. Cf. Hegel's point (c) in this para. and Marx's allusion in *The German Ideology* (text quoted above) to 'a power which baffles the German theoreticians' and which 'turns out to be the world market'. See also the *Zusatz* to this para.; in the Knox translation cited p. 279.

67. Inasmuch as Marx's first statements of his plan for the 'Economics' reflect the influence of Hegel and yet predate his perusal of 'The Logic' at the end of 1857 (the plan was stated by mid-September; Freiligrath only offered the volumes to Marx in October), it is not accurate to characterize that perusal as marking a 'return' to Hegel. Cf. *Freiligraths Briefwechsel mit Marx und Engels.* Published by Manfred Häckel (Akademie Verlag, Berlin, 1968), vol. I, p. 96.

68. *Philosophie des Rechts, Vorrede,* Hoffmeister edition, p. 17; Knox translation, pp. 12–13.

69. See for example his letters to J. Weydemeyer (27 June 1851), F. Lassalle (22 February 1858), F. Engels (2 and 20 August 1862, 15 August 1863, 13 February 1866, 7 May 1867, 16 May 1868), S. Meyer (4 July 1868), Engels (10 October 1868), N. Danielson (12 December 1872 and 17 January 1873), P. Lavrov

(11 February 1875), F. Sorge (4 April 1876), Danielson (15 November 1878 and 10 April 1879), F. Domela-Nieuwenhuis (27 June 1880); also Engels to Sorge (29 June 1883); *MEW*, vol. 27, p. 560; vol. 29, p. 550; vol. 30, pp. 267, 281, 368; vol. 31, pp. 178, 296–9; vol. 32, pp. 88, 55, 181; vol. 33, pp. 549, 559; vol. 34, pp. 122, 179, 359, 370–72, 447.

FRIEDRICH ENGELS – MARXISM'S FOUNDING FATHER
NINE PREMISES TO A THEME

MAXIMILIEN RUBEL
Centre National de la Recherche Scientifique, Paris

> "For the ultimate triumph of the principles established in the Manifesto, Marx counted solely and exclusively on the intellectual development of the working class such as should necessarily result from common action and discussion".
>
> F. Engels, Preface to the Fourth
> German Edition of the Communist
> Manifesto, May 1, 1890

I

Marxism is not an original product of the Marxian way of thought. If today, as in the past, the Marx debate is still the object of general discussion, it is principally concerned with problems which Engels resolved partially or not at all. To the extent that they admit of an answer, these problems demand the aid of Marx himself. This is not to imply that Engels must be excluded from the present discussion, yet we may legitimately ask just how qualified he is to serve as a reference in a debate focused on writings which escaped his attention. In more general terms, this question might be formulated: What are the limits to Engels's competence as the incontestable executor of Marx's intellectual heritage – a heritage which continues to be invoked even today in clarifying the material and moral dilemmas of modern times?

II

This question obliges us to examine the central problem of the intellectual relationship between Marx and Engels, both considered the "founders" of a body of ideological and political conceptions artificially subsumed under the label of "Marxism." The very fact that such a question must be asked reveals a phenomenon most characteristic of our era which we are tempted to designate as the "myth of the twentieth century." What is more, we must not forget that the "founders" themselves at times adopted mythological interpretations in characterizing the peculiar nature of their friendship and intellectual collaboration. Indeed, it was Marx who ironically referred to the example of the antique "Dioscuri" and that of Orestes and Pyladus, and Engels who amusedly remarked on the rumour that "Ahriman-Marx" was said to have diverted "Ormuzd-Engels" from the path of virtue.[1] We also note the inverse tendency, i.e. with growing frequency Marx as the "true" founder is opposed to Engels who is degraded to the rank of "pseudo-dialectician."[2]

III

Any investigation of the relations between Marx and Engels will never progress should it fail to acquit itself of the legend of the "founding" of Marxism and to begin methodically with the *aporia* of the concept of Marxism. Karl Korsch merits special attention for having attempted, two decades ago, during a period of radical intellectual reorientation, to launch a critique of Marxism tantamount to a declaration of war. However, Korsch never wagered the ultimate step: that of ridding this concept of its mythological residuum. Instead, he tried to ride off the difficulty by using linguistic artifices designed to overcome the conceptual problem and conserve "important elements of the Marxian doctrine" in view of "reconstructing a revolutionary theory and *praxis*." In his *Ten Theses on Marxism Today* he speaks interchangeably of "the teaching of Marx and Engels," "Marxist doctrine," "Marx's doctrine" and "Marxism."[3] His fifth thesis, concerning the precursors, founders and continuators of the socialist movement, even omits the name of Engels, Marx's *alter ego*! Korsch was, nevertheless, not far from the truth when he wrote:

> All contemporary efforts to re-establish the unity of Marxist teachings and its primary function as a theory of social revolution for the working class have proved to be reactionary utopias. (Second Thesis)

Korsch would have been even more accurate had he spoken of "aberrant mythology in place of "reactionary utopias."

IV

In view of the evident impossibility of unequivocably defining the concept of "Marxism," the logical conclusion would be to abandon this word altogether, is spite of its current universal usage. Reduced

today to no more than a mystifying catchword, "Marxism" was marked from the very outset with the stigma of obscurantism. In his last
years, after his work had finally penetrated the wall of silence which
had accompanied his first publications, Marx in fact tried to disengage
himself from this term, declaring peremptorily: "Tout ce que je sais,
c'est que *moi* je ne suis pas marxiste." Engels affirmed that this statement was directed against the "Marxism" rampant among "certain
Frenchmen" during the 1880s but was meant as well for the intellectuals and students in the German social-democratic party: they
together with the whole "oppositional" press stirred up talk about a
grotesquely deformed kind of Marxism."[4] That Engels was the one to
pass on to posterity this highly revelatory remark does not relieve him
of the responsibility of having sanctioned this unjustifiable term with
his authority. Tasked with the preservation and continuation of a
theory to whose elaboration he avowedly contributed little,[5] Engels
was persuaded that in glorifying his friend's name he was also righting
a wrong. However, in so doing he willingly risked favoring a superstition whose nefarious consequences were then unforeseeable —
consequences which today, nearly eighty years after his death, are
unmistakably evident. As he decided to adopt the expressions
"Marxist" and "Marxism" coined by his adversaries, so as to change an
injurious label into a title of glory, he was unaware that this gesture of
defiance — or was it an act of resignation? — made him the godfather
of a mythology destined to dominate the twentieth century.

V

The genesis of the Marxist myth can be traced step by step by
following the course of the conflicts which took place within the
International Working Men's Association in the early 1870s. Out of
the need to stigmatize their "enemy" and his partisans, the "anti-
autoritaires," headed by Bakunin, inventively produced terms such as
"Marxides," "Marxiens," "Marxistes."[6] In time Marx's French followers became accustomed to being called by an epithet which they
had not themselves created. This linguistic expediency, which at first
merely distinguished them from other socialist factions, finally became a political and ideological label. Henceforth, all that was needed
was for Engels to sanction with his authority the use of a term whose
ambiguity did not immediately occur to its users. At the beginning
Engels vigorously opposed such terminology; he, more than anyone
else, was conscious that this threatened to corrupt the basic significance of the teachings which were conceived of as the theoretical ex-

pression of a social movement — and not as a doctrine invented by a particular individual for the benefit of an intellectual elite. He persisted in his resistance until 1889, at a time when the internal quarrels between "possibilists," "Blanquists," "Broussists," "collectivists" and "Guesdists" threatened to cause a definitive rupture in the French working-class movement: each faction now decided to organize "its own" international working men's congress. Engels was obviously caught in a dilemma, and this is why he sought to avert further confusion and verbal or ideological corruption by referring to "Marxists" or "Marxism" in quotation marks or prefaced with the qualification "so-called." Answering Paul Lafargue's fear of seeing his group pass for one "faction" among others in the working-class movement, Engels remarked: "We have never called you anything but 'the so-called Marxists' and I wouldn't know what to call you otherwise. If you have another name as short as that, tell us and we shall use it accordingly, and with pleasure."[7]

Once engaged on the path of terminological concessions, Engels was obliged to go the whole way. He decided to take that final step when he thought the victory of the "collectivists," led by Guesde and Lafargue, to be near: "But the position we conquered upon the anarchists after 1873 was now attacked by their successors, and so I had no choice. Now we have been victorious, we have proved to the world that almost all socialists in Europe are 'Marxists' (they will be mad they gave us that name!) and they are left alone in the cold with Hyndman to console them."[8] An irony of sorts, for it was precisely Hyndman whom Marx had advised not to refer to his name in writing the program of the new British socialist party: "In the party programs everything which evidences a direct dependency on any author or any work must be avoided."[9]

VI

In contrast to Nietzsche who published his *Ecce homo* for fear of being one day canonized by undesired disciples, Marx had no need of such a precaution: he had been unable to write and publish more than a fragment of his projected works. Indeed, his published writings and posthumous papers are tantamount to a formal and rigorous prohibition of any effort to attach his name to the cause for which he fought and to the teaching he formulated in the belief that this act bore the sanction of the anonymous proletarian masses. Had Engels respected this injunction and had he, in his capacity as Marx's testamentary executor, vetoed the usage of this ill-conceived term, the world-wide scandal of "Marxism" would never have seen the light. Instead, Engels committed the unforgivable mistake of endorsing this abuse and thus acquired the dubious glory of being the first "Marxist." He thought himself heir but was, in fact, founder, although involuntarily so, and we might be prone to say that this was fate's own punishment. That "irony of history," which Engels so often extolled, played a bad trick on him: with the following words, pronounced on the occasion of his 70th birthday, he ruefully became a prophet in spite of himself: "My destiny wants that I shall reap the honour and glory sown by one who was greater than I, Karl Marx."[10] And today we should accord him both the contestable merit and even more dubious title of being the "founding-father of Marxism."

VII

In the history of Marxism as the cult of Marx, Engels played the principal role. The human, quasi-religious aspect of the relationship between the two men is sufficiently well-known to dispense us from special examination. On the other hand, however, it is necessary to investigate in detail the effects of this behavior both on Marx and on his direct or more distant disciples. Engels, always a willing pioneer for Marx's ideas, expressed many thoughts of his own which the latter was certainly unable to accept without reservation. The fact that he nevertheless said nothing can be explained by his desire to respect scrupulously the bond of solidarity between them. We cannot determine with certitude whether or not Marx identified himself with all that Engels did or said, at least on essential matters, yet in fact this problem is a relatively minor one in view of Marx's declared admiration for his friend's intellectual talents. He even considered himself to be Engels's disciple.[11] In any event what Marx refrained from doing has today become our strict obligation: the task at hand is that of breaking the spell of his legend and determining in view of the destiny of the working-class movement, the true place of Engels's work in developing the intellectual patrimony of socialism.

VIII

Only through an understanding of Engels as a potential founding-father is it possible to recognize why the way in which he fulfilled his task of editing and continuing Marx's writings, offers, today more than ever, serious grounds for criticism. [12] The Marxian texts neglected by Engels (the material for Marx's doctoral thesis, the anti-Hegel manuscript from Kreuznach, the economic-philosophic manuscripts prepared in Paris and Brussels, the first draft of the "Economics" dating from 1857–1858, his numerous notebooks of notes and extracts, the correspondence with third parties, etc.) present problems of radical interpretation to the researcher and specialist; what is more, they generate new categories and new generations of readers who no longer can or will content themselves with the stereotyped phraseology of professional Marxists. And their refusal is all the greater at a time when their goal is to understand, to live and to act in a world threatened by ideology, mechanization and the manipulation of minds, and allied with crude violence to produce a state verging on total self-destruction.

IX

The points outlined here are intended as an introduction to a debate centered on the problem of Marxism as the mythology of our era. Engels's responsibility in creating this worldwide superstition is a secondary issue to the extent that we can − while respecting the teaching of Marx the "materialist" − affirm that ideologies, including Marxism and all its variants, do not fall from heaven but are fundamentally linked to class interests, which are at the same time the interests of power. Moreover, if we recognize in Engels the legitimate heir to Marx's thought, we are justified in denouncing in his name and to his glory that very Marxism which has been established as a school of illusions and confusion for our cataclysmic age of iron.

NOTE TO THE READER

The city of Wuppertal (German Federal Republic) organized, in May 1970, an international scientific conference for Friedrich Engels's 150th birthday. This event drew the participation of nearly fifty Engels-specialists from more than ten European countries, Israel, and the United States. Their task was to resume modern research on the thought of this man who was the closest friend and collaborator of Karl Marx and who is universally considered as one of the founders of "Marxism." I was among those invited to participate in this conference and submitted for discussion a paper consisting of eight critical "theses" or "viewpoints," centered around Engels's responsibility for the foundation of what has now become a dominant ideology of our world. Since I had assumed that this celebration would be more scientific than commemorative in spirit, I thought it imperative to pass on my critical remarks to a scientific audience aware of the problems produced by the evolution of ideas which are linked to this century's own particular events and upsurges. Consequently, I sent the organizers of the conference a paper, written in German, entitled "Gesichtspunkte zum Thema 'Engels als Begründer'."

My surprise was great, on arriving in Wuppertal, to be received by the conference officials who immediately informed me of their predicament: my Soviet and East-German colleagues felt personally offended in reading my "Viewpoints" and threatened to leave the conference unless this contribution be withdrawn from the debates! After tedious negotiations we came upon a formula which seemed to mitigate the irritation of the "scientific" representatives from the so-called socialist countries: henceforth the papers would no longer be read from the podium but simply commented upon and discussed.

There is little interest in recounting here the details of the debate provoked by my "Viewpoints." The objections brought up against them were wholly void of quality, while the conduct of certain participants betrayed their categorical refusal to engage in any discussion which might engender doubts about that scheme of ideological positions known as "Marxism-Leninism." Moreover, this obstinate, if not simply insulting, refusal of discussion was an adequate confirmation of the basic critique to be made of the very use of the concept "Marxism." My "Viewpoints" had been conceived of in particular as a denunciation of the illogical usage of this concept, and of the fanaticism and mythology to which it is attached.[13] The epilogue to the conference again emphasized the relevance of my denunciation, which through a simple exercise in semantics actually defends Marx's social theory against Marxist mythology. The organizers made no scruple to violate the elementary rules of editing policy generally respected in bourgeois democratic states: the text rendered suspect (and which had been submitted *at the request* of the officials) was not included in the volume dedicated to the contributions received in advance of the conference.[14] *Habent sua fata libelli. . . .*

The above is an English rendition, amplified by a number of comments, of the German manuscript which was turned down by the organizers of the Wuppertal conference.

NOTES

1. Cf. Marx to Engels, January 20, 1864, and April 24, 1867; Engels to Bernstein, April 23, 1883. There are instances where even the two friends were spoken of as if they were one: "Marx and Engels says"; cf. Marx's letter to Engels, August 1, 1856.

2. See, for instance, the opposition established by Iring Fetscher between Marx's "proletarian philosophy" and that of Engels. Fetscher also examines their differing perspectives on the "negation of philosophy" and the relation between human history and nature, on the conception of an "objective" dialect of nature and of thought as a reflection of reality, which Marx held to be inacceptable; cf. I. Fetscher, *Karl Marx und der Marxismus. Von der Philosophie des Proletariats zur proletarischen Weltanschauung* (R. Piper Verlag, Munich, 1967), pp. 132 ff. See also Donald C. Hodges, "Engels's Contribution to Marxism" in *The Socialist Register*, 1965, 297–310; Vladimir Hosky, "Der neue Mensch in theologischer und marxistischer Anthropologie," in *Marxismusstudien*, 7, 1972, 58–86; and Jürgen Habermas, "Zur philosophischen Diskussion um Marx und den Marxismus" in *Theorie und Praxis* (Luchterhand, Neuwied am Rheim und Berlin, 1963) pp. 261–335.

3. Cf. Karl Korsch, *Zehn Thesen über Marxismus heute*, 1950. First published in French by M. Rubel, *Arguments*, 16, 1959, 26–27, Paris.

4. Cf. Engels's letter to the editors of the *Sozialdemokrat*, dated September 7, 1890 and published in that journal, September 13, 1890. Engels reported Marx's spontaneous sally each time the occasion presented itself; see his letters to Bernstein, November 3, 1882, to Conrad Schmidt, August 15, 1890, and Paul Lafargue, August 27, 1890. The Russian revolutionary G.A. Lopatin conversed with Engels in September 1883 about the perspectives of revolution in Russia. Recounting this meeting to a member of *Narodnaia voliia*, Lopatin wrote: "You remember, I told you once that Marx himself never was a Marxist. Engels told me that during the conflict between Brousse, Malon & Co. and the others, Marx had said one day with a laugh: "I can only say one thing, that *I am not a Marxist!...*" (Lopatin to M.N. Ochanina, September 20, 1883, in *MEW*. 21, 489.) However, there was no note of amusement in Marx's account of his impressions gathered from the reported quarrels during the two socialist congresses held in France in the fall of 1882, the possibilists at Saint-Etienne and the Guesdists at Roanne. Both "the 'Marxists' and the 'anti-Marxists,' these two types," he wrote to Engels, "have done their best to spoil my holiday in France" (September 30, 1882). On the subject of Marx's disagreement with the Russian "Marxists," provoked by the question of the future of the peasant commune, see Marx's letter to Vera Zasulitch, March 8, 1881, in *Oeuvres*, "Economie," vol. 2 (Gallimard, Paris, 1968), pp. 1556 ff. Material concerning Marx's and Engels's relations with their Russian followers may be found in: *Marx/Engels: Die russische Kommune. Kritik eines Mythos*, edited by M. Rubel (Hanser Verlag, Munich, 1972).

5. Engels's formal declarations to this effect are too numerous to be noted here. Let us simply say that they leave no trace of a doubt concerning the paternity of the great scientific discoveries, attributed without exception to Marx alone. His most significant declaration is perhaps the note Engels introduced into a text with the intention of demonstrating the continuity of German philosophy by raising its most deserving heir, Karl Marx, to the rank of a system-founder (cf. Engels, *Ludwig Feuerbach and the End of Classical German Philosophy*. In German in *MEW* 21, 291–292). It was here that Engels officially christened the theory after Marx: "Since the dissolution of the Hegelian school, a new current has developed, the only one to have truly borne fruit, and this current is fundamentally linked to the name of Marx." And Engels repeated this symbolic act further on, stating explicitly: "I would never have been able to realise what Marx accomplished ... Marx was a genius, while the rest of us, we are at most men of talent. *It is therefore just that this theory bear his name.*" After a remark of that nature we are hardly surprised by the conclusion to this text, in which Marx is ordained as the heir and founder of a philosophic school: "The German working class movement is the heir of classical German philosophy" (*ibid.*, p. 307). With these words, Engels put the final touch on the Marx legend.

6. Cf. M. Rubel, "La Charte de la Première Internationale," in *Marx critique du marxisme* (Payot, Paris, 1974), p. 25–41; Manale, Margaret, "Aux origines du concept de 'marxisme' ", in *Cahiers de l'I.S.E.A.,* série S, no. 17, p. 1397–1430; and "la Constitution du 'marxisme' ", in *Cahiers de l'I.S.E.A.,* série S. no 18, p. 813–840.

7. Letter to Paul Lafargue, May 11, 1889.

8. Engels's letter to Laura Lafargue, June 11, 1889.

9. Marx to Hyndman, July 2, 1881.

10. Letter to the editors of the paper *Berliner Volksblatt*, December 5, 1890 (*MEW* 22, 86).

11. "You know that 1. I always catch on to things late, and 2. always follow in your footsteps" (Marx to Engels, July 4, 1864).

12. Cf. M. Rubel, "Introduction" to vol. 2 of *Oeuvres*, "Economie" (Gallimard, Paris, 1968), pp. cxxi ff. See also *ibid.*, pp. cxxviii ff. for a list of the "discoveries" which Marx acknowledged having made. He never took credit either for the founding of "historical materialism" or for the discovery of "surplus value." Their attribution to Marx was Engels' gesture, tacitly approved by the former. See, for example, Engels's articles in *Das Volk* (London, 1859; in *MEW* 13, 468–477) and the Marx biography which he wrote for the *Volkskalender* in 1877 *(MEW* 13, 468–477.).

13. , A summary of the Wuppertal debates is given in the article written by Henryk Skrzypczak "Internationale wissenschaftliche Engels Konferenz in Wuppertal", in *Internationale wissenschaftliche Korrespondenz zur Geschichte der Deutschen Arbeiterbewegung* (IWK). Berlin, no. 10, June 1970, pp. 62 ff. A resumé of the "Viewpoints" is found on pp. 81 ff.

14. *Friedrich Engels, 1820–1970. Referate – Diskussionen – Dokumente.* Internationale wissenschaftliche Konferenz in Wuppertal vom 25–29 Mai 1970. Hanover, Verlag für Literatur und Zeitgeschehen, 1970.
    We find the following comments on my "position" on pp. 25 ff.:
"In order to be able to fulfill the program foreseen for the final day, the conference council decided to dispense with discussion following the sixth session and to begin with the general debate immediately after the seventh session. First of all, Maximilien Rubel was to continue [?] the exposition of his conception. He had submitted to the conference a text formulated in polemic terms and attacking Engels, but did not present it subsequently to the assembly [and with reason!]. His eight theses which, according to the author's original intention, were to provoke a debate of the actual significance of Marxism today, may be summarized as follows: After Marx's death Engels devoted much effort to the task of transforming the term "Marxism," which had been coined by Marx's adversaries, into an intelligible and definable concept. In so doing, Engels unwittingly founded a system of hybrid thought which had nothing in common with Marx's own intentions. Following Engels's death the germs of this ideological system developed into a conceptual methodology necessarily dependent on certain class relations."
    The report then mentioned a polemic from a precedent session in which my views confronted those of an East-German Marxist, Erich Hahn, regarding the concept of "historic mission," a debate "in which Engels played only an indirect part" (*ibid.*, pp.255 ff.).
    Much could be said about this "abridged report" summarizing my theses and the "polemic" which they provoked. However, I only wish to emphasize that my text was not intended as an "attack on Engels" but rather, through its criticism of a gesture which proved to be historically negative, was directed against a particular school of Marxist thought whose very existence constitutes the negation of all that Marx and Engels had done for the working class movement and for socialist thought. And I continue to maintain that my contribution, more than any other, honored the scientific spirit of this conference: was it not our task to pay our respects in a scientific manner to the originator of "scientific socialism," a concept which he nevertheless equated with "critical socialism." The only true homage the conference might have paid to the man it was celebrating would have been to adopt as its guideline and the basis of its debates the following statement from a letter of Engels to Gerson Trier (December 18, 1889):
    "The working-class movement is founded on the most rigorous critique of existing society. Critique is its vital element. How could it dispense itself from self-critique and prohibit debate?"

WEST-EUROPEAN MARXISM TODAY

IRING FETSCHER
Johann-Wolfgang Goethe University, Frankfurt/Main

In our day, Marxism is not only the political doctrine of communist and socialist parties but is, at the same time, an influential and manifold intellectual current in Western Europe. One could even say somewhat paradoxically that it became a more influential and interesting intellectual current (and undercurrent) precisely when communist and socialist parties abandoned at least some of their (traditional) elements by adapting themselves to the patterns of parliamentary democracy and inter-party peaceful competition. The two subjects of my paper are certainly linked and therefore it will not be possible to deal with them separately; the connections and contradictions, however, may not always be evident.

I. WESTERN EUROPEAN MARXISM – FROM REVOLUTION TO COOPERATION

The evolution of Marxist parties from a revolutionary radical rejection of the existing political (and socio-economic) system to a (partial) acceptance of the political system (and its socio-economic "basis") can be observed today for the second time. It had already been the fate of the German Social-Democratic party after 1914/18 and it was repeated – in a somewhat modified form – by the Italian and French Communist Parties after 1956 when Krushschev opened up new possibilities for the propagation of "peaceful forms of transition" from capitalism to socialism in the developed Western countries. Almost from the very beginning members of radical revolutionary groups (*"groupuscules"*) have criticized these new tendencies as "opportunist" and "revisionist" and as mere repetitions of Bernstein's "deviation" under new banners, and the Chinese Communists have laid strong emphasis on this criticism since their open break with the Soviet leadership of the socialist camp. But in order to consider whether such criticism is justified it is necessary to investigate both the theoretical self-justifications of communist parties such as the Italian and French ones, and the possibility of accounting for their new approach by a new evaluation of the changed historical situation in the world (independent of their arguments). Within the context of this short paper I shall have to confine myself to a few systematic statements which can be further developed in discussion. I shall start with the more general statements and come to the more specific ones step by step:

1. Revolution and cooperation are not necessarily opposites. A revolution in Marxian terms is a transformation of the socio-economic structure of society, a transition from feudalism to capitalism or from capitalism to socialism, for instance. This transition can take place in a more or less violent form (in England the Glorious Revolution achieved this transformation in a peaceful form a century before the French Revolution, whereas in France it had to take a violent form because of the strength of feudal opposition and international interference). It is true that Marx, Engels and later Lenin insisted time and again upon the necessity for the emerging new class of the proletariat to take over the (formerly) bourgeois state and to transform this "instrument" into a means for the emancipation of the workers and the suppression of the bourgeoisie. But according to Marx and Engels this "takeover" could occur in "peaceful forms" in states such as England or the United States where neither bureaucracies nor standing armies were prepared to suppress revolutions (as in Prussia-Germany or Austria-Hungary). It is open to question whether these statements by Marx and Engels can still be applied to contemporary democratic states, all of which have bureaucracies (but of quite a different kind than at Marx's time) and standing armies.

2. In Marx's view the (bourgeois) state is, in the first place, an instrument for holding back the exploited (proletarian) masses. This means identifying the state with police forces, prisons, the army and law courts. But at the same time Marx and Engels knew quite well that state power does not rest on force alone, that it is based on "consent," on a kind of "legitimacy" as Max Weber would call it; this legitimacy in the latter's view was "incarnated" in institutions such as parliament, the "law" (legal rules for the exercise of power) and publicly accepted morals. In other words, the rule of the ruling class does not rest only on repressive state organs but also on an ideological domination of the minds of the "lower classes," the proletariat.

It cannot be doubted that the contemporary bourgeois state has not only progressed in the development of its "material means" of suppression (a much more perfect police system) but also in the elaboration of legitimizing institutions (social intervention for the sake of "public welfare" in general) and ideologies. The strongest and most convincing modern state ideology is just the contention that the state "manages" the whole economy, tries to maintain full employment, economic growth, money stability and the balance of payments. Whereas the old "liberal state" in fact or at least in theory restricted its activity to maintaining the legal preconditions of free trade, namely the predictability of individual and state actions (insofar as both were governed by laws), the new intervention state has (at least in theory) taken over responsibility for the functioning of the economic system itself and its social consequences. This has changed the character of demands for reform. They are in fact (if not in theory, because sometimes, as in Germany during the Erhard period, state intervention is still regarded as a "sin") no longer alien to the existing order, they can no longer be qualified as "the victory of a new principle" over the ruling liberal principle (as Marx called the Ten-Hours Bill in England).

As long as the state in fact (or apparently) fulfills this new function there seems to be no problem of legitimacy and it is difficult to arouse revolutionary tendencies among the people. But, on the other hand, the state (the political system) has now completely identified itself with the economic order and has no longer any "excuse" for an economic crisis. Therefore, both of the following statements are true: 1) the state in late capitalist societies has become to a much higher degree identical with the existing economic order and 2) as this state has already taken over "ideally" the role of public provider of economic goods (and services) it would be no longer a total break if it took over the ownership of the means of production as well. In fact, in all developed European capitalist societies the state already owns a considerable part of the means of production (although they are still managed in similar ways to private enterprises, the only difference being that their deficits are covered by taxes directly and not indirectly as in the case of big enterprises which receive state subsidies in the interest of "public welfare").

It is certainly true that as long as the economy rests on a "capitalist" (market) economy the state is forced to remain within the "rules of the game" and cannot go beyond certain limits (it must not alienate the interests of those who decide on investments, that is the owners of the means of production); nevertheless it has developed a great number of "means" which would certainly facilitate a gradual transformation into a socialist economy. Had Mitterand been victorious in France, he would have been able to utilize the instruments created by de Gaulle to carry out a gradual reform which might have produced, if not a socialist society, at least a mixed economy of a considerable different "quality."

3. Not only the state but also society has undergone profound structural changes since the times of Marx. Within the last two decades the percentage of *manual workers* as compared with *non-manuals* has rapidly declined and is declining still further, in countries such as England, Germany and France. It may now have reached the ratio of 3:2 and soon will be 1:1. This does not mean that our societies have become "homogenous middle-class societies" as the sociologists of the fifties would have it, but that certainly a revolutionary change can less and less be based on the manual workers alone. Marxists both within and outside political parties have therefore re-discovered the Marxian category of *"Gesamtarbeiter,"* the collective worker, which is composed of both manuals and non-manuals and in fact creates all the wealth of contemporary societies. Above all the role of scientists within this "collective worker" is becoming increasingly important.

From this fact communist parties such as the Italian and French draw different conclusions from the left-wing radicals within the student and intellectual movements. Communist parties react tactically to the tendency for white-collar people to become more and more relevant for the creation of popular majorities. They advocate "peoples's fronts" and "common programs" which respect not only the interests of workers (manuals and non-manuals) but also of small farmers and businessmen because they assume that a large part of the white-collar workers will — for the time being — not become revolutionary communists but at most democratic socialists or Christian socialists. The Italian Communist Party has gone so far as to give up its anti-religious bent (at least in its program) and has repeatedly declared that a socialist Italy cannot be built without the help of Italian Christians (!). The *"programme commun"* of French Communists, Socialists and Radicals contains specific guarantees for the small capitalist (rural, commercial and artisan). Despite these tactical concessions, all communist parties still insist "in principle" on the primacy of the working class as the subject of socialist revolution. But this class needs allies, and these can be found among the "anti-monopolistic classes" of society — including parts of the bourgeoisie.

On this point party Marxists and radical Marxists (of the *groupuscules*) differ most. Many of them (since about 1967) claim that *within the working class* a new working class of skilled and sometimes scientifically trained workers can and eventually will become the leading revolutionary force. As their importance within the collective worker is growing day by day and as – at the same time – their intellectual level and their (possible) class-consciousness is much higher than in the rest of the working class (part of which may even become reactionary as part of a "declining stratum"), they form the real nucleus for the future socialist revolution. The students, of whom an ever growing number do not face an independent life in the liberal professions or business become more and more part and parcel of this "new working class" and as such part of a (potential) *avant-garde.*

The opposition of traditional Marxists to this concept of a new working class (Serge Mallet) was articulated by the late Werner Hoffman. He maintained that the so-called rebellion of students was and is in fact a reaction to the social decline they are experiencing, their loss of (economic) independence and their refusal to accept this fate. As part of a declining petty-bourgeois stratum, students were therefore objectively reactionaries rather than revolutionaries but had clad their retrogressive aims in a revolutionary vocabulary. Later communists both in Germany and France tried to adopt a somewhat more positive attitude towards student rebels, but the fact that most student rebels were hostile to the bureaucratic Soviet type of socialism and denounced communists as "revisionists" generally served to prove their point: that there can be no revolutionary movement without the working class, and that, being more or less middle-class, students who denounce the communist party are still under the spell of their class origins and ideology.

4. *Antonio Gramsci* – one of the few Marxists respected by both party Marxists and left-wing radicals – had already stated that in developed capitalist societies the problem of *ideological hegemony* may prove to be more difficult to solve than the problem of mere *political power.* The class struggle therefore, if it is to be successful, will more and more be a struggle "on the ideological front," a struggle for hegemony over minds (and only indirectly over the key positions of power). If this is so, peaceful means of transition will again prevail over violent ones. But this, of course, is not tantamount to "cooperation." Cooperation turns out to be inevitable only because the final success of the ideological struggle is not likely to come so soon. But as the state has to fulfill more and more socio-economic functions, even Marxist revolutionary parties can no longer abstain from participating in sharing responsibility for decisions which are taken in the parliament. A complete rejection of any participation, as was at least theoretically advocated by the Marxist center of the German Social-Democrats before 1914, is no longer possible.

It is not only because bourgeois ideologies have deeply penetrated the minds of the proletariat (as Gramsci stated) but also because a socialist revolution no longer presents itself as the only possible solution to the problem of proletarian survival that a new and more developed kind of ideological struggle seems to be necessary. Revolution will no longer be born of sheer material need but will be based on a concrete and detailed "vision" (a concrete utopia) of the future socialist society. This vision must at the same time ensure that the future society will differ considerably from the Soviet model. Here again are some of the weaknesses of party Marxists who — even if they keep some distance from the Soviet model as do the Italian Communists — have difficulty in accounting for the amount of repression in the Soviet Union during the "personality cult" and even today. Radical Marxist revolutionaries outside the orthodox parties tend to insist on new *democratic forms* of workers' self-management of factories, on direct participatory democracy and decentralization as a decisive means against state bureaucracies. This ideological tendency is sometimes linked with the advocacy of different strategic approaches, namely factory occupation and local violence as means of a direct (decentralized) takeover by the working class; actions out of which, step by step, a revolutionary movement could be created and spread over the whole country. Communist parties are generally opposed to both the strategic device of factory occupation (or terror against factory managers and owners) and the vision of a de-bureaucratized and decentralized socialist society in which the "councils" would be the real centers of class power.

5. The differences between communist-party Marxism and radical non-party Marxism are most fundamental when it comes to defining socialism or a socialist society. Starting from a statement by Frederik Engels according to which "private production" and even the "anarchic way of capitalist production" are already overcome by joint-stock companies which produce "for the associated account of many" (shareholders) and by "trusts which monopolize entire branches of industry thereby doing away with 'planlessness' " (cf. *MEW*, vol. 22, pp. 231 ff). Based on this Engelsian position *Rudolf Hilferding* in his *Finance Capital* and *V.I. Lenin* held that late capitalism (or monopoly capitalism) has in fact more or less freed itself from domination by the law of value (*Wertgesetz*) and produces the "forms of a *transitional* period from capitalism to a higher social and economic order" (*Imperialismus als höchstes Stadium des Kapitalismus*, Berlin 1945 p. 77). It is true that Lenin at the same time stresses the fact that monopoly-capitalism does not completely abolish competition and produces "a series of particularly sharp and flagrant contradictions"

(loc.cit.). But nevertheless *Gert Schäfer*, one of the young Marxist critics of Engels and Lenin is right when he says that "for this conception generally an understanding of 'planlessness' and 'private production' is introduced which has little to do with the exact concept of capital as developed by Marx" (*Karl Marx-Friedrich Engels, Staatstheorie, Materialien zur Rekonstruktion der marxistischen Staatstheorie,* Frankfurt-Berlin-Wien, 1974, *Einleitung* p. 130). The social character of any capitalist production is achieved only behind the back of the producers through the "law of value" *(Wertgesetz)*. Therefore, capitalist production can only be called "social" *"an sich"* (i.e. for the theoretical analyst); it would only become social for itself *("für sich")* if transformed and elevated to the socialist way of production. Engels's understanding (like Hilferding's and Lenin's) confuses the specific kind of social character of capitalist production of commodities with immediate social production. But capitalist private production does not disappear if it is changed into 'production for the associated account of many capitalists' . . . Capitalist planlessness does not disappear when trusts and similar organizations of capital plan on a large scale. . ." (*ibid.* p. 132).

This fallacy of party Marxists has important practical consequences. It could convince Lenin that all he needed was a copy of the German war-economic planning with some kind of complementary workers' control, just as Hilferding had praised the organizational preparation for socialism achieved by finance and monopoly capitalism. The expropriation of the expropriators thus could be condensed in the socialist state's act of taking over banks.

The problems which disappear if one starts from such assumptions as those of Lenin and Hilferding are 1. the role of the law of value in monopoly capitalist economies, 2. the role of international commerce in so-called socialist planned economies which nevertheless participate in the world market and act as a kind of unified "state trust."

Ignoring the first problem leads directly to overlooking the second. And once the law of value as the central category of any capitalist production was ignored it was possible to "rediscover" it as a "means" of a more flexible and decentralized planning within so-called socialist countries.

At this point the criticisms made by the New-Left Marxists may join the much cruder criticism levelled by the Chinese Marxists against the Soviet way to socialism as a kind of neo-capitalism.

Another – more pragmatic – tradition of criticism of the content of so-called socialist planned economies can easily be combined with this theoretical one. *Leszek Kołakowski* in 1956 gave the ironic definition that "socialism does not exist in a country which builds excellent jet-fighters but bad shoes for its citizens." Only recently *Andras Hegedüs* has made a more systematic critique of the Hungarian planning authorities. They take, he said, the aims of their plan either from existing trends in their own economy (extrapolation) or from stages of economic evolution which have already been reached by more developed (non-socialist) societies. In either case one cannot speak of socialist planning. What those bureaucrats do is imitate capitalist industrialists in their own way, and to surpass it only by speed (their secret ideal being: the same but quicker). But in fact what socialism was supposed to do was to free society from the pressure of blind tendencies and to permit the "associated producers" to plan their common future in a concrete and practical way, to decide what kind of production and what kind of everyday life they wish to prepare for themselves and their children, no longer to follow the immanent "tendencies" of an automatic evolution but to make decisions and change the flow of events. All this seems to be completely absent from socialist planning which, in all seriousness, sets itself the task of "catching up with capitalist countries and overtaking them" (!). This mistake is tacitly connected with the misunderstanding of monopoly capitalism and the superficial evaluation of capitalist "planned economy" inaugurated by Engels. Bertolt Brecht in his *"Me-Ti-Buch der Wendungen"* hits the nail on the head when he says that the decisive error of Stalin was "to have made planning an economic not a political problem," that is that he merely saw a pragmatic and technical problem instead of the decisive new aspect of a truly socialist society.

6. Linked with the economic-political questions discussed above are the problems of *pedagogics, psychology and everyday life* as approached by party Marxists on the one hand and non-party New Left Marxists on the other.

It is true that in the beginning the approach of the New Left Marxists was more influenced by Sigmund Freud, Wilhelm Reich and Herbert Marcuse than by Marx, but later these influences were increasingly combined.

Theoretically, the incorporation of psychological categories into Marxist theory is connected with the *discussion of fascism* (which, by the way, has also contributed to the critical approach to the theories of state-monopoly capitalism and socialist planned economy discussed above). Traditional Marxism was not sufficiently prepared to interpret and account for the fascist mass movement. Certainly there was "false consciousness," but how was it able to develop on such a large scale, and why did the labor movement prove so weak when confronted by it? *Wilhelm Reich* was the first to point to the "characterological" aspect of the problem. He thought he had discovered the psychical roots of fascism in the minds of working-class and lower middle-class people. They were to be sought in the sexual repression exercised by the traditional family structure. Therefore, if working-class people were to be enabled freely to develop a consciousness of their real interests (their political class-consciousness) sexual repression had to go. By giving the new generation a non-repressive sexual education, the roots of fascism could be cut. This, however, was of little help against actual fascism and later Wilhelm Reich himself became more and more of an eccentric biological mystic which helped to undermine his reputation, already under severe attack from both Freudian psychoanalysts and orthodox Marxist-Leninists. The revival of Wilhelm Reich among the New Left in Germany (and the U.S.A., and to a much lesser degree in France and Italy) was connected with the general tendency of our contemporary societies towards more sexual freedom and a heightened awareness of all kinds of repression and taboos.

A more subtle and less radical approach to the problem of fascist characterology was developed by Horkheimer, Marcuse, Adorno and their collaborators in their "Studies in Prejudice," above all in their study *The Authoritarian Personality* published in 1950 in New York. Here a kind of fascist "syndrome" is diagnosed in which authoritarian attitudes are linked with anti-feminism, racism and rejection of all kinds of liberal values. Again, characterological aspects are related to the family structures and educational patterns of the (lower) middle classes. Recent studies, however, made at the *Institut für Sozialforschung* in Frankfurt, have made clear that the interpretative patterns of *The Authoritarian Personality* cannot be applied to other social strata and necessarily give distorted images when applied, for instance, to working-class or non-working-class samples alike. A certain kind of authoritarianism within the working class seems to be unavoidable under present conditions. For instance, does the real (and realistic) fear of losing one's job produce a special kind of xenophobia which cannot be equated with middle-class racism. If, however, one accepts these criticisms (as they are formulated in a forthcoming doctoral dissertation by Ursula Jaerisch) one can again ask oneself how working-class authoritarianism might be overcome. And the answer will certainly be that under present conditions it cannot be. The consequences of this diagnosis are: first, to accept an authoritarian workers' party and second, that this authoritarian (elitist) party once in power is hardly likely to produce social conditions under which working-class authoritarianism will disappear.

Behind the decline of "belief" in socialist salvation by working-class revolutions expressed by some of the New-Left Marxists (generally reluctantly and overtly) seems to lie the following line of argumentation:

1. Working-class people no longer *need* a socialist revolution merely to survive; for the time being they can survive under capitalism just as well, at least in the developed countries.

2. If, to mobilize working-class movements, an elitist kind of party remains necessary, the creation of such a party together with working-class authoritarianism (which, in fact, Lenin had already praised and contrasted to the *petit-bourgeois* libertarianism of the intellectuals) paves the way to the kind of bureaucratic state socialism we see in the East-European countries.

All this can be understood as a new and understandable argument in favor of a non-proletarian basis for a socialist revolution. It is not only the decline of blue-collar workers in numbers but also the characterological quality of these working-class people which makes it not only unlikely but also undesirable to hope for a working-class based socialist revolution. As far as I know *no* representative of the new Marxist left goes as far as that, but there can be no doubt that qualms of this kind lie behind some of their ideas.

On the other hand, the traditional party Marxists, whilst at the same time insisting on the necessity for any socialist revolution to have a proletarian character, do not always take the "real working class" of the developed countries very seriously.

II. SOME CHARACTERISTICS OF NON-PARTY MARXIST THEORIES IN GERMANY AND FRANCE

I have already mentioned several times the critical remarks and objections of New Left Marxists in contrast to the positions held by Party Marxists in France and Italy. It is now time to sum up some of these remarks and look at the kind of neo-Marxism they produce:

1. *Critique of political economics.* Some of the authors of the New Left such as Herbert Marcuse, Max Horkheimer, Theodor W. Adorno, and even Juergen Habermas tend to neglect economics completely or to deal with it in a very cursory way. Generally it has been assumed (by Habermas for instance) that in highly monopolized state-interventionist societies the law of value production no longer operates (if it ever did, which Habermas used to deny). The state has entered as a new subject and the problems it faces are now those of *legitimacy* (because the liberal ideology which assumes that everybody receives

his due via exchange of equal value no longer works). Both assertions are, of course, far removed from any Marxist analysis. 1. The assumption that in monopolized economies the law of value production no longer operates mistakes the different ways in which this law operates today for the non-existence of the law itself. 2. The liberal ideology neither objectively nor subjectively served the purpose which Habermas ascribes to it. Problems of legitimacy have always formed part of class dominion and state rule. States of all kinds can function regularly only through a combination of ideological argumentation and brute force (held in reserve). The character of the legitimizing ideologies has again changed, but not the fact that every state needs such an ideology. What is new, however, is that the ideology which now justifies the state in a much more direct and unmediated way, also justifies the socio-economic system. The state, capitalist economy, society, and political institutions have become one.

If some neo-Marxists tend to neglect economics altogether, others, on the contrary — as we have seen — accuse even party Marxists of not being sufficiently orthodox, of confusing Marxian categories with categories of bourgeois economics and of misunderstanding the fundamental differences between capitalist and socialist "economics." Research in this field has not yet reached a conclusive stage, but it is now generally accepted (by people like Helmut Reichelt, H.G. Backhaus and a group of philosophers at Konstanz) that 1. Marx's *Capital* is only an abstract reconstruction of a pure capitalist economy and must not be confused with a description of reality; 2. in the past the *"Wertformenlehre,"* the theory of "forms" in which value appears and above all the money form, has been dealt with inadequately so that, for instance, even today two different and opposed assumptions as to the character of Marx's theory of money are accepted in the Soviet Union (a metallist and a non-metallist theory). 3. (in contradiction to Althusser to whom these German authors are nevertheless partially indebted) Hegelian dialectical categories are essential for an adequate understanding of the inner dynamic character of capitalism.

2. *Base-superstructure.* There seems to be near unanimity that superstructural elements (above all ideas) have a relatively independent role to play and have been too much neglected in the past. Whereas Soviet and East-German Marxists tend to insist on the necessity for a "moral code for the builders of communism," neo-Marxists are liable to stress the necessity for emancipation from traditional social institutions (such as the family) and moral taboos (mostly sexual).

3. *Class — the role of the proletariat.* From the very beginning the Frankfurt School (after a brief flirtation by some of its members with

proletarian Marxism before 1933) separated Marxism from the working class. Many New-Left intellectuals in Germany and France would
probably accept V.G. Kiernan's statement that: "the origin of Marxism is not to be found in the birth of the proletariat alone, and its
identity with the proletariat was always more a wish than a fact" (*The
Socialist Register*, 1968, p. 209). The desire to attribute a larger revolutionary role to intellectuals (and to students among them) has found
additional support in the social development which has led to the
continuous growth of non-manual (skilled) workers and at the same time
to a steady increase in the proportion of students who have to face a
future as wage-earners and cannot even dream of an independent
position.

As a result of this development socialism has become more "moralist;" it is based less on the economic need of the masses than on social
ideals embraced by a new generation that tends to identify itself with
the miserable and downtrodden not only in its own country. It may
be true that declining classes such as the *petit-bourgeois* intellectuals
are traditionally more inclined to become romantics and reactionaries
than revolutionaries, but the fact remains that they (at least a leading
group of them) did become socialist revolutionaries and that their
motives can be found in certain moral needs (or the need for self-
justification which every intellectual feels to a certain degree).

This last point may account for the puzzling fact that in the middle
of never-dreamed-of material plenty (in the sixties in the USA and
Germany, as in France in 1968) large masses of intellectuals and students stood up for socialism. "Moral and cultural reasons for putting
an end to capitalism have become much stronger than any merely
economic ones" (Kiernan *op.cit.* p. 208) — many New-Left Marxists
may agree with this statement, tacitly at least, since they may prefer
to conceal their own moral commitment and present their attitudes as
the outcome of rational argumentation alone. The reasons for advocating socialism have completely changed and some — as Theodor
Adorno already did — may go as far as advocating socialism not because capitalism has lost its inner dynamics before fulfilling the needs
of the majority of its producers-consumers but, on the contrary,
because our economy must come to a half if we are to avert the
complete destruction of our ecological environment.

TROTSKY, MARXISM AND THE REVOLUTION OF BACKWARDNESS

BARUCH KNEI-PAZ

The Hebrew University of Jerusalem

From the endless welter of partisan polemics, diatribes and recriminations which weigh down upon the name and thought of Leon Trotsky, actual stature and character of his contribution to Marxist theory are understandably difficult to unearth. His followers and opponents alike, each for obviously different purposes and in different ways, have for the most part distorted, exaggerated and generally misconstrued his views and ideas. To read the Trotskyist and anti-Trotskyist literature of the 1930s, or even that which to this day continues to appear, is to wonder whether Trotsky was a modern saviour or the incarnation of the devil himself.[1] And as for the recent revival and contemporary re-interpretation of Trotsky amongst young radical circles in the West, the less said the better; the curious transmutation, in such circles, of his theory of the "permanent revolution" into what may be called the existential concept of "permanent revolt", has absolutely nothing to do with any of his writings or ideas. He is hardly to be blamed for such metaphysical acrobatics; they are a caprice and a reflection of our times and concern, not his.[2]

Indeed, therefore, in the thirty-five years since Trotsky's death as during most of his lifetime, the *terribles simplificateurs* of history, of all shades and predilections, pro and con, have had a field day with him. But even if one looks at the less partisan, more scholarly accounts of Trotsky's thought, which are in any case sparse, one finds that his place in the pantheon of Marxist thinkers remains, when not vague and undefined, acknowledged largely on the basis, and under the impact, of the apparent role or image into which history has pigeonholed him. It is clear that his great controversy of the 1930s with Stalin, from which he seemed to emerge as a kind of "conscience" of "true Marxism" — whatever that may mean — has here also cast its long shadow over the whole of his theoretical writings. As a consequence, while it is not unrecognized that the theory of the per-

manent revolution arose as a response to the specific problematics of
the relevance of Marxism to a backward society such as Russia, it is its
internationalist element — which assumed such prominence in the
1930s in confrontation with the idea of "socialism in one country" —
that is taken to be its essential feature. Its other elements are either
ignored or quickly summarized, as if constituting today no more than
a historical curiosity. Accordingly, the most commonly encountered
view of Trotsky is that he was, first and foremost, a theorist of "world
revolution"; that, moreover, he was a Marxist in the "classical" style
and mold, by which it is presumably meant that his fundamental
orientation was Western, that his primary frame of reference was a
world beyond the borders of Russia, that his grasp of the theoretical
substance of Marxism and its translation into a political creed and
movement was in the great European tradition but, thereby, largely
irrelevant or alien to his native milieu. This portrait of Trotsky
emerges in numerous accounts but nowhere more so, or in an ostensibly more credible manner, than in the late Isaac Deutscher's well-
known, and in many ways justly praised, three-volume biography.[3]
Deutscher, of course, is a sophisticated and intelligent historian; he
does not, it is true, confine his account to such a characterization
alone but also duly makes note of such of Trotsky's writings as reveal
very different concerns and attitudes. However, this is largely incidental and marginal to the unifying theme of Deutscher's biography, the
overall message of which is unmistakable: in the long procession of
Russian revolutionary figures and thinkers, Trotsky is to be seen as the
outstanding symbol of Marxist internationalism. Since Deutscher's is a
definitive work, it has been crucial in establishing this "classical"
image of Trotsky and his thought.

Indeed, this image has become so ubiquitous and persistent, and so
seemingly convincing, that hardly a single voice has been raised to take
issue with it.[4] Little wonder, then, that Trotsky has acquired the aura
of a Don Quixote figure, of an idealistic, uncompromising and obsessive servant of great and pure ideals, who, nevertheless, is doomed to be
always defeated. This would seem to make Trotsky in many ways
attractive and certainly dramatically and historically fascinating, but,
as a thinker, far from interesting or original. Put more concretely, the
view of Trotsky we are commonly asked to adopt is that of a European oriented Marxist who was the "odd man out" in the revolutionary regime which arose in Russia and, even before that, essentially a
stranger to his place and times, animated by matters which had only
secondarily anything to do with the abiding concerns of the Russian
Marxist movement.

Now the fact of Trotsky's internationalism is undeniable; he *was* a proponent of world revolution and his interests *did* extend beyond those of many of his sometimes down-to-earth, more provincial, Russian revolutionary contemporaries. Unlike not a few of these, he *did* pay more than lip-service to certain fundamental Marxist axioms and ideals; thus, for example, he never failed to champion the doctrine that the socialist revolution must be the work primarily, if not exclusively, of the working class, whether in Russia, in Europe, or even in Asia, specifically China. And by temperament and intellect he *was* hostile to, and free of, all national, not to mention nationalist, sentiments. But to say all this and to leave it at that is to divorce it from the context in which Trotsky upheld all such precepts. For the truth of the matter is that the significance and character of Trotsky's Marxist thought — whatever some of its traditional or classical aspects — lie elsewhere. And this is so clear from the record of his written work as to be a cause for wonder that it has been so little noticed or acknowledged. To put the matter directly, Trotsky, far from being mired in internationalist concerns, was throughout his life preoccupied with the problem of the relationship and applicability of Marxism to Russia, or, more generally, to backward, non-capitalist societies, and the idea of the "world revolution" was an *aspect of this,* not *vice versa.* In fact, this problem so concentrated Trotsky's mind that in the process he re-worked and extended certain Marxist axioms in such a way as to formulate a theory of the socialist revolution which was specifically applicable to backward societies. In view of the "success" of Marxist movements in the non-European world, it needs to be said, in retrospect, that Trotsky did as much as anyone to postulate such a phenomenon, and to account for it, and to effect, as well, a fundamental re-orientation of Marxism in the twentieth century — though all this was only grudgingly and incompletely acknowledged in his time and has been generally unappreciated since.

In order to establish this significance of Trotsky's thought, I propose, in what follows, to give an account of what I shall call his theory or conception of backwardness and, in terms of it, to briefly explicate his theory of the permanent revolution. The latter, it will be seen, was not, as has sometimes been assumed, primarily a theory of the international or world revolution. It did postulate a European revolution, but it was, first of all, a theory of what I shall refer to as the revolution of backwardness. And because it was firmly grounded in a sociological and historical analysis of backwardness, the theory of the permanent revolution, whatever its defects — and I shall touch upon these as well — cannot be dismissed as simply a clever rationalization

for the autonomy of revolutionary radicalism. In the light of the interpretation to be presented, it may be possible to say that the school or
variety of Marxism to which Trotsky's thought belongs is far more
heterogeneous than that with which it has been hitherto commonly
associated.[5]

* * *

To appreciate the scope of Trotsky's theoretical achievement, it
needs to be recalled that at the time he first formulated the theory ot
the permanent revolution, that is, in the years immediately following
upon 1905, Russian Marxism was in theoretical doldrums. Though
they had readily embraced the theories of Marx and had proceeded to
build a movement upon them, Russian Marxists had hardly resolved
the problem of what the immediate relevance was of such theories to
Russia. And Marx himself had not provided them with any sure guidelines in this direction. Now it is true that the possible relevance to
Russia of his social and political ideas had not escaped the notice of
Marx.[6] But Marx cannot be said to have either considered the matter
systematically or to have pronounced unambivalently upon it. He was,
undoubtedly, intrigued by the peculiarities of the Russian social and
economic situation – witness his decision to learn the Russian language, his efforts to study Russian development, his attempts to
analyse the significance of the Russian commune and his general re-
captivity to inquiries from his Russian followers. He did, in the end,
envisage the prospect of a Russian revolution providing a "signal" for
a proletarian revolution in the West; but since he made the chances of
the Russian revolution turning into a socialist affair dependent on the
– dubious – viability of the Russian commune, it is not clear what
precisely he had in mind nor how optimistic he was about this whole
scenario.[7]

Marx had certainly not produced a variant of his theories which
could be made applicable to a non-capitalist, non-industrialized society such as Russia was in the nineteenth century and would largely
remain into the next. But he had warned against attempts to "meta-
morphose" his account of Western development into one grand "his-
torico-philosophic theory of the general path every people is fated to
tread".[8] Strangely enough, his Russian followers proved to be doctrinaire on this very issue. Plekhanov, for instance, never countenanced
anything but a repetition in Russia of the Western path of development. And the Mensheviks, of course, forever remained adherents of
this position. But not only the Mensheviks; Lenin too was in this
respect an "orthodox" Marxist (however dubious the appellation in

view of Marx's own apparent rejection of such orthodoxy). Until 1917, and except for what was clearly an impulsive deviation in 1905 which he then quickly corrected and abandoned,[9] Lenin also would consistently cling to the view that Russia must traverse more or less the same history as Europe before there could be any real prospects of a Russian socialist revolution. Of course, it is true that Lenin was concurrently propounding a conception of the revolutionary movement which, given its success, would ultimately make largely immaterial his "orthodox", theoretical reservations about the immediate applicability of Marxism or the timing of the socialist revolution. Nevertheless, such "orthodoxy" accentuated the fact that the Marxist theory of revolution had been merely transplanted to Russia, not adapted. And the view, therefore, that Lenin had adapted Marxism to Russian conditions is grossly misleading: what he did, rather, was to harness his conception of the revolutionary party to Marxism; his adaptation, if such it was, of the *latter* to Russia, came much later, after 1917, and in circumstances which were governed by considerations of practice, not theory.

In 1905, consequently, the conjoining of Marxian socialism and Russian backwardness still required a theoretical framework, one which went beyond the simple mechanical projection into Russia's future of the Western historical experience. And it was in that year, under the impact of its revolutionary events, that Trotsky became the first to begin to formulate such a framework — though initially he took his cue from one Alexander Helphand, better known by his pen-name Parvus, an expatriate Russian Marxist whom Trotsky had met a year earlier in Germany. Parvus had published a series of articles in 1904 the gist of which was that Russia, being the "weakest link" in the capitalist chain, especially during a time of war, was most vulnerable to being overextended by war, and thus most susceptible to internal upheaval. He appended to this the rather unexpected observation that such an upheaval stood every chance of culminating with the workers in power. And he concluded, therefore, that a revolution led by the workers could erupt in Russia before it had done so in Western Europe.[10] Parvus later made a brief attempt to explain this phenomenon on the basis of Russia's social development; but he did not go into this very deeply or systematically. And, in any case, when discussing the social character of the workers' government which might arise in Russia, Parvus had stopped short of defining it as a socialist regime; he appeared, rather, to envisage it as a radical vanguard pushing in the direction of the rapid democratization of the country.[11]

The influence of Parvus upon Trotsky was nevertheless profound and Trotsky would in later years often acknowledge this intellectual debt.[12] For, having taken the cue from Parvus and having then witnessed the turmoil in Russia during 1905, Trotsky proceeded, in a number of works written between the years 1905 to 1908 — to which he would add refinements periodically, and especially many years later, in the 1920s and 1930s — to develop a theory of revolutionary change — more specifically socialist revolutionary change — in backward society.[13] To do full justice to this theory it would be necessary to give an account of the careful and cometimes very detailed analysis which Trotsky made of Russian social history and development and of the peculiarities of Russian backwardness as these emerged in the wake of the economic changes at the end of the nineteenth century; but this is clearly impossible in the space afforded by this paper. Instead, therefore, I propose to reconstruct the conclusions which Trotsky, on the basis of his analysis of Russian backwardness, may be said to have abstracted about the phenomenon of backwardness in general. What follows is, admittedly, arranged in a manner more synoptic and systematic than it appears in Trotsky's writings; but the synopsis neither distorts nor oversteps the bounds of Trotsky's meaning and intentions. His theory of backwardness may thus be formulated as follows:

1. Backwardness is a condition (and a term) which characterizes or describes two essentially different types of societies. The one is a static, even stagnant, society whose internal mode of production and social structure remain what they have fundamentally always been and are incapable of generating change from within. This, roughly speaking, is the type of society called by Marx Oriental or whose "mode of production" he defined as Asiatic. The second type is a society which originally may have been of the first type but which in the course of time, and for various historical reasons (military confrontation, economic relations, colonialism), has been subject to the impact of other societies, defined as "advanced" or Western. In this case, change becomes a fundamental characteristic of backwardness and the interrelationship between this backward society and the advanced ones becomes crucial to an understanding of developments in the former particularly. Russia, for example, by virtue of her long interrelationship with the West, belongs to this second category of backwardness and it is this category which is the subject of sociological (and revolutionary) as opposed to anthropological analysis.

2. The impact of an advanced society on a backward one may be said to be traumatic: ultimately, it forces the backward society to adopt new forms of economic production, it undermines the tradi-

tional social hierarchy, it infects and transforms the existing elites, it introduces new patterns of thought and, throughout, it creates comparative norms. To a large extent all this is true even if the impact is the result of a "colonial-imperialist" relationship. But the effect is far more extreme and more rapid where the impact precedes the colonial period (as in the case of Russia) and where the backward society has remained fundamentally independent. In that case, the very exigencies of the struggle for retaining independence lead to a more extensive adoption of new methods of economic and social organization and thus to a more widespread disintegration of the traditional methods and forms of life. The process whereby this occurs may now be traced.

3. The confrontation between the backward and the advanced initially leads the former to seek to adopt, in part at least, those aspects of the latter which are the source of its strength, since only in this way can the latter be withstood, i.e., on its own grounds. This involves primarily the copying of methods of economic production but the latter cannot be affected without simultaneously copying, or unleashing, those social relations which these methods demand. This presents a dilemma to the political authority — the state — of the backward society: how to change methods of production without overly disturbing traditional social relations. The state meets the dilemma by pursuing the former while attempting to take greater control of the latter, through bureaucratic interference, complete domination of the economy and especially capital formation, prevention of the growth of independent economic powers and, finally, force and oppression. In fact, however, new social relations can never be completely suppressed or even controlled and they develop in spite of the state's efforts.

4. In copying an advanced society, the backward society is working according to a ready-made model. This may suggest that it necessarily must reproduce both the paths followed by the advanced society in reaching that model as well as the actual model itself. In fact, of course, the advantage of a "late-comer" is that, with hindsight and through the experience of the "pioneer", it can move directly towards the end-product, skipping various stages, avoiding the *process* of development, imposing upon itself the result of it only. But this not only shortens the time-span; it introduces in fact a *different* process and leads in the end to the creation of a different model, which subsumes that of the advanced society and goes beyond it. This is so because of the previously mentioned disruption of old social relations, the innovative nature of the new ones and the peculiar intermixing of the whole:

The laws of history have nothing in common with a pedantic schematism. Unevenness, the most general law of the historic process, reveals itself most sharply and complexly in the destiny of the backward countries. Under the whip of external necessity, their backward culture is compelled to make leaps. From the universal law of unevenness thus derives another law which, for the lack of a better name, we may call the law of *combined development* – by which we mean a drawing together of the different stages of the journey, a combining of separate steps, an amalgam of archaic with more contemporary forms. Without this law, to be taken of course in its whole material content, it is impossible to understand the history of Russia, and indeed of any country of the second, third or tenth cultural class.[14]

5. The skipping of developmental stages creates curious results for by leaping over forms of production the backward society is also by-passing social forms. Those social groupings which would have come into being had there been no skipping over stages, i.e., had there been an adoption of earlier forms of production, do *not* come into being. On the other hand, such social groupings as are the pre-conditions of the latest model *do* crystallize. Simultaneously, the main elements of the traditional society remain: the old political authority, because of the power it has accumulated and its control over the economy; and the old agricultural sector because its break-up need be only partial and limited in order to make the new sector viable for immediate purposes, Thus, as in the case of Russia, the overall curious result is political absolutism, aristocratic privileges and a large agricultural population, together with advanced industry, urbanization, a working class, but – no middle class.

6. This situation is characteristic of the unique process through which the backward society has travelled, namely, "uneven and combined development." The situation may be broken down into the following attributes:

(a) Backwardness, far from being total, is only partial and in some ways the backward society is as advanced as any other.

(b) Conversely, sectors of the society have not changed at all, ostensibly at least, so that the overall impact is that of lopsidedness, uneven distribution of new forms of production, the polarization of society into various groups not directly or logically related to one another.

(c) The juxtaposition of very old and very new creates stark anomalies and a general non-rationalized economic and social structure, i.e., one that is in many ways counter-productive or self-defeating.

(d) The co-existence within one social framework of two fundamentally different and contradictory "models" of society arouses comparison, awareness of alternatives and, eventually, a *consciousness* of backwardness, i.e., a consciousness of the fact that the society is, in comparison with others, in some important senses defective.

(e) New methods of production create new goals and aspirations which are at variance with previous ones but since the former have not been wholly adopted and the latter not wholly abandoned there is both confusion over goals and a clash between them.

(f) The contradictions inherent in non-uniform development, the growth of a consciousness of backwardness and of alternatives, the conflict over goals, all these create disharmony, instability and a political situation which is potentially explosive. In fact, the peculiar nature and dynamics of backwardness make revolution inevitable. And this revolution, like the backward society from which it arises, will also have the character of an unprecedented, combined "amalgam," that is, one exhibiting both "archaic" and "contemporary" forms.

* * *

The conception of backwardness summarized above was at the basis of that theory of revolution with which Trotsky's name became universally identified, namely, the theory of the permanent revolution. Yet discussions of the latter theory have seldom related it to Trotsky's views about the social dynamics of backwardness; and the result, almost invariably, has been that the concept of the permanent revolution has been interpreted as a variant, albeit an intellectually more satisfying one, of the Bolshevik notion of vanguardism, that is, of radicalization from above, combined with the militant pursuit of revolution abroad. Nothing, however, could be further from the truth. Though the theory of the permanent revolution, like its author, came to be eventually linked to Bolshevism — for reasons I shall presently discuss — and though it *was* directly related to a general European conflagration, it was derived in the first place from what Trotsky took to be the objective character of social developments in a country such as Russia. Whatever its weaknesses — and these too will be presently mentioned — the theory did not divorce politics from society or revolutionary activity from social reality — habits of thought more justifiably associated with Lenin.

The summary I have given already indicates how Trotsky linked Russian politics with Russian society (and history). The central aspect of his view of backwardness was that social development was everywhere different, and nowhere more so than in Russia, and the notion therefore that all historical roads must eventually culminate in a repetition of the West-European experience — a notion so prevalent among Russian Marxists of the time — was for him a purely mechanical, and unhistorical, application of Marx's theories. The point about Russia, Trotsky believed, was not only that her history was unlike anything experienced in the West but that, having had so different a past, her future must also turn out to be unlike anything which had characterized the West. Plekhanov, Lenin and others had taken for granted that Russia must inevitably evolve into a capitalist phase. It is one aspect of Trotsky's originality that he dismissed this prospect as an absurdity of Marxist schematics. Capitalism, he argued, was in fact impossible in Russia; the view that it was taking root grew out of a confusion of capitalism with industrialization. The character of the latter provided, actually, the best evidence for the fact that the Russian economy was unique: industrialization was neither carried out by, nor did it create, a middle class; it had neither transformed Russian agriculture nor resolved the problem of the peasant population — for it had been simply "grafted on" from above, and it had been made to co-exist alongside the traditional agricultural economy, not intermix with it; and industrialization had left the political structure intact, in fact even more powerful, for the autocracy — the absolutist state — now controlled even greater economic resources.

This last, however, was, in Trotsky's view, a temporary phenomenon or rather an illusion created by the immediate, not final, impact of rapid industrialization. The latter had also set into motion longer-term processes of which the most striking was the — relatively — astronomical growth of a working class population; its strength was out of all proportion to its relative size within the population as a whole for it had the power to paralyze industry and thus the Russian state's capacity for pursuing its foreign policy objectives in general, its military ambitions in particular. In a parallel and obviously connected way, industrialization had given rise to significant urban centres; the city, Trotsky believed, was now imposing its hegemony over the countryside and would become the clue to revolutionary strategy. Finally, industrialization, though it had not grown organically via the countryside and the town, was having disruptive effects upon agriculture and the peasants, the ultimate pillars of the autocracy's traditional support. The first effect was economic: industrial capital had been mobilized by the state through huge foreign loans and these had to be serviced by higher taxation and more relentless exploitation of agriculture, so that the lot of the peasant had become worse as a direct result of the policy of industrialization. The second effect was social: industry took its labor force from the village but since the pace of industry was so great, the uprooting of those peasants who entered the industrial orbit was sudden − and in this sense violent − and at the same time both unassimilated and incomplete − thus the social phenomenon of peasants who found themselves simultaneously in two different worlds, the old and the new. The third effect was political: in the absence of a middle class, of a mediating force between city and countryside, between industry and agriculture, a basis had been created for a direct linkage between workers and peasants.[15]

One other aspect of Trotsky's analysis must be touched upon before we conclude this discussion of the manner in which he conceived the relationship between Russian society and politics. This is what may be called the dilemma, which eventually confronted the autocracy and society in general, of modernization. The introduction of industry had created the need for such concomitant changes as would keep industry not only going but developing at a pace necessary to assure Russia's continued viability as a European and Far Eastern power. Could the autocracy afford to give its blessing to such changes − the most important of which was agrarian reform? Trotsky believed that it could not, for the simple reason that changes of this kind were tantamount to the autocracy committing suicide. Thus the Russian state at the beginning of the twentieth century was behaving in a manner reminiscent of its behaviour during previous centuries: having itself championed one element of modernization − in the present case industry − it suppressed and strangled all other elements.

It would be no exaggeration to say that Trotsky's concept of the permanent revolution − the revolution of backward society − was conceived by him as the only possible way out of the dilemma, that is, as the only way to modernizing Russia, and, moreover, as the only possible consequence of the emerging pattern of Russia's economic, social and political peculiarities. How else could Russia be transformed, and her anomalies erased, except through one, uninterrupted leap into the modern world? And who else except the working class could supervise this ongoing transition? The autocracy did not want to do it, the middle class − such as it was − could not do it, and the peasants had no idea how to do it. The Russian proletariat, Trotsky believed, however limited its relative size and resources, was in a position to seize power if it gained the support of the peasantry. But having gained this support and having seized power it would soon discover that it could not solve any of Russia's fundamental problems without organizing society on a collectivist basis. Thus the revolution of backwardness in the twentieth century would issue forth in the form of a combined revolution, bringing together two different, but now related in time, historical eras, that of the bourgeois-agrarian revolution and that of the industrial-socialist revolution.

But Trotsky was not so naive as to believe that out of the largely primitive and impoverished foundations of Russia's economy and society a modern, much less socialist, world could arise; the needs of society and the declared intentions of its revolutionary class, even if followed by immediate institutional changes, would not be enough to assure that the leap culminated with a landing in the socialist millennium. Had not Marx assumed that a pre-condition of socialism was man's capacity — already proven under advanced capitalism — for developing to its ultimate levels the means and organization of economic production? In this sense, Russia, whatever the industrial changes of the last decades of the nineteenth century, was merely an upstart and any attempt, in the post-revolutionary period, to rely on her internal resources alone would end, Trotsky thought, in disaster — either complete chaos or a bureaucratic tyranny. In the light of this premonition, therefore, it is not difficult to understand the emphasis which Trotsky, in the context of the revolution of backwardness, placed upon the European or world revolution. Without such a revolution, he believed, the Russian revolution would be doomed to the vengeance of backwardness. Trotsky was indeed an internationalist by temperament and mentality, but his internationalism was not merely the idealistic frame of mind it has so often been made out to be; it was also an intrinsic part of his conception of the material needs of the *Russian* revolution.[16]

In the event, the European revolution did not, of course, materialize and it is in fact one of the great weaknesses of Trotsky's theory of the permanent revolution that he could find no way of explaining why it *should* materialize (except by mouthing the standard, and in themselves insufficient, general Marxist assumptions about European capitalism). Nothing would be so amusing today, were it not so pathetic, than to parade Trotsky's obsessive misreadings, in the 1920s and 1930s, of developments at the time in Britain or Germany or France.[17] But it would be too simple, and much too kind, to attribute the failure of his predictions for Russian socialism to the failure of the European revolution alone. There is a further, more important, lacuna in his conception of the Russian revolution — and of the revolution of backwardness in general — and it is worth considering briefly for it completes the picture of the scope and limits, and character, of his thought.

I have said nothing so far about Trotsky's view of revolutionary organization, more specifically the revolutionary party, and this is because for a long time the matter of party leadership and strategy played virtually no part in his formulation of the theory of permanent revolution. The whole subject of Trotsky's critique of Bolshevism is a story in itself, but suffice it to say that between 1903 and 1917 no one was more scathingly hostile towards − and, incidentally, more successful in laying bare − the ideas of Lenin.[18] Why is it, then, that in mid-1917 Trotsky suddenly embraced what he had for so long and so convincingly rejected? The answer, I think, is not far-sought. Trotsky had always assumed − is *this,* perhaps, the reason why he has been called a "classical" Marxist? − that social, objective factors were both the necessary and the sufficient conditions for determining the character, the social content, of a revolution. And if the revolution were to be socialist, this meant, among other things, that it was to be led by the workers, or rather that the objective conditions were such as to catapult the workers into a position of leadership. It would be merely superfluous to dwell on the fact that this was too simplistic a formulation of the problem and that, even assuming the workers to be the force *behind* the revolution, it did not resolve two operative questions: firstly, in what concrete sense would the workers actually *lead* or organize the revolution; and, secondly, in what concrete sense were the Russian workers actually socialist. It is clear that these issues had suddenly dawned upon Trotsky after February 1917; and it is equally clear he then concluded that the somewhat glib manner in which he had over the years treated the issues could no longer be defended. It is clear, in other words, that he then recognized that his theory had assumed too much about the capacities of the Russian proletariat, that it had failed to provide for an operative, organizational link between social conditions − the objective revolutionary situation − and political consequences − the seizure of power. What happened in 1917 may thus be described as both a personal and theoretical coming together, between Trotsky and Lenin and between the theory of the revolution of backwardness and the theory of revolution-making in conditions of backwardness.[19]

To put the matter thus is to reject the charge sometimes made against Trotsky that in 1917 he had succumbed to an instrumentalist view of revolution, to the view, in other words, that revolution was a function of personal, organizational factors, in this case Lenin and Bolshevism. In later years he would, it is true, admit that but for Lenin the October Revolution may never have taken place.[20] And he would also argue that the main reason why a workers' revolution had not broken out in, for example, Germany was that the Marxist movement there had not succeeded in creating a Bolshevik-like party and leadership.[21] But in both cases he meant only to say that neither the objective factor — social reality — nor the subjective one — revolutionary leadership — in itself constituted a sufficient condition for revolution. A combination of the two was essential. This, incidentally, is one of the central themes of his major historical work, *The History of the Russian Revolution,* in which he made so monumental an attempt to explain the events of 1917.

Nevertheless, his alliance with Lenin did commit him to an ambiguous position which in the course of time would press upon him but the implications of which he was never quite prepared to recognize, much less confess to, however much he himself did to make them credible. Before 1917, in his attacks against Lenin — particularly in 1903 and 1904 — Trotsky had argued that Bolshevism was a form of Jacobinism — and a degenerate form at that — peculiar to a revolutionary movement in a backward society, that it was itself one reflection of backwardness.[22] Its organizational principles, he had then claimed, like its attitudes to politics and society, were diametrically opposed to those of socialism. Were it to succeed in seizing power this would constitute proof not that socialism had triumphed but that it had been defeated, that the workers' cause was either betrayed or impossible in the first place. Following 1917, of course, Trotsky never raised this theme again; but it must surely have haunted him in the darkening days of the 1930s. It is not only the advantages of hindsight, therefore, which allow us to conclude that the revolution of backwardness which Trotsky had postulated as long ago as 1905 had ultimately assumed an ironic twist and one which he himself had not failed to anticipate; it was already inherent in his own understanding of Russia and of the dilemmas of backwardness in general. Trotsky, in his theory of the permanent revolution, had indeed gone a long way toward showing that the social and political conditions of backwardness were such as to make highly likely the emergence of a revolution in the name of socialism, for no other revolution, he had argued, could cope with the problems of backwardness. Elsewhere, however, he had also shown that such conditions were equally propitious to the growth of a Bolshevik-type party. In 1917, in fact, he came to recognize that the revolution in the name of socialism would emerge as a result, partly, of the existence and strength of such a party. In that case, however, in view of the character he had once attributed to Bolshevism, it could be said — though Trotsky was able to do so only inadvertently — that the conditions of backwardness were such as to make socialism — of the Marxist variety — itself impossible.

This same point may be put in a somewhat different form. Marx, it will be recalled, had frequently called attention to the "universalizing" force of capitalism, to its tendency to modernize the backward societies it came into contact with, and thus arouse them from their centuries-old stagnation.[23] He made no systematic study of the pattern which this modernization assumed, but he claimed to see in it the self-reproduction of capitalism. Trotsky too, as we have seen, was fascinated by the processes of development set in motion by the impact of the West on a backward society. But Trotsky, in analyzing the peculiarities of these processes, may be said to have implicitly denied the truth of Marx's famous observation that capitalism was everywhere creating "a world after its own image". On the contrary, Trotsky argued, capitalism in the West had the long-term effect of transforming backward societies in a direction historically unprecedented; modernization in such societies was thus by-passing the capitalist phase and would ultimately issue in a peculiarly twentieth century revolution. He believed this revolution would be the harbinger of socialism. It was not, and perhaps could not be; but the revolution of backwardness did bring forth a unique form of modern society, a unique form of collectivism. This last resembled nothing imagined in the Marxist canon; yet movements calling themselves Marxist have championed it. Why this should be so − and the irony of it − can in no small measure be comprehended and appreciated through the thought of Leon Trotsky.

NOTES

1. For a recent example of this kind of literature, which, however, is in parts above the customary level of such polemics, see Nicholas Krassò (ed.), *Trotsky: The Great Debate Renewed* (St. Louis, 1972). This consists of a series of articles which originally appeared in the *New Left Review.*

2. Trotsky once declared that the idea of "permanent revolt seems to me simply nonsense" *(Byulleten Oppozitsii,* no. 81, January 1940, p. 13).

3. *The Prophet Armed, The Prophet Unarmed, The Prophet Outcast* (London, 1954, 1959, 1963).

4. A major exception to this rule is the recent work by Richard Day, *Leon Trotsky and the Politics of Economic Isolation* (Cambridge, 1973). But Day, whose book is based almost exclusively on an examination of Trotsky's economic views and writings, goes so far as to deny entirely Trotsky's adherence, before the end of the 1920s, to the idea of "world revolution", a denial which seems to me

insupportable when the whole range and context of Trotsky's writings are taken into account.

5. The subject and issues raised in this paper are discussed in greater detail, and within a larger context, in my forthcoming book, *The Social and Political Thought of Leon Trotsky*, to be published by Oxford University Press.

6. For Marx's writings on backward societies in general and on Russia in particular, see Shlomo Avineri (ed.), *Karl Marx on Colonialism and Modernization* (Garden City, N.Y., 1968) and Paul Blackstock and Bert Hoselitz (eds.), *Marx and Engels: The Russian Menace to Europe* (London, 1953).

7. See his (and Engels's) preface to the 1882 Russian edition of the *Communist Manifesto* (in Marx-Engels, *Selected Works*, Moscow, 1955, vol. I, pp. 22–24).

8. See his 1877 letter (which he did not however send off) to the Russian journal *Otechestvenniye Zapiski*, reproduced in Avineri, *op. cit.*, pp. 442–445.

9. In an article written in September 1905 Lenin had raised the prospect of an "uninterrupted revolution" (see Lenin, *Sochineniya*, 4th ed., vol. IX, p. 213); but before the end of the year he had jettisoned the idea, never to return to it again until 1917, in the form of the "April Theses".

10. Parvus' articles originally appeared in *Iskra* and were later reprinted in his *Rossiya i revolyutsiya* (St. Petersburg, 1906), pp. 83 ff.

11. See his preface to Trotsky's brochure *Do 9-go Yanvarya* (Geneva, 1905), pp. iii-xiv.

12. See, for example, his autobiography *Moya Zhizn* (Berlin, 1930), vol. I, p. 193 and his *Stalin* (New York and London, 1941, issued 1946), pp. 429–430.

13. Trotsky formulated his conception of backwardness and his theory of the permanent revolution in numerous books and articles; but see in particular the following: *Itogi i perspektivy*, first published in 1906 and translated as *Results and Prospects* (London, 1962); *1905*, first published in German in 1910 and in Russian in 1922, it has only recently been translated into English (New York, 1972); *Permanentnaya Revolyutsiya* (Berlin, 1930), translated as *The Permanent Revolution* (London, 1962). See also the opening chapter of his *The History of the Russian Revolution* (single volume edition, reissued London, 1965).

14. Trotsky, *The History of the Russian Revolution*, pp. 27–28.

15. The foregoing is based on the works by Trotsky mentioned in note 13, above and on various shorter pieces, too numerous to list here. But for a partial collec-

tion of his articles and essays on these subjects, see his *Sochineniya*, vol. II, parts 1 and 2 (Moscow-Leningrad, 1925, 1927).

16. He first raised the issue of the dependence of the Russian revolution on the European revolution in *Itogi i perspektivy* (see especially – in the English translation *Results and Prospects* –pp. 237ff.).

17. The most glaring example of such misreadings is his *Where is Britain Going?* (London, 1926), first published in Russian in 1925, as *Kuda idet Angliya?*

18. Particularly in the long pamphlet *Nashi Politicheskye Zadachi* (Geneva, 1904).

19. Trotsky interpreted Lenin's "April Theses" as constituting a tacit, if not explicit, acceptance of his theory of the permanent revolution and he claimed Lenin had acknowledged the correctness of the theory (see *The Permanent Revolution*, pp. 42–43).

20. See, for example, his *Diary in Exile, 1935* (London, 1959), pp. 53–54.

21. See, for example, Trotsky, *Pyat Let Kominterna* (Moscow, 1924), p. 27.

22. See the previously mentioned work, *Nashi Politicheskye Zadachi,* as well as his initial observations on the Bolshevik-Menshevik split of 1903, *Vtoroi Syezd RSDRP: Otchet Sibirskoi Delegatsii* (Geneva, 1903).

23. In this connection, see the introduction by Avineri, *op.cit.*, pp. 1–28, and George Lichtheim, "Oriental Despotism", in his *The Concept of Ideology* (New York, 1967), pp. 62–93.

THE CONTEXTS OF MAOISM

JONATHAN SPENCE
Yale University

In 1971 a new book for the reading of Elementary Chinese was issued in Peking. A post-Cultural Revolutionary work, it contained almost no references to socialism that might embarrass western bourgeois readers: the reader was led into the Chinese language through a traditional world of teachers, pens and pencils, chairs and tables. But on the middle of page 156, in the section on numbers and dates, the compilers made an important statement of ideology in a neat, short-hand way; three examples were given for the student who was seeking to master a year, month and day sequence:

> March 18, 1871
> November 7, 1917
> October 1, 1949.

Though no comment was made in the text, the lesson seems clear enough: if the founding of the Paris Commune was the first great stage in the history of modern revolutions, and the Bolshevik revolution was the second, then the formation of the People's Republic of China was the third. Or, reading the same list through the major analysts of each stage, Marx was the first, Lenin the second, and Mao Tse-tung the third.[1]

It has been a tortuous historical road to this presentation of "Marxism-Leninism-Mao Tse-tung thought", as the Chinese now term it. To this historian, at least, "Maoism" is not so much an ideology as a quest, and the body of writings from Mao's hand that has gradually accumulated does not seem so much a coherent whole – though there are some continuous themes and patterns of emphasis – as a series of contextual responses. In trying to come to grips with "Maoism" we have to consider at least four contexts: the context of party factionalism, the context of China's struggle for national survival, the global context, and the historical roots of Chinese Marxism.

The association of Mao's name with the history of the communist party of China has become axiomatic, and perhaps tends to make us forget that Mao's dominance within his own Party has been regularly and hotly contested. Not surprisingly, many of Mao's ideological statements were responses to specific challenges. At least nine confrontations have been of major importance since Mao gained control of the communist party apparatus at Tsunyi (in January 1935 during the Long March), and each of them played a part in developing Mao's strategies and responses. Chang Kuo-t'ao, one of the founding members of the Chinese Communist Party (CCP), began a feud with Mao during the Long March, that ended only with Chang's defection to the Kuomintang in 1938; their struggle concerned the crucial question of which area was most suitable for the retrenchment and redevelopment of the CCP, which had been driven out of its previous base areas in Kiangsi and Szechwan. The struggle with Ch'en Shao-yü (better known by his pseudonym Wang Ming), that had begun in the Kiangsi Soviet in the early 1930s, flared anew in the early forties and was a central component to the "Rectification Campaign" which Mao launched against his critics in Yenan. Both Kao Kang and Jao Shu-shih struggled with Mao in 1954, apparently over the extent to which semiautonomous development might be permitted to the major industrial centers that they had been charged with developing in Shanghai and in Manchuria. Marshal P'eng Teh-huai was ousted in 1959 because of his fundamental disagreements with Mao over the economic policies of the Great Leap Forward and the organization and training of the army. In recent years there have been a succession of major power struggles that led, in the five years between 1966 and 1971, to the removal of P'eng Chen, Liu Shao-ch'i, T'ao Chu and Lin Piao, during different stages of the "Cultural Revolution".

In every one of these cases, except perhaps that of T'ao Chu, the Soviet Union either played, or is alleged to have played, an important role. Thus Chang Kuo-t'ao had apparently hoped to make a base in the far northwest of China, where he could be in closer contact with the Soviet Union; Ch'en Shao-yü (as leader of the "28 Bolsheviks" who returned to China under the direction of Pavel Mif in 1931) was a loyal Comintern man who lived the later part of his life in the Soviet Union; both Jao Shu-shih and Kao Kang were accused of over-strict reliance on Soviet economic models for development; and P'eng Teh-huai was charged with over-admiration of the Soviet military apparatus and command structure, and with willingness to shelter under a Soviet "nuclear umbrella" as a corollary to his disdain for classic concepts of guerilla warfare. During the Cultural Revolution it had become commonplace to charge party enemies with being "Soviet revisionists", and the factual grounding for all such charges is not yet apparent; nevertheless it seems reasonably well proven that Liu Shao-ch'i and P'eng Chen, at least, may have advocated policies that organizationally leant toward the Soviet Union, and Lin Piao may in fact have been fleeing to the Soviet Union when his plane was shot down in 1971.

If the context of China's struggle for national survival is a crucial one in our understanding of Maoism, it is also one in which – from the Chinese nationalist standpoint – the Soviet Union has played an intensely ambiguous role. Mao (born in 1893) was a youth in late Ch'ing China, aware of the patterns of China's humiliations at the hands of Britain, Germany, France, Japan and Russia; and he grew up in an era in which imperialist pressures continued as the structure of China's new democratic republic crumbled into Warlordism. In retrospect, it seems to historians that Japan was undoubtedly China's major menace at this time, with the sequence of Sino-Japanese war (1894–1895), "21 Demands" (1915), Versailles Treaty spoils (1919), Tsinan Incident (1928), Mukden Incident (1931). and on through the insult of Manchukuo to the final outbreak of war in 1937. But this may be too simple a patterning, and Mao might easily have been more moved by the older forms of arrogance exemplified in the French and British concessions. Like many Chinese, he may have had the exhilaration of the Kharakan manifesto speedily dampened by the realization that Soviet foreign policy in the Far East would not, after all, abandon all the pretensions of Tsarist policy; and like many members of the young Chinese Communist party he must have been torn by the contradictory elements within Comintern China policy. The story of the Comintern-Kuomintang-CCP triangle between 1923 and 1927 is a well-told one, and needn't be dwelt on here, except to reiterate the obvious fact that Comintern policies both directly and indirectly led to the deaths of many of Mao's closest comrades as well as members of his own family. What concerns the historian is rather the levels of ambiguity that must have adhered to Mao's perceptions of the Soviet Union after this date.

In a summary of a new Chinese revolutionary opera called *Azalea Mountain,* which appeared recently in an official Chinese publication, we find this historical sketch:

> In the autumn of 1927 Chairman Mao led the Autumn Harvest Uprising, organized the first detachment of Workers' and Peasants' Red Army and set up the first revolutionary base in the Chinkang Mountains. This was in

keeping with his strategy for the Chinese revolution – building rural bases, surrounding the cities by the countryside and ultimately seizing the cities.

Based on this background the opera *Azalea Mountain* develops. It is the spring of 1928, at the beginning of the Second Revolutionary Civil War. Ko Hsiang, a Communist, has been sent by the Party to the Azalea Mountain to find a Peasant's Self-Defence Guards unit which rose in rebellion under the influence of the Autumn Harvest Uprising. She is arrested on the way. The self-defence unit, having suffered three defeats in a row, is eagerly seeking Communist Party leadership. They rescue Ko Hsiang on the execution ground. Ko Hsiang becomes the Party representative of the guards. She works hard to implement Chairman Mao's revolutionary line and the Party's policies and patiently teaches the leader Lei Kang and other guards to distinguish friend from foe and treat correctly exploited class brothers, ordinary merchants and captives of the reactionary army. She mobilizes the masses and expands the people's militia. The self-defence guards correct their shortcomings and make a fresh start.[2]

This would seem, in current political terms, to be an interpretation that we can safely call "Maoist", yet its relation to actual events is complex. The Comintern, of course, has gone, and Mao has emerged as the master, not the victim, of events. There is no hint, even to the initiated, of the disastrous failure of the Autumn Harvest Uprisings, of the failure of Mao's attack on Changsha, and of the tragedy of the Canton Commune in December 1927. Instead we find an elaborate historical corrective: a peasant's guard unit "which rose in rebellion *under the influence of* the Autumn Harvest Uprising" and is "*eagerly seeking* Communist Party leadership". Mao, who had to smart under the leadership of Ch'ü Ch'iu-pai, Li Li-san and Ch'en Shao-yü in turn, has become "chairman" in this account, and has already elaborated a strategy of "surrounding the cities by the countryside". Ironically – in view of Mao's general insistence on the profoundly constructive elements of struggle and the progression that emerges from "contradictions" – we find any notion of struggle by Mao utterly eliminated; and what was part of an intensely dramatic and difficult struggle over lines, in a poverty-stricken countryside (where theory did, indeed, gradually yield to practice) becomes a commonplace. The opera ends with the peasant unit setting out to find Mao in the Chingkang mountains, transforming Mao's most temporary and dangerous base into a revolutionary haven. This emphasis is presumably not without purpose: the Red Guards, too, seized on the Chingkangshan period of Mao's life as a major epoch, and launched their own Chingkangshan brigades. What does Chingkangshan really stand for? Survival after disaster, certainly, and reliance on military rather than political means;

harsh life in the mountains; independence from the Comintern; a radical "peasant line"; and a rural party composition despite the bow to a "Workers' and Peasants' Red Army".

The subsequent history of Mao's relations with the CPSU is always intimately connected to China's own national priorities – from Mao's initial declaration of war against Japan as he developed his base in the Kiangsi Soviet, through the United Front with the Kuomintang in 1937 to the mutual security pacts of 1949–1950 and the nuclear policy and "de-Stalinization" arguments in the later 1950s. Obviously Mao's most influential writings reflected the ebbs and flows of this relationship, and often had a purely temporary function; one of the most intriguing tasks for a biographer of Mao in the future might be to try and separate out Mao's attitudes to Stalin from Mao's attitudes to the CPSU: as his hostility to the latter has grown ever more vocal, his admiration for the former has apparently stood constant.[3] It is possible that, embedded within that elusive "Maoism", is an admiration for unwavering leadership and great-power chauvinism when that leadership and chauvinism keep the Party in its place and hold the frontiers firm.

At this point we begin to shift from the more immediate context of China's national survival to her perceptions of a role in the world. In current doctrine, China is the revolutionary leader of those nations who resist the domination of the twin "Superpowers" – the United States and the Soviet Union. The non-superpowers are not only the unindustrialized have-nots of the world; they may include also such capitalist countries as France, West Germany, and Britain. Perhaps no other leader of a state could have had such a shift in global perceptions as Mao, who was seven years old when the Boxer expeditionary force entered Peking to lift the siege of the legations, was thirty-two when British troops fired on the Chinese demonstrators outside their Shanghai concession in May 1925, saw extraterritoriality formally ended in 1943, and during the First Five Year Plan of 1953 could seriously consider a programme for surpassing Britain's GNP.

Any such summary is hopelessly simplistic. The global perspective must, in the case of Mao, look behind the Boxers to theorists like Liang Ch'i-ch'ao and the views that they held of European dynamism; and from there must move forward twenty years to the First World War, and to the shattering effect that that conflict had on Chinese scholars who had been pinning their faith and their reputations on European rationalism. The nineteen-twenties and thirties were a period when reassessment of China's own historical stages had to be coupled with assessment of international agencies such as the China International Famine Relief Commission, The League of Nations, Peking Union Medical College, and all the other well-meaning offshoots of technological superiority. And as well as the immediate impact of specific Comintern directives there were the wider problems of adjustment of the Second United Front, the Hitler-Stalin pact, and the anti-Axis line; not to mention fighting a war in China against the Japanese, while the Japanese were in fact being defeated elsewhere and the Chinese were marshalling their own forces for civil war. Since 1949, major determinants have been the United States' intervention in the Korean War, with its echoes in the Chinese mobilization, land reform, and "5-anti campaigns"; and the American bombing of North Vietnam, *combined with* the Indonesian anti-leftist massacres, which may well have acted as catalysts in the planning of the Great Proletarian Cultural Revolution.[4]

The global contexts are in turn enmeshed with the historical. In March 1974 the interconnections could be phrased in this way:

> The bourgeoisie may well believe that the works of the 18th-century Austrian bourgeois composer Mozart embody "bright" and "healthy" sentiments. But we working people know clearly that these sentiments cannot compare with the exuberant and impassioned feelings expressed by the chorus *The Sun Rises* in the seventh scene of *The White-Haired Girl*. Brimming over with jubilation, this chorus extols Chairman Mao, the red sun in the hearts of the Chinese people, as well as the Communist Party, and evokes the soul-stirring scene "of the land of hibiscus glowing in the morning sun" and the emancipation of the down-trodden peasants. No bourgeois music can even remotely compare with this unrestrained healthy burst of joy evoked by this chorus.[5]

In February 1974, in the same issue of *Peking Review* that carried a sharp attack on Antonioni's film *China,* the past and the present had been linked in a dramatically Chinese context:

> By analysing the reactionary ideology of Confucius and Lin Piao, workers unanimously concluded: Lin Piao was truly a faithful disciple of Confucius and his reactionary world outlook was rooted in Confucius' reactionary ideology. Confucius was a spokesman of the declining slave-owning aristocracy more than two thousand years ago and Lin Piao was an agent of the landlord class and the bourgeoisie in contemporary times. Though they lived in different eras, both represented moribund reactionary classes and both tried to turn back the wheel of history. Criticism of Confucius and especially criticism of the crimes committed by Lin Piao and his gang in extolling Confucius and using his ideology to serve their plot for a counter-revolutionary restoration clearly shows that Lin Piao's reactionary ideology was a mixture of the ideology of all reactionary classes in history.[6]

Again, we might see both passages as being in some way "Maoist", and insert them in a brief essay like this, or in an anthology; the interesting challenge, of course, is to gauge what montage of which fragments will yield a historically valid summation.

There is ample documentation on Mao's interest in the past, and he has commented (to Edgar Snow and others) on the influences that affected him. A major attempt to assemble and analyze all these leads has just been made by Frederic Wakeman in *History and Will, Philosophical Perspectives of Mao Tse-tung's Thought,* but it remains an attempt and not an answer because – as Wakeman himself states – the conclusions are rooted in the Cultural Revolution: "At that moment, when history (bureaucratic routinization) and will (Mao's permanent revolution) conflicted so dramatically, the reflections were united at last".[7] The "reflections" Wakemen refers to come, "as in a hall of mirrors," from a huge range of traditional Chinese – as well as Kantian and Marxist – imprints on Mao. Yet the Cultural Revolution is a deceptive focal point, dictated more by the time of writing than by any wider analytical criteria. For Mao, surely, the Cultural Revolution was not meant to unite anything "at last"; it united things only temporarily, for "one always divides into two" in Mao's parlance. It united them "at the first", if we might rephrase Wakeman, so that further growth might ensue.

An extraordinarily forceful and sarcastic speech that Mao delivered on history (in May 1958, just before the Great Leap Forward) reached the West in 1973:

> Comrade Fan Wen-lan has recently written an article, which I have read with great pleasure. This is really standing up and telling them. This article adduces a great many facts in order to demonstrate that "stressing the present and slighting the past" *(hou chin po ku)* is a tradition in our country. He cites Ssu-ma Ch'ien and Ssu-ma Kuang . . . Unfortunately, he did not cite Ch'in Shih-huang. Ch'in Shih-huang favoured the proposal that "those who make use of the past to disparage the present should be exterminated together with their whole families." He was a specialist in "stressing the present and slighting the past." Naturally, I am not advocating that we cite Ch'in Shih-huang either. (Comrade Lin Piao interjects: "Ch'in Shih-huang burned the books and buried the Confucian scholars.") Ch'in Shih-huang didn't amount to much. He only buried 460 Confucian scholars *(ju)*. We buried 46,000 of them. Didn't we execute some counter-revolutionary intellectuals in the course of the campaign for the repression of counter-revolutionaries? I had a discussion with a democratic personage, who criticized us for being (like) Ch'in Shih-huang. That's not correct, we have surpassed Ch'in Shih-huang a hundred times. If you denounce us for being

Ch'in Shin-huang, for being autocrats, we admit everything. The unfortunate thing is that you don't say enough, so that we keep having to complete it for you. (Loud laughter).[8]

This passage is both explicit, and full of echoes. The most ringing of the echoes comes in the phrase "if you denounce us for being . . . autocrats, we admit everything"; almost identical language was used in 1917 when Ch'en Tu-hsiu issued a manifesto in *Hsin-ch'ing-nien (La Jeunesse* or *New Youth)* pleading guilty to the charge of destroying traditional values, but citing in total exoneration the fact that the destruction was wrought in the names of "Mr. Democracy and Mr. Science".[9] Ch'en Tu-hsiu, co-founder of the CCP, is excoriated now for his opportunism in 1927, but his language (and his values) are very much alive in the exuberantly iconoclastic sides of Mao's thought. And the immensely influential *New Youth* magazine that Ch'en edited seems to be a major focus for understanding Mao, not only because it introduced him to new ideas which he later developed, but because it presented ideas (often distinctly idiosyncratic in terms of socialist theory) which can now be found deeply embedded in some of Mao's works.[10]

One example would be the essay "The Foundations of Russian Revolutionary Theory" ("O-kuo ke-ming chih che-hsueh ti chi-ch'u") which appeared in two lengthy instalments in the *New Youth* of April 15 and May 1919 — the May number being the famous "Marxism" issue which historians have seen as a focal revolutionary moment in the May 4th movement.[11] This article is a translation of a portemanteau essay by Angelo Rappaport that had appeared in the July 1917 issue of the *Edinburgh Review*[12] — Rappaport being a voluminous writer whose occasional political works such as his *Dictionary of Socialism* were written along with tasty general histories such as *The Love Affairs of the Vatican* and *Napoleon III and the Women He Loved.*[13] Rappaport's article was not, in fact, a systematic appraisal of Socialism — it was a loosely structured review article which examined a variety of works by Herzen, Tshernyshevski, Lavrov and Bakunin. The Chinese translator noted at the end that he had some reservations about Rappaport's critique but found it in general clear and comprehensive.[14] If the article had a focus, it was anti-Marxist. Thus, writing of Lavrov, Rappaport said:

> The pivots of Marx's theories are economic evolution and development of the productive forces; the central ideas of Lavrov's theories are the progress and development of the individual. Progress, according to his philosophy, consists in the physical, intellectual, and moral development of the indivi-

dual, and in the realisation of truth and justice through proper social organisation. Social happiness, according to Lavrov, is nothing but the happiness of the individuals who compose the society or group or nation, and they therefore have a right to modify the existing forms of society.

He also quoted a brief passage from Lavrov's *Lettres Historiques:*

We are approaching an epoch when the realisation of the human ideal will be possible; when the instinctive tendencies of the individual will be brought to harmonise with the welfare of the collectivity. Only the organisation of men into one harmonious group, united by the interests of collective work and search for justice, can constitute the happiness of the individual.[15]

Bakunin is favorably contrasted with Marx in two other passages later in the article:

Here one notices the differences that existed between Marx and Bakunin. The former was a cold intellectual, the latter a sentimentalist and an idealist, despite his realistic conception of the world. Marx had a deep sense of justice, but no instinct of liberty, whilst Bakunin's soul thirsted for liberty .... Marx believed that the nation that would first give the signal for the social revolution would be the State that was furthest advanced – Germany, for instance. (He seems, however, to have changed his views altogether after his sojourn in England.) Bakunin, on the contrary, was of opinion that the nation most richly endowed with the spirit of revolt and the instinct of liberty would be the first to give the signal.[16]

There is a kind of stirring independence in these passages that separates out the call to action from any ideological specificity. The Chinese, throughout the twentieth century, have drawn on a mixture of thinkers and on the Bolshevik revolution as inspirational forces even while knowing how distant they were from these sources. This combination of eclecticism with exaggeration of isolated trends led George Lichtheim to dub Mao's claims as "patently absurd" and to say that the Chinese had stood Marxism "entirely on its head".[16A] Certainly we move beyond the boundaries of Marxism and Leninism as we look through this last context of historical roots and try to draw the various strands together into something distinctly "Maoist". Do we single out the power of the will in Socialist transformation? The turbulence of the revolutionary quest, its reexamining of its inner-self without end? The transcendance of economically defined classes through the passionate act of the individual declaration? The leadership role of the Third World? Few other countries can have a "Marxist" thinker to match Li Ta-chao, with his theoretical leap that China, although it had almost no proletariat, was yet a proletarian country because of its poverty and its world situation under imperialism.[17] Or a "Marxist" poet like Kuo Mo-jo (still a major figure in China's cultural policy-making) who sang as a bourgeois youth:

> I am a member of the proletariat,
> for besides my naked body,
> I have no property whatsoever.[18]

In 1958, as the Great Leap Forward developed, Mao could praise the size of China's population as increasing these spiritual forces: "The more people the more views and suggestions, the more intense the fervour, and the greater the energy". And in one of his most famous recent passages:

> Apart from their other characteristics, China's 600 million people have two remarkable peculiarities; they are, first of all, poor, and secondly, blank. That may seem like a bad thing, but it is really a good thing. Poor people want change, want to do things, want revolution. A clean sheet of paper has no blotches, and so the newest and most beautiful words can be written on it, the newest and most beautiful pictures can be painted on it.[19]

The poverty and blankness represents the absence of ideological "over-sophistication": education — even socialist education — corrupts and leads to its opposite. In constantly seeking rejuvenation "from below" Mao does, with consistency, threaten the Party by challenging its conception of hierarchy. Yet surely, in insisting that his definitions of reality have the deepest meaning because they most truly represent the needs of the masses, Mao reintroduces his own dogmatisms. Party, nation, world and history enfold him as they do all other Chinese, or other citizens in other lands; the elusiveness of Maoism comes perhaps from the fact that Mao has been influenced by an unusually wide range of phenomena, and also from the paradox that he seems constantly on the edge of seeing that a great trap is there even as he falls into it. The trap, in this case, being that "unflagging vigilance over its own meticulous boundary lines"[20] which Kolakowski has described as afflicting the "sect", and which demands political polarization even as it claims to shun it.[21]

NOTES

This essay, being just a general sketch, is dependent on a mass of background reading which could not possibly be cited in detail here. My main debt, like that of any other scholar of modern Chinese history, is to the work of Stuart Schram, whose *Political Thought of Mao Tse-tung* and biography *Mao Tse-tung* provide essential organization and synthesis. Other books that I found particularly intelligent and useful include Maurice Meisner, *Li Ta-chao and the Origins of Chinese Marxism,* Benjamin Schwartz, *Chinese Communism and the Rise of Mao,* Lyman Van Slyke, *Enemies and Friends,* Mark Selden, *The Yenan Way,* Franz Schurmann, *Ideology and Organization in Communist China*, Donald Zagoria, *The Sino-Soviet Conflict.* I am also indebted to dozens of articles in *China Quarterly,* and to the books of essays edited by Chalmers Johnson, Michel Oksenberg, John Wilson Lewis, Robert Scalapino, and Doak Barnett.

1. *Elementary Chinese,* Vol. 1, Peking, 1971, p. 156.

2. *China Pictorial,* Vol. 1, 1974, pp. 7–8.

3. Schram shows critiques of Stalin, *CQ* 57(Jan/Mar 1974) 161–2.

4. Raya Dunayevskaya, *Philosophy and Revolution* Delta, New York, 1973, pp. 158–59 has a forceful presentation of these ideas, plus a critique of Mao's "retrogressionism".

5. *Peking Review, 9,* March 1, 1974, p. 17.

6. *PR, 5,* Feb. 1, 1974, p. 3.

7. Frederic Wakeman, *History and Will,* University of California Press, 1973, p. xii.

8. *CQ, 57,* January/March 1974, 161–62.

9. Chow Tse-tsung, *The May 4th Movement,* p. 59.

10. Wakeman, *History and Will,* pp. 164–65, makes a step in this direction.

11. Translated by "Ch'i-ming", *Hsin-ch'ing-nien, 6* (4), pp. 365–371, and 6 (5), pp. 470–78.

12. Angelo S. Rappaport, "The Philosophic Basis of the Russian Revolution", *Edinburgh Review,* July 1917, pp. 113–133.

13. British Museum General Catalog 846–48.

14. *Hsin-ch'ing-nien, 6* (5), note, p. 478.

15. Rappaport, p. 120.

16. Rappaport, p. 126.

16A. George Lichtheim, *Marxism, An Historical and Critical Study*, pp. 363–64

17. Meisner, *Li Ta-chao.*

18. Cited in Leo Lee, *The Romantic Generation of Modern Chinese Writers*, Harvard University Press, 1973, p. 195.

19. Schram, *Political Thought*, p. 351.

20. Leszek Kołakowski, *Toward a Marxist Humanism: Essays on the Left Today*, p. 98.

21. Kołakowski, p. 106.

MARXISM IN RUSSIA

LEONARD SCHAPIRO
London School of Economics

The use of the term "Marxism" to denote a certain doctrine gives rise to complicated problems. For example, if "Marxism" is used in its widest and most political sense as it is by the leaders of the Soviet Union then everything that has happened in the Soviet Union since 1917 could be brought under the heading of "Marxism in Russia," and a paper on this subject would amount to a history of Soviet power much more than to the history of certain ideas. The much more modest aim of this paper is to look at the views of Marx and Engels in their relation to Russia, both in the way in which, in the formative years of the Russian revolutionary movement, Marx and Engels understood this movement and in the way in which the Russian revolutionaries, when they first became acquainted with the ideas of Marx and Engels, were influenced by them and attempted to interpret them in relation to their own situation. This is not to say that all discussion of the writings of Marx and Engels that has taken place in Russia since those early years is irrelevant to the question of Marxism in Russia. However, one cannot escape the fact that after 1903, for example, after the split between the Bolsheviks and the Mensheviks as the two factions of the party were to become known, interpretations of what Marx and Engels were supposed to have said or written became an integral part of the political struggle and therefore belong much more to the history of that political struggle than they do to intellectual history. Or to take some other examples of a rather more extreme kind. Stalin's propagandists in the 'thirties were able to find, or claim to find, justification in the writings of Marx for the view that the idea of a Leader, a supreme Leader such as Stalin became, was an integral part of the doctrine of Marxism. They were also able to show that the repressive policy of Stalin, which resulted in the doing to death of many millions of innocent people, was somehow or other justified by doctrines which were supposed to derive from Marx. All this is very interesting for those who study the nature of totalitarian rule. It has nothing whatever to do with the intellectual history of a doctrine.

If one goes a little further back in time in the history of the Soviet Union, there are two periods where much turned or appeared to turn on the political scene on the interpretation of the doctrines of Marx or at any rate on the interpretation of Lenin's interpretation of the doctrines of Marx. Thus, during the period of the New Economic Policy from 1921 to 1928 or 1929, Bukharin developed a number of doctrines, based on the last writings and the last opinions of Lenin as orally expressed to him, which claimed to be a new interpretation of Marx in the conditions of Russia of the third decade of the century. What this doctrine amounted to in short was that the peculiar circumstances, in which the proletariat had been forced to seize power in Russia in October of 1917 dictated the need for a long period of reconciliation between the countryside and the towns, a period lasting generations; that during this period social peace had at all costs to be preserved; that the peasants had to acquire the social consciousness which they had lacked in 1917 before one could even think about socialism; and that the state with its ownership of the principal means of production must meanwhile encourage socialism by example and not by compulsion. All this, which also implied a more humane attitude than had been practiced in the early years after the Bolsheviks had seized power, may or may not have been a reinterpretation or deepening of the views of Lenin. It is very difficult to see what it has got to do with Marx's analysis of the future of industrial societies. Similarly, while the debates between Trotsky and the right wing on the pace of industrialization and later on the relation of Soviet Communism to world Communism may present a great deal of interest for the history of Russia, it is once again very difficult to see them outside the context of the peculiar Russian circumstances, or indeed as related to the general study of a doctrine which is based on the writings of two men in the nineteenth century. It is for this reason that my topic must, in my view, be mainly confined to the first impact of the doctrines of Marx and Engels on Russia and to the part which they played in influencing the course of Russian revolutionary history.

Before the reforms of the sixties and particularly the emancipation of the peasants in 1861, the interest of Marx and of Engels in Russia was mainly confined to the effects of Russian policy on other countries, or to Russia's reactionary repression of revolutions. Marx and Engels saw Russia as the arch enemy of Europe in particular, and of progress in general. However, in spite of their apparent dislike for this bastion of reaction, Engels' interest in language and in the history of culture generally prompted him to start learning Russian as early as 1851. As far as Marx was concerned, it was not until much later that he began to take a detailed interest in the internal conditions of Russia. He began learning Russian in October of 1869 and mastered it very quickly indeed, though even before that date he had been reading a good deal of material on Russia in translation. After 1869 he appears to have read and abstracted voraciously from a large number of books on Russia, and an incomplete list which has been compiled on the basis of his library and of the published extracts from his notebooks runs to very many titles.[1] Marx obtained his material on Russia mainly with the help of the populist economist Danielson. It would seem that the first book which drew an enthusiastic response from Marx was Bervi-Flerovski's account of the situation of the working class in Russia, which was published in 1869 and was regarded by Marx as the first work to tell the truth about internal conditions in Russia.[2] Whatever intentions Marx may have had — and it would seem that he did intend, if he had the time, to write comprehensively on the subject of Russia — he in fact was never able to carry them out. It is an interesting speculation to consider the effect which a complete analysis in depth by Marx of the future of Russia might have had on the development of the Russian revolutionary movement, particularly if one considers the important influence which his fragmentary and usually inconclusive remarks on the subject seem to have had inside Russia.

Although there is no analysis in depth by either Marx or Engels of the nature of Russian society of the pre-Reform period, there are sufficient occasional references to show quite clearly what their view was. They regarded the communal organization of Russia as an example of a primitive form of society which had occurred in every country at some period of its history; they regarded the absence of private property in the Russian village and what Engels used to refer to sarcastically as the primitive communism of Russia as the best foundation for despotism; and Marx, in particular, indulged in caustic diatribes against Herzen's plans for rejuvenating Europe through the influence of Russian primitive socialism — which Engels on one occasion describes as the "pan-Slavist swindle."[3] So far as the commune was concerned, it is clear that neither Marx nor Engels regarded it as having anything to do with socialism. Indeed it seems to have been Bervi-Flerovski's book which persuaded Marx for the first time that the germs of socialism had been sown by the emancipation of the serfs. According to Marx, as expressed in a letter to Engels, this had accelerated the loosening-up process in Russia, with the result that a great social revolution could be regarded as imminent.[4] Marx was drawn into a discussion of the question of the village commune and consideration of the possibility that it might be a distinctive Russian institution and not merely a primitive relic, as Engels believed it to be right to the end. Marx yielded sufficiently to the persistence of the populists to bring his great authority to bear on the burning question of whether the communal land organization and its primitive socialism offered an opportunity for Russia to develop on lines which would avoid the effects which capitalism had had. The best-known discussion of this problem was the result of a request by Vera Zasulich to Marx on the subject of the commune. Her letter was dated from Geneva on February 16, 1881. It therefore came at a period when Vera Zasulich, together with Plekhanov and others, had deserted the populist organizations inside Russia and moved to Geneva, and were on the way to their "conversion" to Marxism if they were not already "converted." One of the reasons which most affected Plekhanov, and therefore presumably Zasulich, in their "conversion" to Marxism was their belief on the evidence before them that the commune in fact was already disintegrating, and that reliance upon it for the future of Russian socialism was therefore a chimera. Thus, in this letter, Vera Zasulich implores Marx to express his opinion on the commune. Was it doomed to decay, as some people in Russia believed? In that case, surely there was no hope for any kind of separate development for Russia, and therefore nothing remained but to wait with resignation for the development of capitalist and proletarian organizations in Russia before there could be any thought of revolution. On the other hand, if the commune could be saved, then its development might be regarded as a favorable factor for the development of a peculiar Russian form of socialism.

Marx devoted considerable thought to this letter, as is revealed by a number of draft replies which indicate the care with which he directed his thoughts to this all-important question. Even so, his ultimate reply was not conclusive, although on the whole it did appear to give more comfort to the populist point of view than to the Marxist point of view of Plekhanov and Zasulich. What Marx in effect wrote, after apologizing for his inability to prepare a really detailed and adequate reply, was first of all to emphasize that his analysis of society and of the course of its development was designed for societies in which capitalist production prevailed. He further emphasized that the basis of this capitalist process is the expropriation of land by the capitalists and the creation of a landless proletariat. Now this, Marx continued, bore little relationship to Russia, where it is not a question of one form of property being transformed into another, but, on the contrary, of the transformation of communal property into private property. However, Marx goes on to say that he had come to the conclusion that the commune could provide a basis for the social transformation of Russia, provided that it was safeguarded from the decay with which it was threatened by various factors and circumstances.[5] It may be doubted whether Marx's cautious support of the populist dogma would have been fully shared by Engels, at all events by the end of his life. It is true that Engels did join with Marx in 1882 in the preface to the Russian edition of the Communist Manifesto, which also gave cautious support to the populist belief in a separate destiny for Russia which would enable it to escape the general fate of European countries. In this preface, Marx and Engels wrote after quoting the great problem with which the Russian revolutionaries were concerned, that if the Russian revolution were to become a signal for a proletarian revolution in the West so that revolutions in the West and in Russia complement each other, then indeed the present Russian communal landholding system might become a point of departure for a development of Russia along communist lines.[6] But whatever may have been Engel's view of the subject in 1882, it is quite plain that his views on the subject had undergone a pretty fundamental change by 1895, if not before.

Of course it is not only views which could have changed in that time but the conditions inside Russia, and in particular the continuing and all the time more evident decline of the village commune as well as the growth of industrialization and the development of a proletariat. In 1894 Engels' opinion seems clear enough that Marx's earlier view, if it could be taken to justify the populist hope for a separate path of development for Russia, had been overtaken by events and that Russia would have to go the way of the other European countries. This, of course, was the view which Plekhanov and Vera Zasulich had been propagating for a decade and during that time they had maintained fairly close contact with Engels and had been encouraged and sustained by him.[7] Whatever the reasoned and closely argued views which were expressed by both Marx and Engels on the subject of the future of Russian development, it would seem that neither of them ever really abandoned a kind of simple inner conviction that the first and foremost priority for Russia was a revolution — revolution of any kind, but above all a revolution which would destroy the influence of this reactionary force and thus might have a beneficent influence on revolutionary development outside Russia. It is clear, for example, that neither of them derived any particular satisfaction from the fact that their own ideas had actually prompted Russians to begin to apply them to Russian conditions, and they showed scant sympathy for Russian revolutionary theorists in general. When Marx heard that Plekhanov and other members of the Russian revolutionary organization "Land and Liberty" had left Russia and emigrated to Geneva in order to form an intellectual group, Marx's indignation found expression in a letter to Sorge in which he wrote (in his characteristic and quite untranslatable style) about those members of the revolutionary organization who have "*voluntarily* left Russia in sharp contrast with those who are prepared as terrorists to risk their own skins, in order to form the so-called party of propaganda (in order to make propaganda in *Russia* they move to *Geneva*! What a quid pro quo!). These gentlement are against all political revolutionary action. Russia is destined according to them to leap through a *salto mortale* into the anarchistic-communistic-atheistic millennium! Meanwhile they are preparing this leap through the means of the most dreary doctrinaire ideas of which the so-called principes *courent la rue depuis feu Bakounine.*"[8] And not very long afterwards, on April 23, 1885, Engels wrote to Vera Zasulich in politer but very similar terms. While expressing his satisfaction that Plekhanov's ideas had been so much influenced by the theories of Marx and stressing how proud Marx would have been had he lived to see it, he nevertheless expressed some doubt as to the relevance of these theories to the present position in Russia. He argued that Russia is on the eve of a revolution and that this could be one of those exceptional circumstances when the "blanquist phantasy" might have some sort of foundation for its existence. He then proceeded to say that such a revolution in Russia might very well start a universal conflagration.[9] In a private letter from about the same time Engels expressed his view even more forcibly when he pointed out that what Russia needed was "not a programme but a revolution."[10]

The question of the future of the village commune and of Marx's views whether or not Russia could escape the evils of capitalism and progress towards an indigenous form of socialism, although of great importance to the Russian revolutionaries and to Russian populist thinkers generally, was not, however, the only aspect of Marx's ideas which appeared of importance to Russians at different periods. The most intense and indeed revealing discussion of Marx's ideas developed in Russia after the publication of the first volume of *Das Kapital* in a Russian translation in 1872. However, this was not the beginning of the influence and discussion of Marx's ideas in Russia and some of these earlier contacts and influences must be examined. The earliest open mention of Marx was in an encyclopedic dictionary published in

1848.[11] It would seem that some of Marx's works were already available in Russia in narrow circles. At any rate, the library which was organized between 1845 and 1848 by Petrashevsky contained a copy of Engels' *Condition of the Working Class in England* and Marx's *Poverty of Philosophy*. Petrashevsky was the leader of a small group of young Russians, which included Dostoevsky, who met mainly for the discussion of socialist ideas and the future of Russia. It was only a revolutionary group in the fevered imagination of the Russian police, and was disbanded with many subsequent arrests in 1848. There was, however, no sign that the ideas of either Marx or Engels had any influence on this group and, as indeed Marx himself says in the *Poverty of Philosophy,* speaking of socialists and communists, that "as long as the productive forces have not yet been sufficiently developed among the bourgeoisie . . . which are necessary for the liberation of the proletariat and for the formation of a new society, these theorists will remain utopians who . . . will continue to think out systems. . . "[12] At about the same time, the literary critic and historian P.V. Annenkov, who is best known nowadays for his account of what he called "The Remarkable Decade," after correspondence with Marx met him on a number of occasions in 1847 and 1848. He has left a very fascinating account of these meetings, which include one occasion in which Marx delivered an all-out attack on Weitling. In the course of this attack he pointed out to Annenkov that Weitling's fantastic ideas for immediate revolution might have some sort of meaning in a country like Russia, but could be of no possible relevance in a country like Germany. When Weitling attempted to defend himself against this savage attack, and among other things pointed out that the great support which he received from humble workmen was perhaps more important than all the theoretical analyses of this study, Marx struck the table with great force, jumped up, and said "Ignorance has never yet been of any help to anyone."[13]

Marx's contempt for Herzen has already been referred to and is in any case well known, as is his very high regard for the work of Chernyshevski. There was no contact at any time between the two men, and, indeed, by the time Marx became familiar with his works Chernyshevski was already exiled. There is also no evidence at all that Chernyshevski had ever read any work of Marx. The main coincidence between their ideas is passionate devotion to atheism and materialism. Otherwise there could be little in common between the views of Marx and those of Chernyshevski, because Chernyshevski believed that Russia was destined to follow an entirely separate and noncapitalist path of development from Western Europe. Marx, on the other hand, ap-

proved of Chernyshevski because he saw in his method of analysis a
similarity to the historical materialist approach. Before the 1870s
Marx also had friendly contacts with Bakunin and even with the re-
doubtable Nechaev — until the character of the latter was fully exposed to Marx by German Lopatin. Lopatin, a prominent populist and
then quite a young man, had a very close relationship with Marx when
he came to London in the summer of 1870 in order to work under
Marx's direction at the British Museum while at the same time taking
English lessons from Marx's daughter Eleanor.[14] There is no evidence
of correspondence between Marx and Lopatin, but Marx's correspondence with Danielson dates from 1868, and Lopatin would have been
well informed of Marx's views and interests through this leading populist economist. In order to complete this story one should also recall
that Marx had a certain amount of correspondence with the Russians
who were members of the Russian section of the First International
whose representative Karl Marx became at their invitation. This correspondence is not very revealing from the point of view of ideas,
though we do learn from it of the very high regard which Marx, after
he learned Russian, had acquired for the works of Chernyshevski and
Bervi-Flerovski.[15]

The earliest work that appears to have influenced the populists in
Russia was Engels's *Condition of the Working Class in England.* A
number of articles, both critical and approving, were published on this
work which seems to have been widely known in Russia. If for want
of a better definition we adopt a description of "populists" as those
revolutionaries and reformers in Russia who rejected the capitalist
path of development for Russia's future, the most interesting early
case of the influence of Engels is that of N. V. Shelgunov. Shelgunov
was one of the most radical of the populists and was of particular
importance as the co-author of a revolutionary proclamation addressed
"to the younger generation" in 1861, in the very first flowering of
Russian revolutionary activity after the emancipation of the serfs in
February 1861. Shelgunov discussed Engels's work at length in an article on the position of the working class in France and in England. His
main purpose in writing this article was, in fact, to illustrate the
misery of the working class under capitalism, and to draw the moral
that the capitalist path was something that Russia should at all costs
avoid. Indeed, in his famous proclamation Shelgunov expressly says
"Who can assert that we must travel the same path as Europe, the path
of some Saxony, or England, or France? ... We believe in our own
fresh powers; we believe that we are called upon to bring to history
some new principle, to say our own word and not to repeat the past

errors of Europe."[16] But perhaps the most important question of the influence of Marx is that of his supposed influence on the Russian Jacobin thinker P.N. Tkachev. Tkachev was a very distinctive Russian nineteenth-century thinker, whom it is in some ways difficult to identify as a populist, though he certainly shared the populist characteristic of wishing to avoid any kind of industrial development of Russia. The interest of discussing Marx's influence on Tkachev is at least threefold. In the first place he claimed that he was a Marxist, whatever he may have meant by this, as early as 1865, asserting at the same time that in his opinion there could scarcely be any objection raised to any of the doctrines of Marx on the part of anyone of any intelligence at all.[17] The second reason why the influence of Marx on Tkachev is of particular importance is because quite a strong case can be made for the proposition that Lenin was influenced by the views of Tkachev.[18] The third reason is that Tkachev engaged in open polemics with Engels. Now in view of the extraordinary acceptance by Tkachev of Marx's views as self-evident and really beyond any contradiction, one is entitled to enquire what it is he understood by "Marxism." One thing that is quite clear is that he never for a moment regarded, either in 1865 or in the following decade when his main activity took place, the work of Marx as having any relationship to revolution at all. The side of Marx's thought which appealed to Tkachev was therefore in effect irrelevant to his revolutionary doctrine. What appealed to him was Marx's materialist interpretation of history. One of the most significant and most "Marxist" of Tkachev's publications, which did not see the light of day until long after his death, was a study of political ideas in their relation to their material base and viewed as a superstructure of their materialist base.[19] How remote Tkachev was from any interpretation of revolution which could in any way be associated with Marx's analysis of society is shown by his polemics with Engels in 1874, in which Tkachev argued that the Russian autocracy was without any support at that time, but that the moment the peasantry beame more prosperous as the result of governmental efforts, the government would then acquire peasant support, and the chance of a revolution effected by a revolutionary minority, as always advocated by Tkachev, would then be gone forever. Tkachev argued that Russia could not therefore afford to wait while the laws of history slowly brought about the desired revolution. In other words, for Tkachev the laws of history were not something to be regarded as inevitable, but were plainly subordinate to the voluntary action of man. Engels in his attack is mainly concerned to argue against Tkachev's view that the minority should seize power in the name of the people and then put

socialist measures into force. But Engels also advanced the view that
the autocracy was already then, in 1874 or 1875, supported by landlords and rich peasants, and he quoted figures to support his thesis.[20]

This debate prompts several observations. In the first place it would
be difficult for a true follower of Marx to regard a revolution as
postponed "forever" if it were not undertaken at the right moment,
though it will be recalled that Lenin got perilously near to arguing this
in his impassioned letters to the Bolshevik Central Committee in 1917
on the eve of the Bolshevik seizure of power. It is also true that Lenin
was seriously disturbed by the thought that the Stolypin reforms
might succeed and create strong support for the government, and that
this would make revolution much less likely to succeed. It may also be
observed, however, that Engels' somewhat superficial argument that
the landlords and the rich peasants supported the government because
they derived economic benefit from their privileged position is a good
deal further away from the historical truth than the position adopted
by Tkachev; it would be very difficult to argue that, whatever their
economic position, landlords and rich peasants exercised any political
influence in the Russia of 1875, or acted as a support that the government could rely on. For completeness, one must note the relationship
between Marx and Peter Lavrov, from 1873 to 1876 the editor of
Vpered, the leading Russian revolutionary paper of the period – if
such it can be called. Lavrov's main influence on the Russian populist
movement was in the direction of gradualism and evolution, and his
was the voice that influenced those who believed in long-term peaceful
propaganda among the peasants rather than in any kind of sudden
revolutionary violence. Lavrov was indeed a great admirer of Marx,
particularly of Marx's erudition as an economist, but it is difficult to
see of what relevance a confirmed opponent of capitalism as far as
Russia was concerned could have found in Marx's analysis of Western
Europe. And it is indeed difficult to see in Lavrov's ideas any direct
influence of Marx other than a belief in gradualism, if indeed this
aspect of Lavrov's thought was influenced by Marx. As far as Marx
was concerned, he seems to have tolerated Lavrov with a certain
amount of condescension, and was probably flattered by Lavrov's
deference.[21] Thus it would seem that the populist revolutionaries,
who have hitherto been considered, valued Marx and Engels either because they offered a good object lesson of what Russia should avoid – a
view which was shared both by Shelgunov and by Tkachev – or because of the exposition of the materialist interpretation of history. As
far as making revolution was concerned, this was regarded as a Russian
matter to which Marx's analysis of society and history was irrelevant

for Russians. Certainly there is nothing in the writing of Tkachev to suggest that any of his *revolutionary* ideas was inspired by Marx; and we know that, as far as Engels was concerned, there was a violent collision of views between Tkachev and him.

None of this, however, prevented Marx from acquiring an enormous reputation as the leading economist of Western Europe among the populist economists, of whom Danielson became the most famous. Hence the somewhat surprising fact occurred that the first translation of the first volume of *Das Kapital* should have taken place in Russia. The translation was first mooted in 1868 and promoted by Danielson (with whom Marx would maintain an extensive correspondence until 1881 and Engels until his death in 1895). But the translation was, in fact, not published until 1872. One of the difficulties was that of getting through the Russian censorship. The import of all of Marx's previously published works had already been prohibited in Russia. But when they came to read *Das Kapital* the censors decided that the book was "abstruse" and "obscure"; that "few will read it and even fewer will understand it"; and that its attacks on the factory system in England were not relevant to Russian conditions where the government protected the workers.[22] The censors proved to be right in their prognosis, at any rate in one respect, namely that in the event no one who was associated with the venture of promoting the translation of *Das Kapital* in fact became a revolutionary (Lopatin never became a revolutionary; and Danielson became one of the main theoretical opponents of the relevance of Marxism to Russian conditions). Marx was particularly scathing about this popularity of his work among Russians. In a letter to Kugelman of October 12, 1868, he attributed his popularity, with characteristic sarcasm, to the fact that the Russian aristocracy brought up in the universities of Germany and Paris was always ready to chase after any kind of extreme doctrine produced in the West. "This does not prevent the very same Russians from becoming rascals the moment they have entered state service."[23] Marx was really somewhat unfair in this comment. The avidity for serious foreign literature among aristocratic or other Russian intellectuals in the nineteenth century could well be explained by the rigorous censorship which prevented them from easy access to the latest developments in Western European intellectual life. However, this still raises the intriguing question of why Marx, whose doctrines in 1872 still seemed somewhat irrelevant to Russian conditions, was so popular in Russia.

The reactions to the appearance in Russian of *Das Kapital*, which remained a subject of vigorous discussion, praise, and criticism for

many years, suggest part of the answer. As far as the populists theorists were concerned, they saw in Marx's work, rather as Shelgunov
had seen in Engels' *Condition of the Working Class in England,* a
terrible warning against the evils of capitalism and a powerful argument for the populist view that Russia must at all costs avoid going
the way of capitalist development. The most influential criticism of
Das Kapital along these lines, or rather welcoming of it, was that of
N.K. Mikhailovsky, the leading theorist of populism, in his article on
Das Kapital published in 1872. According to Mikhailovsky *Das Kapital*
was above all a warning to Russia not to rush into industrialization,
but, indeed, to take steps to avoid it. The alternatives before Russia
were either capitalist industrialization or a form of popular production
based on the commune, and Russia must take steps to see that the
commune did not disintegrate, and that popular production remained
possible. This far Mikhailovsky was, in fact, on a more sophisticated
level, echoing Shelgunov. However, Mikhailovsky now attempted by a
misinterpretation of what Marx had written to suggest that this view
had the authority of the great Marx. He appeared to construe some
sentences from the preface to *Das Kapital* as meaning that it was
possible for one nation to learn from another and thus avoid the fate
which had befallen other countries; and, by inference, invoked Marx's
authority for the populist faith in the Russian "separate path."
Mikhailovsky's interpretation of *Das Kapital* in this article became in
the course of time a powerful argument in favor of the populist point
of view. It was not, however, shared by Marx, who wrote a rejoinder
to Mikhailovsky which remained unpublished for some time, but
which certainly circulated in manuscript. Marx's rejoinder to Mikhailovsky is characterized by the ambivalent or even ambiguous position
on the subject of the future of Russia which seems to have characterized everything that Marx wrote on the subject. He vigorously objected to what he regarded as Mikhailovsky's unjustified attempt to
recruit him as a supporter for the populist view that Russia could and
ought follow a path different from capitalist Western Europe. In fact,
he maintained that his book was limited in its analysis to Western
Europe and could not be used one way or the other as an argument
for what would happen in Russia. Having said this, he then proceeded
to express a view on Russia which, while ambiguous, nevertheless
seems to lean to the populist side. Thus, he said at length that if
Russia is to become a capitalist country (and certainly, according to
Marx the signs of that in recent years were pretty clear) then it will
only achieve capitalism by transforming a considerable number of its
peasants into proletarians. After that, having reached the sphere of

capitalist structure, Russia will be like other unfortunate peoples, destined inevitably to suffer the rigors of capitalism. There are, however, some sentences which suggest that Russia could avoid this fate, as indeed Mikhailovsky argued. Thus he wrote that "if Russia will continue to follow the path which it has been following since 1861, then it will lose the best opportunity which history has ever offered to any people and will experience all the fatal evils of the capitalist régime." It is difficult to interpret this as meaning anything other than the fact that Russia had some kind of alternative, and indeed a desirable one, to capitalism in store for her if she followed the right policy.[24]

The Russian debates over *Das Kapital* were too extensive and too numerous to be summarized here in any detail, and the whole subject has already been extensively treated. However, there are certain trends which should be mentioned. First there were those who saw *Das Kapital*, with its portrayal of the horrors of industrial England, as a timely argument in favor of those who believed in factory reform. Then there were the out-and-out opponents of the argument on economic grounds, who challenged the whole theory of surplus value and other cornerstones of Marx's analysis. The most prominent among these was B.N. Chicherin, the leading liberal lawyer and legal historian of that time, whose criticism aroused much indignation from Marx's supporters in Russia and from Marx himself. Of greater interest for the present investigation are the arguments which were adduced by those who could be regarded as followers of Marx. One of them was the liberal professor of economics at St. Petersburg Kaufmann, who wrote the review which seems to have pleased Marx best of all the reviews which appeared in Russia. The point that distinguishes Kaufmann from other Russian reviewers is that he realized that *Das Kapital* represented a scientific investigation of the basic laws governing the transformation of one social order into another, and that it set forth the essential nature of the materialist interpretation of history.[25]

One of the most important exponents of Marx whose writings did more than those of anyone to make Marx's works known widely among the Russian intellectuals was N.E. Ziber, who at one time taught in the economics faculty of the University of Kiev. Ziber, who was born in 1844 and died in 1888, produced a number of substantial works during his lifetime, including a long study of the comparative views of David Ricardo and Karl Marx. He also contributed a number of articles to the controversy over *Das Kapital*, several of which became part of the regular reading of the Russian revolutionary circles of the 'eighties. The striking feature about Ziber, as indeed of every single one of the Russians whose views on Marx have so far been examined, is that there is no suggestion anywhere in his discussion of Marx that the doctrine of Marx is in any way related to revolution. In fact this is one of the faults which are laid at his door by Soviet critics who otherwise, quite rightly, regard him as having made a great contribution to the spread of the ideas of Marx in Russia. It is evident from Ziber's view of Marx that he regarded the social transformation foretold by Marx as an inevitable process, in which no voluntary activity of any kind by revolutionaries was required, and indeed there is no trace in Ziber of any kind of advocacy of revolutionary activity, nor was he at any time subjected to any kind of persecution by the police. This view, that Marxism was quite unrelated to revolution and indeed did not call for any kind of action of anyone's part at all, was apparently not unusual in the 'seventies, according to the historian B.P. Koz'min. Koz'min recounts one particular example of a follower of Marx who greatly admired and constantly quoted the Master. As a result of his conversion to Marxism, this young man decided that the actions of individuals were totally immaterial in relation to the forces of history which would bring about the eventual overthrow of society, and that nothing could be done either to accelerate or to postpone the historically predetermined event. And so he turned away from his former populist revolutionary convictions and sat quietly chatting to his friends and playing chess, waiting for the moment when the time would be ripe.[26]

The main debate over *Das Kapital* thus took place in the 'seventies. It had the effect of familiarizing the Russian intellectuals with the principal ideas of Marx, but it did not suggest to them as yet that these ideas and the idea of revolution, let alone organization for the purposes of revolution, were in any way connected. The situation in Russia was greatly affected by the breakaway from the bosom of populism of a group of populists which comprised G.V. Plekhanov, Lev Deich, Vera Zasulich, and P.B. Axel'rod. These four had in 1879 broken with the part of the revolutionary populist organization "Land and Liberty" which, under the name of the "People's Will," proceeded to organize the assassination of Emperor Alexander II which took place on March 1, 1881. Under the name of "Repartition of the Land" the dissident group preached for a short time a doctrine of evolutionary social development in which terrorism, and indeed any kind of political activity, was to have no part. However, by 1880 the members of the group were living abroad, much to Marx's indignation, as will be recalled, and by 1881 were beginning to show certain signs of conversion to Marxism. On September 25, 1883, Plekhanov and his supporters announced the publication in Geneva of a series of popular political pamphlets for workers which was to be called the Library of Contemporary Socialism. Thus came into existence the first Russian theoretical group devoted to the exposition of the doctrines of Marx, which became known as the Group for the Liberation of Labor.

This first real Marxist theoretical group was thus the product of revulsion against terrorist action and against conspiratorial theories of revolution. It was inspired both by a deep conviction that conspiracies for the purpose of seizing power were useless — a point of view which the entirely futile assassination of Alexander II would seem to prove conclusively — and by the conviction that the commune was fast disintegrating, thus removing the linchpin of the whole social foundation on which the doctrine of populism was built. Moreover, the rapid growth, or relatively rapid growth, of the Russian working class, as a consequence of the emancipation of the serfs of 1861, increasingly suggested that Russia was irrevocably launched in the direction of industrialization. However, the Liberation of Labor Group remained pretty remote from Russia, as indeed Marx had feared, and this became especially evident after the arrest of Deich in 1884. Deich had been in charge of organizing contact with Russia and as a result of his arrest, regular contact could not be resumed until 1895. One of the consequences of this was that Marxist groups which began to spring up in Russia in the eighties, and especially in the nineties, developed to a large extent quite independently of the theorists in Geneva, and this fact was to lead to serious factional difficulties in the young Russian movement around the turn of the century. With these, however, we are not here concerned. The main doctrines of the group were expounded by Plekhanov both in his vigorous polemics with Tkachev and in two pamphlets, published in 1883 and in 1884, and in two programs, published in 1884 and 1887.[27] Essentially what Plekhanov was advocating was a very long-term, two-stage view of development in Russia. In the first place, the full development of capitalism would take place, and of this the disintegration of the commune and the development of a proletariat were the first beginnings. The advent of capitalism would inexorably be followed by the emergence of bourgeois political parties and of the bourgeois revolution, and this, in the fullness of time, would be followed by a socialist revolution led by the proletariat and its party. It was essential, however, for the proletariat to create its own party as soon as possible. The proletariat would have to cooperate with the liberals in the first phase in order to bring down the autocracy, but, having achieved that, would have separate tasks to pursue and would pursue them in opposition to the liberals. It is fairly clear that this particular adaptation of Marx's analysis to Russia could

not be very comforting to revolutionaries who are in general not endowed with very much patience, but in any case were smarting under
the catastrophic failure of March 1, 1881. Plainly, in Plekhanov's view,
the ultimate socialist revolution was a very long way off.

The association of ultimate revolution with the works of Marx was
already a considerable innovation on the Russian scene. There were
also certain modifications of doctrine made in the course of years by
Plekhanov and his associates, particularly Axel'rod, which were designed to make the delay seem less irksome. One of them was the
doctrine of "hegemony," which meant that the working class party, or
the social democratic party, would in fact take over the leadership
over the liberal parties and exert hegemony over them. This particular
piece of nonsense was very soon disproved in practice, and was
dropped quietly. The second argument, which had rather more force,
was that Russia would benefit from experience of the Western social
democratic parties and would therefore be able considerably to speed
up the process of advancing the workers' revolution in Russia. It was
perhaps a significant and a symbolic fact that the founding congress of
the Russian Social Democratic Labor Party in 1898, which could be
regarded as one indirect result of Plekhanov's influence, played no role
whatever in the future of the Russian party, and that the real history,
both of the Bolsheviks and of the Mensheviks, dates from the Second
Congress of the Party of 1903 which was dominated by Lenin.

While it is true that there were discernible groups of workers in the
eighties which could be described as Marxist, the great majority of
revolutionary groups, in the very broad sense, should more properly
be described as "preparatory." This term owes its origin to the shock
of the failure of the assassination of March 1, 1881, to result in any
kind of national uprising, as was apparently fervently hoped. The
disastrous failure persuaded the revolutionaries who remained at liberty that uprisings were very unlikely to occur unless they had been
carefully prepared — a fact which they might have learned before
1881 if the works of Tkachev had been studied more attentively. Like
Lenin, and unlike any other Russian revolutionary theorist before
him, Tkachev realized the importance of preparing the revolutionary
situation before attempting the dramatic coup d'état. It was a significant fact that the terrorist group headed by Alexander Ulianov,
Lenin's elder brother (the only, or perhaps one of two, active terrorist
groups), did not regard the social democrats as a separate category of
revolutionaries in the broad sense, or consider that their views were
indeed very relevant to revolutionary activity. Ulianov's conspiratorial
group worked out a plan to assassinate Emperor Alexander III on

March 1, 1887, but the plan was foiled owing to a gross breach in security by one of the conspirators, and those conspirators who did not succeed in escaping were hanged. While in prison, Alexander Ulianov reconstructed from memory the program of his group. It is a curious amalgam of Marxism and traditional Russian revolutionary populist theory. Declaring themselves socialists, the group asserts that socialism is an inevitable result of capitalism and of the classes which emerge as a result of capitalism, although it denies that this is necessarily the only path to socialism. It then proceeds to analyze the social classes in Russia and to proclaim that the organization of the working class is the most important task for the future. This, however, is regarded as impossible until some kind of freedom of speech and other civil freedoms are attained. There is therefore nothing left for the group to do but to struggle for a minimum of civil freedoms. This could only be achieved by systematic terror, by which Ulianov meant a continuous sacrifice of the flower of young Russian intelligentsia in the hope that this self-sacrifice would eventually force the authorities to realize that they must make some political concessions to society. The interesting paragraph in the present context is the reference to other parties. The program explains that the group is prepared to make common cause with the liberals. "As regards the social democrats our disagreements with them seem to us to be very insubstantial and merely theoretical."[28] Ten years later, if not earlier, when social democrats and populists were forming themselves into antagonistic groups and engaging in violent debates, this kind of assertion would have been inconceivable: the rival positions were by that time too clearly pegged out.

Lenin's well-known adaptation of Marxism, which in effect replaces social process by the human will, at any rate to a large extent, was plainly of a much more radical nature than Plekhanov's. If one follows Lenin's early revolutionary career, it is significant to note that Lenin (Vladimir Ulianov) began his career at the age of seventeen, in 1887, as a revolutionary without any theoretical label attached to him, very much influenced by the shock of discovering that his brother had been a revolutionary and, of course, the even greater shock of the execution and all the consequences of social ostracism that this entailed for the young Lenin's family. Some years pass before Lenin can be identifiably described as a convert to Marxism, although his study of it may very well have begun quite early. It is certainly the case that his general apprenticeship in conspiratorial revolutionary organizations included some active participation in a Marxist circle organized by G.E. Fedoseev in Kazan. Fedoseev, an early convert to Marxism who, to judge from his writings, was a very remarkable young man, died too early (tragically and by his own hand) to exercise much influence on the development of Marxism in Russia. The few writings that he left suggest that in the main his views were not along the lines that were later to become identified with Lenin. However, in one respect Lenin may have been influenced by Fedoseev, whom he never met, but with whom he corresponded for a long time after the latter's exile.[29] It seems most probable that Fedoseev influenced the young Lenin in implanting in his mind an idea which Lenin expounded as early as 1893, to the effect that capitalism *already* existed in Russia. This was a considerable divergence from the view hitherto held by Plekhanov and other Marxists that capitalism would be a necessary stage in Russia's development, but that it was still some way off. In a series of letters (recently published) dating from 1893, Lenin argued that capitalism did not belong to the future but was actually to be found in the Russian village, in the relationship between the rich peasants and the exploited poor peasants; and that although of a more rustic kind, it was in no respect different from the capitalism described by Marx.[30]

It was indeed in 1893 that Lenin's extensive correspondence with Fedoseev began. It is evident that Lenin's assertion, if accepted, would advance the development of socialism in Russia very considerably, indeed advance it by a whole historical phase as compared with the view of Plekhanov. This, therefore, was the first adaptation of Marxism to Russian conditions which was due to Lenin, who from 1893 onwards became one of the most accomplished experts on Marx in Russia, and one of the most forceful advocates of his views.

But it is not until sometime after his arrest in 1895 that the doctrines particularly associated with Lenin become apparent in his writings. These views, which became the foundation of *What Is to Be Done,* published in March of 1902, only became apparent in Lenin's writings toward the autumn of 1899 and appear to have emerged under the influence of reading the works of Eduard Bernstein, and of the fear that revisionism as advocated by Bernstein was widespread in the Russian Social Democratic movement. The first apprehensions appear in Lenin's writings in 1899, and the organizational prescriptions which are contained in articles published around that time and between then and 1902 culminated in the essential doctrine of Leninism. This expounds the need for organized professional, disciplined, centralized revolutionary activity, and propounds the doctrine that the workers by themselves will never achieve revolutionary consciousness, which has to be brought to them from the outside by their leaders. It is an open question, which it is neither possible nor necessary to discuss here, whether this view must be regarded as a departure from the views of Marx. Certain passages can be found in Marx's works which would substantiate Lenin's interpretation. For example, the last paragraph but one of Marx's *Critique of Hegel's Philosophy of Right* which was much discussed in the Ulianov group and had, in fact, been translated into Russian by one of the members of the group, reads as follows: "Just as philosophy finds in the proletariat its material weapon so the proletariat finds in philosophy its spiritual weapon, and as soon as the lightning of thought has struck deeply into this native popular soil then the emancipation of the Germans to the status of human beings will be complete."[31] Fortunately it is not necessary in this context to consider whether or not Lenin's version of Marx is a perversion, or an adaptation, or an implementation, or indeed a correct interpretation. It is beyond doubt, and suffices for present purposes, that it was an entirely new departure in the Russian reception of Marx. In Russia the doctrine of Karl Marx had hitherto been received as an analysis of society and an interpretation of history quite unrelated to any revolutionary organizational activity except in the remote and almost academic sense of Plekhanov. Lenin's interpretation transformed this into a revolutionary technique of which the consequences are beyond the scope of this study.

A question of great interest, however, is how it is that a doctrine that was so novel was so readily accepted and so little criticized or objected to at the time when it was first propounded. There was, of course, a great deal of controversy between the rival factions of the party, the Bolsheviks and the Mensheviks, after the split in 1903. But this belongs much more to the realm of party polemics than to the realm of doctrine. As far as doctrine is concerned, no one seriously objected to *What Is to Be Done* when it was published, and at the Second Party Congress in 1903 only one speaker pointed out that Lenin's doctrine of bringing consciousness from the outside was, in fact, inconsistent with Marx's doctrine of the class struggle. The ease with which Lenin's interpretation of Marx was accepted is perhaps not difficult to understand. In the first place it was a very welcome relief to revolutionaries, fed hitherto on the diet of Plekhanov's long-term doctrine of a revolution which was possibly generations away. Here was something which provided for action here and now and which very considerably shortened the period of waiting. It must also be recalled that the doctrine of elitist leadership of the masses was by no means new to the Russian revolutionary tradition. It is of course essential to the doctrines of Tkachev, and this revolutionary thinker expressed views on the nature of the proletariat in relation to revolution which were not very different from those expressed by Lenin a generation later.[32] Probably, few Russians were aware of Marx's diatribe against the doctrine of bringing consciousness into the workers' organization from the outside and of treating the working class as material to be worked on, "A chaos which requries the breath of the Holy Spirit of Bakunin's *Allianz* in order to take on form."[33] On the other hand, even if they did know of this remark by Marx they could have been forgiven for wondering why they should prefer this particular diatribe against Bakunin to the very different opinions which had been expressed by Marx in the passage quoted above of some thirty years earlier. Lenin's main proposition was in fact incorporated in a quotation from Kautsky which forms part of the text of *What Is to Be Done;* and indeed, this same view of Kautsky may be cited almost in the same words as those used by Lenin from other works by Kautsky.[34]

If it is true, as has been argued, that after 1903 Marxism as far as Russia was concerned became an organizational technique to which doctrine was subordinate, then it follows that the debates which were to revolve for years around the interpretation of Marx became not so much discussions of Marx and his doctrines as discussions of policies which were made desirable or undesirable as the result of their adoption by Russian revolutionaries of a particular kind of Russian adaptation, or perversion, of the doctrines of Marx. These discussions can therefore no longer be subsumed under the title of "Marxism in Russia" − except of course in the very broad sense in which the term Marxism could be used to cover the whole history of Soviet Russia since 1917 and the whole history of the rise of Bolshevism after 1903, which is clearly beyond the scope of this paper.

The story could be concluded at this point. However, there is one postscript which is perhaps of interest because it represents another attempt to apply the doctrines of Marx to Russia, which ended in a diametrically opposite result from Lenin's. This concerns the intellectual course of Peter Struve. Struve belonged to a group, which included Berdiaev, Bulgakov, and S.L. Frank, that became known as the Legal Marxists. Struve's influential book, published in 1894, was basically a plea for the need for Russia to evolve into a fully capitalist society on the grounds that the necessary consequence of capitalism was the development of freedom, and that therefore the sooner Russia went through the unpleasant stage of capitalism the better because at any rate this would be the means of her achieving the kind of freedoms to the defense of which Struve was to devote his life.[35] Incidentally, Struve expressly throws doubt on the question as to whether

Marx can in any way be regarded as a revolutionary. By 1901, if not earlier, Struve had come to the conclusion that the principles of liberalism need not depend either on the existence of a middle class or on an economic substructure of the type that exists in Western Europe. His historical researches had convinced him, he wrote in 1901, that the doctrine currently accepted in Russia that liberalism had emerged as the political system of the bourgeoisie and in the material interests of the bourgeoisie was false. On the contrary, the origin of liberalism, he wrote, must be sought in the striving of the freedom of conscience, and this was neither the perrogative of any particular class nor dependent on any particular system of economic relations.[36] Consistently with this view, Struve in the following year became the ideological leader of a group formed around a newspaper entitled *Liberation.* His fellow legal Marxists likewise had by then also deserted Marxism in favor of various degrees of idealism and religious doctrine. Here then is one aspect of the failure of the adaptation of Marxist doctrines to Russia to achieve what Marx himself could conceivably have wished them to achieve. If it also be the case, as can be convincingly argued, that Lenin's adaptation of Marx led on directly to Stalin, with all the consequences of that régime, then likewise Marx could have derived little satisfaction from the direct or indirect consequences of the adaptation of his theories to Russia. Perhaps Marx's scepticism in 1880, when he heard of the emergence of a theoretical group of propagandists leaving Russia for Geneva, was a healthy premonition of what the future held.

NOTES

1. See Helmut Krause, *Marx und Engels und das zeitgenoessische Russland* (Giessen, 1958), pp. 85–6, footnote.

2. *Ibid.*, p. 84, footnote.

3. Gustav Mayer, *Friedrich Engels. Eine Biographie,* vol. 2 (The Hague, 1934), p. 57.

4. Letter of 12 February, 1870. Karl Marx and Friedrich Engels, *Werke,* vol. 32 (Berlin, 1965), pp. 443–444.

5. For the original French text of the letter and the drafts which are much more detailed and exhaustive, see *Arkhiv K. Marksa I F. Engel'sa,* Pod Redaktsiei D. Riazanova, Part 1, (Moscow, 1924), pp. 265–286.

6. *Werke,* vol. 2, (Berlin, 1957), p. 576.

7. *Perepiska K. Marksa I F. Engel'sa S Russkimi Politicheskimi Deiateliami,* (Moscow, 1951), second edition, pp. 285–297.

8. *Werke,* vol. 34 (Berlin, 1966), p. 477.

9. *Perepiska . . .,* pp. 309–310.

10. Quoted in J. L. H. Keep, *The Rise of Social Democracy in Russia* (Oxford, 1963), p. 19.

11. A. L. Reuel', *Russkaia Ekonomicheskaia Mysl' 60–70 KH Godov XIX Veka I Marksizm* (Moscow, 1956), p. 182.

12. *Werke,* vol. 4 (Moscow, 1959), p. 143.

13. P. V. Annenkov, *Literaturnye Vospominaniia* (Moscow, 1960), pp. 301–307.

14. David McLellan, *Karl Marx. His Life and Thought* (London, 1973), p. 419; see also Reuel, *op. cit.,* pp. 226–227.

15. *Perepiska . . .,* p. 39.

16. Quoted in Reuel', *op. cit.,* p. 196; and see *ibid.,* pp. 192–195.

17. B. P. Koz'min, *12 Istorii Revoliutsionnoi Mysli V Rossii.* (Izbrannye Trudy, Moscow, 1961), p. 314.

18. I have discussed this question in my *Rationalism and Nationalism in Russian Nineteenth-Century Political Thought* (New Haven and London, 1967), pp. 139–142.

19. "Ocherki iz Istorii Ratsionalizma," probably written in 1865, and published in 1933 in *Literaturnoe Nasledstvo,* 7–8, 1933, 124–162, Moscow.

20. This debate is summarized in an unpublished doctoral dissertation at the University of Indiana in 1964 by Rolf A. W. Theen, entitled "Petr Nikitich Tkavhev. A study in Revolutionary Theory," pp. 89–99.

21. Philip Pomper, *Peter Lavrov and the Russian Revolutionary Movement* (Chicago and London, 1972), pp. 125–128.

22. Albert Resis, "Das Kapital Comes to Russia," *Slavic Review,* 29 (2), June 1970, 219–237, especially pp. 219–224.

23. *Werke,* vol. 32 (Berlin, 1965), p. 567.

24. Mikhailovsky's article is summarized in Resis, *op. cit.,* pp. 232–234; for Marx's rejoinder see *Perepiska . . .,* pp. 320–323.

25. In general, for the debates provoked by the appearance of the Russian translation of *Das Kapital* see Resis, *op. cit.,* passim, and Reuel, *op. cit.,* Chapter 5.

26. Koz'min. *op. cit.,* pp. 381–382.

27. The two pamphlets were "Sotsialism i Politicheskaia Bor'ba" and "Nashi Raznoglasiia." The programes are printed in volume 2 of the collected edition of Plekhanov's works at pp. 357–362 and 400–404.

28. On Alexander Ulianov see *Aleksandr Ilyich Ulianov i Delo i Marta 1887 G.,* edited by A. L. Ulianova-Elizarova (Moscow, Leningrad, 1927). The program appears on pp. 375–380.

29. On Lenin's relations with Fedoseev see the introduction to a collection of his writings published in Moscow in 1958, *N. Fedoseev. Stat'i i Pis'ma.* On the intellectual formation of Lenin see the article by R. Pipes, in *Revolutionary Russia,* edited by R. Pipes (Cambridge, Mass., 1968). I have also drawn on two chapters from the as yet unpublished history of bolshevism to 1917, on which I am working jointly with H. Shukman.

30. For these letters to Maslov see volume 46 of the most recent, ostensibly complete, edition of Lenin's works in Russian, pp. 1–5.

31. *Werke,* vol. 1 (Berlin, 1957), p. 391.

32. Theen, *op. cit.,* p. 91.

33. Karl Marx, *Politische Schriften,* edited by H. J. Lieber, vol. 2 (Stuttgart, 1960), pp. 999–1000.

34. There are several quite striking parallels in Kautsky's writings with Lenin's doctrine of "bringing consciousness from the outside." The late George Lichtheim maintained in a conversation with me that the parallels were more apparent than real. The real point is, perhaps, that Lenin was skilfull enough to make use of Kautsky's authority to bolster a novel view.

35. P. Struve, *Kriticheskiia Zametki K Voprosu Ob Ekonomicheskom Razvitii Rossii* (St. Petersburg, 1894).

36. See P. Struve, "V Chem Zhe Istinnyi Natsionalizm? " in P. Struve, *Na Raznyia Temy (1893–1901)* (Sbornik Statei, St. Petersburg, 1902), pp. 526–555.

MARXISM AND ETHICS – A RECONSIDERATION

EUGENE KAMENKA
Australian National University, Canberra

I

Eleven years ago, when one's serious friends and mentors were almost all *ex*-Marxists, convinced that they had witnessed the end of ideology and of socialism as a significant *radical, revolutionary* movement, I wrote the following:

"To those political fighters whom I have found it in my heart to admire, socialism meant the revolt against a society based on commerce and calculation; it meant the fusion, in a united effort and a single morality, of worker and intellectual, of the productive hand and the productive brain; it meant, above all, the birth of a new humanity, purified and ennobled in struggle and deprivation. If socialism means that – and I believe it does – then socialism is dead. Let us bury it before its last rites can no longer be performed with honour.

"The thought that socialism might die occurred to one of its most perceptive exponents, the great French syndicalist Georges Sorel, as early as 1906. In his *Reflections on Violence* we find the following:

> In a society so enfevered by the passion for the success which can be obtained in competition, all the actors walk straight before them like veritable automata, without taking any notice of the great ideas of the sociologists; they are subject to very simple forces, and not one of them dreams of escaping from the circumstances of his condition. Then only is the development of capitalism carried on with that inevitableness which struck Marx so much, and which seemed to him comparable to that of a natural law. If on the contrary, the middle class, led astray by the chatter of the teachers of ethics and sociology, return to an *ideal of conservative mediocrity* and seek to correct the *abuses* of economics, and wish to break with the barbarism of their predecessors, then one part of the forces which were to further the development of capitalism is employed in hindering it, an arbitrary and irrational element is introduced, and the future of the world becomes completely indeterminate.

   This indeterminacy grows still greater if the proletariat are converted to the ideas of social peace at the same time as their masters, or even if they simply consider everything from the corporative [i.e., trade union – E.K.] point of view; while socialism gives to every economic contest a general and revolutionary colour.
   Conservatives are not deceived when they see in the compromises which lead to collective contracts, and in corporative particularism, the means of avoiding the Marxian revolution; but they escape one danger only to fall into another, and they run the risk of being devoured by Parliamentary socialism.

"Parliamentary socialism, for Sorel, was simply not socialism. It was not socialism because it elevated compromise over conflict, the calculator over the hero, the modest reform over the heroic myth. For working-class independence, violence and strength, it substituted the manipulation and hypocrisy that formed the trade of the politician, the calculation of the bourgeois and the cunning of the *clerc*. Parliamentary socialism, it is true, might menace the capitalist, but it could never transform the worker. At best – and here the best is the worst – it would lead to the worker's *embourgeoisement*.

"Parliamentary socialism and trade union particularism, Sorel feared, could sap the worker's moral fibre, turn him from the heroic values of the confident and disinterested producer to the self-seeking commercialism and concern with security that characterized the consumer; they could kill socialism and the working-class movement. It was for this reason that Sorel threw everything into the idea of the general strike, not primarily as a practical step to facilitate the seizure of power, but as a heroic myth, as an ideal concept illuminating the social situation and promoting working-class education and strength. 'All oppositions', he writes,

> become extraordinarily clear when conflicts are supposed to be enlarged to the size of the general strike; then all parts of the economic-judicial structure, in so far as the latter is looked upon from the point of view of the class war, reach the summit of their perfection; society is plainly divided into two camps, and only into two, on a field of battle. No philosophical explanation of the facts observed in practical affairs could throw such vivid light on the situation as the extremely simple picture called up by the conception of the general strike . . .
>
> The idea of the general strike has such power behind it that it drags into the revolutionary track everything it touches. In virtue of this idea Socialism remains ever young; all attempts made to bring about social peace seem childish; desertions of comrades into the ranks of the middle class, far from discouraging the masses, only excite them still more to rebellion; in a word, the line of cleavage is never in danger of disappearing.

"Two years after writing his *Reflections on Violence,* from which the preceding passage also comes, Sorel published a small but often interesting book entitled *La Décomposition du Marxisme.* Especially interesting for us is the title. For Sorel, whom I have called one of the most perceptive exponents of socialism, was perhaps the first to recognize that the greatest of all socialist ideologies, the socialism of Karl Marx, was not a unified system breathing a single spirit, but contained within it a number of distinct and contradictory strains. Sorel, in seeking to purify the structure and thus strengthen the ideology of socialism, came down on what I, too, take as the most significant ethical strain in socialist thinking — the rejection of commercialism, of utility and calculation, the emphasis on the values implicit in production, in art and rebellion. In doing so, he made a significant, but ultimately vain, contribution to saving 'socialism' — from success. So might some early perceptive Christian have prayed that Caesar would not join the Church, and suddenly found that the Church was striving to join Caesar. All those perversions of the spirit of socialism that Marx feared and Sorel fought have now come to pass.

"To understand what has happened, we must do what Sorel tried to do in a somewhat different intellectual context, and decompose socialism into those elemental but conflicting strains that Marx welded together in a tremendous act of intellectual force and faith, and that have since come apart once more. In doing so, I propose to look at Marx not primarily as a great social analyst, but as an even greater ideologue, as the man who had an enormous influence on the socialist movement throughout the world precisely because he was able to offer it a synthesis of its distinct and conflicting hopes and attitudes.

"Socialism in the nineteenth century was first the rebellion against, and then the consummation of, industrial capitalism. Therein, it seems to me, lies its chief — and fatal — contradiction. The first generations of the new working class looked back with wistful longing to the comparative brotherhood and security of their feudal-agrarian past, comparing it with the misery and intense social atomization of the new industrial settlements. 'What sort of a society is it, in truth,' Marx writes in 1845, reviewing Peuchet's book on suicide, 'where one finds several millions in deepest loneliness, where one can be overcome by an irresistible longing to kill oneself without anyone discovering it? This society is not a society; it is, as Rousseau says, a desert populated by wild animals.' A year earlier, in his 'Critical Glosses on the Article: "The King of Prussia and Social Reform. By a Prussian" ', he had written:

The fellowship *(Gemeinwesen)* from which the worker is isolated is a fellowship of a scope and order of reality quite different from that of the political fellowship. The fellowship from which his own labour separates the worker is *life* itself, physical and intellectual life, morality and customs, human activity, human satisfaction, being human. Being human is the true fellowship of men. Just as irremediable isolation from this fellowship is incomparably more pervasive, unbearable, horrible and full of contradiction than the isolation from the political fellowship, so the dissolution of this isolation from being human, or even a partial reaction or uprising against it, is as much wider in scope as man is wider in scope than the political citizen, as human life is wider in scope than political life.

"Capitalism, for Marx and for tens of thousands of the new industrial workers, had decomposed and atomized man. It had torn him out of the bondage but security of feudalism, in which his material and his political life were welded together, in which he was oppressed but also protected, and thrown him into an arena of wild animals, into a society in which the liberation of man's mind and status had also meant the complete liberation, from all restraints, of man's greed, acquisitiveness and economic power over others.

"The tendency to look back wistfully to the comparative security of an essentially non-commercial society expressed itself violently, in the early generations of industrial workers, in the Luddite smashing of the machines. Intellectually, it expressed itself in the nineteenth-century Romantic movement and in the work on those late nineteenth-century and early twentieth-century sociologists who contrasted the unity and fellowship of the primarily non-commercial community, the *Gemeinschaft,* with the narrow, utilitarian individualism and loneliness of the commercialized society, the *Gesellschaft,* ruled as Spengler put it, by the sterile super-city, the megalopolis, and its inhabitant, the intellectual nomad.

"The tendency to look back to the security of the feudal-agrarian fellowship and of the non-commercial society most socialists think of as ultra-conservative. But remember that the society of Communism was for Marx above all the society without money, the society in which economic transactions were no longer 'mystified' by being converted into something other than the direct production and distribution of goods, the society in which production had become directly for use and had thus become the servant and no longer the master of man. The longing for a society in which men would be brought together in production as peasants working a single field are brought together, in which the disturbing effects of commercialism would disappear and men would become assimilated to a way of life that embodied the best features of a crew of fishermen working together, and of a community of artists or scientists living as such, was always an essential part of the socialist vision. The only quarrel between socialists, on the one hand, and romantics and ultra-conservatives, on the other, on this issue lay in the fact that the socialists saw the truest expression of such a society in the future, the romantics and ultra-conservatives saw it in the past.[1]

"It is in this ethical conception of a fellowship in which men transcend and dedicate themselves in the common process of production that the whole mystique of socialism, the moral force that enabled the movement to bring together workers and intellectuals, lay. In my *The Ethical Foundations of Marxism* (Routledge and Kegan Paul, London, Praeger, New York, 1962) I have tried to argue that this conception is not utterly utopian, that men do display the characteristics that socialists sought to exalt and will, in certain situations, always go on to display them. But all the evidence is against the belief that such a spirit of spontaneous, cooperative immersion in production can catch up a whole society, pervade every corner of it and banish the conflict and distinction between means and ends, between my ends and yours. This spirit occurs rather, as Edward Shils has somewhere suggested, in sectional groups, in 'dedicated companies' pursuing a limited interest, and in unusual moments of wider crisis and effort. The chief features of twentieth-century society — the constant extension of calculation and the constant process of levelling associated with calculation — militate strongly against its extension.

"For a considerable period, the socialist movement was able to maintain its ethical force and its moral mystique precisely because it was a movement of opposition, a movement shaped in struggle and crisis. The revolution that Marx preached in the *Communist Manifesto* of 1848 was to a very great extent the democratic revolution, the revolution against police states, foreign oppression and feudal privilege. In the struggle against censorship, oppression and privilege, in its contempt for immediate material welfare and the security to be found in the bosom of authority, socialism could liberate precisely those dormant ethical qualities which it strove to vindicate. It could become a movement with a certain spirit, a spirit which — for a limited historical period — could unite the rebellious worker and the rebellious intellectual.

"The spirit, however, was not enough. The free intellectuals from whom Marx took his departure were a specific historic phenomenon, made free not only by their own intrinsic qualities, but rather more by their lack of social opportunities within the existing system, by their bearing the brunt of the oppressive police state, by the disparity

between their expectations and the rewards they might actually acquire. (They survive today [*i.e.,* in 1963], as we might expect, in that
last fortress of the Europe of 1848, Salazar's Portugal.) The workers,
too, were equally far from finding the heroic values of enterprise,
disinterestedness, exactitude and lack of concern with reward merely
as a result of their work. They were driven, as Marx himself saw,
largely by their need — they have remained militant almost only in
those occupations (coal-mining, dock-working, etc.) where the conditions of their work are peculiarly unpleasant, dangerous or insecure. If
the socialist movement had relied simply on the morality of the wor-
ker-producer, it would have failed at the very start, as anarchism and
anarcho-syndicalism failed in all conditions short of the critical.

"The fantastic success of Karl Marx as a socialist ideologist — and
his failure as a radical moralist — lay precisely in the fact that Marx
did not merely rely on the vision of brotherhood in the non-commercial society and on the moral values of the rebellious worker and the
free intellectual. Marxism succeeded where the Luddites and anarchists
failed, precisely because it seemed to solve the contradiction between socialism's appeal to the solidarity and non-commercialism of
the past and its looking forward to a glorious future. The glorious
future would be brought about not by smashing machines, as the
Luddites had done, or by withdrawing into Utopian socialist and
anarchist colonies, but by the very process of industrialization itself.
There is no ultimate conflict between the worker's hopes and his daily
life because the very machines that seem to enslave him are secretly
working toward his restoration. Communism or socialism will be the
inevitable result of the machinery set in motion by capitalism.

"Much of what seems to Western socialists most interesting and
most relevant in Marx's serious economic work, especially in the
second and third volumes of *Capital,* is devoted to the theme of economic rationality and to the inescapable socialization of capitalism
from within. Schumpeter has taught us, I think, that Marx's long-range
predictions about capitalism were largely correct, though Marx based
them on reasoning that was at least partly unsound. To this point I
shall return later. For the moment I want to stress the ideological
values implied by Marx's emphasis on the historic march toward
rationality, by his view that the bourgeoisie was doomed because it
was becoming a fetter on economic development and had ceased to be
its agent. This side of Marxism had quite extraordinary appeal. It is a
side that shows the intimate connection of Marxism with the ideology
of industrial society — an ideology of which Marxism was in many
ways the most consistent and confident expression. Marxism, as I have

written elsewhere, professed to speak for the proletarian against the capitalist; but it also spoke, far more effectively, for industrialism against merchant enterprise: for economic rationalism and efficient management against the individualistic vitality, independence and flair of the merchant-adventurer and *entrepreneur*. Marxism mobilized into the service of socialism the whole ideology of economic calculation and rational planning against which earlier generations of workers had rebelled — it became the final and consummated ideology of industrial society and technological advance.

"So long as industrial enterprise was still run by men with entrepreneurial values along entrepreneurial lines (the mill-owners who appear as the paradigm capitalists in *Das Kapital*) socialism could present the struggle between economic rationalism and self-seeking individualism as a struggle between workers and capitalists. But with the creation of the limited company — 'the dissolution of the capitalist mode of production within the capitalist mode of production' as Marx wrote — the vast spread of planning procedures and the tremendous increase in the range of the calculable, and with the increasing mechanization and institutionalization of industrial 'progress' through teamwork in research departments, etc., the lines of cleavage are no longer clear, and planning can no longer be posed as the obvious contradictory of capitalist competition. To preach social planning thus becomes one thing, not particularly inimical to the fundamental economic structure of our society; to preach class war becomes another.

"Many socialists today profess to be content with the ideology of social planning and would willingly leave the class war and the moral mystique of the movement that once looked as though it would radically humanize and transform the working classes to the museums of history. In doing so, they can point to sixty years of Fabianism, with its administrator's morality and its banker's outlook, as an all-too-respectable and successful progenitor. But let us recognize that we are then turning one of the great movements of history into a periodic rise in real wages, that we transform one expression of the great moral conflicts that take place in the heart of man and in society into a technical and far from clear-cut argument about economic efficiency. The values that Marx and the great socialists detested, and which the Fabians have always worshipped as a banker's clerk might worship them, we have left untouched.

"Marx believed that technological advance and economic rationality were important, because he believed that man could not be free until he had been liberated from economic necessity, from the domination and limitation imposed upon him by his unsatisfied 'animal needs'.

But Marx also believed that the class war was important, not merely as a way of overthrowing the capitalist constriction of technological advance, but as a way of destroying capitalist values, of radically transforming society, of purifying the working classes from any taint of bourgeois calculation and self-seeking. Because he was wrong in predicting the ever-sharpening tensions of capitalism and the ever-increasing situation of crisis for the working class, socialism has been brought back to that insipid mixture of planning and philanthropy, of economic rationalism and distributive justice, which Marx, above all people, transformed into an ideology that could make men — for a short time, at least — greater than they were.

"The contempt for the gains which socialist planning and economic calculation might make is typical, no doubt, of the free intellectual, of the artist, the scientific researcher, the peasant or craftsman involved in his work. It is not typical of twentieth-century man. What seems to me the failure of socialism may seem to many its success. We have seen the coming of a society that has averted the prospects of class war and institutionalized economic and industrial progress, a society that has significantly distributed wealth and made possible ever-increasing consumption. It may be, as Engels believed, that the development of technology, by virtually freeing man from unpleasant labour and opening up to him an incredible range of new enjoyments, will produce a society in which man is a fuller and freer being than he has ever been before. But if this should prove to be so, the efforts of the socialist movement in the present decade and in future decades will have had nothing to do with it. The end will have been the result of a technological advance pioneered and largely carried out — I believe — by the techniques and the ideology of industrial capitalism; socialism in the West will have been one of the great moral movements of mankind that may one day inspire future moral movements in renewed days of adversity or in a new flowering of productive life; socialism in the East will have been an intermediary stage of ideological labour discipline designed to usher in the era of industrialization and capitalist plenty."[2]

II

Not long after these words were written, we began to witness, in the latter half of the 1960s, a remarkable revival and revitalization of revolutionary enthusiasm and revolutionary rhetoric, stretching from Peking and Shanghai to Tokyo, Paris, Berlin and New York. The tumult came from various quarters, the slogans were drawn from many competing and conflicting radical traditions, but they did seem to put a decisive 'finis' to the period of the end of ideology and to the charge that socialism as a radical, revolutionary ideal, as a protesting ethical stance, was dying or dead. Nevertheless, I — and so many of us who admired Ben Compton in Dos Passos' *U.S.A.* — felt unable to welcome the movement. It lacked, for us, historical dignity and historical understanding; it lacked a genuine concept of moral and of intellectual responsibility. "The guerilla makes the leader and the revolution makes itself" was not the content of our understanding of freedom or of history; Marxists, for many of us, were still to be distinguished from anarchists by their capacity to *think,* to ask "what will happen next," to consider seriously the life of society and the course of the revolution after the initial frenzy had passed and the old world had fallen into ruins. We were witnessing, many of us felt, not a revitalization of Marxism, but a further disintegration — a shift, in its fundamental concern, from the proletarian to the drop-out masquerading as nihilist or as peasant. This indeed is what I urged, together with most — but not all — of my fellow contributors to the Australian National University's series of University lectures for 1970. There, taking up themes also found in the work of George Lichtheim, Adam Ulam and Shlomo Avineri, I argued thus:

"The existence of the Soviet Union and the most recent developments within it have not only helped to discredit Marxism as a movement in the West, but are now seriously hampering the role of Marxism as an ideology of industrialisation in backward countries. It has become all too evident that the enormous sacrifices demanded by the Communist policy of forced industrialisation do not produce a new stage in the history of mankind, a utopian society of freedom and co-operation, but merely strive to give to agrarian countries what the West already has. The product seems in many respects inferior, and the sufferings are no less than those imposed by the initial stages of capitalist industrial development. To a society still far removed from the living standard of advanced industrial civilisation, the aim and the means may still seem attractive; the closer such a society moves to the achievement of industrialisation, the less plausible the aim and the less attractive the means.

"The difficulties created by already having an example of the aim you are working toward become evident when we consider the role of Marxism in China. It is to some degree important for the Chinese revolutionary with a genuine attachment to the utopian side of Marxism to persuade himself and others that Russian society will not be the ultimate upshot of the Chinese revolution. Recent events in China suggest that — for a time — the anarchist component of Marxism to

some extent broke loose from the rest of the ideology, that the Red
Guards have reverted, in part, to Luddite peasant anarchism with its
hostility to industrialisation and specialisation, and that there is in
consequence a serious risk that Marxism as a westernising ideology
may fail. Yet what else has it to offer?

"The same, it may be argued, has happened — also, I believe, only
temporarily — in the rest of the world. Thus, in recent years, in
socialist humanism and student radicalism, the ethical presuppositions
and implications of the work of Karl Marx, long neglected by classical
Marxists and Leninist Communists, have once again moved to the
forefront of the discussion of Marx and Marxism. The 'classical' Marxist preoccupation with the abolition of private property, increased
economic production and rational social planning as the necessary and
sufficient condition for human happiness has lost much of its appeal;
the forces of history and of factory production are not obviously and
inexorably working toward that final ideal society in which the whole
of humanity will be joined in the free, co-operative and creative satisfaction of common human requirements and skills. The incredible
sufferings that men have gone through in the Soviet Union in the last
fifty years are leading them, at best, into a shabby, second-rate copy
of Western society, subject to far greater dictatorial pressures, more
pervasive controls and a ubiquitous secret police, still socially incredibly
backward in relation to England, or Germany or Japan. Socialist-
Communist states have then shown themselves to be at the very least
as oppressive as bourgeois-capitalist states: the industrial revolution
under Communism — e.g. in the period of Stalin's five-year plans —
has proved itself at the very least as horrible, and has imposed as high
a price in human suffering and waste of human resources, as any
industrial revolution under capitalism. Its striking achievements lie in
strengthening the state rather than in revolutionising the capacities
and expectations of the people or in making them happier than they
could otherwise have ever hoped to be. International tension, geno-
cide, colonial exploitation, invasion and military oppression are no
longer the prerogatives of non-socialist or non-Communist states; the
myth of the socialist brotherhood of man and of new Communist
norms in international relations between socialist nations was finally
shattered in Hungary, Czechoslovakia and on the banks of the Amur.
As both Ulam and I have argued, once the initial (and very severe)
strains of industrialisation in an agrarian setting have been overcome,
once a peasantry learns confidence and new habits in the discipline of
factory production and begins to appreciate and enjoy its very real
economic and cultural rewards, Marxism as a thorough-going affirma-

tion of industrialisation combined with a radical critique of private property and the urban *Gesellschaft* loses its relevance to the problems and its appeal to the attitudes of the industrial proletariat. The pro- letariat no longer needs an ideological palliative for industrialisation and no longer dreams of the idealised village *Gemeinschaft* that forms the empirical content of the promised Communist utopia. Hence we have in advanced industrial societies a growing recognition that both the benefits and the evils of the industrial process transcend any ab- stract division between societies based on private property in the means of production and societies based on state ownership or control, that bureaucratisation and dictatorship need not be based on private ownership and are in fact to some extent limited by it, and that centralised economic planning guarantees neither increasing prosperity nor a generally welcome distribution of resources. In non-Communist industrial societies this has expressed itself, as we have seen, in the long-term deradicalisation of the 'conscious' industrial proletariat; in the industrially advanced Communist countries it has expressed itself in the crisis of legitimacy faced by ruling Communist parties in the Soviet Union and in Eastern Europe. The simple faith in the primacy of the economic, in the historic, liberating role of the industrial pro- letariat and in the all-pervasive significance of the distinction between private control and public or social control, which characterised most Marxists and Marxist intellectuals until the end of World War II, has probably gone forever.

"In these circumstances, then, it is not surprising that Marx the economist and scientist of society is being ousted — in radical thinking — by Marx the moralist and the philosopher of the human condition on the one hand and by revolutionary opportunism, the deification of tactics, on the other. In post-industrial 'technetronic' society the con- cept of alienation is replacing the concepts of private property and commodity production as the central category in Marxist thought; at the same time, though without real logical connection, the struggle between the world of the cities and the world of the countryside (as it is called) has claimed the attention and the emotional commitment once devoted to the struggle between bourgeois and proletarian. Yet the role of the proletariat — the universal class that would take up and supersede the civilisation of capitalism — was crucial, as we have also seen, in the old Marxian system. The proletariat, through its sheer numbers, through the fact that the vast majority of mankind would have become workers, would ensure that the revolutionary dictator- ship would be transitional and a dictatorship *of* the majority, not a dictatorship *over* the majority. Through its involvement in factory

production, through its appreciation of the vastly increased productive potential and of the rationality and economic calculation introduced by capitalism, the proletariat becomes the heir to the values of
the Enlightenment, to its confidence in human capacities and human
skills, to its elevation of rationality and freedom. This affirmation of
the industrial process and of the rationality associated with it distinguished Marx and Marxists from peasant anarchists and from the nihilistic cult of violence. Anarchist revolutionaries, like the Luddites before
them, relied on outrage rather than rationality, on disaffected minorities and the *Lumpenproletariat* rather than on those trained and
shaped by their involvement in production. They sought to reshape
society by a romantic act of will, to 'negate' (i.e., burn and destroy)
everything that they could not cope with or think out of existence. If
the moral 'constructive' anarchism of a Godwin and Proudhon was a
peasant proprietor's and petty-bourgeois shopkeeper's flight into fantasy, away from the realities of the world-shaking industrial upheaval,
the proudly amoral irrationalist nihilistic anarchism of Nechaev and
Bakunin was the ideology of the *Lumpenproletarian* (whether he be
an aristocrat or a pauper) who stands outside the process of production and seeks to abolish its consequences by terror. Marx, in a world-
historical act of intellectual force and revolutionary faith, strove to
hold together in one coherent system the Rousseauan belief in community, the commitment to freedom and individual development that
lay at the base of the European Enlightenment and the emphasis on
rational economic planning that characterized the socialist Saint-
Simonians. Marx was, at least for much of his life, a revolutionist, but
he was also a scientist of society. For him every positive, significant
social protest was also an act of rational criticism, every true revolutionary was also an analyst of the social situation. He rejected completely the attempt to achieve social transformation by a romantic
glorification of the purely political will; he exposed the nameless
authoritarianism of the anarchist cult of violence and its deification of
an undifferentiated, characterless, mass or mob. This is the whole
force and point of Marx's fundamentally important distinction between political emancipation and social emancipation. Political emancipation, when abstracted from the material social context in which
the revolution takes place and in which the victorious party will operate, is illusory emancipation. The historical role of the proletariat,
closely linked – for Marx – with its concrete social situation, cannot
be thrust into any hands whatever. 'Burn, baby, burn', as I suggested
in the first lecture in this series, is not a socialist slogan and the
universities are not the power centres of modern industrial society.

That is why they can be wrecked by chanting students who mistake their own turmoil and insecurity and intellectual confusion for the alleged turmoil insecurity and confusion of an industrial process that is in fact growing stronger every day. The focus of radical activity, indeed, has shifted from those who were critics of industrial society from within, recognising its possibilities and its weaknesses, to those who feel a confused rage at being left out of industrial society or at no longer being impressed by its benefits. The result is that Marxism, the heir presumptive of capitalist civilisation, has become, in confused and irrational form, an ideology for the industrial drop-out, for students, for peasants in pre-industrial society and even for witch-doctors. It attempts to find a revolutionary base in capitalism among those who, for one reason or another, stand outside the productive process of advanced industrial civilisations, i.e., the depressed urban negro, the deprived Australian aboriginal and above all the student who is freed – for a period – from the responsibilities and cares of productive labour and whose elitist expectations are in marked disparity with his incomplete socialisation and his related adolescent sense of insecurity. The result is temporary alliance – in the name of a pseudo-Marxism – between the pre-industrial Luddite of China's cultural revolution and America's urban ghettoes with the post-industrial Luddite of the universities in Tokyo, New York, Paris and Berlin. In all these new foci of attention, moral and philosophical questions play the central role once played by the concept of surplus value and the alleged 'laws' of the materialist interpretation of history. In Communist countries, the Marxian humanist is likely to use Marx's concern with freedom and self-determination and the overcoming of alienation as a basis for protest against the crude emphasis on social discipline preached by the Party theologues; in non-Communist countries which are either too advanced or too backward for Marxian economic doctrines, the Marxist revolutionary is now becoming much more at home with the postures of moral outrage and the tactics of guerilla warfare and violent confrontation than with serious analysis and planning of the economic and social future of his nation. To him, the revolution is no longer the product of economic forces or an act of social analysis and criticism; it is primarily a moral revolt, a romantic act of will born of moral outrage and purely political consciousness which, he thinks, will never fall into thralldom to purely economic forces and the inevitable hierarchies of industrial and economic organisation. To others still, Marxism becomes a vessel for nationalism that shades readily into fascism. In pre-industrial societies, such as China, the nation and the collective become the substitute for the creative individual; in Poland

and less obviously in Hungary there is a return to the modernising conservative fascist life-style of the 1930s, replete with anti-semitism and distrust in all intellectuals.

"It is easy to counterpose Marx's own writings and the rational social and political criticism of classical Marxism to the romantic radicalism of industrial society's new *Lumpenproletariat* and to the overweening pretensions of a theoretically confused, politically vulgar and practically authoritarian Maoism. Nevertheless, the confusions of the new neo-Marxism have been made possible only by the significant failures and inadequacies of the old Marxism, failures as evident in its theoretical treatment of capitalism in a post-industrial society as in its practical conduct of revolutionary struggle and socialist upbuilding. The tension always present in Marxism — tensions that led to the splits between the 'orthodox' and the 'revisionists', the 'revolutionaries' and the 'economists', the Mensheviks and the Bolsheviks, democratic socialists and Communist Party elitists — have been brought to crisis point by the growing strength of the Welfare State, by the recognition that the historical role of Communist regimes has been that of brutal engine of industrialisation, very limited in its capacity when society outgrows the stage of crash programs, and that the Communisms in advanced societies have been *imposed* by military conquests and subsequent chicanery. Above all, the growing social significance of the 'salariat' or the white-collar workers, the shift of employment from heavy industry to services, and the whole scientific-technological-electronic revolution of the 1950s have produced a new post-industrial society in which many of the classical Marxist analyses seem not merely false, as they proved to be in the period 1890–1939, but irrelevant. We are going through a social and technological revolution as great in its implications as the industrial revolution of the eighteenth century and we are as lost as the first generations of pre-Marxian socialists were in the period from 1790–1840. Marx, as George Lichtheim reminded us, was the great theorist of the industrial revolution in its European-bourgeois phase, a phase which is now over. The greatness of many of his insights and the historical importance of his enterprise remain, but the ideological unity and coherence of his system have gone forever. It is a sign of the bewilderment and confusion and helplessness of the young radicals in advanced industrial societies today that they flee back to the pre-Marxian strains of the socialisms and radicalisms of the 1840s, that they return, in the midst of one technological revolution, to the outrage and despair and the utopian fantasies initially provoked by another. The Marx who had come to terms with the industrial process, who sought to understand its place in human history, is not for them."[3]

The lecture from which I have just cited was delivered four years ago; the events from which it took its departure occurred some two years before that. Their significance has proved to be both more temporary and more lasting than at first expected; if they did not herald the bursting forth of a new society no longer able to exist in the womb of the old, they did dramatize, through hysterical and opportunistic overemphasis, new attitudes and new problems and new circumstances that have in reality driven yet another nail into the coffin of classical Marxism, especially into the coffin of classical Marxism as an ideology of industrialization, rational endeavor, and subservience to historical processes. For a period, indeed, Sorel had once more come into his own. In the last few years, it is true, there has been a shift of attention, among intellectual Marxists, from Marx's early philosophical works to his *Grundrisse*, with a consequent reintegration into intellectual neo-Marxism of some of Marx's sense of history. But the *Grundrisse* are attracting attention because they deal, in large part, with *pre-capitalist* and *non-capitalist* socio-economic formations; they are taken to provide a corrective — as Mrs. Sawer in her paper to this seminar argues — to the Eurocentrism and faith in the industrial process displayed in the *Communist Manifesto;* they are taken to reinforce the message that Dr. Rubel found in Marx's decision to come out on behalf of the Paris Commune,[4] the message that history is open, that backwardness can be an advantage, that the ideal of the future, the poetry of revolution, can itself be a historic force. The real problems that have emerged, and that have made much of what I wrote about contemporary society in the preceding pages now seem over-glib and too time-bound — the changes in human attitudes, lifestyles and expectations, in optimal forms of planning and bureaucratic supervision, in the nature of political and economic problems — are obscured rather than clarified by the new mysticism and the new romanticism, by the flight from complexity, responsibility and intellectual and physical discipline, to which they have given rise.

III

"To preach morality is easy, to give it a foundation is difficult," is the motto which Arthur Schopenhauer took for his essay on the basis of morality, unsuccessfully submitted for the Royal Danish Society prize. Schopenhauer thought that the difficulty could be removed only by ridding ethics of the theological imperativism introduced into it by the Old Testament and consummated in the ethical philosophy of Kant. The first task of the ethical scientist was to turn his eyes away from prescriptions and commands and to look at the actual quality and foundation of human behavior. For ethics, if a science, could not be concerned with that which men *ought* to do; it could only study those actual, existing motives, feelings and acts of will which *in fact* produce conflict or cooperation between men. At one level, Schopenhauer believed, ethics was concerned with the distinction between 'egoism' and 'altruism', between that which is divisive and that which is cooperative or uniting in human life. At a deeper level, the distinction between bad and good, between egoism and altruism, rests on the liberation from particularity, from what Schopenhauer saw as 'the will-governed' way of life, and the ability to recognise that other individuals are 'ourselves once more', homogeneous with our own nature and being. Ethics, like art and culture generally, is contemplative perception; it rests on the recognition of universality, on the rejection of the primacy of the will and of the self-sufficiency of the individual here and now. Morality is thus closely linked with literature, music and art; it is connected with knowledge rather than desire, with the character of culture rather than the strivings of abstract and abstracted individuals.

What is the relevance of this to Marx and Marxism? Certainly, Marx himself had no time for and no interest in Schopenhauer's philosophical constructions: Schopenhauer's conception of universality in art ends in a Platonic dualism of 'ideas' or 'archtypes' which transcend empirical 'will-governed' reality and are counterposed to it — a dualism hinted at, as a result of Schopenhauer's influence, in the ethical passages of Wittgenstein's *Tractatus Logico-Philosophicus,* and all too uncomfortably linked with the Kantian dualism of noumena and phenomena, though it has been revived as 'neo-Marxism' by Marcuse. Certainly, too, Schopenhauer's distinction between egoism and altruism is a crude and unexamined one which presupposes the very individualism that he is anxious to overcome: for what is altruism but servitude to the egoism of others, and what sense can be made of the whole concept of egoism if men are not simple atomic individuals or pure particulars? The attempted distinction between egoism and altruism, or between self-love (self-interest, if you will) and benevolence, requires much more careful and critical consideration than has been given it either by Schopenhauer or by the majority of moral and political philosophers: it will not survive in that form in any philosophy that has looked closely and critically at the concept of an 'interest' or 'desire' or at the concept of 'the self', let alone of 'a society'. Nevertheless, Schopenhauer has something to teach us that is crucial in appreciating where Marx stood on the question of moral and political obligation. First, he helps to remind us that not all moral or political theorists have been convinced that ethics or political theory is concerned with what men *ought* to do. Schopenhauer believed, as Hume did before him, that an *ought* could never be derived from an *is,* that a science or empirical study of what men ought to do was a contradiction in terms. As a determinist, he also believed that exhortation and 'rational' decision played a minor role in life; ethics was not concerned with guiding choice, but with examining human activities and character and the behavior that results from them. On the second point Marx would have agreed entirely; on the first, he would have agreed that neither ethics nor politics is concerned with what men *ought* to do, with either moral or political obligation. Further, Schopenhauer reminds us of the central role that empirical features of the distinction between cooperation and conflict, confusedly portrayed as those of the distinction between egoism and altruism, have played in moral theory and moral discussion. They do play, as I have argued in *The Ethical Foundations of Marxism,* a central role in Marx's vision of man and in his judgment of social systems. Finally, Schopenhauer helps to suggest to us the possibility that ethics is concerned with production and communication rather than consumption and the distribution of resources, with tradition and ways of life rather than individuals, with culture rather than commerce or, more broadly, economics and the science of 'satisfactions'. Paradoxical are, as it may seem that, in the upshot, was also Marx's belief, though it was a belief inconsistent with many other themes and beliefs to be found in Marx's work.

The difficulty men have encountered in 'giving ethics a foundation' is, in the first place, the product of confusion and uncertainty about what they are trying to do, of confusion and uncertainty about the subject-matter of ethics and its character as a discipline. It is this confusion and uncertainty, and not any character of ethics as the study of 'values', which explains why ethics or moral philosophy is still thought of as a department of philosophical studies and not as a separate discipline in its own right, why political philosophy flourishes in remarkable isolation from that much more genuine subject, social theory, and why the contribution of Marxism to ethics, or of ethics to Marxism, remain fundamentally obscure. The view that philosophy is concerned with 'values' or the 'ultimate significance' of things, while science is concerned with facts, and that all 'value-fields' such as ethics, aesthetics and the 'determination' of economic and political ends that 'ought' to be pursued are therefore departments of philosophy, is still sometimes heard; in special allegedly 'dialectical' or 'critical' forms it has indeed become extremely influential in recent years, especially in that home of intellectual confusion, the radical campus. In any case the abstract counter-position of 'facts' and 'values', I would hold, is nonsense. There are no 'values' — there are only things, activities, traditions and people that *are valued* by other things, activities, traditions and people in a normal, empirical and observable way. There are not *values,* but *valuations,* which are as much a fact, and as describable and as subject to scientific investigation, as any other empirical fact. Ethics has not remained a part of philosophy because of the peculiarly philosophical nature of its subject-matter. It has remained part of philosophy because of confusion and disagreement about its subject-matter, because it has stood in need of critical clarification of its premises and presuppositions before further empirical investigation could fruitfully be undertaken. Almost all departments of human knowledge have passed through a stage, or stages, when the main impediment to their further development has been a problem or uncertainty calling for logical or philosophical analysis, a problem or uncertainty concerning the *relevance* of empirical information, or the sort of empirical information required, which must be settled or side-stepped before further empirical information can be sought. Ethics has been too long in that stage.

The difficulty, the uncertainty about ethics, stems precisely from the contradiction that has lain at the heart of most traditional moral theories — their uncritical mingling of science and advocacy in the concept of a *normative* science, their attempt to give ethical judgments the objectivity of scientific descriptions and the imperative, exhortative force of recommendations, attitudes, or commands. The imperative side of moral theory is essential to those who see ethics as a prescriptive theory of conduct and morality as a theory of *absolute obligation.* For them, 'good' cannot represent 'merely' a quality which some of us display (or seek) and others lack (and reject); it must be a relation as well, something *demanded, pursued, required,* which it is illogical (or 'wrong') to reject. So long as we think of good as simply those qualities which 'are demanded' or 'required', there is a superficial plausibility; it disappears the moment we ask the question that must be asked of an incomplete relation — "demanded or required by whom or by what? " The concept of an *absolute* obligation or demand is, as Schopenhauer noted in his *Grundprobleme der Ethik,* a contradiction in terms. To become intelligible, the statement of an obligation or a demand requires two terms: that which obliges or demands as well as that which is obligatory or demanded. "Laying a foundation for morality" has all too often been seen as finding an 'authority' to which these demands may be brought back: God, conscience, reason, the nature of man, the nature of society, the 'law' of the universe. But apart from the inevitable vagueness of these 'authorities', there is nothing unconditional about them; it is always possible to ask why I ought to obey this or that authority and always impossible to give a satisfactory reply without invoking some further, questionable authority. To the man who rejects the Constitution, I cannot demonstrate why he should obey the law. In fact, men have exhorted or commanded obedience to moral and legal norms precisely because these norms are not part of the 'nature of things', because there are no universal ends or standards which we all *must* follow, and (one might add), no universal 'true' humanity for which we all must strive. What is made obligatory or demanded by one authority, may be rejected by another. The illusion of a single, binding morality thus vanishes; it has to be replaced by the recognition of competing interests, competing demands, and competing codes that cannot be brought before one tribunal. We can study how such interests, demands and codes arise, what conditions are favorable to them and what conditions are not; but no such study will show that we *have* to obey them. The advocative moralist, of course, has an interest in preventing the recognition of the sources from which moral exhortation stems or on which it depends: the normative function of moralism has partly depended on the adoption of a moral language particularly suited to obscuring the sources of the demands it makes by dealing in incomplete relations. "You ought to do this," "Stealing is wrong," "Children must obey their elders" all suggest authority without specifying it: in many cases they thus successfully invoke the terrors of any anonymous authority, or of one filled in by the hearer himself, simply by leaving the relation incomplete. Ethical discussion and enquiry, on the other hand, require the completion of the relation and thus threaten the foundations of moral obedience much as a close acquaintance with officers and the general staff threatens the foundations of military obedience. It is here that the moralist is driven back on hierarchical, anti-empirical, conceptions of reality. If ethical propositions are to have prescriptive force, the source of moral demands must be elevated above 'the world' to which the demands are addressed. It is thus that the relational, prescriptive treatment of 'good' readily leads moralists to a dualism of 'facts' and 'standards', 'actions' and principles', 'apparent interests' and 'true interests', mere 'reality' and ideal 'potentiality'. This is patently obvious where the source of moral obligation is treated as supra-empirical, as god, soul, or an unhistorical faculty of reason or conscience. It is equally true, however, where the source is allegedly 'natural' — human nature, human interests or social de-

mands. These, too, have to be given a primacy in which moral advocacy masquerades as logical priority, and left imprecise to avoid conflict and incoherence. It is here that we find the reappearance of
constitutive relations to protect the source of moral authority from
criticism. Just as 'conscience' becomes that whose nature it is to ap-
prove of good, so 'principles' become that whose nature it is to be
obeyed, and the 'true' that which is 'better'. For the social and historical investigation of moral attitudes, we find substituted the attempt to
bind conduct with tautologies, for the empiricist's rejection of doctrines of 'higher' and 'lower' realities, for what Feuerbach called scientific republicanism, we find substituted the aristocratic-monarchical
principle of dualism. It is precisely that dualism — the dualism of the
'real' versus 'the merely empirical', of the 'essential' versus the 'accidental', of the 'true consciousness' versus the 'ideology' or 'false
consciousness' — that constantly breaks out in the work of Marx and
in the history of Marxism.

Marxist dualism, paradoxically, is the result of Marxist monism, of
the attempt to establish a common good, which will be pursued, and
recognized as 'good' by all. For if 'good' is treated as that which is
demanded or pursued, there can be no systematic or coherent ethical
science. The nature of the things demanded or pursued will vary with
the demands or interests concerned; what is 'good' in terms of one
morality may be 'evil' in terms of another. There is, however, a second
strain in Marx's own work and in traditional moral theory and moral
conceptions which does seem to emphasize and portray a positive,
intrinsic distinction between goods and evils which is independent of
whether we pursue them or not. The distinction may be approached —
though not defined — in terms of cooperation and conflict, assistance
and resistance. Goods cooperate with one another, evoking and assisting other goods; evils conflict not only with goods, but with each
other; they enforce and compel instead of evoking and assisting.
Taking up distinctions suggested in Georges Sorel's contrast between
the producer's and the consumer's morality, and worked out in the
ethical writings of the late Professor John Anderson,[5] we may say that
goods are those mental activities which are 'free' or enterprising, activities which are disinterested, possible under all conditions, com-
municating themselves with a spontaneity radically distinct from the
enforced imitation enjoined by evils, cooperating with each other and
displaying internal progress and development in a way that evils cannot cooperate or progress. (Compare the history of science with the
history of religion or of tyranny.) Evils, though ineradicable, are para-

sitic upon goods; they conflict not only with goods, but also with each other; they are interested as opposed to disinterested, repressive as opposed to free, consumptive as opposed to productive. Goods carry with them a characteristic devotion to movements 'transcending the individuals', to ways of living in which he is 'caught up', evils elevate the particular and produce such egoistic attitudes as hope, guilt, and despair. The qualities characteristic of goods are displayed in love and courage, in the scientific, artistic, and productive spirit, in the enquirer's and creator's honesty, detachment from self, and immersion in his work. Goods require no censorship, no punishments, no protection as part of their ways of working. Evils, on the other hand, display their characteristics in obscurantism, superstition, the demand for censorship, luxury, commercialism, tyranny and the "sheltered hell of bourgeois existence" (Anderson). They require censorship, suppression, punishment, and protection; they seek prior guarantees of security; they display a fundamental instability and incoherence. Moralism itself, on this view, it will be noted, is the product of evil motives, and the necessary instability of moralistic theories is characteristic of evils in general. Goods require no protection or commendation; the question whether any person, movement, or code supports goods is irrelevant to their character, while the suggestion that their ethical character itself *requires* support is exposed as an illusion. In general, the extent to which men display goods and engage in good activities will depend not on exhortation, but on the goods they already have and their communication with other goods.

Marx was not a moral philosopher. He concerned himself with none of the traditional problems of moral philosophy; he never analyzed critically the meaning of moral terms, he never considered carefully the concept of moral obligation or how one could distinguish moral demands from other demands. He rejected − quite soundly − the dualism of ought and is; in his conception of good as freedom and self-determination he came close to the recognition of positive ethical qualities. His theory of alienation implies his personal rejection of the subordination of activities to (egoistic) ends which is characteristic of evils; his emphasis on the 'complete man' and his *Gattungswesen* suggests, or evokes the coherence, cooperation, and immersion in an activity characteristic of goods. His lifelong contempt for servility, his respect for the moral character of the proletariat, his own uncompromising refusal to serve or to seek security show how strong his perception of ethical qualities could be.

"The social principles of Christianity," he wrote in the *Deutsche-Brüsseler Zeitung* in 1847, "preach cowardice, self-contempt, abasement, subjugation, humility, in short, all the properties of the *canaille;* and the proletariat, which does not want to be treated as *canaille,* needs its courage, its consciousness of self, its pride and its independence far more than its bread." But Marx himself was not able to develop this into a coherent theory of positive ethical qualities, logically independent of men's interests or attitudes towards them. For all his suppression of the dualism of 'ought' and 'is', historical 'progress' remained for him a normative conception, 'rationality' something which one *ought* to support. Yet, at the same time, he professed to be a determinist and a 'pure scientist'. Since he was not able to purify ethics of its normative and advocative overtones, the result is a contradiction in his work and a fundamental weakness in his social theory which hides, beyond the pluralism of appearance, an essential monism. Precisely because Marx never freed himself from this advocative strain, because he never ceased to think of ethics as connected with the fulfillment of demands, he was quite unable, for all his materialism, to work out a coherent naturalistic theory of ethics as concerned with qualitative differences in *activities,* in the nature of those activities which, incidentally, do the demanding. Marx does say in a well-known passage of *The Holy Family:* "It is not a question of what this or that proletarian, or even the proletariat as a whole, may imagine for the moment to be the aim. It is a question of what the proletariat actually is and what it will be compelled to do historically as a result of this being"; from time to time he also emphasizes, as Sorel has pointed out, the *moral character* of the proletariat, its rugged honesty, independence, and striving for knowledge. But Marx was simply not able to stick to the sound 'materialist' view that the character of a thing is prior to its aims; the influence of Hegel was too strong. The working out of a naturalistic, 'materialist' theory of ethics was smothered by Marx's teleologism and cast on the dungheap by his tendency toward economic reductionism. The direct result was a failure to come to grips with ethical problems and moral qualities which not only reduced the Marxist critique of ethics to incoherence, but in its failure to grasp positive ethical distinctions and the conflict of activities seriously weakened Marx's social theory.

IV

Karl Marx confronts us as a thinker of world-historical dimensions. Nineteenth-century European socialism and perhaps nineteenth-century European social theory found in him their greatest and most penetrating mind. The position of Marx as the greatest of the socialist ideologists and as the posthumously proclaimed founder of one of the world's great religions is assured. In itself it is no guarantee of his stature as a thinker and as a theorist of modern society. Nevertheless, Marx has such stature. Few would now seriously contest the proposition that he was the greatest thinker in the history of socialism. He gave socialism its intellectual respectability and its theoretical self-confidence. From diverse sources and materials, from phrases in radical pamphlets and slogans at socialist meetings, from German philosophy, French politics and English economics, he created a socialist system of thought, a total socialist critique of modern society. He refined and systematized the language of socialism; he explained and expounded the place of socialism in history; he reconciled, or seemed to reconcile, its conflicting hopes and theoretical contradictions. His work — itself a process of self-clarification — set the seal, as Lichtheim liked to emphasize, upon the transition from the romantic revolutionism of the 1840s to the working-class movement of the 1860s, 70s and 80s. It fused into a single body of connected doctrine moral criticism and economic analysis, revolutionary activism and social science, the longing for community and the acceptance of economic rationality and industrial progress. It clothed the interests and demands of a still largely nascent and despised working class in the dignity of a categorical imperative, pronounced by history itself. Marx's attempt to explain socialism to itself thus laid the foundations for a critical account of the birth and development of modern society. For Marx correctly recognized the world-historical importance of the French Revolution and the Industrial Revolution. He saw that, in Europe at least, they were part and parcel of the one development. He realized that they had inaugurated a new era in history, an era in which civil society — the world of industry and trade — had moved to the center of the stage and was being driven by violent internal compulsions to ever more rapid change and expansion. Marx recognized, more clearly than others, the birth of modern society and the tensions and conflicts involved in its internal dynamic. Since the Napoleonic wars set the seal of destruction upon the old order and the old regime in Europe, we have been living through a continuing crisis that has spread outward from Europe until it engulfs the world. Marx was the first and in many respects greatest student of that crisis. His predictions have proved at least partly false; his presentation of the issues may now seem far too simple; but he saw where the issues lay.

The perennial appeal of Marxism, nevertheless, has depended on its weaknesses as well as its strengths. It speaks to us, like Christianity, with many voices and in accents that are at best suggestive and at worst deliberately seductive rather than precise. Any ideology that survives for one hundred years and takes root in a wide range of social and historical settings and conditions will undergo large and small changes of emphasis, content and thrust. But Marxism, like capitalism, has a logic of its own. The varieties of Marxism — the historical, political and moral shifts of emphasis within it — are not mere external accretions or distortions; they stem from ambiguities and tensions that lie at the very heart of Marx's thought. There is the tension between the normative and the descriptive, between revolutionary activism and historical and political realism, between determinism and free will, between reliance on history and technology on the one hand, and reliance on class struggle and the proletariat on the other; the tension between romantic elitism and recognition of the dawning age of mass parties and mass politics, between an ideology directed to rebellion and one which, at the same time, is supposed to represent the 'scientific basis' of the transition to the new society. Precisely those categories which appeared to hold these contradictions together — the concepts of 'scientific socialism' and of 'consciousness', of the industrial process, of the proletariat, and the ideal concept of the community — have proved to be the least examined and/or the most time-bound and abstracted categories of Marxist thought. Marxist advocacy and Marxist essentialism have prevented the resolution of these difficulties, have prevented Marxists from developing the founder's thought into a genuinely naturalistic and pluralistic theory of society and into a world-view that recognizes genuine complexity and independence and thus guarantees no success and no inevitable rewards for the constantly agonizing life of ethical honesty, cultural and social creativity and social and moral responsibility. For the real problem of morals is not merely, as the defeated Trotsky thought, that history confronts us with one outrage after another and that we can only fight back with our fists. It lies in the fact that man and society are infinitely complex, that situations cannot be totally controlled and that the effects of actions cannot be fully foreseen. Life appears to us, at best, as a series of choices between lesser and greater evils; there is no total social plan, no general moral handbook, that will remove the necessity for decisions which are as agonizing as they are often ultimately pointless, i.e., bound to produce something quite different from what the actor intended, and undertaken for motives that we ourselves often misunderstand or repress. It is not by 'overcoming' the division of labor, by seeking to reduce all goods to a common or ultimate good, by striving to plan for a social totality which does not exist, that ethical and social freedom and responsibility can best be maintained.

This is done, on the contrary, by resisting the reduction of social life to a common currency, by maintaining specific traditions, specific institutions, specific values and ways of life — traditions, institutions, values and ways of life which, despite Kant and Marx, cannot be universalized logically or empirically and which, despite Mill and the utilitarians and their heirs, the proponents of 'welfare', cannot be reduced to a common measure. The desire to make the world safe for goods before or instead of engaging in them directly is itself an evil and results in evils: cynicism, dishonesty, repression and the attempt to 'deny' or 'overcome' the pluralities of social life. It is in the pursuit of particular, specific goods, and not in the pursuit of the spurious universality of an ahistorical 'common good', that men reveal their ethical qualities and the extent to which knowledge and disinterestedness can shape or permeate their lives.

The failure or inadequacy of Marx's thought as the foundation for a theory of ethics, then, lies in Marx's inability to overcome or resolve the fundamental tensions or paradoxes inherent in the morality of the Enlightenment, with its elevation of 'man' as the 'subject' of history and society, as inherently or potentially cooperative, 'rational' and 'progressive', and its attempt to smother its own accompanying sense of pessimism, a pessimism that breaks out sharply, if inconsistently, in the work of all of the greatest proponents of the Enlightenment. The classical antinomies are not resolved, the dualisms are not overcome; the Marxian solution remains a pseudo-solution and the 'dialectic' becomes little more than a way of restating the problem while pretending it does not exist. We have, in Marx and Marxism, all the traditional unresolved dualisms and contradictions — between the 'particular' and the 'universal', the 'real' and the 'empirical', the universally co-operative and the universally divisive, the 'free' and the 'coerced', the 'Promethean' subjectivity and the recognition of genuine independence and objectivity, the 'descriptive' and the 'advocative', pluralism and monism. These contradictions break out constantly, both in the thought of Marx himself and in the thoughts and actions of his followers, as theoretical contradictions, as incoherencies. The genuine solution of these problems requires a critical examination and restatement of the very terms that purport to make up the two sides of the dualism, an examination of which Marx's work conspicuously stops short. The attempts to 'supplement' Marxism — with an evolutionary ethic, a utilitarian ethic, a humanist ethic that seeks to convert the concept of man into a normative concept, a 'social' ethic that elevates the 'collective' interest and 'collective' will — are all intellectually far inferior to the thought of Marx himself, but they arise

directly from the conscious or unconscious recognition of the inadequacies we have sought to bring out. The attempt to make Marx a
'phenomenological' or 'existential' or 'critical' theorist is simply to
proclaim that his vices are virtues; that the obscure can be illuminated
by elevating obscurity itself into a category.

To say all this — to charge that Marx has failed to evercome the
dualisms and logical incoherencies that have bedevilled the philosophy
of morals — is not to say that he gives us no insights, insights, indeed,
that no subsequent ethical theory should ignore. Nevertheless, any
development of ethical theory that will constitute a genuine breakthrough will not come, I believe, from any attempt to grapple with the
theory of man, of society, or of freedom, in its Marxian formulation,
especially in its Young Marxian formulation. It will require logical
analysis of a sharpness and rigor which, in this field, is foreign to
Marx; it will also require a concern with the economy, or economies,
of the mind, in particular with the origins and characteristics of love
and hate, and with the characteristics of culture, science, literature
and the arts, that were not part of Marx's concerns and that would
have threatened his ultimate monism and his tendencies toward reductionism, as well as his historical optimism.

Ethical theory, I believe, does not and cannot tell men how to act;
history may, at least, make certain suggestions. Marx had a shrewd, if
somewhat biased, eye for historical precedent, historical context and
possible historical outcome. It is the sense of historical reality that
George Lichtheim always saw, and helped me to see, in Marx; it is
without ignoring that historical reality itself that Marxism as a political ideology and theory of society has to be judged. To Marx's moral
hopes and to his sociology of morals, history has not been kind; it is
for this reason that the idea of revolution, as Raymond Aron has said,
flees constantly to untried pastures, that Marxists now yearn to believe that history is really open and that Marx must be seen as the
prophet, and not as the scientist, of a new humanity and a new world
order. Today, as in past ages, moralities compete, and they do so not
as expressions or variants of a timeless human spirit, but as the moralities of social provinces, functions, institutions and classes. However,
they compete as much within socialism as outside it. Marx's theory of
classes, and Marx's form of a materialist interpretation of history, are
not adequate to provide a coherent account of this conflict or an
explanation of its roots. Marx was right, I believe, in seeing the historicity, the quite specific time-boundedness, of the overwhelmingly confident appearance of the morality of liberalism, of the commercial-
individualistic *Gesellschaft,* as the ultimate voice of progress. He was

quite wrong in seeing its downfall as coming at the hands of the proletariat, with its own specific morality. It is threatened, as Professor Tay and I have argued elsewhere,[6] by a most complex set of social developments to which Max Weber provides a better key than Karl Marx – developments that still hold in unresolved tension the concept of the community and that of the socio-technical norm, the morality of the *Gemeinschaft* and that of bureaucratic-administrative *étatisme*. This contradiction lies at the very heart of socialism and of Marxism; its very existence and the vacillations from one side to the other are determined by social and historical developments that Marx may have taught us to look for, but which he himself failed to see. In ethics and in social theory, we can neither ignore Marx nor remain in the circle of his positions: the necessity to think, to grapple with new problems in the light of past errors and difficulties is still with us. For the theory of twentieth-century society, Marxism provides the beginning, not the end of thought; for philosophical and ethical theory in general it does not even do that.

NOTES

1. And, of course, in the fact that socialists showed what little relation there was between the real, historical feudalism of the past and the idealized version of the *Gemeinschaft* elevated in conservative fantasy, while conservatives made and can still make, the same point about the socialist vision of the *Gemeinschaft* and its relation to actual or conceivable socialist societies.

2. Cited from Eugene Kamenka, "Karl Marx and Socialism Today", in *Quadrant* (Australia), Vol. VII, No. 4, Spring 1963, pp. 37–44.

3. Eugene Kamenka, "The Relevance – and Irrelevance – of Marxism", in Eugene Kamenka (ed.), *A World in Revolution? The University Lecture, 1970* (Canberra, 1971), pp. 66–70.

4. See Maximilien Rubel, "Socialism and the Commune", in Eugene Kamenka (ed.), *Paradigm for Revolution? – The Paris Commune 1871–1971*, (Canberra, 1972), pp. 31–48, esp. pp. 43–48, where Rubel insists that Marx was not a scientific thinker in the strict sense of the word, that he came to socialism as the result of a value judgment, and that he put aside the materialist interpretation of history, at least for a brief period, in deciding to write on behalf of the Commune.

5. Published in the *Australasian Journal of [Psychology and] Philosophy* from 1927 onwards and collected – in part – in John Anderson, *Studies in Empirical Philosophy* (Sydney, 1962), esp. pp. 214–363. See especially his "Determinism

and Ethics", Vol. 6 (1927), p. 241ff. and "The Meaning of Good", Vol. 20 (1942), p. 111ff., on which I have drawn heavily, and, for my own attempts to elaborate the position, Eugene Kamenka, *The Ethical Foundations of Marxism*, esp. part 3, pp. 89–117.

6. See Eugene Kamenka and A.E.S. Tay, "Beyond the French Revolution: Communist Socialism and the Concept of Law", in *University of Toronto Law Journal* 21, 1971, pp. 109–140 and Kamenka and Tay, "Beyond Bourgeois Individualism: The Contemporary Crisis in Law and Legal Ideology", in Eugene Kamenka and R. S. Neale (eds.), *Feudalism, Capitalism and Beyond* (ANU Press, Canberra, 1975), pp. 126–144; also published in *Die Funktionen des Rechts, Vorträge des Weltkongresses für Rechts- und Sozialphilosophie* (Beiheft no. 8 to *Archiv für Rechts- und Sozialphilosophie*, Wiesbaden), pp. 15–30.

THE CONCEPT OF TOTALITY IN LUKÁCS AND ADORNO

MARTIN JAY
University of California, Berkeley

At a conference dedicated to the memory of George Lichtheim, it is a risky undertaking indeed to attempt an analysis of the relationship between Georg Lukács and the Frankfurt School. For in so doing, one must traverse much of the same ground that Lichtheim crossed with such agility in *From Marx to Hegel* and elsewhere.[1] Rather than try to match the integrative sweep and synthetic power which characterize the essays in that collection, I have set myself the more modest task of focusing on one facet of that relationship which seems central to an understanding of the development of Marxist Humanism in this century. The issue I have chosen is the different uses of the concept of totality in the work of Lukács and Theodor W. Adorno, who represents the most radical antipode to Lukács among the first generation of Frankfurt School theorists.[2] More specifically, my concern will be with the implicit clash between *History and Class Consciousness*[3] and *Negative Dialectics* and the implications of that clash for Marxist theory today.[4] Although many of the same questions were treated in the aesthetic writings of both men — Lukács in fact first used totality in *The Theory of the Novel*[5] — limitations of space preclude an examination of the implications for Marxist aesthetics. No study of aesthetic theory, however, could proceed without a prior grasp of the philosophical issues underlying the approach of both men, which is what I hope to provide in this essay. I will try to show that *Negative Dialectics* represents a serious, perhaps fatal, challenge to the assumptions of the early Lukács, assumptions which, combined with the recovery of the *Economic and Philosophic Manuscripts,* led to the rise of Marxist Humanism. In fact, I will suggest some surprising similarities between Adorno's critique of *History and Class Consciousness* and that of Louis Althusser,[6] who is usually seen as an opponent of both Lukács and the Frankfurt School. Adorno, from within the walls of the humanist camp, and Althusser, from without, have jointly presided over the dismantling of the problematic introduced into Marxist theory by Lukács (and Karl Korsch)[7] in 1923.

*   *   *

> It is not the primacy of economic motives in historical explanation that constitutes the decisive difference between Marxism and bourgeois thought, but the point of view of totality. The category of totality, the all-pervasive supremacy of the whole over the parts is the essence of the method which Marx took over from Hegel and brilliantly transformed into the foundations of a wholly new science. . . . *The primacy of the category of totality is the bearer of the principle of revolution in science.*[8]

With these now familiar words from his January 1921 discussion of "The Marxism of Rosa Luxemburg," the second essay in *History and Class Consciousness,* Lukács announced a new paradigm in the history of Marxist theory, whose exploration was to occupy Western Marxists for the next half century. All of the other major characteristics of what has been variously known as "Western Marxism," "Para-Marxism," "Marxism with a Human Face," or simply "Marxist Humanism," have been integrally connected to the concept of totality. No serious discussion of alienation, reification, *praxis,* the critique of everyday life, or critical theory in general has failed to recognize that totality (or totalization) is an essential category of the discourse in which these issues are meaningful. Even among the recent advocates of a structuralist Marxism, it is assumed to be a necessary component in any dialectical theory of the social world.[9] What I hope to demonstrate, however, is that its meaning underwent a very crucial alteration in the usage of the Frankfurt School, especially of Adorno, so that much of its power had been eroded by the time of the Althusserian challenge to Marxist humanism. To do so, I will develop five different meanings of totality − longitudinal, latitudinal, expressive, decentered, and normative − which will be defined in the course of the argument.

Before tracing the development of the concept after 1923, it will be necessary to glance at the antecedents which precede its adoption for Marxist purposes by Lukács in the postwar period. Strictly speaking, Lukács' claim that the Hegelian concept of totality was preserved solely by the Marxist tradition was incorrect. His reasoning, which was more logical than historical in any empirical sense, was as follows: Marxism is the theoretical expression of the *praxis* of the proletariat. Because the proletariat was the universal class by virtue of its uniquely constitutive role in the production process, it (and its spokesmen) possessed the epistemological vantage point necessary to grasp the totality of social relations, which were ultimately of its own creation. Implicit in this claim was Vico's now familiar argument against Descartes that knowledge of the historical world was superior to knowledge of the natural world because men could know what they've made better than what was merely given to them. To Lukács, the bourgeoisie was thus precluded from a totalistic view, even though it dominated capitalist society:

> The tragic dialectics of the bourgeoisie can be seen in the fact that it is not only desirable but essential for it to clarify its own class interests on *every particular issue,* while at the same time such a clear awareness becomes fatal when it is extended to *the question of the totality.* The chief reason for this is that the rule of the bourgeoisie can only be the rule of a minority.[10]

Although bourgeois hegemony may well have meant minority control, this did not prevent bourgeois thinkers from employing totality in their work. The traditional German obsession with the alleged harmony of Greek culture still had a powerful impact in early twentieth-century thought, despite Nietzsche's exposure of its illusory qualities;[11] indeed, Lukács' own pre-Marxist *Theory of the Novel* adhered to the Greek epic as the ideal of aesthetic totality against which the fragmented modern novel might be measured. More significantly from the point of view of social thought, totality was a potent category in the historicist tradition, which persisted until the Second World War.[12] Dilthey, Simmel, Troeltsch, and Mannheim all used the term in one fashion of another. For Dilthey, history as a whole still had an inherent meaning, although this meaning was inexpressible in rational terms, as Hegel had believed. The historical world, he wrote, is "a system of interactions centered on itself; each individual system of interactions contained in it has, through the positing of values and their realization, its center within itself; but all are structurally linked into a whole in which, from the significance of the individual parts, the meaning of the whole context of the social-historical world arises."[13] To Dilthey, the meaning of this irrational whole was accessible through a process of hermeneutic interpretation, which to be sure remained incomplete until the end of the story. Like Hegel, he believed that totalistic knowledge was only a retrospective possibility.

A similar belief in an irrational *Lebenstotalität* can be found in Simmel, Troeltsch, and Mannheim, although in a more modest sense than in the quasi-Hegelian Dilthey. Instead of seeing universal history as a meaningful totality, they restricted their use of the term to what

Troeltsch called "individual totalities," the specific historical configurations that have emerged throughout history. Closer to Ranke than
Hegel, they refused to extend the concept beyond the boundaries of
these irreducible cultural wholes, a reluctance that Spengler was also
to share. This usage of totality we will call "latitudinal," in opposition
to the "longitudinal" use which will be reserved for the belief that
universal history was itself a totality.

Still other examples of holistic thinking can be found in the literary
criticism of Friedrich Gundolf, the biology of Hans Driesch, the art
criticism of Max Dvořak, and the anti-associationist psychology of
Oswald Külpe and his students at Wurzburg, who anticipated the
Gestalt psychology of the 1920s. In short, there was, to borrow a
phrase from Peter Gay, a "hunger for wholeness"[14] in late Wilhelmian
Germany which expressed itself in bourgeois as well as proletarian
terms. That Lukács's own world view developed in the context of a
bourgeois culture in crisis, a culture anxious about fragmentation and
absurdity, has now become a commonplace.[15]

If then Lukács was overstating the case by saying that only Marxist
theory possessed the point of view of totality, it was nonetheless true
that his use of the term did set him apart from the majority of his
non-Marxist competitors. First, Lukács returned to the Hegelian stress
on rationalism that the *Lebensphilosophs* had repudiated. Although he
was not yet as hostile to their irrationalism as he was to become by
the time of *The Destruction of Reason,*[16] it is clear that the essence
of history to Lukács was the collective realization of a rational
society, a project that had been at the heart of German idealism at
least since 1784 and Kant's "Idea of a Universal History from a Cosmopolitan Point of View." His notion of reason, of course, was essentially Hegelian — that is, reason was understood in the substantive
sense of reconciling contradictions between essence and appearance,
"is" and "ought," particular and universal, potential and actual, rather
than in the formal and instrumental sense employed by neo-Kantians
such as Max Weber. Formal reason meant the separation of reason from
ethics and its restriction to a set of shared procedural rules. Instrumental reason signified an efficient choice of means to reach ends which
were irrationally selected.

Lukács also differed from the later *Lebensphilosophs,* although not
from Dilthey, by extending the idea of totality beyond the boundaries
of individual cultures to include the entire historical process.

> The question of universal history [he wrote] is a problem of methodology
> that necessarily emerges in every account of even the smallest segment of

history. For history as a totality (universal history) is neither the mechanical aggregate of individual historical events, nor is it a transcendent heuristic principle opposed to the events of history.... The totality of history is itself a real historical power — even though one that has not hitherto become conscious and has therefore gone unrecognized — a power which is not to be separated from the reality (and hence the knowledge) of the individual facts without at the same time annulling their reality and their factual existence.[17]

In so arguing, Lukács adopted what we have called a "longitudinal" view of totality, which carried with it the possibility of a theodicy in the manner of Hegel and Kant, who argued that strife and antagonism were necessary components in the process of historical development. It was the danger of such a theodicy that aroused the skepticism of the Frankfurt School about the notion of "longitudinal totality," as we shall see shortly. Lukács, to be sure, did not endorse the Hegelian use of universal history without serious reservations of his own. One of the most fundamental was his rejection of the belief, shared by Dilthey as well as Hegel, that knowledge of the whole comes only at the end of the process; for Lukács, Minerva's owl flew at midday, not at dusk, which meant that the constitutive role of subjectivity in creating the totality and the cognitive process of knowing it were essentially the same.[18]

Lukács departed from the post-Hegelian bourgeois use of totality in yet another way. For the social whole, as he understood it, was a concrete, complexly mediated totality, which did not stand opposed to the isolated individual as an abstract, collective other. Instead, as his student Istvan Meśzáros has succinctly put it:

"Social totality" without "mediation" is rather like "freedom without equality": an abstract — and empty — postulate. "Social totality" exists in and through those manifold mediations through which the specific complexes — i.e., "partial totalities" — are linked to each other in a constantly shifting and changing, dynamic overall complex. The direct cult of totality, the mystification of totality as an immediacy, the negation of mediations and complex interconnections with each other, can only produce a myth and, as the Nazis have proved, a dangerous one at that.[19]

Because of his stress on mediation, Lukács's notion of totality still contained a moment of that personal wholeness so extolled by previous German thinkers. Thus, *History and Class Consciousness* contains a description of "authentic humanity," of "man as a perfected whole who has inwardly overcome, or is in the process of overcoming, the dichotomy of theory and practice, reason and the senses, form and content . . . for whom freedom and necessity are identical"[20] which bears a striking resemblence to Nietzsche's analysis of Goethe in *The Twilight of the Idols:*

> What he wanted was *totality;* he fought the mutual extraneousness of reason, senses, feeling and will (preached with the abhorrent scholasticism by *Kant,* the antipode of Goethe); he disciplined himself to wholeness; he *created* himself.[21]

Although Lukács was to neglect this aspect of totality far more than, say, Sartre, it remained in dialectical tension in his work with the more frequently used notion of social totality.

Nietzsche's reference to Kant as the antipode of Goethe leads us to one of the key functions of totality in *History and Class Consciousness:* a means to overcome what Lukács called the "antinomies of bourgeois thought." The most important of these was the irreconcilability of theoretical and moral knowledge, of facts and values, which had most recently been expressed in the work of Weber. Science and ethics to Kant and the neo-Kantians required two separate modes of cognition, one "pure" — that is, contemplative — the other "practical" or active. This division was retained by the neo-Kantians, with the further complication that for many of them, no truly cognitive approach to ethical or "practical" knowledge was possible. Weber, to take one example, could only face the relativist implications of historicism with stoic resignation. For Weber, the idea of a substantive rationality positing ends as well as means was an absurdity. Nor did the concept of totality appeal to him as a means to overcome the gap between "is" and "ought," as it did to his friend Troeltsch (and to the Lukács of *History and Class Consciousness*).

A second antinomy posited by Kant, which Lukács saw as characteristic of all bourgeois thought, was the gap between the phenomenal and noumenal worlds. Our knowledge was inevitably imperfect because of our inability to perceive things-in-themselves. Weber's celebrated method of ideal types was an attempt to deal with this problem, but one which did not restore the epistemological confidence of the Hegelian-Marxist tradition, a restoration Lukács was anxious to achieve. Before 1917, however, he was unable to find the means to do so and his attitude closely paralleled Weber's in many respects.[22] Like Weber, he seemed to regard the "disenchantment of the world" an irreversible process. Both *The Soul and Its Forms* (1911) and *The Theory of the Novel* (completed in 1916) expressed a profound pessimism about regaining the sense of wholeness and harmony that provided a social-cultural precondition for the Greek epic.[23]

But with the Russian Revolution and Lukács's subsequent entrance
into the Hungarian Communist Party, all of this suddenly and dramatically changed. With the special fervor of a recent convert, Lukács
proclaimed the imminent rise of the proletariat to power as the source
of a new totality. The age of "transcendental homelessness"[24] now
seemed nearing its end; the antinomies of bourgeois thought were to
be resolved as the bourgeoisie lost its hegemony in the forthcoming
revolution. For a Marxist intellectual, this meant *inter alia* that a
radical rethinking of traditional Marxist categories was on the immediate agenda, a task Lukács set himself in the essays he wrote during the
early 1920's. The need was urgent as even Marxist theory had been
tainted by the antinomies of bourgeois thought during the prerevolutionary era. Revisionists like Bernstein, Otto Bauer, and Tugan-
Baranovsky were clearly weakened by their neo-Kantianism, but even
Engels with his scientistic dialectics of nature and Rosa Luxemburg
with her overly economistic theory of spontaneity were severely
deficient. "Economic fatalism and the reformation of socialism
through ethics are intimately connected," Lukács argued; "the 'ethical' reformation of socialism is the subjective side of the missing
category of totality which alone can provide an overall view."[25]

The category was missing in both bourgeois theory and in its Marxist counterpart during the Second International because, as we have
already noted, only the proletariat could totally create society and
become conscious of its self-creation. Capitalism, to be sure, had laid
the groundwork: "with the mounting socialization of society it becomes increasingly possible and hence necessary to integrate the content of each specific event into the totality of contents."[26] But the
crucial step towards a real totalization of society could only be taken
when a universal class took power, an event that Lukács thought
imminent in the heady climate after 1917.

The fundamental reason for this totalistic overcoming of the several
antinomies of both bourgeois society and bourgeois thought must be
found, so Lukács argued, in the new relationship between subject and
object that emerged with the ascendency of the proletariat. For once
the historical world was understood as the objectification of an historical subject, it could no longer stand opposed to that subject as a
reified other, a "second nature," which could only be passively contemplated. Values also gain an objective quality when this new relationship emerges, although they never can be seen as eternally
immutable. Values are more than mere subjective whims because they

exist in the objective (or more correctly, objectivized) world of institutions and mores, a world which is historically created.[27]

The "sense of totality" Lukács introduced here, however, was very different from that which we have seen in Hegel and the historicist tradition. For instead of seeing all of history as a totality or individual periods as totalities, Lukács was talking about a totality as the product of a creative act. Here he was anticipating the distinction postwar French Marxists were to make between a given totality and the process of totalization.[28] In fact, in *Adventures of the Dialectic,* Merleau-Ponty interpreted Lukács solely as a theorist of totalization rather than totality.[29] Here a new use of totality, which following the structuralists we choose to call "expressive," appeared for the first time. In *The Theory of the Novel,* this usage had been completely absent, even in the discussion of the Greek epic: "In the epic, totality can only truly manifest itself in the contents of the object; it is meta-subjective, transcendent, it is a revelation and grace."[30] The subject of the epic, he wrote at that time, is a "purely receptive"[31] one. In *The Theory of the Novel,* Lukács was thus in the tradition of what Dilthey called "objective idealism," rather than that of the "idealism of freedom," which was to surface in his positive remarks on Fichte in *History and Class Consciousness.*[32] For both Fichte and the Lukács of those years, the subject was a meta-individual who created the social world through will and action. Although Lukács was to move away from this position and explicitly criticize Fichte in his 1925 review of a new edition of Lassalle's letters,[33] it is arguable that the "expressive" use of totality in *History and Class Consciousness* derives as much from Fichte as from Hegel. Here history is understood as the product of a creator-subject, not as a constellation of structures or processes whose origins cannot be traced to human agency, either partially or wholly. One crucial result of this assumption was that the totality was understood to have a genetic center which was reflected in all of its various aspects.

Lukács was able to embrace the "idealism of freedom" to the extent that he did only because of his radical separation of history and nature, a consequence of his overzealous, if essentially justified, critique of Engels's dialectics of nature. This distinction of course reveals Lukács's indebtedness to the Diltheyan tradition of setting the *Geisteswissenschaften* apart from the *Naturwissenschaften,* as well as to the more conservative dichotomy of *Kultur* and *Zivilisation.* In *The Theory of the Novel,* Lukács had chastised Tolstoy for seeking totality in nature, whereas "a totality of men and events is possible only on the basis of culture."[34] This attitude persisted in *History and Class*

Consciousness, where Hegel is praised for seeing that "the dialectics of nature can never become anything more exalted than a dialectics of movement witnessed by the detached observer."[35] To Lukács, totality was a solely historical-social concept because only the most extreme idealism could argue that nature was the objectification of a creator-subject.

In confining totality to the nonnatural, Lukács thus avoided the embarrassment of trying to marry Descartes and Vico, an obviously unnatural match. But in so doing, he also skirted the issues raised by Kant's antinomies, or at least seriously weakened his answer. For Kant's recognition that phenomenal and noumenal knowledge were not identical rested in his acceptance of a Newtonian scientific world view in which natural objects could not be understood as the objectifications of the observing subject. That men were in fact rooted in such a natural world, as well as capable of transcending it through history, eluded Lukács's grasp. Any totality that limited itself to the historically changeable "second nature" that was society without dealing with the "first nature" could only be an idealist notion, as Lukács himself later came to believe.[36] The result of this failing, as Paul Piccone has acutely argued, was that Lukács's dialectic was "not between form and content, but between form and *formed* content."[37] History for Lukács thus became a reified category itself because of its overly stark opposition to nature, or if a phenomenological vocabulary is preferred, to a precategorical *Lebenswelt.* As we shall see shortly, one of the most serious charges laid against Lukács by the Frankfurt School concerned his inadequate handling of the society-nature question.

Before turning to their critique, one more issue must be clarified: the political implications of Lukács's use of totality. Here the ground is particularly slippery as, Lenin notwithstanding, it is extremely difficult to derive political positions directly from philosophical ones. This is especially the case when the theory itself is supposed to reflect dialectically on the practice which is its only verification. Still, efforts to see a link between totality and Lukács politics have been made and must be discussed. In the article quoted above, Piccone asserts a direct link between Lukács idealism and his defense of Soviet dictatorship, in both its Leninist and Stalinist forms:

> That substitutionism so often charged by Trotskyists whereby the proletariat substitutes itself for humanity, the party for the proletariat and the leader for the party, receives in Lukács its theoretical justification precisely in those works that "Western" Marxism has always contraposed to his later Stalinist contributions. The *Zeitgeist* that Hegel had already identified in

Napoleon, Lukács identifies in Lenin and, after his death, in whomever happened to follow him *precisely through the same idealistic dialectical methodology.*[38]

To Piccone, the very use of totality as an expressive category, combined with the idea of "imputed class consciousness," is a license for tyranny. Similar charges have been leveled against Lenin by previous anti-Bolshevik critics such as Max Eastman and Neil McInnes.[39]

Although this argument has a certain logical validity — Lukács could have derived his Stalinism from a distorted idealism — it appears that the historical reality was somewhat different. For it was precisely at the time that he began to move away from the notion of expressive totality that the more sinister political turns of his career began. A glance at his attitude towards the most significant political models of his life, Lenin and Rosa Luxemburg, will clarify the issue. Although it would be a mistake to oversimplify Lukács's evolution and see a Luxemburgist (or Sorellian or left communist) phase superseded by a Leninist one,[40] a clear change occurred in his thinking between January 1921, when "The Marxism of Rosa Luxemburg" was written, and September 1922, when "Towards a Methodology of the Problem of Organization" appeared. With Lukács's shift towards a more Leninist notion of a vanguard party came a subtle movement away from expressive totality. In the first essay, he commended Rosa Luxemburg for using totality in her analytical work:

> Just as the young Marx's concept of totality cast a bright light upon the pathological symptoms of a still-flourishing capitalism, so too in the studies of Rosa Luxemburg we find the basic problems of capitalism analysed within the context of the historical process as a whole.[41]

Similarly, he praised her insight into the true function of the party as the *"bearer of the class consciousness of the proletariat and the conscience of its historical vocation."*[42] Although unwilling to fall back into fatalistic economism, Lukács was still arguing for a continuum between economics and politics, which he saw accurately expressed in Rosa Luxemburg's thought and practice.

Nineteen months later, however, Lukács was no longer as sure that the party's role was that of mere bearer of proletarian class consciousness. Now Rosa Luxemburg was criticized for failing to see that the party was something more than the voice of the working class. Although still superior to the left communists and the revisionists, she shared one major flaw with both of them: a belief in the "illusion of an 'organic,' *purely proletarian* revolution."[43] Lenin in contrast was now praised by Lukács for acknowledging the need to exploit a revolutionary situation in which the demands of other discontented factions can be manipulated to destroy the system. As a result, the party was not to be understood solely as expressing working class consciousness, even if the notion of imputation was still used to veil its departure from that role. Moreover, the Soviets or *Räte*, which Lukács had once seen as the link between the masses and the party, had faded from view. What was left was a vision of the party as "an *autonomous form* of proletarian consciousness serving the interests of the revolution."[44]

Lukács' hasty retreat from the Fichtean elements in his notion of totality can be more clearly seen in his 1924 *Lenin, A Study on the Unity of His Thought*, where Lenin is frequently praised for his adherence to the idea of totality, but without a concomitant stress on the proletariat as the subject-object of history.[45] The successful experience of the Bolshevik revolution, which could not be construed as a purely proletarian affair, in combination with the failure of its German counterpart, where spontaneism had been completely discredited, sobered Lukács considerably. His new realism, which expressed itself theoretically in his critique of Fichte in the 1925 essay of Lassalle and in a piece he wrote during the next year on Moses Hess,[46] reached its peak in the rightist "Blum Theses" of 1928, which earned him the calumny of the Comintern and led to his subsequent political silence. Significantly, his subsequent recantation of the Theses, unlike that following *History and Class Consciousness*, did not really come from the heart.[47] Thus all throughout the period he supported Stalinism, it was a nonexpressive view of totality – a view that can be justly called "decentered" – that was operative in his reasoning. In embracing the Leninist position that consciousness must be brought to the workers from without, he returned to the very stance that Pannekoek and the Council Communists had condemned in Kautsky, a condemnation that had been shared by the early Lukács.[48] This position may have been more "realistic" in a way that earned Thomas Mann's caricature of Lukács as Naphtha in *The Magic Mountain*, but it was a far cry from the utopian expectations contained in his previous use of expressive totality. If expressive totality was retained in Lukács's thought at all, it was in the guise of a future possibility, as a normative idea, not a descriptive one.

Be that as it may, it was the ideas in *History and Class Consciousness*, confirmed as they seemed to be by the recovery of the 1844 manuscripts, that set the terms of the Western Marxist discussion for the next generation. The members of the Institut für Sozialforschung grouped around Max Horkheimer played a crucial role in that discussion. Their adherence to the general tenor of thought expressed in *History and Class Consciousness* has been frequently asserted, as has their unalloyed repudiation of the compromises with Stalinism that the later Lukács made. What has not been fully clear, however, is the extent to which their development in the years from the founding of the *Zeitschrift für Sozialforschung* in 1932 to the publication of *Negative Dialectics* in 1966 saw a gradual but decisive rejection of the early Lukács as well. The Institut member whose work best represents the distance, as I have noted before, is Adorno. Anticipations of his argument in *Negative Dialectics* can be found in many places in his earlier writings, including specific critiques of Lukács in his 1931 speech "Die Idee der Naturgeschichte" and in the essay entitled "Erpresste Versöhnung," reprinted in *Noten zur Literatur II* in 1961.[49] But it is in his intellectual testament, as *Negative Dialectics* has been seen by many that the full force of his repudiation of *History and Class Consciousness* can be felt. At the center of the dispute is the concept of totality.

The intellectual sources of Adorno's new use of totality, prime among which must be counted his friendships with Walter Benjamin and Siegfried Kracauer, cannot be dealt with here.[50] The basic non-intellectual stimulus can be more simply stated, as Adorno himself has done in the frequently quoted first sentence of his book: "Philosophy, which once seemed obsolete, lives on because the moment to realize it was missed."[51] In other words, the revolutionary optimism of the period from 1917 to 1923, which served to dispel the gloom of *The Theory of the Novel,* has since been revealed as premature. In fact, *Negative Dialectics* revived the tone of despair of that very book, without, however, expressing any of its nostalgia for a lost wholeness.[52] "Transcendental homelessness" in Adorno's eyes had become a far more permanent reality than the Lukács of *History and Class Consciousness* had believed. Any hopes for change that might have survived the defeats of the working class movement were irrevocably silenced by Auschwitz:

> The earthquake of Lisbon sufficed to cure Voltaire of the theodicy of Leibniz, and the visible disaster of the first nature was insignificant in comparison with the second, social one, which defies human imagination as it distills a real hell from human evil. . . . Auschwitz confirmed the philosopheme of pure identity as death.[53]

Adorno's rejection of identity, which long antedated Auschwitz, did not, however, mean he ceased using totality in his work. As in the writing of his Institut colleagues,[54] the concept still functioned as a corrective to positivist nominalism or vulgar Marxist economism. In 1938, for example, Adorno chastised Benjamin, in what is fast becoming one of the most celebrated editorial disputes in recent history, for reductionism in one of his *Passagenarbeit* manuscripts:

> I regard it as methodologically unfortunate to give conspicuous individual features from the realm of the superstructure a "materialistic" turn by relating them immediately and perhaps even casually to corresponding features of the infrastructure. Materialist determination of cultural traits is only possible if it is mediated through the *total social process.*[55]

As late as the 1960s, he wrote in a piece on society that one must understand "the dependency of all individuals on the totality which they form. In such a totality, everyone is also dependent on everyone else. The whole survives only through the unity of the functions which its members fulfill."[56] Other examples could be adduced to show that Adorno still used the term, but what must be understood is the way in which his usage differed from Lukács'. This will be easier to see after a review of what appears to me as the five ways in which Lukács employs the word. Unfortunately, these usages were never very clearly differentiated in his writing, which accounts for much of the confusion surrounding the meaning of the word.

(1) *Longitudinal totality:* A synonym for universal history, which, as I have already noted, connects Lukács to Hegel and Dilthey.

(2) *Latitudinal totality:* The specific constellation of social structures and tendencies in effect during any one period in history or in any one culture over time. Here the usage is close to Troeltsch's idea of "individual totalities," although without the irrationalist emphasis. Still diachronic and process-oriented, this use of the term suggests a somewhat more stable set of relationships which define one totality as opposed to another. Although he did not use the word, Jacob Burckhardt's study of the Renaissance demonstrates this use perfectly.

(3) *Expressive totality:* This concept rests on the assumption that a totalizer, a genetic subject, creates the totality through self-objectification. This essentially Fichtean idea was important in Lukács' work only for a brief time — after *The Theory of the Novel* and before the concluding chapters of *History and Class Consciousness* — but it was to have a profound impact on the later development of Marxist Humanism. The concepts of reification and alienation, which Lukács failed to distinguish from objectification *per se,* were intimately tied to the expressive use of totality, which also served in the ways we have

examined to overcome the antinomies of bourgeois thought. Possible synonyms for this usage are "centered" or "reflective" totality in that all of the significant manifestations of the expressive totality reflect in miniature its genetic center, somewhat like Leibnizian monads.

(4) *Decentered totality:* A force-field of relationships whose constituent elements cannot be understood without reference to the whole, but a whole which is irreducible to one expressive or genetic center. In other words, the totality is not seen as the objectification of a creator-subject, but rather as a constellation of interactions without a specific origin. This revised use of totality appears, albeit without fanfare, in the essays following Lukács' repudiation of his extreme leftism and in *Lenin, A Study on the Unity of His Thought;* it underlies his criticism of Rosa Luxemburg's notion of a purely proletarian revolution. Its usage in these works suggests a narrowing of the gap between Lukács and Althusser, who uses totality in precisely this way.[57]

(5) *Normative totality:* Totality as a desirable goal towards which humanity should strive in an age of fragmentation. Whereas the other uses of totality can be said to be descriptive, here Lukács uses the word in a value-laden way as a state of integrated harmony in which all social contradictions are reconciled. In *The Theory of the Novel,* nostalgia for a past totality and yearning for a future one indicate that the word has normative rather than merely descriptive power. The integration sought in that early work is essentially a passive one in which the subject can surrender himself to a meaningful whole. In *History and Class Consciousness,* the whole that is desired is an expressive, active one, but the yearning is just as strong. Thus when Lukács writes that "what is crucial is that there should be an aspiration towards totality,"[58] he reveals a "hunger for wholeness" worthy of any *völkisch* critic of *Zerrissenheit.*

If the same set of categories is applied to Adorno's use of the word totality in *Negative Dialectics,* the following contrast with Lukács emerges:

(1) *Longitudinal totality:* In conscious opposition to Hegel, Marx,[59] and Lukács, Adorno vehemently inveighed against the concept of universal history. The only sense in which the historical process as a whole might be viewed was negative:

> Universal history must be construed and denied. . . . No universal history leads from savagery to humanitarianism, but there is one leading from the slingshot to the megaton bomb. . . . It is the horror that verifies Hegel and stands him on his head.[60]

To Adorno, as to Horkheimer, who once remarked that past suffering can never be redeemed no matter how utopian the future, the longitudinal use of totality smacked of a theodicy which must be exposed as an illusion.

(2) *Latitudinal totality:* This is perhaps the most frequent use of the term in Adorno's lexicon. Bourgeois society, an individual totality of unfortunately elastic boundaries,[61] is the main target of his opprobrium. It is an "administered world," whose still unreconciled contradictions are covered by a veneer of what his former colleague, Herbert Marcuse, made famous as "one-dimensionality." Adorno's famous pronouncement in *Minima Moralia* that "the whole is the untrue," a deliberate play on Hegel's "the true is the whole," must be understood in the sense that our present totality makes a mockery of true reconciliation.[62] Our "satanic" system, as he called it in his 1957 study of Hegel,[63] is the dialectical negation of an expressive totality.

(3) *Expressive totality:* The very possibility of a totality based on an identical subject-object was anathema to Adorno. The idealism at the root of this notion derived from human domination of nature, from "rage" against the irreducible otherness of the nonhuman:

> the system in which the sovereign mind imagined itself transfigured, has its primal history in the pre-mental, the animal life of the species. . . . Idealism — most explicitly Fichte — gives unconscious sway to the ideology that the not-I, *l'autrui,* and finally all that reminds us of nature is inferior.[64]

An outgrowth of this rage was the conceptual imperialism which arrogantly identified thought with its object. In contrast, negative dialectics sought "the disenchantment of the concept."[65] Lukács' revival of the subject-object identity argument was thus as fallacious as the Cartesian dualism it was intended to overcome.

Expressive totality contained other dangers as well, so Adorno suggested. Perhaps chief among them was the absolutization of the collective subject in opposition to the empirical individual; dialectics, he maintained, must always preserve a tension between the universal and the particular, thereby avoiding the liquidation of the latter in the name of the former. The very search for a transcendent subject, whether in idealist or materialist form (the proletariat), was thus a potentially hazardous undertaking. A truly materialist dialectics adhered to what Adorno called the "preponderance of the object."[66]

In so arguing, Adorno was explicitly minimizing the importance of reification and alienation, those mainstays of any Marxist Humanist analysis. Although he used the former concept frequently in his writings (far more so than alienation), he was reluctant to accord it primary importance:

> The thinker may easily comfort himself by imagining that in the dissolution of reification, of the merchandise character, he possesses the philosophers' stone. But reification itself is the reflexive form of false objectivity; centering theory around reification, a form of consciousness, makes the critical theory idealistically acceptable to the reigning consciousness. This is what raised Marx's early writings — in contradistinction to *Das Kapital* — to their present popularity, notably with theologians.[67]

Adorno did not have to go far to put his finger on one of the main culprits for this distortion:

> There is a good deal of irony in the fact that the brutal and primitive functionaries who more than forty years back damned Lukács as a heretic because of the reification chapter in his important *History and Class Consciousness*, did sense the idealistic nature of his conception.[68]

Yet another manifestation of his rejection of expressive totality was Adorno's denial that labor constituted the social world out of its own objectifications, an idea that Horkheimer had criticized as early as 1934.[69] Here too he called on the mature Marx to bear witness against his earlier incarnation:

> When Marx, in his critique of the Gotha Program, told the Lassalleans that in contrast to the customary litany of popular socialists labor was not the source of social wealth, he was philosophically . . . saying no less than that labor could not be hypostatized in any form, neither in the form of diligent hands nor in that of mental production. Such hypostasis merely extends the illusion of the predominance of the productive principle.[70]

Although labor had not been at the center of *History and Class Consciousness*, a failing Lukács was to bemoan in his 1967 preface, it is clear that the notion of *praxis* in that book was beholden to the same "production principle" whose hypostatization Adorno found objectionable.

Finally, Adorno rejected the notion of expressive totality because of the assumption behind it that the historical and natural worlds were separate and distinct spheres.[71] While thoroughly endorsing Lukács' insight that society under capitalism was falsely perceived as a "second nature," Adorno felt that Lukács had neglected the "first nature" which man could not entirely escape. To Adorno, the total socialization of the world, which both Marx and Lukács had celebrated, threatened a new regression to a socialized barbarism. The revenge of exploited nature was one of the main Frankfurt School explanations of fascism in the 1940's.[72]

A corollary of this position was the abandonment of Lukács's answer to Weber's relativism, an answer rooted in the Vician distinction between history and nature. "The concept of sense," Adorno wrote, "involves an objectivity beyond all 'making': a sense that is 'made' is already fictitious."[73] Once again, the idealist rage at nature was involved: "The permanent *reductio ad hominem* of all appearance prepares cognition for purpose of internal and external domination."[74] In short, the antinomies of bourgeois thought could not be overcome through Lukács' desperate gamble to relativize both subject and object and unite them as an historically changing subject-object. No stronger condemnation of Lukács's belief that the gap between "is" and "ought" was transcended by the proletariat could exist than the sorry spectacle of Lukács's endorsement of Stalinism. How to avoid falling into the relativism that Lukács had attempted to overcome without at the same time resorting to an "extorted reconciliation," Adorno could not really say. *Negative Dialectics* ends with a weak plea for an uneasy alliance between a nonabsolutist metaphysics and the negation of identity. The ghost of the Kantian antinomies remained unexorcised.

(4) *Decentered totality:* Like Lukács after *History and Class Consciousness,* Adorno implicitly adopted the belief that totality could not be reduced to a genetic center. Also like Lukács, he came to believe (or had believed from the beginning) that the proletariat by itself could not rise above trade union consciousness. But in direct opposition to Lukács, Adorno refused to appeal to an "autonomous" proletarian organization, the party, to direct the revolution from above. Instead, he rested content with the much debated belief that theory was itself a form of *praxis* in an era when no historical subject could be located. In constantly demanding adherence to the principle of nonidentity, Adorno cast doubt on the possibility that such a subject could ever be found.

(5) *Normative totality:* Despite the clear pessimism of his vision, Adorno did not entirely abandon the idea of an integrated, reconciled totality in the future. In at least two places in *Negative Dialectics,* he permitted himself to indulge his own, albeit faint, "hunger for wholeness." In a section entitled "Noncontradictoriness Not To Be Hypostatized," he wrote: "Dialectical reason's own essence has come to be and will pass, like antagonistic society."[75] And in his closing remarks, he

adopted a view reminiscent of Ernst Bloch in saying that "it lies in the definition of negative dialectics that it will not come to rest in itself, as if it were total. This is its form of hope."[76] Despite these isolated comments, however, it is clear that the concept of totality did not become an affirmative category in his thought, but remained a perpetually critical one.

What emerges from this comparison between Lukács and Adorno is a sense that the problematic introduced into Marxist theory with *History and Class Consciousness* is now approaching its end. For although a certain continuity has often been assumed between Lukács and the Frankfurt School because of their common reliance on the Hegelian notion of totality, the very different uses to which they put the concept suggests a radical disparity in their thought. Moreover, one can find other examples in recent Marxist thinking, even within the humanist camp, to illustrate the exhaustion of the Lukácsian problematic. Leszek Kołakowski is just one prominent instance among many.[77] But the most vigorous polemic against Lukács's notion of totality has, of course, come from the structuralist Marxists such as Louis Althusser, Maurice Godelier, Nicos Poulantzas, and Göran Therborn. Although their own alternative has serious problems that cannot be discussed here, it will be illuminating to finish this essay by casting a glance at the surprising similarities that unite Adorno's critique of Lukács with Althusser's.

These similarities are unexpected because the differences between the Frankfurt School and the Althusserians have been so thoroughly explored. Göran Therborn has assimilated Critical Theory to the humanist, historicist Marxism so disliked by the structuralists.[78] And Alfred Schmidt, Adorno's successor to the chair of Philosophy at Frankfurt, has inveighed against structuralism in general and Althusser in particular in several places.[79] The battle lines have been unmistakably drawn. Althusser's political Leninism, adulation of science, quasi-religious appeal to the authority of the real Marx (read, of course, "symptomatically"), and undialectical rejection of all subjectivity are clearly irreconcilable with Critical Theory. Although both camps criticize empiricism, Adorno was unwilling to sacrifice the reality of appearances in the name of a higher reality allegedly to be found in deep structures or essences. For all his hostility to identity theory, he was clearly in the Hegelian-Marxist problematic reintroduced by *History and Class Consciousness*.

And yet, the antipathy that we have seen in *Negative Dialectics* to many of the fundamental premises of that book suggests a common ground with Althusser and his followers. What has obscured the similarity is the seeming irreconcilability of Adorno's essentially positive attitude towards Hegel with Althusser's obvious hostility.[80] The difficulty is resolvable, however, if one realizes that their interpretations of Hegel differ radically, with the result that what Althusser attacks in Hegel is precisely what Adorno thinks Hegel has himself overcome. More specifically, in his *Aspekte der Hegelschen Philosophie,* Adorno strove to exorcise the Fichtean idea of "expressive totality" from Hegel's work. In fact, he went so far as to say that Marx's *Critique of the Gotha Program,* with its rejection of the absolute constitutive power of labor, was implicit in Hegel as well.[81] Whether or not this is valid (Marcuse thought not in *Reason and Revolution*)[82] is not at issue. What is significant is that Althusser has seized on precisely the same work of Marx for a similar purpose: to attack the notion of "expressive totality."[83] Although Althusser's "ever pre-given complex whole" consists of structures without genetic subjectivity, whereas Adorno's "force-field" involves an unreconciled dialectic of subject and object, both clearly reject as an idealistic residue the idea of a collective, constitutive subject. Both clearly employ a concept of overdetermination that maintains the irreducibility of one causal chain to another. Both share a considerable coolness towards the usefulness of such humanist categories as alienation and reification, although Adorno is not as unqualified in his disavowal. Moreover, Althusser's assertion that "the last instance never comes," which qualifies and perhaps even undermines his argument that the economy is always determinant "in the last instance," suggests a reticence to make any centered totality, even an economistic one, an historical possibility, which corresponds to Adorno's retreat from the normative idea of totality. Further evidence of this caution is Althusser's argument that ideology will exist even after the revolution, which is paralleled in a number of statements in Adorno's work.[84] Similarly, when Althusser speaks of a "theoretical praxis" distinct from other *praxes,* he is reinforcing Adorno's claim that theory can itself be a form of *praxis* (although, of course, the method of the theoretical *praxis* in the two cases is very different). Not surprisingly, this assertion has earned Althusser the same reproach so often leveled against Adorno for elitism and covert idealism.[85]

Such similarities can be extended further, but I hope the point has been made. For what Adorno and Althusser together signify is the exhaustion of the problematic introduced into Marxist theory by *History and Class Consciousness.* Both represent the Marxism of a more sober and disillusioned time. For with Althusser's reluctance to see ideology and the division of labor end after the revolution, we have come a long way from the utopian expectations of both the early Marx and the early Lukács. As Lucien Goldmann, himself an uneasy interpretor of the Lukácsian notion of totality, once noted:

> All of the great Marxist works which stress the powers of man, his possibilities of changing society and the world through action, are found in the great revolutionary epochs, around the years 1848, 1871, 1905 in Russia, and 1917. It is enough to mention the philosophical writings of the young Marx (1841–6), his essay on *The Civil War in France* (1871), *Gosudarstvo i Revolutsia* by Lenin (1917), the *Juniusbroschüre* of Rosa Luxemburg (1916), and *Geschichte und Klassenbewusstsein* by Georg Lukács (1917–1922). Conversely, the epochs during which the dominant classes are stable, epochs in which the workers' movement must defend itself against a powerful adversary, which is occasionally threatening and is in every case solidly seated in power, produce naturally a socialist literature which emphasizes the "material" element of reality, the obstacles to be overcome, and the scant efficacy of human awareness and action.[86]

Whether or not a new revolutionary era will emerge is still uncertain. But if it does, one thing is clear: no future Lukács will be able to see totality as "the bearer of the principle of revolution in science" without having answered, if he can, the devastating critique of the concept, in particular of its expressive mode, so skillfully and painfully made by Adorno and his unwitting allies in the structuralist movement.

NOTES

1. George Lichtheim, *From Marx to Hegel* (New York, 1972), and *Georg Lukács* (New York, 1970).

2. By the first generation of Frankfurt School theorists, I mean the inner circle of the Institut für Sozialforschung which coalesced around Max Horkheimer in the 1930s. Included in their number were Herbert Marcuse, Leo Lowenthal, Friedrich Pollock, Erich Fromm, and Adorno. See Martin Jay, *The Dialectical Imagination: A History of the Frankfurt School and the Institute of Social Research, 1923–1950* (Boston, 1973) for their history. The second generation's most important members are Jürgen Habermas and Alfred Schmidt.

3. Georg Lukács, *History and Class Consciousness,* translated by Rodney Livingstone (Cambridge, Mass., 1971).

4. Theodor W. Adorno, *Negative Dialectics*, translated by E.B. Ashton (New York, 1973).

5. Georg Lukács, *The Theory of the Novel*, translated by Anna Bostock (Cambridge, Mass., 1971). For a discussion of the use of totality in Lukács' aesthetic work, see Roy Pascal, "Georg Lukács: The Concept of Totality" in *Georg Lukács, The Man, His Work and His Ideas*, edited by G.H.R. Parkinson (New York, 1970). See also Fredric Jameson, *Marxism and Form* (Princeton, 1971).

6. The best exposition of Althusser's position can be found in *For Marx*, translated by Ben Brewster (New York, 1969).

7. Karl Korsch, *Marxism and Philosophy*, translated with an introduction by Fred Halliday (London, 1970).

8. Lukács, *History and Class Consciousness*, p. 27.

9. See, for example, Karl Klare's statement in *The Unknown Dimension: European Marxism Since Lenin*, edited by Dick Howard and Karl Klare (New York, 1972), p. 8. See also Serge Latouche, "Totalité, Totalisation et Totalitarisme," *Dialogue, Canadian Philosophical Review*, 12 (1), 1974.

10. Lukács, *History and Class Consciousness*, pp. 65–66. Italics in the original.

11. For a discussion of the German fascination with Greece, see E.M. Butler, *The Tyranny of Greece over Germany* (Cambridge, 1935).

12. See Georg G. Iggers, *The German Conception of History* (Middletown, Conn., 1968) for a history of historicism. See Sylvie Rücker, "Totalität als ethisches und ästhetisches Problem," *Text + Kritik*, 39/40 (October 1973) for Lukács debt to the historicist use of totality.

13. Wilhelm Dilthey, *Pattern and Meaning in History*, edited and with an introduction by H. P. Rickman (London, 1961), p. 82.

14. Peter Gay, *Weimar Culture: The Outsider as Insider* (New York, 1968), Chapter IV.

15. For a discussion of the early Lukács that sees him as an anticipation of existentialism, see Lucien Goldmann, "The Early Writings of Georg Lukács," *TriQuarterly*, 9 (Spring 1967); for a critique of this argument, see Paul Breines, "Lukács, Revolution, and Marxism, 1885–1918: Notes on Lukács' 'Road to Marx,' " *The Philosophical Forum*, 3 (34) (Spring–Summer 1972).

16. Georg Lukács, *Die Zerstörung der Vernunft* (Berlin, 1954); for a critique of

the book, which Adorno once said expressed "the destruction of Lukács' own reason," see H.A. Hodges, "Lukács on Irrationalism," in Parkinson, *op. cit.*

17. Lukács, *History and Class Consciousness,* pp. 151–152.

18. For a critique of this assumption, see Alfred Schmidt, *Geschichte und Struktur; Fragen einer marxistischen Historik* (Munich, 1971). Schmidt distinguishes between an historical "Darstellungsweise" and a structural, agenetic "Forschungsweise."

19. Istvan Meśźáros, "Lukács' Concept of Dialectic," in Parkinson, p. 65; reprinted as a separate book with the same title (London, 1972).

20. Lukács, *History and Class Consciousness,* pp. 136–137.

21. Friedrich Nietzsche, "Twilight of the Idols," reprinted in *The Portable Nietzsche,* edited by Walter Kaufmann (New York, 1968), p. 554.

22. For Lukács' relation to Weber, see Andrew Arato, "Lukács' Theory of Reification," *Telos,* 11 (Spring 1972); Andrew Feenberg, "Lukács and the Critique of 'Orthodoc' Marxism," *The Philosophical Forum,* 3 (3–4) (Spring–Summer 1972); and Fritz J. Raddatz, *Georg Lukács in Selbstzeugnissen und Bilddokumenten* (Reinbek bei Hamburg, 1972).

23. The novel, Lukács argued, was the appropriate genre for an age of irreconcilable subject-object dualism, an age Fichte had correctly called an "epoch of absolute sinfulness." In it the "conflict between what is and what should be has not been abolished and cannot be abolished in the sphere wherein these events take place – the life sphere of the novel" (p. 80). Only at the very end of his study did Lukács offer the tentative and undefended hope that in Dostoevsky a possible herald of a new age of wholeness might be seen.

24. Lukács, *The Theory of the Novel,* p. 41.

25. Lukács, *History and Class Consciousness,* p. 38.

26. *Ibid.,* p. 198.

27. As Merleau-Ponty recognized, Lukács answered Weber's relativism not by absolutizing values, but rather by carrying relativism as far as it could go:

> The old problem of the relations between subject and object is transformed, and relativism is surpassed as soon as one puts it in historical terms, since here the object is the vestige left by other subjects, and the subject – historical understanding – held in the fabric of history, is by this very fact capable of

self-criticism. . . . Would not a more radical criticism, the unrestricted recognition of history as the unique milieu of our errors and our verifications, lead us to recover an absolute in the relative? This is the question that Georg Lukács asks of his teacher, Weber. He does not reproach him for having been too relativistic but rather for not having been relativistic enough and for not having gone so far as to "relativize the notions of subject and object." For, by so doing, one regains a sort of totality.

Maurice Merleau-Ponty, *Adventures of the Dialectic,* translated by Joseph Bien (Evanston, 1973), pp. 30–31.

28. Jean-Paul Sartre, *Critique de la raison dialectique* (Paris, 1960) contains the most extensive discussion of totalization and de-totalization in the postwar French literature.

29. Merleau-Ponty, *Adventures of the Dialectic,* p. 31.

30. Lukács, *The Theory of the Novel,* p. 50.

31. *Ibid.,* p. 75.

32. Lukács, *History and Class Consciousness,* p. 123. Here Lukács praises Fichte for going beyond Kant and putting "the practical, action and activity in the center of his unifying philosophical system." As a Marxist, of course, Lukács could not then fail to chastise Fichte for neglecting to "enquire after the *concrete* nature of this identical subject-object." (Italics in the original.)

33. Lukács, "The New Edition of Lassalle's Letters," in *Political Writings, 1919–1929,* edited by Rodney Livingstone and translated by Michael McColgan (London, 1972).

34. Lukács, *The Theory of the Novel,* pp. 146–147. In his later work, Tolstoy was to be seen in a much more favorable light. See *Studies in European Realism* (New York, 1964).

35. Lukács, *History and Class Consciousness,* p. 207.

36. The 1967 preface to *History and Class Consciousness* contains the most extensive expression of his self-criticism on this point.

37. Paul Piccone, "Dialectic and Materialism in Lukács," *Telos,* 11 (Spring 1972), p. 108. Italics in the original.

38. *Ibid.,* p. 124. Italics in the original.

39. For a discussion of Eastman's argument, see John A. Diggins, "Getting Hegel

out of History: Max Eastman's Quarrel with Marxism," *American Historical Review*, 79 (1) (February 1974). McInnes makes the same point in his article, "From Marx to Marcuse," *Survey*, 16 (1) (Winter 1971), where he writes:

> Lenin wholeheartedly takes over Hegel's absolute idealism, the notion that everything is in touch with everything else in one vast moving totality. This is that "total movement" that is to be so useful in Lenin's political writings. It is the overall picture to which the Party has privileged access, and in terms of which other peoples' political actions can be declared too Left, too Right or even (this happened also) too Center (p. 143). This article is reprinted in his book, *The Western Marxist* (London, 1972).

For a more positive assessment of Lenin's discovery of Hegel, see Raya Dunayevskaya, *Philosophy and Revolution* (New York, 1973).

40. See Feenberg, p. 423, for a critique of this periodization of Lukács' development.

41. Lukács, *History and Class Consciousness*, p. 32. Italics in the original.

42. *Ibid.*, p. 41. Italics in the original.

43. *Ibid.*, p. 303. Italics in the original.

44. *Ibid.*, p. 330. Italics in the original.

45. Georg Lukács, *Lenin, A Study on the Unity of His Thought*, translated by Nicholas Jacobs (Cambridge, Mass., 1971). In his 1967 postscript, Lukács made the implications of his shift away from expressive totality clear:

> Without orientation towards totality there can be no historically true practice. But knowledge of the totality is never spontaneous, it must always be brought into activity "from the outside," that is, theoretically.... As Lenin well knew, the totality of being as it unfolds objectively is infinite, and therefore can never be adequately grasped. A vicious circle seems to develop between the infinity of knowledge and the ever-present dictates of correct, immediate action. But this abstract-theoretical insolubility can — like the Gordian knot — be cut through practically. The only sword suitable for this is that human attitude for which once again we must refer to Shakespeare: "The readiness is all."

46. Lukács, "Moses Hess and the Problems of Idealist Dialectics," in *Political Writings, 1919–1929*, cited above.

47. Lukács, *History and Class Consciousness*, p. xxxi.

48. Stanley Aronowitz, "Left-wing Communism: The Reply to Lenin," in *The*

Unknown Dimension: European Marxism Since Lenin, edited by D. Howard and K. Klare, p. 176; for a discussion of Lukács early adherence to a similar position, see Raddatz, p. 49.

49. Adorno, "Die Idee der Naturgeschichte," *Philosophische Frühschriften, Gesammelte Schriften,* Vol.1 (Frankfurt, 1973); *Noten zur Literatur* Vol. 2 (Frankfurt, 1961).

50. For a discussion of the intellectual influences on Adorno, see Susan Buck-Morss, "The Dialectic of T. W. Adorno," *Telos,* 14 (Winter 1972) and Martin Jay, "The Frankfurt School's Critique of Marxist Humanism," *Social Research,* 39 (2) (Summer 1972). For a specific discussion of Kracauer's role, see Adorno, "Der wunderliche Realist: Über Siegfried Kracauer," *Noten zur Literatur,* Vol. 3 (Frankfurt, 1965).

51. Adorno, *Negative Dialectics,* p. 3.

52. The meaningful times for whose return the early Lukács yearned were as much due to reification, to inhuman situations, as he would later attest it only to the bourgeois age. Contemporary representations of medieval towns usually look as if an execution were just taking place to cheer the populace. If any harmony of subject and object should have prevailed in those days, it was a harmony like the most recent one: pressure-born and brittle. The transfiguration of past conditions serves the purpose of a late, superfluous denial that is experienced as a no-exit situation; only as lost conditions do they become glamorous. Their cult, the cult of pre-subjective phases, arose in horror, in the age of individual disintegration and collective regression.

Adorno, *Negative Dialectics,* p. 191. Lukács' nostalgia for a lost past and Adorno's lack of the same might well have something to do with their respective ages. Lukács was born in 1885 into a wealthy, patrician family; Adorno's family background was no less fortunate, but he was born in 1903. Thus, whereas Lukács matured in an environment that still seemed relatively secure, even if bourgeois culture as a whole was in decline, Adorno came of age during the war when it had completely collapsed. Like Brecht, who was roughly of the same generation, he had no nostalgia for the prewar era, which may account for their common interest in the modernist art that Lukács abhorred. See Eugene Lunn, "Marxism and Art in the Era of Stalin and Hitler: The Brecht–Lukács Debate," *New German Critique,* 3 (Fall, 1974).

53. Adorno, *Negative Dialectics,* pp. 361–362. For a discussion of the impact of Auschwitz on Adorno, see Arnold Künzli, *Aufklärung und Dialektik; Politische Philosophie von Hobbes bis Adorno* (Freiburg, 1971).

54. See Max Horkheimer, *Kritische Theorie,* 2 volumes, edited by Alfred

Schmidt (Frankfurt, 1968), *passim,* and Herbert Marcuse, *Negations: Essays in Critical Theory,* translated by Jeremy J. Shapiro (Boston, 1968), *passim,* for examples of their use of totality.

55. Adorno, "Letters to Walter Benjamin," *New Left Review,* 81 (September–October 1973), p. 71.

56. Adorno, "Society," in *The Legacy of the German Refugee Intellectuals,* edited by Robert Boyers (New York, 1972), p. 145.

57. Althusser, *For Marx,* p. 256. Althusser tries to avoid relativism by saying that the "Marxist totality is a decentered structure in dominance," (p. 256), which means that the elements of the whole are autonomous, but asymmetrically related with one of them dominant at a particular juncture in history.

58. Lukács, *History and Class Consciousness,* p. 198.

59. Adorno, *Negative Dialectics,* p. 321. For a defense of Marx against Adorno, see Helmut Fleischer, *Marxism and History,* translated by Eric Mosbacher (New York, 1973), p. 64.

60. Adorno, *Negative Dialectics,* p. 320.

61. In Adorno's *Dialektik der Aufklärung* (Amsterdam, 1947), he and Max Horkheimer extended the sway of the exchange principle, the chief characteristic of bourgeois society, as far back as Ulysses.

62. Adorno, *Mimina Moralia: Reflexionen aus dem beschädigten Leben* (Frankfurt, 1951), p. 80. Hegel's statement was made in the preface to *The Phenomenology of the Spirit.*

63. Adorno, *Aspekte der Hegelschen Philosophie* (Frankfurt, 1957), p. 33.

64. Adorno, *Negative Dialectics,* pp. 22–23; also see the remarks on p. 189.

65. *Ibid.,* p. 11.

66. *Ibid.,* p. 183.

67. *Ibid.,* p. 190; also see his remarks on p. 374.

68. *Ibid.,* p. 190.

69. Max Horkheimer [Heinrich Regius, pseud.], *Dämmerung* (Zurich, 1934), p. 181.

70. *Ibid.*, pp. 177—178.

71. He also rejected the absolute separation of the methodologies appropriate for the exploration of the natural and social worlds. Lukács had condemned the natural scientific method as contemplative and contrary to *praxis*. But to Adorno, post-Newtonian physics suggested the possibility of a nonpassive scientific method in both spheres. See his remarks in *Negative Dialectics* on Einstein (p. 188).

72. See Adorno and Horkheimer, *Dialektik der Aufklärung*, and Horkheimer, *Eclipse of Reason* (New York, 1947).

73. Adorno, *Negative Dialectics*, p. 376.

74. *Ibid.*, p. 387.

75. *Ibid.*, p. 141.

76. *Ibid.*, p. 406.

77. See the essays in Kolakowski's *Towards a Marxist Humanism*, translated by Jane Zielonko Peel (New York, 1968), in particular, "In Praise of Inconsistency." To adopt Kolakowski's well-known distinction, Lukács is a Marxist "priest," whereas both Adorno and Kolakowski himself are "jesters."

78. Göran Therborn, "Frankfurt Marxism: A Critique," *New Left Review*, 63 (September—October 1970). I have tried to refute Therborn's position in "The Frankfurt School's Critique of Marxist Humanism."

79. Schmidt, "Der strukturalistische Angriff auf die Geschichte," in *Beiträge zur marxistischen Erkenntnistheorie*, edited by Alfred Schmidt (Frankfurt, 1969), and *Geschichte und Struktur; Fragen einer marxistischen Historik.*

80. For Althusser's attitude towards Hegel, see *For Marx*, pp. 202—204.

81. Adorno, *Aspekte der Hegelschen Philosophie*, p. 28.

82. Herbert Marcuse, *Reason and Revolution: Hegel and the Rise of Social Theory* (revised edition) (Boston, 1960), p. 173.

83. Althusser, *Lenin and Philosophy and Other Essays*, translated by B. Brewster (New York and London, 1971), pp. 93—94.

84. See, for example, Adorno's assertion in *Prisms*, translated by Samuel and Shierry Weber (London, 1967), that "humanity includes reification as well as its

opposite, not merely as the condition from which liberation is possible, but also positively, as the form in which, however brittle and inadequate it may be, subjective impulses are realized, but only by being objectified" (p. 262).

85. See, for example, Norman Geras, "Louis Althusser — An Assessment," *New Left Review*, 71, January—February 1972, p. 84.

86. Lucien Goldmann, *The Human Sciences and Philosophy*, translated by H.V. White and R. Anchor (London, 1969), pp. 80—81.

DIALECTIC WITHOUT MEDIATION
ON SARTRE'S VARIETY OF MARXISM AND DIALECTIC

YIRMIAHU YOVEL
The Hebrew University of Jerusalem

In a famous passage at the opening of his *Critique of Dialectical Reason,* Sartre declares that Marxism is the authentic philosophy of our time, reducing his own existentialism to the status of an "ideology."[1] This statement, however, is misleading.[2] Sartre does not mean that existentialism is simply to play the role of rationalizing Marxism, or that it represents, in the form of ideas, the basic social ills most properly analyzed by Marxism. As a matter of fact, he assigns existentialism a vital role in correcting and even in *grounding* the Marxian theory itself. Especially, it should supply Marxism with a fundamental anthropology; it should modify the historical determinism of the Marxists; it should provide it with a proper philosophy of action; and, above all, it should do justice to the category of the particular – both the particularity of human existence, and particular historical facts – within the framework of Marxist interpretation of history. Sartre sees, in fact, a certain analogy between the role which existentialism plays with respect to Marxism, and the corrective ingredient which Kierkegaard had introduced with respect to the former Hegelian *Zeitgeist.* Yet whereas Kierkegaard's view of the individual was conceived as exclusive of the Hegelian dialectic, existentialism is to be incorporated within the Marxian outlook, and become a moment in a new, richer synthesis.

This synthesis is offered by Sartre's *CRD.* While Sartre does not claim that his new doctrine is a continuous development of his early *Being and Nothingness (BN),* he views them at least as compatible – the latter being a kind of Marxian *Aufhebung* of the former. In the first part of this paper, I shall outline the main points in Sartre's criticism of actual Marxism, and the way in which they invite modification by such theoretical concepts as the existential project, and by the method of existential psycho-history. In the second part, I shall analyze Sartre's version of Dialectical Reason, as against his early doctrine of *BN* on the one hand, and the Hegelian model of dialectic on the other. I shall argue that, as long as Sartre adheres to his basic existentialist principles, he cannot give either dialectic or reason their proper due, and the very possibility of a social philosophy becomes questionable. This will lead to two conclusions. First, that the systematic gap between the early and the later Sartre is greater than he is willing to admit and, secondly, that Sartre's existential variety of Marxism does not (and cannot) recognize the logic of dialectical mediation. It works instead with a notion of a necessary *correlation* between terms that, in principle, cannot be reconciled.

While the first conclusion indicates a systematic flaw, the second does not necessarily require criticism. Sartre's quasi-dialectic – or, *dialectic without mediation* – may be better suited to account for human action and human reality than the classic model, from which he departs even beyond his own admitting.

I. PSYCHO-HISTORY AND THE SINGULAR UNIVERSAL

Sartre's main complaint against the Marxists is that they have neglected the category of the particular, reducing it to a mere universality. This is a serious objection to a theory that regards itself as dialectical. A dialectical approach is one of totalization, and a totality is a "concrete universal," in which the particulars necessarily mediate the universal and make it possible through their diverse interrelations. The relation of universal and particular within a totality is not based on subsumption but on mutual constitution. The universal has no significance outside what is constituted by the occurrence and interplay of actual particulars – each of which, according to Sartre, retains its irreducible "dark side." But this does not make the universal a simple inductive generalization; first, because it is constituted as the holistic (or totalizing) *meaning* of the system, which comprehends and transcends the aggregate of mere particulars; and, secondly, because it is not as such posterior to the occurrence of particulars, but already inherent in them, as their guiding and organizing principle.

Thus, Sartre's first corrective step is to go back to the basic Hegelian concept of dialectic, as the logic embedded in "concrete universals." This is a correction of the main body of Marxist literature which, Sartre holds, has made the universal a mere abstract generality (as shown in its use of "Bourgeoisie," "Idealism," or "Commercial Capitalism," etc., as sufficient explanations for actual historical occurrences, or for grasping the meaning of an individual life). But Sartre also wants to go beyond Hegel, by introducing two further and related corrections. In the first place he rejects the Hegelian idea of an actual or accomplished totality. This he replaces with the notion of *ongoing totalization*. By virtue of their constitution — which goes back to the freedom of human projects — all totalities must be incomplete, unachieved, and their meaning susceptible to radical transformation. In Sartre's jargon: they are "detotalized" totalities. Secondly, while bearing in mind the necessary role which the particular fulfills in the concrete universal (the totality), this particular should be interpreted in the light of Kierkegaard's objection to Hegel, namely, that no complete *Aufhebung* of the particular is possible. There remains a living, spontaneous subjectivity which is necessary for generating the historical universals and yet cannot be absorbed in them. Sartre thus ascribes to human *praxis* and to historical reality a new dialectical structure in which *no full mediation of the particular and the universal is recognized.*

Sartre discusses the problem of the particular in Marxism in several contexts. One is the relation of theory and practice, another the explanation of historical *praxis* itself. In dealing with the latter, Sartre usually concentrates on the substantive question, how our particular freedom regenerates historical structures while at the same time shaping itself through them; and sometimes he stresses the historiographic problem, how an historian should approach particular lives and events in order to permit their universal historical meaning to show *through* them. The term itself ("particularity") is sometimes used in the sense of diverse facts, but more frequently — and much more pertinently — in the sense of individual existential freedom. And in all these contexts, Sartre's criticism is mainly directed at Marx's contemporary disciples and sometimes, through them, at the Master himself.

Sartre's most obvious criticism concerns the divorce between theory and practice in Marxism, which led Marxist politics to become bureaucratic, while its theory evolved into rigid formalism. (Sartre calls this "Marxist idealism".) These two forms of degeneration go together and reflect one another. The fact that Marxist theoreticians do not appreciate the irreducibility and relative autonomy of the particular is reflected in the policy of despotic governments. The analyst who does violence to facts because of his rigid *a priori* universals and the bureaucrat who does violence to people for the sake of similar universals, are two complementary sides of the same system. The politics of terror are the practical manifestation of a theoretical position which reduces the particular to some abstract generality, while pretending to do so in the name of a "dialectic." Severed from its original theory, actual Marxist practice becomes simple, empirical pragmatism, finding its ideology in formalistic abstraction.

Sartre also makes a number of more theoretical criticisms. He objects to the reification of historical universals, as if they were entities in themselves. Historical factors cannot be viewed as "things," and equating them with semi-natural "forces" is equally an ontological fallacy. Yet Marxists, in what Sartre calls their "bad faith," alternate between a mechanistic and a teleological conception of history, using both in the same explanation. In the same vein, Sartre objects to the crude materialism which sees the concept of "matter" in physical or epistemological terms, as something absolutely alien to man, when it should be explicated in historical terms, as the remnant of past historical *praxis* (Sartre's category of the *pratico-inerte*). And, needless to say, Sartre objects to historical and economic determinism, keeping his old notion of existential freedom at the center of his new theory of *praxis* — even if his notions of "facticity" and "situation" have now been historicized and greatly expanded.

Sartre's criticisms are directed not only against those who have departed from Marxism, but also against the original theory itself. To be sure, he credits Marx with the attempt to form the universal as the integration of its diverse particulars. But Marx did not have an adequate theory to deal with particularity and to account for its special status. In fact, Marx's concepts of *praxis* and of human individuality are too crude and remain unanalyzed; he lacks a *fundamental* theory, upon which to base them (and by which they will necessarily be modified). Marx takes such concepts as action, work or need too much for granted; and he starts with man as a species-concept. To ground the Marxian theory of action and history, what is needed is an existential anthropology which roots historical and practical concepts in *a more fundamental theory* of man. This is what the key principles of Existentialism are supposed to do. By giving a detailed explication of human particularity, existentialism is to establish and *explain* the special weight to be assigned to the contingent freedom and irreducible subjectivity of the individual within the dialectical self-shaping of history.

Existential Psychoanalysis

Here the crucial concept in *Existential Psychoanalysis* comes to the fore. Sartre concluded his *Being and Nothingness* with a psychoanalytic theory that rivals Freud's determinism, and summarizes the main ingredients of his early book. Although he remained faithful to his concept of human existence as free, contingent self-transcendence, Sartre nevertheless had to account for the fact that there are indeed consistent behavior and personal traits in the individual's biography. This he explained by the concept of the existential *project* by which individual freedom shapes itself against the background of the given facticity of the world. This project is a primordial choice, or intention, which I perform non-reflectively; its scope is global, and thus it anticipates my future particular behavior although it cannot determine it causally. In fact, this is a teleological explanation of the possible regularities in personal behavior, and of the existence of meaningful relations between different particular choices, moves and gestures in the individual's life. Although the presence of this totalizing project makes it possible to interpret an individual life — or long spans of it[3] — in a psychoanalytic manner, the project is not to be understood as "character," that is, as a set of fixed properties which inhere "in" my person. It is rather the specific intentional form in which my consciousness projects itself into the world and the future, while itself retaining the "emptiness" and "transparence" which distinguish it ontologically from "things." And since consciousness consists in this activity of self-projection, the fundamental project is *my very particular mode of being;* it is the specific determination which my freedom assumes in the factual "situations" in which it is *ontologically* involved.

The doctrine of the existential project includes almost all the elements of *Being and Nothingness* and may be seen as summing up their import. As such, existential psychoanalysis is now to complete Marxism, and to serve as the axis for Sartre's transition to a Marxian philosophy of society and history. In the first place, the existential analysis of man provides the non-empirical (or ontological) anthropology, which Marxism hitherto lacked, and in which the concepts of action, work, need, or historical totalization have to be rooted. But secondly, and more specifically, existential psychoanalysis is now used by Sartre as psychohistory. *Its task is to "anchor" the individual in his historical context, instead of simply "placing" him there* (as Marxism is bound to do). This means that we should not simply subsume an individual life under some historical universal, but trace the particular ways in which an individual's existential freedom projects itself (from early childhood) *through* these universals, and thus constitutes a featured personality, while regenerating (and modifying) the universals themselves. This existential approach is to do justice to the full concreteness of the category of particularity, while serving as a warning that the historical universal can neither determine the individual nor fully capture the meaning of his life. It is existential freedom that constitutes the universals: historical "facticity" is the product of *praxis.*

History and Biography

Historical universals are "inert" structures (classes, institutions, periods, traditions, etc.), into which I am necessarily born. These I both interiorize and negate in the process of my self-constituting, "personalization,"[4] and choice of social role. Since they are the contents through which my "empty" freedom must project itself, the historical universals play a constitutive role in the shaping of my personality; as such they are also expressed and re-exteriorized by individual and group *praxis*. Yet my freedom also *transcends* every given content and state, reasserting its irreducible spontaneity in the face of the same universals which it helps to constitute. This introduces an element of instability into historical universals; their integration is undermined by the same principle that generates them, and so, in Sartre's words, their very constitution is "detotalized." And on the other hand, I, the individual, retain a *trans*-historical particularity in the midst of my historization.[5]

Existential psychoanalysis is thus supposed to show in some detail, *how* history and biography become intertwined in a non-deterministic process. I shape history by shaping myself and shape myself by shaping history, yet in such a way that I am not fully integrated into history and history is not fully integrated in itself. Neither moment in this dialectic can fully mediate the other. But they interrelate sufficiently for Sartre to say that we do not *confront* history but exist *within it*. By interiorizing the historical configurations and re-exteriorizing them in our *particularized* ways, we both form our own personalities and keep history going. In all this we preserve our relative autonomy and irreducible particularity, which, moreover, is not a merely residual factor — an historical fallout — as is Hegel's *faule Existenz*, but belongs to the very principle of history. Historical totalities are possible only through the irreducibly particular ways in which they are generated from the existential project; and this irreducible particularity belongs therefore to their very source and constitution.

This is why Sartre cannot be satisfied with the statement that *some* particularity — as a *general* moment — is necessary for historical totalization. This is the trivial half of a truth which, by itself, must be misleading because it suggests that history's *actual* particulars are dispensable. For the Existentialist, however, who does not recognize anything but contingent existence, nothing that has taken place in history is dispensable. Take away the particular ways through which a Danton, a Flaubert, or their mediocre contemporaries have actually projected themselves in the world, and history as a meaningful universal becomes inconceivable. Sartre ridicules Plekhanov who said — in typically Marxist fashion — that had Napoleon not existed, the same historical stage would have arisen by means of other particulars. This counterfactual conditional is meaningless in existential terms. To make such a statement one has not only to assume that the individual is fully determined by the universal but, moreover, that some *a priori* scheme is working by itself in history, regardless of the actual facts; and although it must be particularized *somehow,* it does not matter how. For Sartre this represents the abstract formalism he set out to abolish. History is only *actual* history. Even historical universals are contingent products of actual historical totalizations; and these go back to the existential project which makes the universals possible in *precisely the same particular ways which they happen to assume.* Remove the actual historical particulars and no universal will be left at all.

Even those Marxists who, unlike Plekhanov and like Marx, wish to do justice to actual individuals, start their analysis when the game is already over. They discuss adults who have already acquired a productive function, a social role and a fairly featured personality, and thus miss the critical stage at which the individual's socio-historical relations are *actually* constituted. Sartre, on the other hand, wants to penetrate into the individual's *pre*-reflective project and into the early stages of life in order to trace the interrelation of freedom and history in *its most crucial moments.* In this, too, he offers a method to meet a major problem in Marxist theory. The Marxists have to assume that the agent is conscious of his major class interests and values; or, if they wish to avoid this over-simplification, they find themselves without an adequate theory to explain *how* these interests and values become reflected non-consciously in the agent's behavior — beyond the crude deterministic generalization that "material conditions determine consciousness." Sartre's existential psychoanalysis is supposed to provide a method for answering this "how" question, and at the same time to modify the crude generalization itself.

Sartre's dialectic of existence and history is summarized by the category of the "*singular universal,*" which he offers as a key concept for understanding history.[6] Universals, as we have seen, should not be approached in the abstract, but through their singularized expression in a unique individual life. We grasp the "singular universal" when we watch a person totalizing the historical meanings of his time and class in his lived singularity, while retaining his irreducible trans-historical particularity which no universal can capture. And the individual (like Flaubert) himself becomes a "singular universal," in that he manifests the historical universal as something *singularly lived (vécu)*. Thus, the category of the "singular universal" and the method of existential psychoanalysis complement one another, the second being the means of applying the first.

To conclude, it should be observed that although existential psycho-history has a theoretical basis, it is not a self-contained doctrine but basically a hermeneutic *method*. It therefore has systematic significance that Sartre did not leave this method on the merely programatic level, but actually put it to work. In his short autobiography, *The Words,* he tried to perform an existential psychoanalysis on himself, and through it, to shed light on an entire milieu − the bourgeois culture in which he grew up. But Sartre's most daring attempt in this direction is his monumental biography of Flaubert *(L'Idiot de la Famille)* − an opus that may unfortunately no longer be completed. Despite the literary deficiencies of this work (it is cumbersome and much too verbose as opposed to the splendid style of *Les Mots* − which is, however, too short), the *systematic* importance of these works lies in the fact that they do not allow the idea of existential psycho-history to wither into a merely programatic formulation. By its own statement and basic meaning, this method demands *to be used;* and so, exemplifying its theoretic assumptions in actual research must be considered an integral part of the theory itself.

II. SARTRE'S DIALECTICAL REASON RE-EXAMINED

Sartre presents his variety of Marxism as a Critique of Dialectical Reason. In the second part of this paper I should like to analyze the three ingredients of this concept: critique, dialectic and rationality.

Sartre uses "critique" in the Kantian sense, implying a restriction of the false and over-reaching claims of rationalism. In Sartre's case, the restricting move consists in his "Kierkegaardian" modification of the concept of historical universals (or, totalities), as they were portrayed by Hegel, Marx, and − needless to say − by the formalistic (or "lazy") Marxists. In this sense, the critical ingredient in Sartre's theory has been viewed, in essence, in Part One.

But Sartre also adheres to the other Kantian sense of a "critique of reason," meaning the formation of a positive, legitimate rational theory. For Sartre, however, this theory must be fundamentally rooted in the key existentialist principles; it has to be governed by dialectical logic; and it must have society and history for its genuine subject-matter. Can all these requirements be consistently met within Sartre's own theory?

To explain my doubts, let me re-examine Sartre's concept of Dialectical Reason with respect to both the Hegelian model and Sartre's own doctrine of *BN.*

Totality vs. Correlation

(A) In its first sense, "Dialectic" suggests the classic Hegelian idea that every concrete is the result of reciprocal mediation between opposing moments. Neither moment is independent or self-sufficient; neither is primary or simple; and each regains its differentiated status and its very meaning through its transformation into its other. This also means that the duality involved is not primordial, but a split in a more fundamental unity. But this unity is initially abstract; it has still to actualize itself by the process of bifurcation and external particularization through which it reconstitutes itself as a concrete unity (or a totality). Within this reconstituted unity the opposing moments no longer retain the independent meaning that they at first seemed to have but are now modified by each other. More precisely, they are modified by their synthetic unity, so that neither can signify within the synthesis what it signified before and outside it. This can also be expressed by saying that the synthesis is not simply a juxtaposition of the moments (as in Kant), or even a necessary correlation between them (as in Sartre's *Being and Nothingness*), but rather an "internal" mediation, in which they lose their supposed heterogeneity. Their synthesis is in fact nothing but this reciprocal mediation; it does not indicate an additional factor, but only the circular process, in which each moment is reconstituted through its passage to its other, gaining a richer (and truer) significance from its function in the synthetic unity.

In conclusion, in the dialectical model (1) no heterogeneous duality is admitted; (2) no moment has the same meaning within the synthesis that it has outside it; and (3) each is actually reconstituted through its other, instead of merely pointing to this other or being externally correlated with it.

In contrast, the basic ontological scheme of *Being and Nothingness* is one not of dialectical mediation but of external negation. Human existence-in-the-world is explained in terms of a necessary correlation between two modes of being, Being-For-Itself (or consciousness) and Being-In-Itself (or thinghood). Neither of these modes-of-being penetrates the other or generates an inner modification in the other by virtue of being correlated with it. Their absolute ontological heterogeneity is retained throughout; there is no mediating unity between intentionality and its object, between absolute lucidity and absolute opacity, self-transcendence and self-identity, spontaneity and passivity, etc., and this makes Sartre himself wonder at the end of his book what justifies the use of the same generic term ("Being") for both. Being In-Itself is in fact like Parmenides' "One": undifferentiated immovable self-identity, which allows of no inner negativity. Negation can only appear as an external projection originating in human consciousness (the "For-Itself"). Thus, Being In-Itself can have no inherent meanings or essential forms, no temporality, change or particularization and, needless to say, no privation, potentialities or other forms of possibility. For actual existence to include all these, Being In-Itself must be affected from without by the negating (or "nihilating") activity of consciousness. Yet this activity does not explicate or actualize some fundamental feature within Being In-Itself; it does not induce its other to develop towards its inherent possibilities, and it is not affected by this other. Instead, Being In-Itself must remain the passive, undifferentiated moment that it is, and enters into no dialectic of its own. Thus, the two types of being remain absolutely alien to each other, even in their necessary correlation (which alone explains concrete existence and actual phenomena).

The Human Predicament

This is also the reason why, according to *BN,* ontological alienation is something that cannot, in principle, be overcome. Man cannot reconstitute his true being in and through his other, first, because the other of consciousness remains permanently severed from it. Consciousness is a perpetually self-transcending power, that cannot come to rest and become identified with any state, content, or specific determination. Man can have no identity without ceasing to be a man, and all his attempts to gain such an identity are therefore doomed to end in self-deception. On the other hand, man is basically a privation or a passion — the passion to overcome his self-transcendence and the alienness of the In-Itself by reconciling the two opposites and finding rest and self-identity. This is the ideal of "for-itself-in-itself," which is to assume the attributes of mere being while retaining those of consciousness and humanity. Yet this ideal is fundamentally void and man is thus a "useless passion."

Because of the absolute heterogeneity of For-Itself and In-Itself, and because neither can be synthesized dialectically with the other (in the form of internal mediation), human freedom must remain a hopeless enterprise, finding the eternal alien in its other rather than a possible means for its own actualization. The human predicament according to *BN* can therefore be summarized by saying that *what makes it ontologically impossible for man to reconcile himself to himself and to the world is precisely the non-dialectical structure of the basic model.*

The Origin of Negation

The fact that Sartre's ontological scheme competes with dialectics can also be seen by examining Sartre's answer to the time-honored metaphysical question of the *origin of negation.* Since the Greeks, this problem has haunted everyone who wished to avoid the Parmenidean results (and contradiction), and to assert the reality of particulars, change, temporality and modality (possibilities). If being *is,* where can its negative principle stem from? The dialectical answer ascribes the negative principle to Being itself, whereas Sartre opts for a dualistic solution, ascribing the origin of negation to an absolutely new principle — human consciousness. Sartre deals with consciousness as an ontic principle in its own right and can therefore present the negations which consciousness generates as having an ontic import and function, namely, as "nihilations" *(néantisations).* Yet given the duality he presupposes, all these ontic negativities neither stem from being itself nor can really affect it, since being has and retains an "in-itself" dimension that escapes all modification and remains eternally the changeless opacity it is. Thus not only is Sartre's conception anti-dialectical in the last analysis, he is also unable to account for the fact that negation somehow succeeds in reaching being and thus in producing a differentiated, specified experience. Just as his "synthesis" of static heterogeneities, *mutatis mutandis,* resembles Kant's, so Sartre faces a fatal problem of ontic "schematism," which he is even less able to solve than Kant. The obscure metaphors that Sartre uses to indicate the relation between the two modes of being (such as "le néant *hante* l'être," or nothingness is a "hole" within being), belong to Sartre's glossary of indispensable metaphors; they do not merely serve as suggestive abbreviations of an intelligible idea, but rather as a cover for or leap beyond systematic *un*intelligibility.

Idealism With an Alibi

Finally, the non-dialectical nature of Sartre's ontology is also the reason why, in the last analysis, his attempt to reconcile idealism and realism ends in a new form of idealism, which I shall call an idealism "with an alibi." The alibi is the concept of Being In-Itself. Since by definition this being stays unaffected and unchanged, it cannot be seen as fulfilling any systematic function. Its existence makes no difference except to enable Sartre to say that there is also something independent of human consciousness beyond and above concrete existence (which is shaped or mediated by human consciousness), although we cannot say anything about it, and although it does not indicate a possible separate world but only a moment of the human reality. As a hypostatization of the moment of passivity in experience, Sartre's In-Itself is close to Husserl's concept of *hylé:* both are vague categorizations of the element of sheer passivity within a world which is supposed to be shaped by the constitutive and interpretative work of consciousness.

The Marxian Connotation

(B) Another major connotation of "dialectical reason" derives from the Marxist context. It indicates a concern with social and historical problems, not as a special branch of philosophy but as its most comprehensive theme. In this Sartre is following Marx, as opposed to the Hegelian primacy of speculation. Yet when he comes to modify the Marxist doctrine, Sartre does not take the same historical standpoint as the Marxists, but the more fundamental standpoint of his own theory of man. His approach thus remains basically existential, although he now wants to give his former existentialism a social and historical thrust.

Can this shift work? Sartre does not claim that his new philosophy of history is a straightforward explication of the early existentialism, but that the two are at least basically consistent and that they could be synthesized. I think, however, that even this less ambitious claim must give rise to some serious doubts. It is questionable whether the basic principles of *BN* can meet the demands of a rational and dialectical social philosophy. In fact, all three concepts (rationality, dialectic and society) seem to be at odds with the implications of *BN*. I shall arrange my comments in three general points.

The Contingency of Historical Choice

As long as Sartre retains the notions of existential project and arbitrary freedom and even makes them the basis of history, both historical *choice* and historical *comprehension* must count as purely contingent. On the one hand, no historical choice can be preferred or justified *a priori*. I have no rational grounds for determining my own choice, much less for universally commending it to others. From this viewpoint, fighting for or against imperialism, for or against alienation, or for or against the Jews are equally arbitrary choices through which my freedom projects itself in the context of certain historical universals. All that the Existentialist philosopher of History can say is that any such action involves the interiorization of the meaning of these universals, as well as their transcendence. But this may take place either by my accepting the trend and the role in which I find myself, or by refusing and fighting it. The interrelation of freedom and historical situation will obtain no matter what particular direction my choice has taken.

Historical Comprehension

The contingency of historical choice would obtain even if History could be construed as an objective rational process which my freedom faces. Yet history cannot be so conceived for the same reasons that make historical choice arbitrary. As long as everything is rooted in the existential project, history must be seen as a web of existential totalizations with which my freedom is intertwined. And this must taint historical comprehension with the same contingency that affects historical choice. In other words, according to existentialistic principles, historical intelligibility itself becomes unintelligible or at best a happy chance. It may well be, as Sartre claims, that History allows us to detect some universal meanings or a deciferable pattern (such as the movement toward and from alienation). But this result is obtained *ex post facto*, from a glance at the facticity of the past. In this respect, historical universals must be considered as contingent no less than any particular aggregate of facts. Our ability to give history meaningful structures does not make them any more rational, necessary, or expressive of the human essence than, say, an imaginary story or any interpretable play of chance. If history were "a tale told by an idiot,"[7] we might still be able to detect a structure in it.

Modes of Retrospective Rationality

It may be countered that Hegel, too, can find meaning in history only in retrospect (and Hegel is the genuine philosopher of rationality). But in Hegel, rational meaning is not assigned to the object as an external projection. Instead it is the rationality embedded in the object which attains subjective self-consciousness through its development and actualization. This is why in Hegel, as opposed to Sartre, the retrospective view indicates that the contingency of the historical past has been *sublated (aufgehoben)*. Hegel can take this view by virtue of his dialectical version of Aristotelianism, which Sartre must reject. Aristotle conceived of development as a movement from potentiality to actuality, which a latent rational concept (or essence) guides and underlies. Hegel gave this model a dialectical interpretation: the latent concept *becomes* rational only by actualizing itself by its "return to itself" (as actual) through the sequence of its empirical manifestations. Thus, it is the *actualization* of the system that makes it rational and sublates its past history into a rationally-necessary moment of the whole. In the accomplished totality, a synthesis takes place between factual and logical necessity *(vérité de fait* and *vérité de raison)* which cease to be mutually opposed and become dialectically mediated, in the higher concept of rational[8] necessity.

Sartre's Existentialism, however, must reject the presuppositions which make such a view possible. It cannot accept the Aristotelian notion of a latent *a priori* essence; it must exclude all forms of rational necessity from the realm of being; it cannot admit of closing the dialectical cycle, which creates a totality; and it does not recognize a fully dialectical mediation, in which the moments are mutually reconciled and their heterogeneity *aufgehoben*. Thus, it is precisely the difference of dialectic which accounts for the fact that although both Sartre and Hegel can only give history meaning in retrospect, in Hegel the retrospective view sublates the contingency of the facts within a rational universal, whereas Sartre must regard the universal itself as merely a contingent fact.

Sartre and Hermeneutics

Analysis shows that Sartre's account of history's intelligibility is closer to the hermeneutic approach than to Hegel. Although history may *de facto* reveal a number of interpretable wholes, these do not manifest any rational necessity. Their meaningful unity is closer to that of literary works, or of psychoanalytical interpretations. But even here a distinction must be made. We can assume that a unifying subjective intention underlies psychoanalytic structures or literary texts. In history, on the other hand, we must proceed without such an overall intention. Here we are subject to what Kant called *Zwecklos Zweckmässigkeit.* In other words, while we may recognize teleological patterns, we may not ascribe them to any single totalizing mind or intention.

It is true that, in Sartre, history is motivated by human intentionality; but the latter belongs only to the *individual* human beings from whose arbitrary freedom it springs. Any attempt to hypostasize this moment of intentionality into some trans-personal intention constitutes a gross philosophical fallacy. Thus historical intelligibility becomes even more problematic in Sartre than personal biography. Sartre was confronted with the following problem in establishing his existential psychoanalysis at the end of *BN:* given the spontaneity of consciousness, and the fact that human freedom has no essential content, how can we account for the unity of the person, and for the fact that there is a certain interpretable consistency in his behavior, particular choices, and even gestures. The problem was to establish the concept of a free character[9] and to account for the (partial) intelligibility of whole historical contexts. Here, the problem no longer concerns a single individual and his project, but successive generations of collective groups — and no single intention or project can be attributed to these. And yet, Sartre attempts to base the intelligibility of history on the same existential concept of project, showing how my own project interiorizes the inertia of the past while at the same time transcending it. It is this practical-inertia that gives history its continuity and serves as a substratum for the formation of historical universals. This, in turn, is the major significance of "Reason" in the late Sartre: the intelligibility of history through its universal structures. But these universals are born of contingent freedom and continue to be contingent even in their inert crystallization; and they certainly cannot be ascribed to any single principle of totalization (there is no human essence, no historical *a priori,* no divine will, no super-historical Ego, etc.). History is to be read and interpreted *ex post facto,* without ascribing its unity to any single intention, and in fact, *without sufficiently explaining the occurrence of universals in terms of the theory.* Their appearance is itself a happy *de facto* chance. Sartre's claim to base history on Dialectical Reason is, therefore, questionable, to say the least.

Social Groups and the "Other"

The second point concerns the claim to develop a social philosophy. In *BN,* social groups are not conceived as having any inner integration of their own. Their unity is purely external, stemming from the "look" of another, rival group.[10] This conclusion was derived from the existential analysis of the "Other" *(autrui)* in general. While consciousness is existentially related to the consciousness of the other —

that is to say, my being "for the other" is a condition or a dimension of my being "for myself" — this other is necessarily conceived as opposed to me. Not only is he a rival focal-point for organizing the world and assigning meanings to it; he is also basically an alien subjectivity incompatible with mine, so that I must either regard him as an object if I wish to assert my own subjectivity, or, conversely regard him as a subject, and relate to myself (through the other's look) as an object. The master-slave relationship in Hegel's *Phenomenology* obtains in Sartre's model, but without its dialectic. The state of conflict is not a phase of the development but a fundamental structure. The perspective can be transposed (I-subject, you-object, or vice versa) but the essential rivalry cannot be abolished. I cannot reveal (not to say: realize) my own subjectivity by recognizing the subjectivity of the other, just as I cannot become a For-Itself-In-Itself (i.e., regain a constant identity while still being conscious).[11] Otherness in both its ontological dimensions — as thinghood and as another-subjectivity — is eternally opposed to me. And what obtains in personal relations is reflected in inter-group relationships. By its very ontology, the group is not individuated by some common inner content (interest, origin, culture, etc.), but only by the external "look" of a rival group; and this is the basic relation, which neither action nor history can change.

It is impossible to develop a positive philosophy of society and history on this basis. If groups have no inner integration, and if their interrelation is subject to no dialectical process, all that can be said about them is contained in the negative picture painted in *Being and Nothingness* — with a possible application to concrete cases.[12] The group-ontology of *BN* has no possible continuation; it cannot provide a basis for the *Critique of Dialectical Reason*, and is in fact incompatible with it.

Groups and Alienation

This is the most apparent incompatibility between the early existential doctrine and the new Marxian philosophy. Sartre recognized it, and tried to explain that the inter-human conflict which makes it impossible to reconcile both sides as subjects is true only of the historical era of alienation.[13] Yet this is definitely not the view of *BN*, which presented the issue as a basic ontic structure. Sartre came to think that this "ontological" claim was itself a symptom of the ideology of alienation which he manifested as a bourgeois philosopher. It is certainly part of the Marxian theory of alienation — at least in its refined form — that alienated man tends to ignore the historicity of his state and to interpret it as a "natural" fate (with which he may even be content). This explanation may well be consistent with the Marxian outlook, but it is not consistent with Sartre's basic existentialism. Systematically, *one cannot modify BN's doctrine about groups, without also changing the whole analysis of the "other,"* and this no longer constitutes a minor modification, but is a real upheaval in the original existential doctrine. Moreover, if the view that the other is ontologically severed from me is to be changed, arguing that some subjective communion or reconciliation is possible between us after all — the same change may be required also for the In-Itself! A major reason why the other and Being-In-Itself are eternally severed from me as opposing, non-dialectical correlates, lies in Sartre's theory of intentionality, and a change in this theory will affect Sartre's whole picture of consciousness. In the last analysis, to say that positive communality in groups is possible may require that Sartre abandon his concept of freedom and consciousness as "empty" and "outward directed" — and this is a heavy systematic price to pay. Changing his theory of groups to meet the prerequisites of a Marxoid social philosophy may in fact force Sartre to throw his existential baby out with the bath water.

The Lack of Historical Reconciliation

(C)   My earlier analysis of *BN's* non-dialectical structure recurs also with respect to the problem of society: the irreconcilability of opposing correlates and the inherent break-down of totalization. In the present context, this analysis will explain why the historical process cannot play for Sartre the role of human redemption it plays in both Hegel and Marx. Not only is such redemption impossible in principle, but history itself is a contingent universal, and does not embody a human ideal or essential task. The element of utopia, the ideal of reconciling man to himself, to his other, and to his natural and social environment, is not only inherently void; even if a series of historical events should show, for example, that certain types of social and economic alienation are actually disappearing, this will have to count only as a historical accident — a happy chance. And, needless to say, Sartre must also reject any quasi-eschatological concept of the "end of history" — the conclusion of the age-old effort — which again was a powerful motive in both Hegel and Marx. Human consciousness is always a self-transcending principle; it cannot come to rest in any state or situation, whether personal or historical. In fact, to Sartre — as he stated in a conference held in Jerusalem[14] — the end of history must seem as the absolute death — the worst nightmare he could imagine.

Sartre's sober conception of history, the absence of any disguised theology and eschatology, may well be more adequate and concrete than the old dialectical optimism. But it must be recognized that this view involves a curious form of dialectic — a dialectic without mediation and without reconciliation — which should in fact be considered a dualistic theory of correlation.

The author wishes to thank C.N.R.S. for their support of this research.

NOTES

1. *Critique de la Raison Dialectique,* Paris, NRF, 1960, p. 18 (henceforth *CRD*).

2. The statement occurs in Sartre's introductory essay to *CRD* (translated into English as *Questions of Method*). This essay had just appeared separately as "Existentialism and Marxism" in a Polish magazine: a fact which may account for Sartre's blunt words.

3. This reservation is necessary, since the project is always "fragile": grounded in an arbitrary choice, it can in principle be always overthrown. This would constitute a whole "*conversion* of the individual's life" (as Sartre tried to show in his play "Le Diable et le Bon Dieu.") In such a case, only the span of life that lies within a specific project could be interpreted in its terms, while the next global project cannot in principle be grounded in its predecessor.

4. Or what is otherwise called "socialization." (The terms "constitution" and "personalization" are taken from the main chapters in Sartre's psycho-history of Flaubert.)

5. This trans-historical moment is stressed by Sartre as against the full historization of the individual, which he ascribes to both Hegel and Marx. The point is mainly stressed in his late essay on Kierkegaard: "L'Universel Singulier."

6. Sartre suggested this category by name in an essay devoted to Kierkegaard and written after *CRD*. He reverts to the category in the preface to his psycho-history of Flaubert.

7. As it may well be upon the existentialist principles.

8. Also: "speculative" or "dialectical" necessity. The term "rational" has to be understood here in terms of *Vernunft,* as opposed to *Verstand,* which is the principle of formal logical truth. Hegel is suggesting a *substantive* logical truth here — a mode of logical necessity that obtains in reality itself. And this has to be actualized by History.

9. As opposed to the deterministic notion of character, as a set of psychological facts.

10. *L'Etre et le Néant* (Paris, Gallimard, 1943), Pt. III, p.484ff. (This was again the basis for Sartre's analysis of the Jews). English translation by Hazel Barnes (New York, Washington Square Press, 1966), p. 500 ff.

11. See p. 17 above.

12. Such as Sartre did with respect to the Jews.

13. Sartre, I suspect, reaches the borders of honesty when he says in an introduction to an LP record of his *Huis Clos,* that by the dictum "Hell is the Other" he did not mean an ontological generalization, but a truth that is relative to the era of alienation. This is definitely not the sense of the same doctrine in *BN.*

14. During his 1967 visit.

PCI STRATEGY AND THE QUESTION OF REVOLUTION IN THE WEST

STEPHEN HELLMAN
York University, Ontario

INTRODUCTION

For a communist party, the Italian Communist Party (PCI) enjoys a remarkably good reputation among scholars and intellectuals. Although it is the largest party of its type in the West, this image obviously reflects much more than electoral or organizational success. The party's flexibility, independence, and overall "liberal" nature have all reinforced its reputation, especially when it is compared to its French counterpart. These positive qualities have most often been apparent to non-Italians with regard to the PCI's relationship to the Soviet Union and what used to be called the international communist movement. Indeed, the PCI's claims about this movement being polycentric, as well as the very title it chose for its strategy, "The Italian Road to Socialism," seem to suggest that the strategy basically concerns the PCI's relationship to its external, international environment.[1] Recently, however, more attention has begun to be paid to the strategy's pretensions with regard to its internal environments, both organizational and domestic.[2] This is extremely important, for the aims of the *via italiana al socialismo* have always been most ambitious on the level of domestic strategy. It is surely on this level that the *via italiana* raises the most interesting questions for students of Marxism — as opposed to students of the communist movement. For the Italian Road to Socialism is, above all else, a formulation which claims to be an original prescription for socialist revolution in the West.

The PCI has habitually contended that the question of a socialist strategy appropriate to the conditions of Western capitalism has been on its agenda longer than that of any other communist party. It does this with pride, pointing to Antonio Gramsci, claimed as a theoretical fountainhead. While what actually remains of Gramsci in the *via italiana* is the subject of considerable dispute,[3] the PCI is certainly correct to underline that its strategy does represent something other than the polarized choice between passive reformism or violent revolution which has plagued European socialism for nearly a century.

Largely because of its pretensions to originality, the Italian Road to Socialism has been the subject of considerable ideological debate almost since its comprehensive elaboration in the period beginning in 1956. All too often, however, critics of the strategy have approached it from a purely abstract and almost scholastic perspective. Armed with rather rigid models of what Marx, Lenin Gramsci, Trotsky, or some other authority said about the transition to socialism, they find, not surprisingly that the *via italiana* falls short on numerous counts.[4] While often of intellectual value, these exercises fail to address the strategy on its own terms, terms, for example, which readily admit departures from the "classics," but claim nevertheless to remain within the revolutionary Marxist fold. Furthermore, this type of criticism often obscures the fact that a much richer ideological debate has been taking place within and around the PCI for nearly two decades. This debate is infinitely more interesting, for its participants largely share the *via italiana's* major assumptions. These are that advanced capitalism – and hence a socialist strategy for advanced capitalism – represent qualitatively different developments than those which are implied in models drawn from the past.

Departing from the belief that this assertion is an intrinsically important one, this essay will examine the Italian Road to Socialism in its own terms. Our analysis will be restricted to those aspects of the strategy which relate most directly to the transformation of an advanced capitalist society. Special emphasis will be placed on the theoretical problems raised by this formulation, for the latter part of this essay will examine whether and how these problems have been raised in debates over the *via italiana,* and how they have eventually been refined, absorbed, or dropped by the PCI in its constant updating of the strategy. Underlying this analysis is the belief that, whatever the weaknesses of the PCI's theory, the issues which have been debated are much more relevant to the question of socialism in the West than are formulations which rest, in the ultimate analysis, on merely one form or another of ideological purity or orthodoxy.

I. THE THEORETICAL FOUNDATIONS OF THE PCI'S STRATEGY

The Postwar Period

Both the PCI and its critics agree that the series of proposals which eventually were labeled The Italian Road to Socialism first made their appearance in the waning days of World War II.[5] To the PCI, this represents proof of continuity in its theory; to critics, it demonstrates a lineage which goes back to Soviet postwar interests, which in turn were more or less a re-hash of the popular front policy of the 1930s.[6] To be sure, the policies enunciated by Palmiro Togliatti in the immediate postwar period were very much in line with those of other communist parties.[7] The call for "progressive democracy," with its emphasis on immediate reconstruction and the postponement of most radical alterations of society; the decision to construct a mass party; the extremely broad definition of allies of the working class which excluded only fascists, collaborationists, and large or monopoly capital; the emphasis on an antifascist rather than an anticapitalist regime were common to all Western communist parties and essential to the USSR's foreign policy.

But does this make the *via italiana* and its less explicit forerunner of the late 1940s nothing but a slavish return to the contentious popular front formula of the Comintern's 1935 Seventh Congress? Along with Dimitrov, Togliatti was the major spokesman for the new policy at the Seventh Congress, but it is also well known that he was never very enthusiastic about the wholesale condemnation of all noncommunists even when this was the Comintern's policy during the "Third Period" (1928–34).[8] These facts suggest that if he found the popular front and "progressive democracy" periods congenial, Togliatti did so not out of a desire to please the Kremlin, but because they corresponded better to his own assessment of an appropriate strategy for Italy. To cite a final, telling example: the slogan of antifascist unity was an international one in the late 'forties, but it was most appropriate in a country where fascism has scored its earliest success against a divided opposition and was eventually swept out, in part, as a result of a united Resistance.

Furthermore, many of Togliatti's earliest postwar proposals went a good deal beyond the prevailing orthodoxy, and they suggest the calculations of a politician keenly aware of his party's historical limitations (above all, the defeat by fascism) and future obstacles (a relatively advanced country in the Allied sphere of influence). These considerations help explain why Togliatti was so insistent about making the PCI a large *mass* party, and also why he was committed to the creation of an extremely dense network of mass organizations in civil society. If we add to this his well-known conciliatory attitude on the religious question, we arrive at a composite, if incomplete, picture of a strategy which was taking no chances, either in terms of a reactionary wave sweeping away the workers' movement as had happened a quarter-century earlier, nor of an adventuristic assault on the pinnacles of state power.[9] His obsession with organization, alliances, and civil society in general indicate that Togliatti was digging in for the long run. In spite of numerous contradictory elements in the PCI's position, it is clear that the policies of the postwar period were not seen as merely a tactical interlude to be ridden out. As a perceptive analyst of European communism has noted, while this may have been an interlude for other communist parties, it was a constitutive period for the PCI after two long decades of exile and underground politics. Thus, in spite of surface similarities, the PCI line from 1944 differed *strategically* from other Western communist parties, and comparison with the PCF makes this evident. The Italian strategy can be called one of "presence and transformation" (although I would emphasize the former), while that of the French is labelled as a model of "encadrement and perseverance."[10] Even those critics who most strenuously criticize the PCI for its popular frontism, moreover, admit that Togliatti's original postwar formulations represented an "elaboration and qualitative alteration" of the original formula.[11]

Why should an excursion into the lineage of the *via italiana* concern itself with the popular front policy at all? Primarily because, as a socialist strategy, this policy raises more questions than it answers. Even in its most successful incarnations, it was defensive in nature, standing for a common front against fascism, not for socialism. It is of course true that the decision to form this type of alliance represented a giant step forward for communist parties which earlier had equated social-democracy with fascism, but the adoption of the popular front only meant that a suicidal path had been abandoned, not that a revolutionary one had been discovered.

Indeed, the difficulties involved in a theoretical justification of the popular front have not escaped even those who interpret this experience in terms more positive than those I have used above. Communists in particular have always dealt with this issue in an awkward fashion, usually concluding with a mechanical and somewhat hypocritical distinction between actions appropriate to the "bourgeois-democratic" and "socialist" stages of the revolution. Since the front involves reassuring noncommunist partners of the communists' good intentions, explanations based on a two-stage analysis can often be embarrassing.

Furthermore, even the two-stage analysis leaves open a variety of interpretations of the popular front, all of which seem to have been used, at one time or another, by major communist parties. The popular front can be seen as (a) a *tactical* expedient which simply holds bourgeois democracy to be more tolerable than fascism, therefore making it worth defending; (b) a *strategic* innovation which requires the participation of the working class for the completion of a flawed bourgeois revolution which will move toward socialism at some unspecified future date; or, as generally occurred in practice, (c) a combination of both of the above. To resolve these theoretical issues would require considerable effort, but under the extraordinary historical circumstances which confronted the left with Hitler, Mussolini, and the like, the fine points of doctrine took a back seat to the more pressing questions of survival.

Now, if we had to force Togliatti's postwar formulations into one of the above slots, (b) would clearly be the most appropriate.[12] But would it be entirely adequate? There is no doubt that Togliatti's interpretation of "progressive democracy" transcended the rigid distinction between bourgeois-democratic and socialist stages of Italy's transformation. He in fact (over) optimistically foresaw Italy's postwar future in terms of a society which was not yet socialist, but which was already more than a classical bourgeois democracy.[13] This may sound like the mechanical repetition of the Soviet line in the forties. but the historical record fully bears out Togliatti's dedication to these principles, and even helps explain why he was so optimistic about the future. The Resistance had been successful, and an institutional referendum had thrown out the monarchy. With the Socialist Party, the PCI had not only an apparently unshakable unity of action pact, but 40% of the popular vote in 1946. These two parties of the left formed a tripartite government with the Christian Democratic Party (DC), and Italy seemed to be on the road to extensive reforms and a progressive constitution. Moreover, Italian capitalism seemed to be on its last legs: major economic groups were not only in a shambles because of the war, but they were also in disgrace because of their collaboration with fascism.

All of the factors discussed above lead, on balance, to a rather original, mixed bag of domestic strategic projections in the PCI's postwar position. Togliatti's domestic proposals are marked by a heavy dose of defensiveness and a fear of a reactionary resurgence. At the same time, he appears to have made a very positive assessment of future potentialities, so much so that he seems to have been convinced that most needed reforms could be carried out within Italy's existing institutional framework. This optimistic outlook was fed by the assumption that Italian capitalism was irreparably decrepit: a PCI leader looking back on this period said that the prevailing assumption was that Italian capitalism represented "pure stagnation and putrefaction,"[14] Finally, Togliatti's optimism about being able to utilize existing institutions meant that very little was said in terms of a coherent socialist program for Italy, or about extra-institutional ways that society might to transformed.[15]

Complementing these factors is the mass party formulation where we also often find more the suggestion than the substance of profound theoretical innovations. With the aim of being present "in every crease and fold" of Italian society, Togliatti's "New Party" could quite easily be interpreted as the organizational extension of frontism, given its stated objective of rooting the party so solidly in the social structure that no reactionary storm could ever again sweep away the workers' movement.[16] The same rationale lies behind the creation of a vast network of mass organizations and associations, as demonstrated by Togliatti's detailed attention to the creation and extension of alliances between the proletariat and other social strata.[17] But here, too, the formulation is not purely defensive: at the same time that the party was to represent a bulwark against fascism, it would also furnish much of the leverage that would help exert enough pressure to transform society. Just as there is little documentary evidence which goes beyond an institutional framework where the domestic strategy is concerned, so is there a paucity of material which goes beyond a relatively narrow organizational perspective where the party is concerned.[18] Here, again, on balance, the legacy of the immediate postwar period is rather mixed.

Even a superficial reading of the PCI's ambivalent postwar legacy would suggest that the party strategy that was being evolved in that period contained numerous points of internal tension, if not outright contradiction. I have emphasized these aspects not only because they help put the origins of the *via italiana* in historical and theoretical perspective, and not only because they represented obvious limits on the PCI's analyses in 1944—47. The striking thing about the party strategy which emerged after 1956, as we shall see, is that it brought all of these tensions from the past with it, even those which seemingly were so historically contingent.

1956: The Strategy Reemerges

In the period between the XX Congress of the Communist Party of the Soviet Union and the VIII Congress of the PCI (March to December, 1956), the PCI dusted off and elaborated the positions outlined in the preceding section. The party's ability to move so swiftly in this direction while other communist parties floundered in the swamp of ideological de-Stalinization underscores the importance of the 1944–47 period to the PCI. The Italians, with a largely united top leadership, had the advantage of falling back on the postwar period's positions, which served both as an ideological anchor and a theoretical patrimony in the turbulent times that followed Khrushchev's revelations about Stalin and the uprising in Eastern Europe. In very short order, the main issues of contention at the summit of the Italian party centered around the speed and ways in which the *via italiana* was going to be put into practice.[19]

The return to orthodoxy of the Cold War had allowed the PCI to dodge comprehensive explanations of its strategic vision, but now the course of events demanded a clarification. And, especially with respect to the question of a socialist strategy for the West, many central aspects of the PCI's theory soon moved considerably beyond "progressive democracy" and the positions assumed in the immediate postwar period.

Perhaps the most significant departure of all concerns what the PCI calls its Strategy of Reforms. Togliatti took great pains after 1956 to distinguish a radical reform strategy from social-democratic reformism. The latter is both deterministic and passive: social-democrats assume that socialism will somehow "happen" when capitalism reaches a high stage of development; they thus generally present loose, piecemeal programs which in any event are not integrated into an overall analysis of a future society. The PCI, on the other hand, knows that socialism does not simply fall from the sky, but can only come about as a result of constant and highly conscious struggle. Reforms cannot be piecemeal but must instead consist of an integrated, organic whole. If successfully pressed in this fashion, structural reforms of Italian society would undermine monopoly capital's power bases in the country by increasingly restricting capital's maneuvering room. At the same time, success would broaden and make more combative the alliance of progressive forces.[20]

In other words, in the frontist and postwar formulations, democratic reforms usually were envisioned only in terms of *opening the way* to the eventual socialist transformation of Italy. The Reform

Strategy transcends the rigid division of the bourgeois-democratic and socialist stages of the revolutionary process. Now, under the correct conditions, Togliatti's claim was that *the very process* of transforming the country's political and economic structures in an advanced direction would itself be a part of Italy's socialist transformation. Where democratic traditions are relatively well rooted, the era of monopoly state capitalism means, in Togliatti's words, that "reforms become something different than what they were in the past."[21] Aside from superceding the often paralyzing two-stage analysis of revolution in the West and an artificial distinction between socialism and democracy, the Reform Strategy, in the PCI's view, also eliminates another false and paralyzing distinction inherited from the past. This is the dichotomy, "either reform *or* revolution." In the complex conditions of advanced capitalism, Togliatti argued, this formula leads one inevitably into either adventuristic, sectarian sterility, or the ineffectiveness of a passive accommodation to the existing system. Only the radical reform strategy elaborated above offers a way out of this dead end.[22]

A related innovation of the *via italiana* concerns not only Italian society, but the state as well. As the citations above make clear, in fact, it is only the existence of "monopoly state capitalism" that makes the Reform Strategy possible. But this raises some nettling questions about the way the party views the state in Italy. "Monopoly state capitalism" denotes a state which is the unrelenting instrument of monopoly capital, and hence a pure instrument of class rule. The problem with using this traditional definition of the state in conjunction with something as innovative as the Reform Strategy is that the latter assumes a state which can be altered in a progressive direction. This implies something akin to a neutral state, the exact opposite of a class instrument. The PCI's approach to this question has often been to avoid it, for it does not like to admit that its rather obscure formulation departs from both the letter and spirit of Leninism, which it clearly does. When it does address the issue, as a result, it is often quite evasive. In the PCI's view, just as it would be difficult to classify Italy as fully capitalist or fully socialist once major structural reforms are underway, so too will it be difficult, if not impossible, to classify the Italian state one way or another; it would be neither bourgeois nor proletarian.[23]

"Justifications" of this nature appear at first glance to be exercises in definitional acrobatics, or worse. But it is important to recognize a mitigating factor: the PCI, in analyses of this type, is not talking of the Italian state as it currently exists, but as it might become. Because the Italian Constitution is not a classical bourgeois document, but the product of the Resistance, and hence laden with clauses of a socialist or at least progressive nature, its full implementation would make the Italian state qualitatively different than other bourgeois-democratic regimes. Only under these conditions can the state be utilized progressively.[24]

As this synopsis of the Reform Strategy makes clear, there are numerous inherent problems, or at least tensions, in the *via italiana.* With regard to reforms, for example, how determining is the extra-institutional pressure of the mass reform movement? Is it and the organic nature of the reform proposals ultimately the determining factor in shifting the real balance of power in the country, as Togliatti seems to say in some places, or do *all* reforms, whatever their programmatic nature, take on a "socialist content" under monopoly capitalism, as he says elsewhere? Does the determining factor in the Italian state remain its generation-old genesis? If so, what is one to make of its increasing subordination to monopoly capital, and what borders on its structural identification with the Christian Democratic Party? Questions of this nature often make the PCI's analyses look like little more than a neat bit of fence-sitting. References to a society neither socialist nor capitalist and a state neither bourgeois nor proletarian hardly address such central theoretical problems. In fact, the PCI's often obscurantist language (at its worst, it is a curious mixture of Leninist remnants, Gramscian snippets, and Italian political circumlocutions) often raises more questions than it answers.

But if the PCI's positions on reforms and the state are riddled with problems, they at least offer several theoretical novelties. Where the *via italiana* becomes truly contradictory is the point at which Marxism is supposed to be most firmly grounded, i.e. in its view of the economy. It seems to me that the most basic question is, simply, how the PCI is able to insist on the continuity of its strategy from the 1940s to the 1970s when this period covers such wildly different sets of socioeconomic conditions in Italy. In 1944, when the strategy was first incompletely enunciated, Italy was shattered by war and was a predominantly agricultural country; by the late 1950s, she was undergoing a transformation which made her primarily industrial, and enjoying an economic "Miracle" besides; by the 1970s, she had reached a stage of very high monopoly concentration along with a bloated state sector. One would expect a revolutionary strategy to change significantly as socioeconomic conditions and indeed historical epochs change, but the underlying assumptions of the Italian Road to Socialism have been reaffirmed at every turn.[25]

What all of this reflects, of course, is the fact that the PCI's analysis never really proceeded in the "classical" fashion of first analyzing objective conditions and then developing an appropriate, made-to-order strategy. If anything, the process has followed exactly the reverse pattern for the PCI. This reversal in turn is the result of two previously noted conditioning factors, or ideological constraints, which are direct holdovers from the immediate postwar period. The first of these is the persistence of the postwar mentality which essentially ignored the more subtle aspects of Italian capitalism, or any need to proceed with a serious analysis of it, because it was considered to be so incompetent and moribund in any event. Strangely, this attitude appears to have remained dominant in the PCI during and long after the expansion of the late fifties – and, as we shall see, it was the cause of considerable debate by the beginning of the sixties. At any rate, the presence of such an attitude makes the absence of a serious economic analysis much less puzzling. The second holdover from the postwar period militates even more strongly against any attempt at a penetrating analysis of the Italian economy or social structure and is particularly helpful in aiding our understanding of why political, institutional analyses have always had the upper hand in elaborations of the *via italiana.* This, of course, is the fundamentally antifascist, defensive orientation that so strongly colored the postwar prescriptions and continues to remain, at base, the point of departure for the Italian Road to Socialism.

The intrinsic tensions in the *via italiana,* and the seemingly incongruous "primacy of the political moment" are nowhere more painfully evident, and consequently more easily understood, than with regard to the PCI's policy of alliances with nonproletarian strata. In its efforts to construct a bloc of disparate social forces which have little in common to bind them together, the party is often forced studiously to avoid any coherent socioeconomic analysis of the country, for that might suggest that the interests of its alleged allies were actually irreconcilable.[26] Since 1956, the PCI has steadfastly stood by its original postwar position, claiming that the broad antimonopolistic alliance posited then remains as valid as ever. Workers of the factories and fields, smallholding peasants, the urban *petite bourgeoisie,* and even small and medium factory owners are all seen as legitimate components of the broad alliance which will transform Italy. While paying lip service to the enormous differences that divide these strata and classes, the PCI has nonetheless consistently considered them all in rather undiscriminating fashion. The PCI's fear of alienating these strata, which comprise fascism's classic mass base, is far from an abstract concern in a country with Italy's history and current problems.

But the party's desire to win over sizeable portions of the *petite bourgeoisie* — a desire which many consider unrealistic in any event — has the unquestionable effect of forcing it to define its alliances first and then, in somewhat limping and often post hoc fashion, create proposals designed to appeal to these potential allies.

The foregoing should alert us to the fact that while many advances may have been made after 1956 in the PCI's domestic strategy, many of the same ambiguities of the postwar period reappeared a decade later. These ambiguities did not escape the attention of many party leaders, but it would take a series of jarring and unexpected events before even a partial challenge to prevailing interpretations was launched.

II. THE MAJOR IDEOLOGICAL DISPUTES OVER THE *VIA ITALIANA*

The Perspective After 1956

The most immediate stimulus to a debate over party strategy quite naturally came from abrupt changes in the USSR in 1956. The revelations about Stalin generated an extensive discussion which touched not only on the construction of socialism in the East but, logically, how the construction of socialism in the West could avoid the errors of the "socialist fatherland." These considerations in turn led to lively arguments about the nature of the party, its internal structures and operations, and its assumed role in the transformation of Italian capitalism. The debate was thus launched quite rapidly, with Togliatti playing a leading, if at first cautious, role in raising some of the most pertinent issues.[27]

A number of events prevented this discussion from becoming a sustained one in the PCI for several more years. Some events were international: the crushing of the Hungarian revolt forced communist parties to hasten to defend the Soviet Union's actions, which seemed to signal a return to some earlier formulations and allegiances. It certainly had the effect of dampening criticism of the USSR, especially since the PCI was literally under siege at home from all political parties on account of its identification with the Russians' acts. Inside the party as well, these events gave the sectarian old guard a breathing spell in their obstinate resistance to any suggestions of establishing some distance between the PCI and the USSR. Moreover, the party leaders had to fight against more than sectarian tendencies within the ranks, for there were also numerous elments who seemed ready to abandon Marxism-Leninism altogether in favor of an immediate accommodation to the system. Under these strained circumstances, an extended ideological debate among supporters of the *via italiana* was a dispensable luxury.[28]

In fact, it would take roughly another five years before an overlapping series of events — most of them outgrowths of Italy's rapidly changing economic and social structure — would force the PCI to come to terms with at least some of the most glaring gaps in its analysis.[29] While the party had already attributed some serious setbacks on the labor front to changing economic conditions, its full attention seems to have been attracted only when the dimensions of economic growth became collossal and, at the same time, a menacing series of *political* developments appeared on the horizon. The most disorienting of these was the unmistakable drift of the Socialist Party toward the DC and the vaunted Center-Left experiment. The resiliency of the economy, and the isolation of opposition, had evidently convinced the bulk of the PSI's leaders that the system was quite capable of carrying out important reforms which they felt they could influence. With equal ambition, PSI leaders also believed that, once provided, these reforms would erode the PCI's mass base in their favor.[30] As if this threat of isolation and erosion were not distressing enough, the PCI also found itself faced with what many considered to be a full-fledged organizational crisis characterized by waning membership and activism, and nonfunctioning grass-roots party units. A good deal of this crisis could be attributed to the disorientation and reflux following 1956, but it also was directly related to society's changing structure outstripping the adaptability of party organization and tactics.[31]

As has already been pointed out, even in the face of these events, the party's response largely consisted of a more or less peremptory "reaffirmation" of the validity of its analysis of the transition to socialism in the epoch of monopoly capitalism. At most, adjustments would be needed to take into account changes which had occurred. It took until the early 1960s for the party to pay more than superficial attention to the profound changes which had occurred, but its analysis of the situation, locked as it was into largely postwar formulations, moved with glacial slowness.[32] Ironically, after bandying the term "monopoly state capitalism" about for so long, when it was confronted by the genuine item, the party's intellectual apparatus seemed to become disoriented.

It was at this point chronologically, and on the issue of advanced capitalism's new qualities ideologically, that critics within the party began to grow increasingly restive. As the party came under increasingly penetrating scrutiny, divergent ideological positions became increasingly discernible within the PCI. Present since 1956, a "Left" and a "Right" within the party suddenly began to gain a good deal of attention, and it is with the disputes that involved these two tendencies that we will be most interested in our discussion. The importance of these two tendencies for this study is the fact that they represent logical extensions of the tensions in the *via italiana* that I have already pointed out.

The reader should be warned against making a number of inferential leaps which the terminology used in the next section may suggest, but which are not warranted by real facts. Because our interest is in the theoretical ramifications of the *via italiana,* our examination will focus on the most coherent and complete expressions of Right and Left in the PCI, and not on an exhaustive analysis of all positions in the party: it is important to remember that a predominance of leaders in the PCI can be clearly identified with neither leftist nor rightist interpretations of the *via italiana* but are, in the tradition of Togliatti, "centrists." It is also important to note that while various sectors or areas of the party have often quite correctly been identified with the Left or Right in a given dispute, it is risky to label them as entirely on one side or the other, or as coherent ideologues fighting for a set of firm principles. Organizational, regional, and personal factors all have contributed to what can only loosely be defined as leftist and rightist tendencies within the party organization.[33] Finally, these tendencies have only on extremely rare occasions — inevitably followed by expulsions — taken on organizational characteristics.

The Ideological Debate Within the Party

The internalization of the *via italiana* among top party leaders is nowhere better illustrated than by the fact that the major spokesmen for both the rightist and leftist tendencies in the 1960s were together, in 1956, pressing for as rapid a break with the Stalinist past as possible. Only with Stalinism largely behind them did the "Renovator's" latent differences become manifest.

The Right's leading exponent, Giorgio Amendola, interpreted the renovation of the PCI to mean a return to the "New Party" and "progressive democracy" of the 1944—47 period. De-Stalinization and the turbulent events of 1956, for the Right, were proof in themselves that the PCI had been renewed. The task then became simply to pick up where everyone had left off nearly a decade earlier, and this could best be accomplished by informing militants and potential adherents alike of the profound scope of the postwar formulations.[34] As should be obvious from so restricted an interpretation of the events of 1956, the Right has also always been reticent about calling for a more profound analysis of the shortcomings of the CPSU's XX Congress, or the PCI's VIII Congress.

For the Left, on the other hand, the VIII Congress was of extreme importance but represented only the first step the PCI would have to travel on the long path of renovation. Both it and the XX Congress hardly were seen as providing definitive explanations of the PCI's (or the CPSU's) limitations, nor did they provide really clear guidelines for future progress. Thus one item always very high on the Left's agenda has been its insistence on the need for deep probing into the historic and programmatic causes of the weaknesses of both Soviet and Italian communism. The underlying rationale is not one which favors exposés, but it is felt that only such probing can clarify the central problems related to the construction of socialism.[35]

Because the Right views the *via italiana* as needing no fundamental alterations, whenever it acknowledges problems it is forced to interpret them as failures in implementing or applying a correct line. The Left has been much more inclined to question underlying assumptions, even though it does not appear eager to reject cardinal principles completely. Nevertheless, the Left is willing to push where the Right is not. An early and important illustration concerns party organization and democracy. As early as 1956, Pietro Ingrao was arguing that the PCI could not place all the blame for its shortcomings on something simply labelled "bureaucratism"; nor was it very helpful to repeat mechanically that correct principles were being applied erroneously. In the face of an internal life which was so consistently stifled, the party's shortcomings could not be blamed on mere distortions of correct organizational principles. Instead, these principles themselves had to be reexamined.[36] Among the policies which were specifically denounced was the passing down of already-made decisions which lower levels of the party were expected to ratify automatically. This was responsible in large part for the rank-and-file's lack of comprehension of the party line, Ingrao pointed out, and he added that until real participation was stimulated from below, one could expect this ignorance to continue. In spite of the problems that so profound a reform of the party would raise, Ingrao warned in 1956 that it would be better to face them sooner rather than later.[37]

The more conservative emphasis of the Right in the PCI means that little time is spent discussing rank-and-file decision-making and qualitative changes in the mechanics of internal party democracy. The

Right has, in fact, generally assumed a very "hard line" on internal dissent in the party. But the question is not whether one interpretation is more democratic than another. It is, rather: What is the underlying vision that informs these interpretations? The Left puts its emphasis on ideas and initiatives in the party originating "from below"; the Right defines party democracy much more formally and institutionally, with decisions – and effective power – flowing from the top down.

Precisely the same emphases are evident in the Left's and Right's respective analyses of the forms and role that grass-roots participation ought to play in society as well as in the party. Ingrao has consistently criticized the PCI for discussing only institutions which already exist when it speaks of the structural transformation of Italian society. He complains that there is little interest in developing new forms of grass-roots democracy. On the societal plane as well, then, "democracy from below" has gotten only lip service from the party: it has been "posited as a mere 'adjunct,' and not as one of the levers needed to transform the state."[38] For Amendola and the Right, the role assigned to the masses as protagonists in winning reforms is extremely limited. Even when using phrases like "mobilization from below" or "democratic and unitary grass-roots organizations," the Right does not transcend the framework of traditional party structures and allegiances. "Unitary" means bringing together the parties of the left *as parties*.[39] For the Left in the PCI, the term "unitary" generally connotes a *movement* which is not hampered by party labels.

It should be apparent that these are neither minor nor mere semantic differences, but expressions of profoundly different interpretations of the party and the revolutionary process. In the arguments of the Right we see quite clearly the logical extension of "the primacy of the political (or institutional)," which we have already pointed out as one pole in many of the *via italiana's* tension-ridden propositions. The Left is equally consistent in the opposite direction, i.e. toward the "social" moment of the equation. These emphases, as we have noted, color all levels of analysis, and it is not hard to deduce from them two very different models of revolution.

Schematically, the Right's position can be defined as favoring a majority revolution from above. It sees the *via italiana* in essentially linear, nondialectical terms, emphasizing formal organizations and institutions rather than any process which first transforms society. Its ultimate goal seems to be the entry of the PCI into the Italian government, rather than the realization of a specific program, and, to this end, it is fairly undiscriminating in its search for the widest possible range of support for the PCI.[40] As far as radical reforms are concerned, only *after* the PCI has entered the government does it see reforms with a truly socialist content being possible to realize.[41]

The Left's emphasis is centered much more around the role that social forces will play in the transformation of Italy. Related to this emphasis is a good deal of skepticism about the radical potentialities of Italy's existing institutions. This position is much more aptly summarized as favoring a majority revolution from below. But the majority that the Left seeks is necessarily quite different from that of the Right which, with its belief in the paramount need to enter government, hopes for the proverbial fifty per cent plus one.[42] The Left's is a more militant, active conception of the relationship between the masses, democracy, and socialist content, and, as a result, the majority they seek must be of a strategic, and not simply a numerical nature. Although all elements in the PCI wantonly cite Antonio Gramsci to legitimize their positions, the Left's interpretation of alliances certainly seems to be much closer to what Gramsci called the "historic bloc" *(blocco storico)* of forces that would make the Italian revolution.[43] Many truly radical changes, as well as a qualitative collective leap of consciousness among the masses, will have to have occurred *prior to and as conditions for* the PCI's entry into any government, in this view.

The contrast between the differing interpretations of the *via italiana* becomes irreconcilable on this point. It once again brings us back to the distinction between an anticapitalist and an antifascist strategy. In practical terms, this distinction determines whether one welcomes or fears a serious crisis of the Italian political and socialist system. The more aggressive interpretation of the party's aims would view such a crisis as one of its eventual goals (assuming, of course, that the movement had built up an organizational and political alternative to the regime as it went along). The conservative interpretation, on the other hand, reacts defensively to the suggestion of a serious crisis. Any such crisis automatically carries with it a threat from antidemocratic and fascist elements, and this threat, as we have seen, has always been the primary concern of the least militant elements in the PCI. Hence when the Left is inclined to step up the attack on the system, the Right tends to call for the system's preservation in the name of broad democratic and antifascist unity. More often than not, this defensive reaction leads to attempts to moderate social tensions and to curb the more radical demands of the labor movement and of the Left in general.

The truly profound theoretical differences between Left and Right have obviously been most clear when they and others have been able to lock horns directly. This frequently occurred in the past, in the relatively rarified pages of the party's theoretical journal, *Critica marxista*. Lively and often bitter debates covered such disparate and interesting topics as popular fronts, the party in Marxism, and the construction of socialism.[44] But the most fascinating and instructive clashes, not surprisingly, took place and continue to take place on questions of direct relevance to party policy. The earliest of these encounters, and the one which most clearly fixed the terms of the entire ideological debate until the end of the 1960s, occurred, as has been observed, at the start of the sixties.

While the Left did not abandon any of its precepts, it expended most of its energy in the early sixties in an attempt to get the PCI to reassess its economic interpretations and the alliance strategy which seemed wedded to them. In the Left's opinion, the "Economic Miracle" demonstrated that Italian capitalism, far from being putrefied, was both mature and cunning. Monopoly expansion and rationalization raised a number of qualitatively new problems for the workers' movement, problems involving not only the immediate needs of the working class, but the entire political structure of the country. With the increasing shift of real power to monopolies, the state sector of the economy, and the bureaucracy, it therefore became increasingly important to define clearly democratic forms of control which would keep the dictation of priorities out of the hands of the monopolies or the supposedly "neutral" bureaucracy and technocracy.[45]

To the Left, the Center-Left represented a threat not so much because it threatened to solve Italy's problems or steal the PCI's votes. Rather, its real menace was that it represented a design for a rationalization of advanced (neo)capitalism. This threat could not be met by stating, as Togliatti had done, that the PCI would look with interest at the works of the Center-Left and perhaps even support the most worthwhile reform proposals. A piecemeal approach of this type greatly increases the threat of rationalization and increased monopoly control. Instead of responding in a vague, "counterpunching" way, approving this, opposing that reform, the Left felt that a much more precise response was necessary.

This analysis goes straight back to the role that an organic reform program and mass mobilization is supposed to play in the *via italiana*. A number of writers stressed the dangers in any sort of piecemeal approach for social-democratic, partial reforms are too easily reabsorbed by the system. They may not truly undercut capitalism's real power bases; or they may only be accepted or implemented in part, with their key elements ignored or perverted; or the working class may ultimately be bought off with marginal rewards; or the bosses may, if allowed breathing space, regroup and make up their losses in some way. Only with mass mobilizations to keep up unrelenting pressure, and a coherent program of truly strategic reforms can the risk of absorption be minimized.[46] Thus the Left claimed that only this kind of "global alternative" to the Center-Left would offer a truly radical alternative to Italy.[47]

Demands for this "global alternative" were a sharp and direct slap at the bulk of the PCI leadership — not only the Right — which brushed aside any suggestions that the party be more specific about its vague slogans extolling progress, democracy, and justice. Amendola made it clear that he viewed any program to be an incumbrance. He went back to the period of "progressive democracy" to justify this claim with a variety of citations.[48] He similarly had little patience with the Left's opposition to piecemeal reforms, and argued that if the PCI always proposed reforms which could not be reabsorbed by the system, "we would be fighting, in today's concrete conditions, simply to be defeated at every turn."[49] As we have noted, even Togliatti had put emphasis on the need to have an organic reform program, but to Amendola, with his belief that the only reforms that really count will come later, this was an incomprehensible distinction which people made to be "fashionable."[50] If Togliatti's silence during this period suggests a desire to avoid the issue, Amendola's response shows that the only way he could address this question was by denying its relevance.

Not all of the Left's challenges were met in this evasive and often curious fashion. The "global alternative" was often very adroitly countered, in admirable Marxist fashion, with the claim that a truly revolutionary strategy could not draw up a "blueprint" of future society. Moreover, Amendola made some telling criticisms of some of the leftists whose arguments, he said, were altogether too schematic. For one thing, they seemed interested in only worker-boss differences; for another, they seemed to have reduced everything in their analysis to the development of the monopolies. This latter position completely ignores the wretchedness of Italy's backward areas, like the South, with its implicit argument that only mature capitalism's developments are important.[51]

For the Left, the alliance strategy with its roots in the antifascist reconstruction was made obsolete by postwar economic development. For one thing, many new groups (technicians, white-collar workers, teachers, and students, to name a few) were numerically and strategically more important to a transformation of Italy than the artisans and shopkeepers whom the PCI seemed to spend the bulk of its time trying to court. Moreover, the indiscriminate lumping together of so many disparate elements reduced the program which they could be expected to support to one of the lowest common denominator. Instead, distinctions had to be made and only those groups with an objective interest in a socialist Italy should be part of the party's progressive bloc.[52] Amendola — and in this case the rest of the party — drew a different conclusion from the expansion of monopoly power. There had indeed been changes as the monopolies expanded, but these changes did not call for a more discriminating alliance policy. On the contrary, they create "new possibilities for the *expansion* of our system of alliances," extending "the basis for alliances with the working class to *all of the strata* victimized by monopolistic expansion."[53]

I have dwelled extensively on the early sixties in part because I feel that this period has not received the attention it merits, in part because I have dealt with other contentious periods elsewhere,[54] but primarily because the fundamental differences between the Left and the Right in the PCI are so vividly apparent in that debate. Lest one get the impression that the issues discussed a decade ago were so specific as to be outdated by now, a brief reference to the PCI's most recent ideological travails will demonstrate that this is decidely not the case.

Although Italy is not Chile, and the *via italiana* differs in many important respects from the Popular Unity government and program of Salvador Allende, enough similarities remained to make the PCI an extremely interested observer of Chilean events. Allende's attempts to carry out structural reforms with respect for parliamentary methods, — or at least within the framework of bourgeois legality — his initially successful attempts to court at least some elements of the *petite bourgeoisie,* and his Christian Democratic opposition hardly escaped the PCI's attention. It is thus not suprising that the tragic end of this experiment made the PCI leadership very reflective about its own strategy. It is also not suprising (although it may be disappointing) that the blatant failure of Popular Unity's attempts to resolve its most fundamental problems on a purely institutional level, its courtship of the DC long after this was productive, and its wooing of the middle classes did not cause the PCI's top leadership to reflect on the similarities between these events and their own approach. After all, one can hardly expect a party to consider dropping its entire ideological baggage after nearly thirty years. What was somewhat surprising, however, was the haste with which secretary-general Enrico Berlinguer reasserted, in unequivocal terms, the party's alliance strategy, as well as the broad, antifascist unity which was the well-spring of the *via italiana*. He also pointed out that the events in Chile demonstrated that even a majority for the left was not sufficient to offset a reactionary offensive. The only way to achieve the truly broad consensus which would make progress possible, therefore, was to arrive at an "historic compromise" with the Christian Democratic Party.[55]

Most of Berlinguer's formulation sounds extremely familiar, though even the "historic compromise," as inappropriate as it sounds given the context, is not a bolt out of the blue.[56] But what interests us here is not to dissect the *via italiana's* latest qualifications. It is, instead, to examine how an alternative interpretation of this strategy would be likely to emphasize different aspects and draw different conclusions.

Interestingly, in Pietro Ingrao's reaction we have not only a contemporary re-statement of the Left's fundamental concerns, but we also have the Left's major spokesman of the sixties. And Ingrao's response minces few words.[57] Whereas the party's official interpretation emphasizes the divisive extremism of some of the elements in Popular Unity, and whereas some of the PCI's more conservative members expressed reservations that the Popular Unity program may have been too ambitious, Ingrao does not feel that these were its basic shortcomings. The Chileans were not too advanced. If anything, they were not advanced enough: "They moved ahead without a plan for the political unification of the bloc of forces they wanted to create, and in fact, they even were totally devoid of an organic economic plan." In a more general comment on the problems of alliance building, Ingrao stressed that

> The key to the problem rests, that is, in the construction of a system of alliances which is not simply a compromise between interests which diverge with respect to a process of the transformation of society, but which works to unify popular forces by means of a democratic dynamic based on a project for restructuring production and the state. [This will have to be done] employing all the tactical compromises that may be necessary, but the aim must be the construction of an alliance which is strategic in nature, and thus capable of withstanding even traumatic crises, even that general confrontation to which the adversary might resort.

He adds that if one really wished to undertake a process of transformation, the party structures and the manipulative party-mass relationships which presently exist in Italy would never allow a progressive coalition to survive the kind of crises it would have to withstand.

These comments refer not only to noncommunist parties: elsewhere, discussing the same topic, Ingrao decries what he calls the erroneous conception of party-union relations as "a summit meeting of leaders which bypasses the masses."[58]

This analysis should demonstrate the continuing existence, and viability, of an alternative application of the tenets of the *via italiana* after more than ten years. On one level, this suggests a continuing tension and dialectic in the party strategy. On another level, however, the continued existence of the leftist interpretation on the fringes, if not entirely outside of, the prevalent interpretation of the *via italiana* within the party suggests not a dialectic, but a waltz without a partner. This does not necessarily mean that the Right has won an unquestioned victory in the PCI's ideological wars, but it at least suggests that the Left may have lost. That suggestion, in turn, leads to very troubling conclusions for anyone who sees in the more dynamic, "social" interpretation of the party strategy the really original theoretical potential of the PCI. It would in fact imply, and perhaps represent an open admission, that the PCI had abandoned its radical potential.

Obviously enough, one is not likely to find someone drawing these conclusions and remaining in the party. But at least some members of the Left eventually did reach just these conclusions. In the course of their intellectual journey, they were involved in the most spectacular debate over party strategy that the PCI has had since the war.

The Debate Moves Outside the PCI: The Case of Il Manifesto

Nothing ever occurs in a purely linear fashion in the PCI, and the trials and tribulations of the Left within the party are not an exception. In 1966, Ingrao and the entire Left seemed to have been roundly rebuked by the XI Party Congress, which repudiated demands for both a "global alternative" and a more democratic party structure. In addition, Ingrao was attacked, often viciously, by ranking party leaders.[59] But, just three years later, the XII Congress appeared to sanction many of the Left's well-known positions and the party seemed to be moving significantly leftward.[60] Several of the most vocal critics of party strategy at the XII Congress, most of them long identified with the PCI's Left, began to publish a monthly journal, *Il Manifesto*, just a few months after the congress ended. Because of the fact that they were publishing a political magazine outside the party's auspices, but especially because of the things they were saying in that magazine, the major exponents of the "Manifesto" group were expelled from the PCI late in 1969.

What explains the apparent turnabout of the PCI in three short years? Why would it undergo such a clamorous attack from the left precisely when it appeared to be moving in a more radical direction? What was *Il Manifesto* saying that was so intolerable? As one might suspect, the answers to all those questions are quite closely inter-related.

Whether the PCI moved only far enough to accommodate itself to the rush of events, or whether it actually intended to embark boldly on a modified course is a question we cannot possibly address in adequate fashion here, but it is undeniable that 1968–69 saw it move consider-ably. A simple enumeration of the most significant events of that period will provide some idea of what their cumulative impact must have been. It also explains why the theses of the Left could hardly be brushed aside.

1. The Italian labor movement was more militant and united than it had been for a generation.

2. The Center-Left, having neither isolated the PCI nor reformed Italy, was moribund.

3. Students, as well as labor, were extremely militant. Across the border, the May-June "Events" of 1968 had left the PCF in the lurch.

4. The Czech Spring, which the PCI had strongly supported, came to an abrupt end in August, 1968, and the PCI openly and strongly condemned the Soviets' actions.

Although the PCI responded quite flexibly to all these events, its actions were still liberally sprinkled with its characteristic caution and ambiguity. Moreover, it quickly found itself in trouble with some of the middle strata on account of its brief flirtation with the labor movement in its most militant moments. Particularly with the extreme right beginning to show signs of revitalization, the party rapidly backed away from some of its more radical postures almost as quickly as it had assumed them.

But while this period may have seemed like a particularly "hot" interlude to most of the party's leaders, it was viewed in a different light by a handful of leaders within the party which shortly would form the "Manifesto" group. They attributed exceptional importance to the events which were unfolding and, partly as a result of this, they interpreted the PCI's reversion to form as definitive proof of its loss of revolutionary elan.

Long before the XII Congress, in fact, two future members of this group were led by the student movement and the French "Events" to a series of radical critiques of the PCI's structure, its related ability to respond to the contradictions of advanced capitalism, and its international system of alliances.[61] One of these efforts could generously be interpreted as entirely within the Left's language and perspective.[62] The other, however, was filled with rather more heretical observations, e.g. that the French "Events" have shown "that the revolution certainly cannot be carried out with the theoretical and organizational instruments which the workers' movement currently has at its disposal"; or, that to work with and coordinate the new movements typical of advanced capitalism, "the revolutionary party cannot be the one that we presently know."[63] These observations should not have been altogether surprising, coming as they did from the man who years earlier had written in the party press that Togliatti's postwar formula was, at best, an attempt to breathe life into the popular front.[64] But they do suggest the urgency that he and his comrades felt.

Thus, by the time *Il Manifesto* hit the stands, its ideators already seemed convinced that the PCI was vacillating and on its way to backsliding (a proposition that seems at least arguable to me). It began to criticize the USSR heavily from the very first issue. In addition, it looked favorably on Chinese events and lambasted the PCI press for its biased coverage of China. In an editorial which won it no favor in the hierarchy or among the rank-and-file of the PCI, *Il Manifesto* said that a cultural revolution was needed in the PCI.[65] It condemned the elitism and manipulation of the party's ruling circles in an article which is probably the best description of decision-making in the PCI ever written.[66] This type of consistent fare, spiced with numerous accusations of "neofrontism" directed at the PCI, shortly sealed the group's fate in the party.[67]

With the group outside the PCI, and with their conviction that the party as it currently exists is a nonrevolutionary force, the polemical tone of many articles increased, but *Il Manifesto's* analysis also moved in an entirely unhindered fashion, following only the logic of the group's assumptions. In short order, the journal moved to an outright condemnation of the USSR. Until the leadership was entirely replaced, it argued, the situation in the Soviet Union would be hopeless. In addition to this, the Soviet Union's global aims were flatly stated to be counterrevolutionary.[68] In the PCI, the Right is seen as having triumphed, and labels like "a new kind of revisionism" and "a new type of reformism" are applied to the party.[69]

These bitter attacks are part of the constant fare of *Il Manifesto* (which changed its format to a daily in 1971). They are no doubt the product of the group's sincere belief that the PCI has betrayed its historic mission, but their tone often reinforces the impression that only ex-members can hate the former source of their allegiance with such intensity. But it would be an error to dismiss *Il Manifesto* out of hand, for, aside from its sometimes excessive rhetoric and occasional blunders on the political scene (e.g. its humiliating defeat in the 1972 elections), its insights into the PCI's innermost workings, limitations, and contradictions are superb.[70] Moreover, the passage of time has tempered their more strident attacks on the PCI.

Indeed, another reason for the bitterness of *Il Manifesto's* attacks on the PCI may well lie not only in their historic proximity to the party, but in their fundamental assumptions about a revolutionary strategy for advanced capitalism. The limitations of the PCI's theories have certainly been laid bare by members of the group. But the fact remains that they are not only products of, but remain quite close to, the basic assumptions that inform the strategic vision of the PCI's Left as it has been presented in this essay. Perhaps the fact that they see themselves as Gramsci's heirs makes them forget that at least some others in the PCI share this ambitious presumption. On one issue, at least, some distance has been established quite convincingly between *Il Manifesto* and the PCI's Left. This is the question of Workers' Councils and the role they might be presumed to play in the revolutionary process.[71]

But it is simply impossible to ignore the bulk of commitments which seem to be common to both sides.[72] Surely there must be a common ideological source when both strategic visions include:

(a)   a primary role assigned to social forces;

(b)   an emphasis on extrainstitutional, grass-roots participatory forms;

(c)   an open, flexible party, the organic outgrowth of a mass movement it is able to coordinate and direct without manipulation;

(d)   an aggressive reform strategy which emphasizes the importance of intermediate objectives, but insists that they be an integral part of a unified, coherent program which aims at the total transformation of capitalist relations;

(e)   an historic bloc of forces which is the expression of society's most combative elements, linked strategically on the basis of their anticapitalist interests.

To the extent that these assumptions remain at the core of the strategic perspective of the Left which remains within the PCI, then the quandary it faces is at least as great as that of the "Manifesto" group. The latter at least have recognized that the PCI is neither willing nor able to translate these assumptions into reality.[73] Given more than ten years of frustration (in some cases closer to twenty), and given the need to apply this strategy in a total fashion, it must be obvious to the internal Left that radical turnabouts are not forthcoming from the PCI. Or perhaps it is not so obvious: many other varieties of revolutionary theory depend, in the ultimate analysis, on some sort of gigantic crisis. But this does seem to leave those inside the PCI with a forlorn hope; meanwhile, those on the outside seem condemned to frustration. In light of the truly advanced nature of this strategy, and its tantalizing promise that a revolution in the West is possible, neither of the current options offers much consolation.

NOTES

1. One must naturally interpret these events in their proper context. In 1956, any kind of distance established between a communist party and the Soviet Union was, *ipso facto,* of primary concern. There was, at least originally, also a natural tendency for scholarship to follow this line in the English-speaking world, in light of the obvious focus on the USSR in communist studies prior to and somewhat after 1956. The definitive study of the PCI's international involvements in this period is Donald L.M. Blackmer's *Unity in Diversity: The Italian Communist Party and the International Communist Movement,* (M.I.T. Press, Cambridge, Mass., 1967).

2. An early and solid analysis is that of Giuseppe Tamburrano, "Lo sviluppo del capitalismo e la crisi teorica dei comunisti italiani," *Tempi Moderni,* V, (luglio-settembre, 1962), 5–36. See also P.A. Allum's brief and incisive *The PCI Since 1945* (University of Reading Occasional Monograph, Reading, England, 1970). An extremely valuable synthetic analysis is Alessandro Pizzorno's, "Il PCI e il ruolo dell 'opposizione in Italia" (mimeograph, 1972). Sidney Tarrow has made numerous excellent contributions; for his most recent effort, see "Communism in Post-Revolutionary Europe: Some Generalizations from the French and Italian Cases" (mimeograph, 1973), especially pp. 10–37.

3. The PCI's blatant manipulation of Gramsci to justify each and every turn in its policies has led to something of an anti-Gramscian revolt in Italy. For an interesting discussion see Massimo L. Salvadori, "Orientamenti dell'attuale storiografia del Partito comunista d'Italia," in his *Gramsci e il problema storico della democrazia* (Einaudi Turin, 1970).

4. There has been so much of this literature since the late 1960s that it would serve little purpose to enumerate such repetitive productions. Two of the earliest and best examples of this type of criticism can be found in Livio Maitan's (Trotskyist) *PCI 1945–69: Stalinismo e opportunismo* (Samonà e Savelli, Rome,

1969), and Lucio Libertini's (Leninist) *Capitalismo moderno e movimento operatio* (Samonà e Savelli, Rome, 1965).

5. Even the term "an Italian Road to Socialism" appeared in this period. See Palmiro Togliatti, Address to the 1947 National Conference of the PCI, "La nostra lotta per la democrazia e per il socialismo," reprinted in *Critica marxista*, II (luglio-ottobre, 1964), 192.

6. These are obviously criticisms "from the left" of the PCI. For a sample of accusations of "neofrontism," see almost any issue of *Il Manifesto*, 1969–71.

7. Togliatti's earliest enunciation of what was to be the PCI's position in the postwar period can be found in Togliatti, *La politica di Salerno*, (Editori Riuniti, Rome, 1969). Especially important is an April, 1944, speech delivered in Naples almost as soon as he arrived back in Italy; cf. pp. 3–41.

8. For a brief, excellent summary of PCI friction with the Comintern during the "Third Period," see Ernesto Ragionieri, "Il giudizio sul fascismo. La lotta contro il fascismo. I rapporti con l'Internazionale comunista," in Paolo Spriano, et al., *Problemi di storia del Partito comunista italiano* (Editori Riuniti, Rome, 1971), pp. 39–42.

9. For Togliatti's earliest full statement on the party, see "I compiti del Partito nella situazione attuale," *Critica marxista*, I, (settembre–dicembre, 1963), 327–357; this is a reprint of a speech delivered in Florence on October 3, 1944. On mass organizations, civil society, and alliances with the middle classes, see his speech in Reggio Emilia, September 24, 1946, "Ceto medio e Emilia rossa," reprinted in *Critica marxista*, II (luglio–ottobre, 1964), 13–46. For Togliatti's speech at the Constituent Assembly in which the PCI's support for the Lateran Treaties was announced, see "Sui rapporti tra la Chiesa e lo Stato," *Discorsi alla Costituente* (Editori Riuniti, Rome, 1973), pp. 41–56.

10. Tarrow, *op. cit.*, p. 11 and p. 20.

11. Lucio Magri, 'Il valore e il limite delle esperienze frontiste," *Politica e teoria nel marxismo italiano 1959–1969*, edited by Giuseppe Vacca, (De Donato, Bari, 1972), p. 180.

12. Ragionieri, *op. cit.*, pp. 49–50 offers convincing arguments to the effect that the PCI's choice for the popular front in the 1930s was an "irreversible choice."

13. Note, for example, the interesting balance of optimism and pessimism in "I compiti del Partito nella situazione attuale," pp. 342–44.

14. Pietro Ingrao, "Il XX Congresso del PCUS e l'VIII Congresso del PCI," in Spriano, et al., *op. cit.*, p. 142.

15. By "extra-institutional" I mean not so much illegal tactics as organizational forms not directly tied to the country's formal political and parliamentary structure. Examples would be the Committees of National Liberation, workers' factory councils, or, more generically, mass protest movements and popular mobilizations. Some of these issues actually were the subject of serious discussion in postwar Italy, but they were rapidly dropped with little objection from the PCI.

16. Togliatti, "I compiti del Partito nella situazione attuale," pp. 339ff. See also Pietro Secchia, "I Cln al potere in un dibattito della sinistra," *Critica marxista*, III (marzo–aprile, 1965), 39.

17. The question of alliances is dealt with extensively in Stephen Hellman, "The PCI's Alliance Strategy and the Case of the Middle Classes," in *Communism in Italy and France*, edited by Donald L.M. Blackmer and Sidney Tarrow (Princeton University Press, Princeton, N.J., 1975).

18. See, e.g., *La politica di Salerno, op. cit.*, pp. 17–18.

19. This is not to suggest that the PCI was spared the trauma of de-Stalinization, but only to note that the bulk of the national leadership, in 1956, was not Stalinist and the party thus avoided both vertical divisions and a paralyzed – because Stalinist – top leadership. There was tremendous resistance to de-Stalinization in the *middle and lower* leadership cadres of the PCI, and this eventually resulted in widespread purges of the old guard in the late 1950s.

20. See Togliatti's address to the VIII Congress and the 1960 IX Congress in Togliatti, *Nella democrazia e nella pace verso il socialismo* (Editori Riuniti, Rome, 1963), p. 52 and pp. 146ff. A good synthetic statement is Togliatti's "Capitalismo e riforme di struttura," in *La via italiana al socialismo* (Editori Riuniti, Rome, 1964), pp. 263–268.

21. Conclusions to the IX Congress, *Nella democrazia e nella pace. . .* pp. 172–173.

22. "Capitalismo e riforme di struttura," *Ibid.*

23. See, e.g., Emilio Sereni, "Antifascismo democrazia socialismo nella rivoluzione italiana," *Critica marxista*, IV (settembre–dicembre, 1966), 5–9. See also Luigi Longo, "E' possibile in regime capitalistico eliminare il potere economico e politico dei monopoli? ", *Critica marxista*, I (marzo–aprile, 1963), 94–108.

24. See Togliatti's justification to this effect in his address to the X Congress, *Nella democrazia e nella pace. . .* p. 223.

25. See, for example, the Political Document of the 1969 XII Congress, which

underscores "the full validity of the reform strategy and the alliance strategy as the line for advancing toward socialism in the phase of monopoly state capitalism," *XII Congresso del PCI: Atti e risoluzioni* (Editori Riuniti, Rome, 1969), p. 783.

26. Cf. Hellman, *op. cit.*

27. Ingrao, *op. cit.*, pp. 153–57, concisely discusses and analyzes Togliatti's somewhat uneven approach immediately following the XX Congress.

28. For a detailed discussion, see Blackmer, *Unity in Diversity.* . . .

29. There had, however, been alarms sounded by high-ranking party leaders as early as 1956. Fabrizio Onofri, expelled in 1957 for his "pessimism," recounts his early experience and analysis in *Classe operaia e partito* (Laterza, Bari, 1957). See especially, p. 28 and pp. 33–34.

30. The historic background and the various parties' positions with regard to the Center-Left are perceptively analyzed in Giuseppe Tamburrano, *Storia e cronaca del centro-sinistra* (Feltrinelli, Milan, 1971).

31. The best comprehensive statement of the PCI's problems and aims for this period is Enrico Berlinguer, "Lo stato del partito in rapporto alle modificazioni della società italiana," *Critica marxista*, I (luglio–settembre, 1963), 186–213.

32. Tamburrano, "Lo sviluppo del capitalismo e la crisi teorica dei comunisti italiani," p. 21, puts the PCI's acceptance of profound changes in society at 1961.

33. For instance, areas of great industrial concentration like that around Turin have generally been "leftist" on domestic strategy, while those with strong social-democratic traditions and little large industry like the "Red Belt" in Emilia-Romagna have generally been "rightist."

34. See, e.g., Giorgio Amendola, "La crisi della società italiana e il Partito comunista," *Critica marxista*, VII (marzo–aprile, 1969), 28.

35. See Ingrao, *op. cit.*, for the leftist view. An excellent comparison of Left and Right on this issue can be drawn from the single issue of *Critica marxista*, VI (luglio-ottobre, 1968), where articles by Amendola and Ingrao appear back-to-back. See Amendola, "Venticinque anni dopo lo scioglimento dell'Internazionale comunista," pp. 63–87, and Ingrao, "Problemi dell'edificazione socialista," pp. 88–103.

36. "La democrazia interna, l'unità, e la politica dei comunisti," *Rinascita* (May–June, 1956), 315.

37. *Ibid.*, pp. 317–318.

38. Ingrao, "Il XX Congresso del PCUS e l'VIII Congresso del PCI," p. 165.

39. Amendola, "Lotta di classe e sviluppo economico dopo la liberazione," in *Tendenze del capitalismo italiano: Atti del convegno economico dell'Istituto Gramsci,* Vol. 1 (Editori Riuniti, Rome, 1962), pp. 205ff.

40. See, for example, "Partito di Governo," *l'Unità,* August 21, 1969. For intelligent summaries of Left-Right differences in the PCI, see Jon Halliday, "Structural Reform in Italy – Theory and Practice," *New Left Review,* 50 (July–August, 1968), 73–92, and Gino Rocchi, "Il PCI dall'XI al XII Congresso," *Relazioni sociali,* IX (marzo–aprile, 1969), 234ff.

41. Amendola, in my opinion, would not deny this at all. See "La crisi della società italiana. . .," p. 44.

42. Note the mechanical, additive approach and discussion in Amendola, "Movimento e organizzazione delle masse," *op. cit.,* p. 162. See as well his introduction to *Il comunismo italiano nella seconda guerra mondiale,* edited by G. Amendola (Editori Riuniti, Rome, 1963), pp. xxxviii–xxxix.

43. This is not the place to examine Gramsci's complex theories and terminology. A discussion of his *blocco storico* is in Giorgio Bonomi, *Partito e rivoluzione in Gramsci* (Feltrinelli, Milan, 1973), pp. 33–35. An excellent clarification in English is Grant Amyot, "Gramsci as a Political Scientist," (mimeograph, 1974), pp. 14–16.

44. On popular fronts, see, for the Left, Lucio Magri, "Il valore e il limite delle esperienze frontiste," cited in note 11, which originally appeared in *Critica marxista,* III, (luglio–agosto, 1965), 36–63. For the Right, see Amendola, "Insegnamenti del VII Congresso dell'Ic (Rileggendo Dimitrov)," *Ibid.,* 21–35. See also Emilio Sereni, "Appunti per una discussione sulle politiche di fronte popolare e nazionale," pp. 6–28. For a series of disparate articles on the nature of the party, see *Critica marxista,* I. (settembre–dicembre, 1963). For the construction of socialism, refer to note 35.

45. See especially Bruno Trentin, "Le dottrine neocapitalistiche e l'ideologia delle forze dominanti nella politica economica italiana," *Tendenze del capitalismo italiano, op. cit.,* Vol. 1, pp. 97–144. This two-volume set is an excellent document of contemporary concerns about neocapitalism and the threat of the Center-Left in 1962.

46. Alfredo Reichlin, "Aspetti della politica unitaria col Psi," *Critica marxista,* I (luglio–agosto, 1963), especially p. 28. Filippo Di Pasquantonio, "Il capitalismo di

Stato nel quadro generale delle tendenze del capitalismo italiano," *Tendenze. . . ,*
Vol. 2, pp. 241–242.

47. Ingrao, "Un nuovo programma per tutta la sinistra," *Rinascita,* (December
25, 1965), 6–7. Trentin, *op. cit.,* p. 139.

48. "La lezione dei CLN" (written in 1963), in *Comunismo antifascismo resist-
enza* (Editori Riuniti, Rome, 1967), p. 305.

49. "Conclusions," *Tendenze del capitalismo italiano,* Vol. 1, p. 439. See also
Halliday, p. 85.

50. *Tendenze. . . ., Ibid.*

51. *Ibid.,* p. 423 and pp. 426–427.

52. Trentin, pp. 141–143.

53. Amendola, "Conclusions," p. 427. Emphasis added.

54. "The PCI's Alliance Strategy and the Case of the Middle Classes."

55. Two articles by Berlinguer are particularly relevant. "Via democratica e viol-
enza reazionaria," *Rinascita* (October 5, 1973), 3–4; and "Alleanze sociali e
schieramenti politici," *Rinascita* (October 12, 1973), 3–5. The latter article closes
with the appeal for an "historic compromise."

56. The PCI has quite openly been seeking a rapprochement with the DC since at
least 1970.

57. All of Ingrao's comments – with the exception in note 58 – come from his
contribution to "Cile: Quattro domande," A Round Table discussion sponsored
by and printed in *Rinascita,* (October 19, 1973), 19.

58. Comments to the Central Committee of the PCI, printed in *l'Unità,* October
19, 1973.

59. Cf. the various interventions in *XI Congresso del PCI: Atti e risoluzioni*
(Editori Riuniti, Rome, 1966), pp. 337–338; pp. 466–467; pp. 594–595; pp.
638–640.

60. Enrico Berlinguer's conclusions, *XII Congresso,* pp. 750–754 and 768–769;
Cf. also the Political Document, pp. 784–789.

61. Rossana Rossanda, *L'Anno degli studenti* (De Donato, Bari, 1968). Lucio
Magri, *Considerazioni sui fatti di maggio* (De Donato, Bari, 1968).

62. Rossanda, *op. cit.*

63. Magri, p. 286 and p. 289.

64. "Il valore e il limite delle esperienze frontiste," *op. cit.*

65. *Il Manifesto,* I (giugno, 1969), 4.

66. Magri and Filippo Maone, "Strutture e metodi di direzione," *Il Manifesto,* I (settembre, 1969), pp. 28–40.

67. For the Central Committee meeting at which the "Manifesto" group was formally "read off the rolls of the party," see *L'Unità,* November 27, 1969, 11–14. For an earlier extensive debate in the Central Committee of the PCI, see *La questione del "Manifesto:" Democrazia e unità nel PCI* (Editori Riuniti, Rome, 1969).

68. Luigi Pintor, "Normalizzazione globale," *Il Manifesto,* II (marzo–aprile, 1970) 5–9. See also Theses 31, 36, and 39 in the special issue, *Per il Comunismo,* II (settembre, 1970).

69. Especially Thesis 16 in *Ibid.* See also Pintor, "Partito di tipo nuovo," I (settembre, 1969), 22–27, and Magri, "Il PCI degli anni '60," II (ottobre–novembre, 1970), 6–13.

70. Cf. Theses 185–192. See also Theses 164–166 for an excellent analysis of how the PCI's alliance policy – and that of other parties as well – have helped make the conditions of the middle strata even more complex.

71. Magri, "Risposta a Ingrao," II (gennaio, 1970), 36–46.

72. I have drawn these assumptions – which often are quite explicit – from the theses and articles cited above. But concrete political developments in the 1970s further reinforce these conclusions. The "Manifesto" group joined with other leftist forces to form the small Democratic Party of Proletarian Unity (PDUP) and it has clearly emerged *within* the PDUP as the faction with (a) a more tempered assessment of the PCI's potentialities, and (b) a less catastrophic interpretation of Italy's political and economic crisis.

73. For a very good synthetic analysis of the forces acting on the PCI to favor "the political moment" of its analyses and actions at the expense of "the social moment," see Pizzorno, *op. cit.*

ZIONIST MARXISM

ISRAEL KOLATT
The Hebrew University of Jerusalem

It seems particularly appropriate to devote a lecture to Zionist Marxism in a symposium in memory of George Lichtheim, in whose life Zionism and Marxism met but did not mingle.

For the past seventy-five years, Zionist Marxism has played a significant role in shaping the history of the Jewish people. Various Marxist interpretations have been applied to crucial questions, such as the claims to or denial of Jewish nationhood; support or rejection of Zionism; agreement or refusal to cooperate with the diverse groups within Jewry and the Zionist movement.

The attitude of the labor movement in Palestine and Israel towards Marxism and Marxist theoreticians has dictated its internationalist socialist orientation and its position in the Arab-Jewish confrontation, as well as its very organization.

However, the great extent of the practical implementation of Marxism in contemporary Jewish history has not been equalled by its purely intellectual achievements. It is difficult to find a single Marxist-Zionist ideologist of note, with the exception of Ber Borochov, who flourished at the beginning of this century.

The different versions of Zionist Marxism related to historical and social problems rather than to philosophical expositions. Zionist Marxism confined itself to a few basic formulae, i.e. "historical process," "historical materialism," "surplus value," "classes," "class struggle" — and attempted to apply them to the problem of Jewish existence and to the objectives of Zionism. The theories of Marx and Engels were quoted indiscriminately along with those of Kautsky, Plekhanov, Lenin, Max Adler, and other popularizers of Marxist ideology. It is only in recent years, after Marxism has lost its political impact, that attempts have been made at a more thorough philosophical analysis.

The conditions of the Jewish people threw the focus of Zionist

Marxism onto problems different from those considered vital by
European Marxists.

Zionist Marxism was not chiefly concerned with the direction of
capitalist development, the changes in class structure entailed thereby,
or revolutionary strategy; it did not even emphasize the class nature of
the state. The problem for Zionist Marxists was Jewish existence
within the framework of capitalist economy and the class state. The
alienation of Jews from the economic and political life of the state
appeared to combine both national and class elements.

Zionist Marxist discussion proceeded on various levels. One fundamental issue was the ideological significance of nationalism in general
and Zionism in particular. Another was the social aspect of Zionism
and the social order to which its realization would give rise. Third was
the relationship between the objectives of Zionism and the class
struggle and world revolution.

Russian Marxism penetrated the Zionist movement at the end of
the nineteenth century, after striking roots in the Jewish workers'
circles and their organization, the Bund. By a historical coincidence,
the emergence of the Jewish workers' movement and the establishment of political Zionism came about in the same decade, in the
1890s.

The social change which was gathering momentum through the
processes of industrialization and proletarization, the intellectual
impact of secularization, and the penetration of socialism into Jewish
society combined to erode traditional Jewish loyalties. While the
socialist theories that reached Jewish society were a mixture of Populism and Marxism, their common denominator was the weakening of
religious influence, criticism of the particularism of Jewish culture,
and emphasis on class interest and universal brotherhood. Zionist
socialist thinking at the turn of the century could not therefore base
itself *a priori* on Judaism as a religion or as a cultural and historical
entity, nor could it regard anti-Semitism as a perpetual and intensify-
ing phenomenon. The exponents of Zionist Marxism had to use new
terminology in order to justify and explain Jewish existence in terms
of economic progress, class, society, and increasing fraternity among
the international proletariat.

Marxism checked Jewish nationalist aspirations and ideology, yet it
also proved able to furnish a basis for Zionism. At the beginning of the
twentieth century, the specific position of the Jewish people in general and the Jewish proletariat in particular, especially with regard to
denial of Jewish rights, was given a Marxist formulation. In addition,
Marxism drew attention to the processes and sociological analysis of

Jewish social reality. The specific and unique nature of the Jewish social reality lent itself to ready formulation in Marxist terms.

Zionist Marxism can be characterized by its considering the Jewish people as a whole to be its relevant field. It was not confined to the particular circumstances of Palestine, and it sought to define the link between Diaspora and homeland in Marxist terms.

I

The self-awareness of the Jewish workers' movement was phenomenally influenced by the actual inculcation of Russian Marxist doctrine into its philosophy in the late 1880s and early 1890s. In Jewish socialism, just as in Russian socialism, Marx's theories were known before their crystallizing into a Marxist doctrine relating particularly to Russia; however, at this stage, Marxism was but one of the available socialist theories, serving as an economic foundation for socialism or as an analysis of the capitalist system, but not as the basis of a separate political organization.

Pre-Marxist thinkers were able to state that Russia, owing to her special status, was able to bypass the capitalist stage and pass from traditional rural organization to socialism. Russian Marxism, as formulated by Plekhanov, established certain well-known innovations in Russian political theory. Plekhanov claimed that capitalism was a stage through which Russia could not pass on her way to socialism; he based his theories on the proletariat, rather than the peasants, and emphasized the former's political role in effecting a change of regime. On the theoretical plane he replaced the theories of Lavrov and Mikhailovsky with the concept of historical materialism.

The Jewish workers should have accepted Russian Marxist doctrine with open arms; it gave importance to the proletariat at a time when the Populist (Narodnikist) philosophy was directed towards the peasants. Indeed, the Marxist doctrine did eventually refer the Jewish intelligentsia to the Jewish workers, who were destined to carry out the revolution. However, the proponents of Marxist doctrine among the Jewish workers' movements, ought to have fought hard for the adoption of such a theory. Jewish workers in the early 1890s supported theories drawn from Russian Populist thought, such as that of Lavrov, which stressed the advancement of a workers' elite rather than mass organization. In Russia, at the beginning of that decade, this meant Russian education for Jewish workers.

The final adoption of Marxism by Jewish workers' movements in Russia around the mid 1890s had many significant effects upon

Jewish nationalism. Marxism changed the Jewish labor from an organization of educated workers' groups to a wider-ranging
organization, which moved from "propaganda" to "agitation," so
obliging Marxists to abandon Russian and switch to Yiddish.

In addition, the broader-based organization turned its attention to
the conditions distinguishing Jewish worker from his non-Jewish
counterpart. The emphasis upon the political deprivation of the rights
of the Jewish proletariat led to the creation in 1897 of a separate
Jewish workers' organization, the "Bund." As the Bund developed, so
grew the demand for Jewish political and cultural autonomy.

In one respect, Jewish Marxism in the 1890s led to the emergence
of the proletariat as the front-line fighter in the Jewish people's battle
for their rights. L. Martov, who was one of the harbingers of the Bund,
although he did not join later on, declared in 1895 that only the
individual who is prepared to fight for his national rights will be capable
of fighting for the rights of his class as well. On the other hand,
Marxism, in its Russian form, maintained an attitude of contempt for
the Jewish bourgeoisie, which supposedly would fight neither against
the Tsarist regime, nor for the national rights of the Jewish people.

Marxism gave the Jewish people not only the idea of organizing and
directing the proletariat, but also the concept of historical materialism. This doctrine was supposed to eliminate the basis of Jewish
historical continuity − a spiritual succession common to all Jews − a
purpose indeed realized among a sizeable proportion of the Jewish
intelligentsia in Russia, which had joined a revolutionary movement
with no Jewish character whatsoever. The Bund did recognize that
Jewish uniqueness existed with regard to denial of language rights
(Yiddish), and certain character traits and experiences, but Zionist
Marxism made historical materialism a basis for Zionism. In the hands
of the Zionists, Marxism was transformed into a tool for defining the
special economic fate of the Jewish people.

II

Zionist Marxism was not a direct continuation of the concept of
nationalism, which sprang from the very organization of the Jewish
proletariat in the Bund. The Bund understood Jewish nationalism as
an autonomy of language and culture. It did not accept the idea of
territorial concentration, politically independent or otherwise, in
Palestine; nationalism itself seemed to it, at least in theory, more of a
fact than a value. Officially, the Bund proclaimed "neutrality" with
regard to the Jewish national future.

Zionist Marxism grew out of the permeation of historical materialist concepts and class struggles into the workers' groups which aligned themselves with the Zionist Organization. These groups, called "Poalei Zion," came into existence at the turn of the century, and were first centered in Minsk, White Russia.

The first such groups were neither theoretically nor practically Marxist, according to the Russian definition. They based their nationalism and socialism on a conglomeration of theories, including Marxism, which suggested a political destiny for the working class, a destiny, however, applied by the Poalei Zion to the workers within the Zionist movement.

Opposed to political Russian Marxism on specifically Jewish grounds, the groups claimed that the national Jewish interest, common to all classes, was to become free and to establish an independent Jewish society. As long as Jews were an oppressed minority, unable to participate in the political revolutionary struggle in Russia, their class activity in the Diaspora could only be economic in nature. The Jews could engage in class struggle only after an independent Jewish center had been established.

Marxism indirectly influenced the stand of the Minsk Circles with regard to the Zionist movement; they desired democratization of the movement and even envisaged the Jewish proletariat's leading the entire nation.

Marxism proper entered Poalei Zion not as a doctrine *per se* but rather made its entrance as a facet of an actual political topic, the disagreement concerning the "political struggle in Russia." We have seen that the political content so characteristic of Russian Marxism was rejected by the early Poalei Zion Minsk groups; Marxism was made acceptable by the stirrings of revolutionary Russia at the beginning of the century and by the Kishinef pogrom of spring 1903.

Some Poalei Zion groups differed with the Minsk Center, and claimed that even within the Diaspora there is class identification and class struggle of an independent nature, and that these are not bound to any general Jewish political organization (i.e. Zionism).

The necessity to relate Zionism to the Jewish class struggle, as well as to that of Russia and the rest of the world, served as a starting point for the development of the various theories of Poalei Zion, including those of Ber Borochov. Every theory, Marxism among them, was tested for its response to this integration into the general class struggle.

At this point, the older members of the Minsk Circle challenged both the theoretical basis of Marxism in Zionism and the practical results. They claimed that Marxism was brought to the Poalei Zion movement by "orthodox socialists," decisively dogmatic, whose credo was a perfect faith in the words of Marx.

With regard to practical Marxist strategies related to the Russian political revolution, the senior members of the Minsk Poalei Zion claimed that these were merely in imitation of the Bund. Actual participation in the Russian revolution would ultimately sound the death-knell for Zionism, in that it would bring about identification with the Russian proletariat and thereby eliminate the consciousness of the individual identity and fate of the Jewish working class.

The struggle for the permeation by Marxism of Poalei Zion philosophy was indeed a difficult one. According to their opponents, the Bund, it was only in December 1904, at a conference of southern Poalei Zion organizations in Ekaterinoslaf, that the formulae of "historical materialism" were accepted.

Yitzhak Ben-Zvi, a former disciple of Borochov and later a leader of Poalei Zion in Palestine, explained why Marxism was adopted during a dispute, not related to Marxism *per se*, about participation in the political struggle. According to Ben-Zvi, the tendency of the intelligentsia to accept the Marxism of the Social Democrats (SD) arose from the fact that it was largely urban, whereas the theories of Mikhailovsky and Kropotkin were based more on the village and the interests of agricultural workers. He did not see the differences between the Bund and Poalei Zion as being germane to Marxism itself, but rather to its interpretation vis-à-vis the Jewish people. Poalei Zion claimed that the Bund placed the Jews in a position inferior to that of other nations.

It was only the stand of the Russian Marxists regarding the question of national identity which led some of the intelligentsia to abandon Marxism and turn to other socialist theories, such as that of the Social Revolutionaries. Others, following Borochov, gave nationalist interpretations to Marxism. In the end, however, Ben-Zvi established that the differences of opinion within Poalei Zion circles with respect to abstract ideology were significant, but not decisive; differences regarding reality were much more crucial.

Marxism's primary effect on the Zionist workers' movements was therefore to engender a tendency to participate in the general revolutionary struggle, and its second effect was to base Zionist philosophy upon the concept of "deproletarization." This theory expounded and developed the contentions of the Minsk workers' circles with regard to the special position of the Jewish worker. Poalei Zion created the idea of the "national economy," as opposed to the Bund's notion of international economy, propounded in the social democratic theories of

Kautsky. Since the life of each and every member of the nation is in this concept bound up in the national economy, while under the special conditions of the Diaspora, in which territory was lacking, minority life and anti-Semitism prevented Jewish workers from entering industry, such workers were thus doomed to deproletarization. This idea did not originate with Poalei Zion; it began with the Bund and with the general Zionist movements. Poalei Zion only expanded and subsequently included it in its philosophy. This has been done by Jacob Leshczynsky.

This theory led to two possible conclusions: that it was not possible for a Jewish proletariat to be created in the Diaspora – thus undermining the very possibility of a proletarian party; and that the establishment of a national economy was necessary and most urgent.

The third effect of Marxism was actually a result of the second, i.e. the concept of deproletarization. At the time of the debates on Uganda and territorialism, Marxism was the primary tool for challenging loyalty to the Land of Israel. Zionism was presented as a movement basing itself upon metaphysics or emotion rather than upon historical reality and the direct needs of the Jewish proletariat.

The inculcation of Marxist philosophy and the concept of Jewish deproletarization were expressed in the "Red Declaration," which, composed by Poalei Zion territorialists (S.S.) in 1905, articulated the changes which Marxism had brought about in Zionist-socialist circles. It adopted a general socialist position, including the concept of "class struggle," in which it demanded Jewish participation, while on the other hand it contradictorily noted that the absence of a national economy among Jews made a Jewish proletariat impossible. All political link with Eretz Israel* was renounced in favour of the needs of the Jewish masses and the establishment – in any territory possible, even outside Palestine – of a Jewish economy, which was seen as an expression of "Jewish democracy," while the connection with Eretz Israel was viewed as sentimental and bourgeois.

A pamphlet published by the Bund, opposing the Red Declaration, shows clearly the advantages of Marxism in the intellectual atmosphere of Russia at that time during the debates in Zionist circles at this time. It derisively remarks that only in 1904 did the concept of "historical materialism" supplant those of "justice" and "truth," which had previously reigned supreme in Poalei Zion philosophy. Even after the adoption of "historical materialism" by Poalei Zion, the Bund claimed that "Socialist Zionists" (who were in essence territori-

*Land of Israel

alists) utilized the concept unfairly. The Bund rejected the concept of a national economy, as used by territorialists, Zionists and non-Zionists alike, to explain Jewish inferiority and the Jewish need for territory, and contended that territorialists err in their very definition of "proletarian" when they speak of the deproletarization of the Jews. They refer only to the factory worker, while the Marxist concept embraces all those compelled to sell their labor because of lack of the means of production. Even if there was no great Jewish manufacturing proletariat, there was still a significantly expanded role for all salaried workers.

The Bund was not sparing with proofs that Poalei Zion was not true either to its claim of supporting historical materialism, or to the solidarity of the proletariat, and that it mingled other non-materialistic elements in its philosophy. The Bund indicated particularly that there was a lack of consistency in the theories of Poalei Zion; Marxist revolutionary activity did not lead to Zionism nor vice versa — the two theories were in fact contradictory. This was obviously one of the more difficult problems which Zionist Marxism had to face. Zionist foreign policy, i.e. contact with the Powers, was considered as invalid by the Bund; instead of a class struggle, Zionists relied upon diplomatic influence or upon the purchase of land with money.

III

The strength of the intellectual and mass influence of Marxism, which affected Poalei Zion through the Bund, is evident from the fate of a group which developed into a Jewish Workers' Party (Yiddishe Socialisten — YS). This party, formed in 1906, practically abandoned Zionism and stressed the struggle for Jewish autonomy in the Diaspora. It began with a group of intellectuals, coming chiefly from southern Russia, who challenged what they saw in Zionism as "utopian" elements. To base Zionism upon the will, as in Herzl's famous statement, "If you will it, it is no dream," was in direct opposition to its scientific and objective claims, as well as to its wish for an ideology founded in reality. This group changed Herzl's doctrine to "If it is no dream, then desire it!" It wished to display the direct connection between the Jewish Diaspora reality and the concentration of Jews in Palestine. In a series of conferences from 1903 on, as well as in various publications, it attempted to set Jewish nationalism and Zionism on a scientific foundation.

This search for a basis in real life could have led this group, named "The Revival," to Marxism. However, its system of concepts was

variegated. It did not deny Marxism, and in fact used Marxist terminology, but did not pledge absolute allegiance to it; and there were
those within it with different ideologies. In later publications, two
leaders of "The Revival", Ben Adir and M. Zilberfarb, asserted that
they had not strayed from the path of orthodox Marxism, and did not
have any ties with the "subjective idealism" of Lavrov and
Mikhailovsky. Only one of the leaders, M.B. Ratner, had had an idealistic view of history and a Social Revolutionary ideology, and his
influence was minimal. The two men admitted, however, that their
political strategy tended to base socialism on the class situation not
only of the workers but also on that of the intellegentsia and small-
scale farmers, and that they supported the federal concept of a national state. However, Marxism's power was so great that the suspicion of
Social Revolution dug a virtually unbridgeable gulf between this group
and the workers themselves.

Actually, there were many non-Marxist elements in its philosophy.
Borochov, whose differences with it were based not upon a scholastic
background of Marxism, but on the real background of
"Palestinianism" or Jewish autonomy in the Diaspora, attempted to
uncover its principles as non-Marxist, seeing them as vulnerable points
for debate. In fact, its position on Marxism was common to those
socialists who did not join the Russian SD, and regarding political
realities.

It may be said that during the years 1903–1905, Marxism played a
rather destructive role in Zionism. It called attention to the revolutionary struggle in Russia, challenged interclass cooperation in
Zionism, and even advocated the abandonment of Palestinian Zionism
altogether, on grounds of territorialism.

IV

The man who transformed Marxism from a deleterious to a constructive factor for Zionism was D. B. Borochov. He changed the
function of Marxist theory for Zionism: from a purely destructive
force in relation to Palestine-oriented Zionism, Marxism became its
ideological justification. This founding of Zionism on Marxism
allowed it to be defended in universalist terms and to be judged by a
universal socialist criterion.

Generations of Zionist socialists used Borochov's philosophy as an
intellectual basis for Jewish nationalism and as a means for explaining
the special position of Jews in the Diaspora and their need for territory and a national economy. Zionism, according to the Borochovist

doctrine, was not set up outside the domain of the Jewish, Russian, and international class struggles, but became the clearly recognizable expression thereof. The Jewish proletariat was involved directly in general socialism and the revolutionary movement at large; Borochov created a historical picture in which a "spontaneous process" was taking place that translated the Jewish class struggle into an emigration to and concentration in Palestine.

However, the universal basis for Zionism had an opposite meaning as well — Palestinian Zionism was justified only because it enabled proletarization under national "conditions of production" or participation in the class struggle; this was liable to become undermined so long as there were other ways of accomplishing those goals or when it became clear that Zionism is not the best method of class struggle participation. The various movements of revolution in Russia, especially those of 1917, provided a serious challenge for Borochovist Zionism.

For many years, up until the 1950s, Borochov's doctrine reflected the ambivalent relationship between Marxism and Zionism, a two-way street which led both towards and away from Zionism, and branched into many different directions even within Zionism itself.

Borochov's theory had two points of departure, one political and the other intellectual. From the political point of view, his Marxism operated against the Bund, which had denied the need of the Jewish proletariat for its own territory and economy, and claimed that Zionism was Utopian and not realizable in the historical framework expressed by the class struggle. But his Marxism also made against the territorialists' extreme definition of the deproletarization of Diaspora Jewry and its need for a national economy. Since the territorialists claimed that traditional, Palestinian Zionism replaced the real requirements of the masses with an emotional devotion to Eretz Israel, Borochov had to prove that the attachment to Palestine was not merely sentimental and historical.

A third stance which Zionist Marxism attacked was that of the Jewish (autonomist) Socialists, who sought to create a direct link between the class struggle and the demand for autonomy in the Diaspora and the ultimate establishment of a territorial center in Palestine, and who, in essence, ignored the idea of Palestine.

Borochov's theoretical point of departure was that of a Marxism which was rather free with its intellectual content — as borne out by his profound knowledge and by his tendency to use the term "historical materialism" far more than "Marxism" — although its political content became increasingly rigid and dogmatic. The political platform of 1906 was indeed one of the stages in his intellectual development. However, the theory underwent dogmatization on being accepted by the party and the formulations of Borochov from the years 1905–1907 became obligatory doctrine within the movement.

Defining his philosophical standpoint, Borochov wrote: "The author is a historical materialist, just as Bogdanov is a historical materialist." He objected to historical materialism "which is known only through the vulgar speech of the Marxists," and denied that the basing of history on materialism was equivalent to seeing hedonistic and utilitarian ends as being decisive in history.

In one of his arguments, he claims: "We are not required to become Marxists; however, we have decided to do so because of our positive research into the principles of Marxism."

In a later period, in 1907, Borochov explained Marxism not only as a theory but as the basis for a party. Parties which were clearly Marxist were those "which recognized the historical materialistic view of society and the Marxist analysis of capitalistic economy and its development." In accordance with accepted Marxist views, he connected this recognition with the class definition of hired laborers as a separate class. As this definition became clearer, he held, idealistic philosophy was neglected and materialistic philosophy adopted.

The question of a place for Marxism within the self-definition of Poalei Zion concerned Borochov when he stayed in the United States in 1915 and participated in the debates among the various ideological factions there. At the same time, he distinguished two basic ideological trends within Poalei Zion – "socialist" and "social democratic." The former demanded realization of Zionism and socialism through national unity. The latter was defined, in accepted Russian terminology, as one which did not discount the class struggle within the process of realization of Zionism and Socialism or cover it up with national unity. "Marxism," at that time, was thought by Borochov to be a philosophical rather than political trend. It stood on the same level as "materialism," "Kantianism," or "critical empiricism." He declared himself to be a "critical empiricist," neither materialistic nor idealistic, who opposed any kind of metaphysics. "A Marxist without matter," in his terminology. According to Borochov, the "social democratic" outlook allowed for different approaches to the future socialist regime, collectivistic and anarchistic alike. He defined himself personally as a socialist anarchist.

In 1905, Borochov joined the criticism of Zionism by the territorialist Marxists. He also opposed the basing of Palestinian Zionism on "eternal spiritual essence," "the Jewish spirit," or race, geography, or historical individuality, describing his credo as follows: "The content of the social ideal should be drawn from the material conditions of the particular society, and not from the remnants of a past ideology."

Even in his debates with non-Marxists in Poalei Zion, he negated the independent position of a "national culture" or "tradition" which is faced by the individual. He saw these concepts as remnants of a populistic outlook, and himself rooted his nationalism in territory as a "condition" of production. Territory is the common means for material living among all classes.

Borochov objected to concepts such as "the content of national existence" or "the goals of national development," which were oppressed by the "form" of a foreign economy (capitalism) or a foreign state. The meaningful content of nationalism is territory as a basis for a national economy, from which political autonomy follows, political unity being simply a protective device. The inclinations of the various classes towards the nation are merely inclinations towards the national territory. Feelings of sacrifice and tradition are only secondary.

Borochov's nationalism did not relate particularly to the Jewish people. It was a general nationalist doctrine which attempted to explain nationalism on the basis of concepts inherent in historical materialism. He claimed that to the Marxist terms "forces of production" and "relations of production," which explain the existence of classes and their struggle, one should add "conditions of production (territory)," which are common to all classes. He indicated that from a historical point of view nationalism is a relative phenomenon supported by the bourgeoisie.

In the first stage of his political theory (1904–1905), Borochov defined Zionism as a "therapeutic" and not a "normal" movement; that is, it creates the pre-conditions for the Jewish class struggle but does not itself express this struggle. The movement combines three factors – people, land, and national culture – which cannot be eliminated or reduced to one another, and is not realized by the proletariat but by pioneers – who are pioneers for the entire nation and not members of a particular class.

At the second stage of development (1905–1906), the class outlook was sharpened with respect to both the content of nationalism and the realization of Zionism. This sharper view came about through the debates among socialist trends within the Jewish community, among nationalists and non-nationalists alike. Borochov's national and Palestinian Zionist theories were presented as the most consistent conclusion to be drawn from historical materialism and the class struggle. He objected to the idea of deproletarization of Diaspora Jewry, claiming that proletarization exists, although suppressed and handicapped, in a form leading to the unique Jewish class struggle, which both involves the Jews in the world revolutionary struggle and propels them to Palestine.

At this stage, nationalism was shown to be of interest in that it laid down the conditions for the national Jewish proletariat. It was put in a radical class formulation: "The national question of the proletariat is the product of the conflict between the need for developing its creative powers, i.e. the class struggle, and the conditions of the strategic base." The primary reason for the troubled state of the Jewish people was no longer its ex-territorialism, but the class structure of society. Thus when private property and the class society disappear from the world, the problem of nationalism may vanish as well.

Borochov wanted to show that Zionism is the highest level in the consciousness of the Jewish worker. Using the accepted scale of the Russian Social Democracy, he defined the position of the Bund as "economism," while proletarian Zionism was an expression of political social consciousness, which viewed the problem in its broadest scope. His explanation of anti-Semitism was also nationalistic and class-related, in terms of a "national rivalry" among the parallel classes of different nations occupying the same territory, so that a rivalry may exist between the Jewish proletariat and that of other nations.

Borochov explained the attachment to Palestine, and not just the need for territory, through historical materialism. By analysis of the trends towards both Jewish emigration and the development of colonial areas, he tried to show that Palestine is the most suitable place for establishing a Jewish society based on concentration of the Jewish people. The attachment to the land of Israel is "prognostic," and not "principle," is based, that is to say, on the historical process and not on eternal values.

The flow of Jewish capital and emigration of labor to Palestine create a Jewish capitalistic economy. The task of building up an economy is for the bourgeoisie, while that of the proletariat is obtaining political and economic freedom.

This doctrine of Borochov strengthened the territorial and economic elements of Jewish socialist nationalism and the development of a Jewish labor movement in Palestine. Thus the essence of national existence, which was based on historical materialism, was not necessarily expressed primarily through sovereignty or tradition and culture, but through territory and economy. This was to have political consequences in the future.

The stage in Borochov's thought of radical class explanation was the one particularly adopted by his movement. In 1909 the Russian Poalei Zion left the Zionist Congress, refusing to cooperate with the "bourgeois Zionists."

Borochov's Marxist thought was not necessarily culled from Russian Marxism; his education and intellectual abilities enabled him to absorb European Marxism directly. His position on the question of nationalism was even in opposition to the Russian Marxist view at that time. To some extent it colored Ukrainian nationalist thought, and he was indeed close to the Ukrainian nationalist movement in 1917. Stalin's 1913 nationalist theory contained principles similar to Borochov's, although it would seem that there was no direct influence. However, there is an indirect connection between Borochov's position on several Zionist topics and the problems which concerned Russian Marxism. That of the relation between the spontaneous process, which nurtured the revolutionary forces, and conscious action became expressed in Russian Marxism as the relation between the development of capitalism and the working class on the one hand and revolutionary action on the other. Within the Zionist field, this was the question of the relation between the plight of Diaspora Jews and emigration to Palestine. The Poalei Zion party was faced with the dilemma of how far to go in encouraging emigration of its members and the Jewish proletariat to Palestine, and to what extent merely to stand at the forefront of the process and guide it.

Russian Marxism even considered the questions of the relation between the two revolutions — the bourgeois and the socialist — and the amount of cooperation necessary and/or desirable between the bourgeoisie and the proletariat. Similar problems were raised in the Zionist field, as regards the justification of cooperation among different classes in the Zionist Movement in order to realize the aims of Zionism.

The third topic which greatly concerned Russian Marxism was connected with the first two. The argument between the Mensheviks and Bolsheviks on whether to have a broad-spectrum or an elitist party did not directly concern Poalei Zion. However, at the time of these debates on the Duma, Borochov indicated his own attitude, and hence implied his views as to the Poalei Zion party. In an article of 1907, before the dissolution of the Second Duma, he assessed Bolsheviks as a group which desired to set the revolution in motion in a technical manner, before spontaneous historical development had paved the way for it. On the other hand, he saw the Mensheviks as the artificial organizers of the proletariat, even before its class organization had come about through spontaneous historical processes. From this we see that his own party, Poalei Zion, was, in Borochov's opinion, one which advanced, led and organized the spontaneous development of the Jewish proletariat.

It could be said that Russian Marxism had a deleterious influence on the Russian Poalei Zion, whose followers became the Palestinian Poalei Zion during the first few years of their operation there, in that it confined the role of the party to the class struggle and the taking over of the political regime. Indeed, options for political activities were closed to them, while they had to prove their capacity in the field of economic activity, since the spontaneous process did not provide jobs and "class struggle" was meaningless.

V

Borochovist Marxism was not the only brand prevalent in Poalei Zion circles. In addition to the Russian party, influenced by him, and the Palestinian party, similarly influenced during its first few years of existence, there was also the Austrian party, which contained one outstanding proponent of a different brand of Marxism, Shlomo Kaplansky.

Despite his Russian origins, Kaplansky was greatly influenced by both German Revisionist Marxism and Austrian Marxism. He was less dogmatic than the Russian Marxists, in the philosophical sense, and less rigid in his devotion to class activity. His Marxism was fundamentally less monistic than Borochov's, and supported interclass cooperation and constructive economic activity. For him the nation was established not on material bases alone, but also on the appeal to the common will, described by Fichte and Lasalle.

Kaplansky's position on nationality was profoundly colored by Austrian Socialism. He did not necessarily found his nationalism on territory, but stressed the abnormalcy of the Jewish economy and proletariat, which was hurt more than any other class by anti-Semitism and the lack of territory.

According to Kaplansky, the proletariat was not intended merely to become integrated into the spontaneous economic process, nor to show its initiative only at the stage of political revolution. Rather, it ought to lead the Jewish people and the Zionist movement through the first step as well, that of economic construction.

Consequently, Zionism as portrayed by Kaplansky was the

movement of the Jewish proletariat, which required neither charter nor legal rights, as Herzl had believed, in order to emigrate to Palestine; and since the stream of private investment of capital could not create enough work, a cooperative settlement might provide jobs for immigrating workers. Such a settlement would present Zionism as a proletarian movement, and would thereby create cells for a future socialist society. This interest of the proletariat, to emigrate and settle collectively, would be realized through interclass cooperation within the Zionist movement, a concept especially important with regard to Palestine activity. In the Diaspora, the Austrian Poalei Zion was in the forefront of the battle for a Jewish national identity and autonomy, while also insisting upon a local Jewish class struggle.

Kaplansky's thought was thus essentially Marxist. Zionism for him was not a political or spiritual longing; it was anchored in economic development and national and international class relations.

The differences of opinion on Marxism and its relevant conclusions among the various Poalei Zion parties did not prevent their establishment in 1907 of a world union. The parties' cooperative efforts in Zionism and in operations in Palestine, and attempt to gain acceptance into the Socialist International, were far more important than doctrine.

An even greater influence was the belief in the proletariat as the expression of the spontaneous process, which increased the desire for unity, on the assumption that the very act of unification would bring about acceptance of the doctrine. Indeed, the articles of the World Federation of Poalei Zion speak of the hope of ending the rule of the property-holders through "class struggle, both economic and political, by the working class." In reality, there were parties whose members objected to historical materialism and viewed the realization of socialist Zionism as the result of national activity and moral influence, rather than class struggle. This view was held especially by the American party and its mentor, Nachman Syrkin.

The test for the various theories in Poalei Zion was the Palestinian party, which was at first influenced by Borochov and envisaged a great flow of Jewish capital to Palestine, as a result of the spontaneous process of class interests and class struggle. This capital was to initiate the development processes of the Jewish and Arab settlements alike, establish a Jewish working class, and make possible the class struggle which would lead to a socialist society.

However, even in the years before 1906, it became clear that Borochov's forecasts were not borne out by reality, and that Jewish capital was not streaming to Palestine. It appeared that the Russian

Marxist and Borochovist models were not suitable for Palestinian conditions. The revolution of the Young Turks in 1908 aroused hopes for some sort of socialist political action within the Ottoman Empire. The content of this socialist action was taken to be primarily the attainment of national autonomy.

The Poalei Zion party in Palestine found that the class struggle against the small and unstable Jewish private property in Palestine was meaningless, and took off in another direction; it turned to the establishing of workers at places of employment and to joining with the Zionist Movement in founding cooperative settlements. Immi-gration to Palestine was no longer considered as owing solely to economic and class-related reasons, but as requiring a conscious voluntary effort. The party began to see itself less in terms of global processes, and instead emphasized the particular needs of the Palestinian Jewish proletariat, which were so pressing that direct interests and reality took preference over Marxist theory.

Under Borochov's leadership, orthodox Marxists objected both to interclass cooperation within the Zionist Movement, and to cooper-ative institutions. The Austrians, Americans, and Palestinians, however, did not think this cooperation impugned the class socialism of Poalei Zion. Borochov's free attitude towards theoretical Marxist doctrine, as well as his orthodoxy regarding class struggle as a way of realizing socialism and Zionism together, were expressed in the renewed debates on the attitude towards cooperation at the Fourth International Convention of the United Poalei Zion parties in 1913.

Speaking about the theoretical side of Marxism, Borochov said: "It is a great mistake to claim that Marxism recognizes only that which was written by Marx himself; our attitude towards the question of nationalism is different from Marx's. Marxism gives us only the standards by which we assess ourselves and the events and phenomena of social life."

The actual explanation for class theory was that socialism in Palestine could come about only in the wake of a class struggle by the proletariat and its taking over of political rule. Because of this, Borochov believed that the constructive economic activities under-taken by the proletariat would not lead to socialism; he saw cooperation merely as an enterprise which had little to do with the realization of socialism.

VI

The First World War placed the Marxism of Poalei Zion in the inter-national arena. Until 1914, Poalei Zion had not been accepted into the

Socialist International; and it therefore did not have to take any stand
on international problems. The Russian Revolution was not yet
feasible, so that the debates on Marxist topics centered on the
question of Zionism.

During the war, Poalei Zion concentrated its political efforts on the
question of Jewish nationality, its rights and recognition, rather than
on the "world class struggle." There were many views within Poalei
Zion with regard to the war itself; there were internationalists
neutralists, and those who favored active participation. The Russian
Poalei Zion members tended to align themselves with the Zimmerwald
group. However, it was generally agreed that the international
workers' movement had failed to prepare its members to face war
danger, since it had avoided the question of nationalism.

During the war, Poalei Zion applied to various international
socialist fora, and in 1916 were accepted into what was left of the
Socialist International. In 1917, it appeared before the Dutch-Scan-
dinavian committee, in preparation for the proposed Stockholm
convention. At these meetings, it formulated its stand and its demands
in the nationalist sphere in universalist and largely Marxist terms. The
question of the Jewish proletariat and its special fate, which would be
resolved only through the establishment of a national Jewish economy
in undeveloped Palestine, was presented as part of the more general
problem of the right of economically dispossessed and oppressed
peoples to emigrate to underdeveloped areas. For the first time this
claim gained wide acceptance and support among socialists in general.
The Bolshevik Revolution and the British Mandate in Palestine evoked
within the Zionist Marxist camp varied attitudes with regard both to
the revolution itself and to Zionism.

In the years 1919 and 1920, debates on the content and meaning of
Marxism accompanied the greater debates which split Poalei Zion into
those who adopted Communism and those who dissociated themselves
from it. On the socialist plane, there was a debate as to whether the
communist takeover of political power is the only way to realize the
aims of the socialist idea. It was agreed that this was a revolutionary
era, and that capitalism would never recover from the wounds
inflicted by the War. However, the Marxists, such as Shlomo
Kaplansky and some members of the Polish party of Poalei Zion,
continued to hold the accepted Marxist position that the revolution
must base itself on the large proletariats of great industrial nations,
and has no chance of succeeding without them. They therefore
supported the reestablishment of the Second International, although
they wanted to give it a more revolutionary demeanor. They were

prepared to abandon democracy, but only in favor of a dictatorship of the whole proletariat, and not of that of one party ruling through terror.

Sections of the Russian, Austrian, and Polish parties adopted the Bolshevist position. They claimed that in the age of revolution, the avant-garde determine the policies of the entire proletariat, and that the parties of the Comintern were indeed the very pioneers who would bring about the socialist revolution.

Along with the debate on communism in the socialist sphere in Poalei Zion, there came an even sharper debate on the meaning of communism in the national and Zionist spheres.

Borochov's key position combined class radicalism with the demand for national autonomy. He estimated that the rise of the proletariat to power would bring about much self-determination for the various nations, whether on a territorial or a personal basis. At the advent of the Bolshevik Revolution, Borochov himself led a campaign for national rights in Russia, until his premature death at the end of 1917.

This revolution established an ambivalent position towards nations. The Bolsheviks theoretically supported their right to self-determination, but saw them as subject to the higher revolutionary interests. The meaning of a separate Jewish existence and its nationalist format became a problem in and of itself, different from the problems of attitude towards nationalism and revolution in general.

In the specifically Jewish and Zionist areas, there were more heated arguments on the meaning of Marxism within Poalei Zion. The basic tenets of Borochov's theory were subject to a new test. The revolution appeared as a universal authority for which all particular interests were to be sacrificed. Moreover, the concept of "national economy" and the interests of the working class within it were not considered unquestionable. Borochov's contention was that Zionism would be realized before the socialist revolution. When the socialist revolution actually came first, his theories were looked upon with doubt. Some members of Poalei Zion claimed that revolutionary processes in fact supported Borochov's theories, in that they uncovered the special damage done to the Jewish economy at the time of the revolution. Others suggested that the revolution could solve the particular problems of Jewish economy by organization of the ruling government, which would bring about economic changes or would itself initiate territorial concentration of the Jewish masses.

Even the concept of the spontaneous process, spontaneous immigration of Jews to Palestine, was put to the test. According to some circles in Poalei Zion, there is no place in the revolutionary age for processes not directed by the supreme revolutionary command. Similarly, the idea of interclass cooperation received new meaning during the age of revolution. The cooperation of Jewish proletariat with the bourgeoisie in a voluntary organization such as the Zionist Congress went against the principles of class struggle and was considered counter-revolutionary. The Zionist Movement was condemned for cooperating with "imperialist" forces when it worked together with Great Britain.

The meaning for Poalei Zion of Marxist doctrine could therefore be taken in various and even conflicting ways, Zionist and anti-Zionist, during the revolutionary era. The struggle of the proletariat to seize political power and to realize socialism could be interpreted as emigration to Palestine in order to establish a Jewish proletariat and carry out the socialist revolution, or, conversely, as the abandonment of Zionism. The Jewish proletariat gathering in Palestine appeared as a solution to the Jewish problem either by creating a Jewish majority and a Jewish economy in Palestine or by its constituting an expeditionary force for the revolution in the midst of an Arab proletariat.

The attitude towards constructive institutions prior to political takeover also changed during the revolutionary age. Orthodox Marxists were prepared to recognize their importance as experiments, even before proletarian control, although Borochov dissented.

Similarly, opinions on a political party necessarily underwent a new test — Poalei Zion did not establish prior to the revolution whether it supported a broad-based workers' party or a smaller party rendered more cohesive by doctrine. Actually, it chose the German Social Democratic model, of a party crystallized through ideological unity and political activity. It was in 1919 that the type of organization in Palestine changed, and the local Poalei Zion party merged with other groups creating a wide-ranging organization called "Ahdut Haavoda," which was both a political party and a trade union.

VII

The Central Workers' party in Palestine — Ahdut Haavoda ("Unity of Labor") — was not based on the Marxist model, but regarded Marx as one of its mentors, as was evidenced by its very foundation on a class basis. Similarly, the Jewish laborers in Palestine took over the attitude to Marx as one of the prophets of the destiny of the workers in the fabric of history.

However, Ahdut Haavoda itself was established as a result of the criticism of many of the practical foundations of Marxism which permeated the Zionist workers' movement. Zionist Marxism began with objection to Marxism and its chief exponents, K. Kautsky and G. Plekhanov, with regard to the question of nationalism in general and the Jewish question in particular, although Borochov anchored his Zionism in a process of class struggle and political takeover by the proletariat. Ahdut Haavoda strayed from this path as well when it declared that the primary purpose of a workers' movement is not to seize political power but to construct a socialist workers' economy without a capitalistic phase.

Another heretical idea was interclass cooperation, since, according to Ahdut Haavoda, the workers' economy was to be built by the immigration of pioneers from all sectors of the Jewish people especially the young, and by the collection of funds from all social classes, organized in the Zionist Movement. Marxism was further challenged in its Borochovist formulation by a lack of faith in the "spontaneous process" of the natural immigration of capital and labor, to result from the class struggle. Ahdut Haavoda stood for the deliberate promotion of immigration.

A fourth area in which Ahdut Haavoda deviated from the accepted Marxist line of Poalei Zion was in the question of party structure. AH was established in 1919 as a trade union and political party. Its founders did not want to separate the objective class status of the workers from that of those who were consciously united into the party itself. They stipulated that there was to be no distinction between concept and reality, party and class. Here they differed even with their non-communist colleagues outside Palestine in Right Poalei Zion. These AH allies objected to any change in the German SD model, which separated the trade union from the party and rendered the former subject to the latter. They saw in the structure of AH a form of syndicalism, which, by 1919, had spread throughout Europe and had gained the support of the Bolsheviks. AH responded by a tendency to refer to the model of organization of the period of the First International, for workers, a form trade-based, and approved by Marx himself.

AH's ideological outlook was similarly divergent. Marxism was viewed as only one of the possible foundations for socialism, and Borochovism as only one of the possible foundations for nationalism. The many interpretations applied to Marxism after World War I allowed the members of AH to escape any compulsory ideological model. Historical materialism, which was thought by many Zionists to be destructive to them, despite Borochov's version, ceased to be the accepted discipline.

Berl Katzenelson, one of the leaders of AH, expressed his objection to dogmatic ideology as follows: "Marxism and Darwinism were undeniable in serving as compasses of human thought ... however, when these laws are accepted as articles of faith, when they become fixed commandments which are not to be questioned, do they not lose their enlightening content and become a kind of modern-day fetishism, and the source of a frightening fanaticism, obstruction and oppression?" This viewpoint remained that of the mainstream of workers in Palestine. Of course, the concept of "class struggle" did indicate a sort of inclination toward Marxism, but it was so reinterpreted as to lose its universalist interpretation and take on a unique Palestinian meaning, one constructive rather than militant.

While the leaders and ideologists of AH were presenting their organization as a Zionist-socialist workers' organization which was free from dogmatic definitions, Marxists were calling it anti-Marxist. Its abandonment of the idea of a party with a clearly delineated doctrinal line, in favor of a broader-based union, struck at the social-democratic party model and stood in evident opposition to any revolutionary party model.

The gap between Marxist ideology and the idea of overall incorporation of the workers into one party had been growing steadily since 1919. The supporters of such association viewed Marxism at its best as *one* of the possible systems within the Zionist socialist world. Unity was more important than dogmatic coherence. Marxists on the other hand, preferred ideological clarity to the scope of such unity. Some of them gave explicit preference to a "vanguard party" over a "class party." The ideological controversy within the workers' movement in Palestine did not therefore center on the various creeds of Marxism (orthodox or reformist) but on the idea of workers' unity and the absence of theoretical dogmatism, as against orthodox Marxism.

The politics of AH made it even more suspect than did its structure, according to the Marxist viewpoint. The idea of building a socialist economy in Palestine could, for economic reasons, succeed only in part. However, the arguments against such an economy, according to socialist criteria, were even stronger. Isolated cells of producers within agriculture and industry were suspected by Marxists, of being disloyal to socialist principles and of offering an inadequate foundation for the future socialist revolution. In 1920 the Histadrut was founded and it took over the professional and cooperative functions.

VIII

In contrast to AH, the "Leftist Poalei Zion" maintained its Zionist Marxist orthodoxy and gave it new meaning within the Palestinian reality.

In 1920, Poalei Zion was divided over the questions of immediate alignment with the Comintern and of interclass cooperation at the Zionist Congress. "Leftist Poalei Zion" wanted to leave the Congress and join the Comintern, whose refusal to recognize Zionism led several to abandon the group and join communism outright. Another faction remained loyal to Zionism, although maintaining a theoretical inclination to communism within the general socialist field, despite being completely opposed to communism in the politics of Palestine.

Their meaning of Marxism within the Palestinian reality was not the advancement of the Arab proletariat (which scarcely existed) under the leadership of the Jewish minority, in preparation for the revolution, as was desired by anti-Zionist communists. "Leftist Poalei Zion" continued to support the Borochovistic notion of the need and right of the Jewish proletariat to emigrate to Palestine. However, in contrast to AH, it claimed that Palestine would be built as a capitalist state and could not initially be constructed as a socialist one, and established its position vis-à-vis the structure and purpose of the labor movement in Palestine accordingly. It demanded energetic political activity among the workers' parties and objected to any obscuring of the special nature of such a policy within the general policies of Zionism. The workers should stand out in their objection to British imperialism. It called for active trade operations and decried "moderation" with regard to the constructive tasks of the workers in their responsibility for the economy.

It demanded a separation of the trade and constructive tasks of the Histadrut in order that the latter should not interfere with the former. The principal front of the class struggle was, it felt, the professional front. It also believed in class solidarity among Jewish and Arab workers and wished for improvement of these mutual ties, although not at the expense of Jewish emigration to Palestine.

It was not only communism on the one hand and AH on the other which established the position of the Marxist Zionists of Leftist Poalei Zion. The realities of Palestine presented a problem for orthodox Marxists which eventually led to rifts, in 1928 and 1934, and to the establishment of two separate parties.

The orthodox Leftist Poalei Zion continued to rally round the cause of the spontaneous process as a reason for immigration; it did not support a wider voluntary immigration. The failure of its members to participate in the Zionist movement made it difficult for them to receive immigration visas, since the Zionist organization was responsible for their distribution. Palestine was considered by them to be the future land of concentration of the Jewish proletariat, although at present most of their members were in the Diaspora.

On the other hand, there was in Palestine a group of Marxist members of Leftist Poalei Zion who sought to make the Borochovist doctrine into a basis for a territorialist-Marxist workers' party. They emphasized not the global Jewish prolatariat of Borochov's theory, but the territorial aspects. They believed in combining Zionist activism with Jewish-Arab solidarity. They encouraged Jewish immigration and fought "British imperialism."

During the thirties the Palestinian capitalist economy grew, and British-Zionist cooperation began to show signs of strain. The Palestinian Marxist party claimed that it would unite the Jewish and Arab proletariats in their struggle against British imperialism. These "Marxist circles" were Zionist, and calculated that the Arab proletariat would agree to Jewish immigration and even be interested in it, since it would develop the local economy and prepare the way for the struggle of the proletariat and the socialist revolution.

The fate of the Jews in Nazi-occupied Europe changed the attitudes of the two factions. In 1939, they abandoned their objections to interclass cooperation and rejoined the Zionist movement, from which they had seceded in 1920 (and the Russians in 1909).

IX

At the time when Marxism was not considered compulsory for Ahdut Haavoda, and when Leftist Poalei Zion aspired to adapt Marxist orthodoxy to world, Jewish and Zionist realities, a new trend of Zionist Marxism appeared on the scene.

The "baptism" of Hashomer Hatzair into Marxism in the 1920s is one of the most exciting intellectual chapters in the modern history of Zionism and Palestine. It bears testimony to the historical essentiality of Marxism in those years, which saw a new wave of Marxism that was to grow and intensify until it reached its political peak in the 1950s, whereupon it would disintegrate in face of the political reality.

Hashomer Hatzair developed from a youth movement which was devoted to the ideas of Nietzsche, Wyneken, Blüher, and Freud on the perfection of the ideal individual and the good community. At one particular stage, HH's subjectivism reached its limits, and it began to seek the connection with Palestinian and global realities, whose respective influence on HH in the first half of the 1920s is difficult to determine. In the former, there was the central problem of the failure to build up Palestine as a socialist society according to the constructive method of Ahdut Haavoda. Leftists in the "Labor Brigade" concluded from this that socialism would be realized through a class struggle in which the task of the Kibbutzim was partial but decisive. They began to claim that Zionism by itself does not advance socialism, and that therefore one should not place the burden of building Zionism upon the workers.

Hashomer Hatzair itself agreed that the identity between Zionism and socialism which Ahdut Haavoda was trying to create did not really exist any more, although its conclusions from this were different from those of the above-mentioned "Labor Brigade."

Borochovism was essential to HH, just as it was to the older generation, although the former had certain additional reasons. Borochovism interpreted Zionism in an objective manner which was not anchored in the individual's will or spiritual assets, but in the all-powerful process taking place in reality. The productive and territorial elements became the mainspring of nationhood. These bases were considered to be firmer than the historical link. In addition, Zionism became associated with the world-wide class struggle, although at the first stage it was realized capitalistically and within the framework of the British Empire.

Hashomer Hatzair differed in several basic respects from the Marxist creed of Leftist Poalei Zion. It viewed aliya (immigration) as a volitional act, not a spontaneous process, and brought the idea of the realization of Zionism by the Jewish proletariat in the Diaspora (as expressed by the early Poalei Zion at the beginning of the century) to the Jewish youth of the middle class, who were becoming impoverished. HH even used Leninist terms and claimed that the Jewish workers' movements in the Diaspora, Zionist and non-Zionist alike, were tainted by "economism," concerned only about the present and not interested in the future revolutionary situation of Palestine; whereas Jewish youth would fulfill Zionism by emigrating to Palestine. Borochov's claim against the Bund was now directed to the class at large.

HH stressed the importance of building a workers' economy ("constructivism") more than did the older Marxists. It saw itself as the vanguard for the establishment of such an economy, although it did not believe that this would by itself lead to socialism, as did Ahdut Haavoda.

In contradistinction to the Marxists of Leftist Poalei Zion, HH did not participate in the Zionist movement and recognized the need for cooperation with different classes within the Jewish people. It criticized the Borochovist theory which stated that the proletariat does not possess the status of national leadership before seizing political power. Even the rightist members of Poalei Zion were condemned for their inadequate activity in the executive branches of the Zionist federation.

However, HH refused to accept constructivism as the main content of class war in the Palestinian reality, or to contend that socialism could be realized without revolution. It therefore had to dissociate itself from traditional Borochovism, on the one hand, and the concept of Zionist unity with socialism of Ahdut Haavoda on the other. It solved the contradiction between orthodox Borochovism and its own position by creating the "Etapist Theory," according to which Jewish socialist society would be realized in two stages. In the first stage, the Jewish national home would be established in Eretz Israel, based on a productive and self sufficient economic foundation. In the second stage, the social revolution itself would be accomplished.

The function of the Zionist movement and Zionist cooperation was limited to the first stage only; it would be terminated after the economic, cultural, and political foundations had been laid in Palestine, and after the national funds, based on national donations, were no longer required. Partnership with the Zionists was therefore considered as only temporary. The social revolution was to be realized, however, by the international organization of the workers, i.e. Jewish-Arab collaboration.

This "theory of stages" formulated by Meir Yaari had many advantages for HH. It could continue to participate in the Zionist Organization, to build socialist cells within the framework of the existing regime, and, at the same time, to maintain revolutionary radicalism. It could sustain its criticism of AH in the 1920s and of Mapai in the thirties by contending that the idea of realizing Zionism in collaboration with the Zionist movement and the building of a workers' economy were an illusion and constituted "social reformism," which blunts the edge of class struggle and obscures the goals of socialism.

However, every attempt by HH to explain the class struggle in such a manner as would lead to the realization of socialism in Palestine without putting Zionism out of mind entirely was doomed to failure. The Palestinian reality made it necessary to maintain the development of all kinds of Jewish capital and to limit the class struggle so that it would not destroy the foundations of the Jewish economy. Enmity between Arabs and Jews prevented their cooperating in the class struggle. Members of Mapai, on the other hand, asserted that such division into stages invites a division of allegiances. They maintained that Zionism and socialism were intertwined, if not identical processes. According to Mapai, HH's contention that its collaboration with the Zionists was only temporary, and that there existed "tragic contradictions" between the process of national liberation and participation in the socialist revolution, pushed it towards anti-Zionist communism. The doctrinaire controversy was closely linked to organizational disagreements. Paradoxically, the Marxist revolutionaries of Hashomer Hatzair did not endeavor to find organizational expression in broad party or union organizations. They retained the collective organizational model which was being created even before the adoption of Marxist doctrine. The mid-20s' party was, in their eyes, a ruling body which sought to govern the working class itself. They maintained that AH and Mapai's contentions that they were fulfilling socialism were but a means for setting up a ruling mechanism.

The majority within the workers' movement in the country was defined by HH as adhering to "social democracy," which to it represented a combination of two negative manifestations; a political machine divorced from the community (Kibbutz) and from creativity, on the one hand, and abandonment of the socialist revolution, on the other. However, HH felt the tension of the endeavor to maintain community of primary relations, which builds the economy (a Kibbutz), and at the same time to act within the political reality.

The incompatibility of Marxism to Palestinian realities, and the internal and external conflicts as to content which were pointed out by HH, lead us to ask why Marxism was adopted at the end of the 1920s not in the real Palestinian framework, but in the ideological, sociological, and psychological spheres of HH. We may see in this a solution to the tensions between the attractive forces of communism on Jewish youth from Eastern Europe and the settlement organizations in Palestine.

Meir Yaari himself explained the adoption of Marxism in psychological terms as the expression of youth from the small bourgeois class who had been forced to descend in social status, and therefore seized hold of the theory which would give direction to the working class, the new class into which they were absorbed; while Eliezer Hacohen, one of the ideological leaders of HH, described the reasons for it as follows: "For us, Marxism was the key to renewing our spiritual creativity, the melting pot of desires, aspirations, beliefs and opinions in all aspects of life, molding them into a comprehensive universal outlook which not only served for direct self-gratification but would also become an active part of objective existence and enterprise and give us access to the universe." The adoption of Marxism may be interpreted as a result of the immanent development of the concepts of a youth movement and the community which establishes it; it may be interpreted against the background of the reality of Jewish youth in the Diaspora and their confrontation with the communist and socialist trends — which set up norms for national loyalty and revolutionary activity.

However, the test of Marxism for Hashomer Hatzair was the political reality of Palestine. The "two-stage" theory in itself did not define HH's position on the appropriate form of organizational body for the labor movement or for Zionist and Palestinian politics.

X

In 1930, AH and Hapoel Hatzair merged and formed Mapai, which was set up as a "class party," i.e. one which would unite all members of the working class, or at least the active elements thereof. A political union of workers would suit well with Marxism. At the same time, Hashomer Hatzair retracted its former opposition to a political body separate from the community of producers at large. It recognized that one should not equate the cooperative cells (Kibbutzim) with the entire scope of political activities, and that there is indeed a place for a political party separate from the economic organization.

Even more, within HH itself there emerged a group (from the Austrian HH in particular), which saw itself as Marxist and, along with this, supported participation in a broad-based political party.

As against this, the HH leadership, headed by Meir Yaari, interpreted Marxism not as a motivation for establishing a wide political party but as one for crystallizing a party based on a clear program and avant-garde groups. This position rested upon the special conditions of Palestine and basic general principles which stated that when one tries to equate a class with a party, there is always a danger that the class will take precedence over ideas and ideals. In addition, the continuing differentiation between the social democratic (reformist) world and that of revolutionary socialism prevented any kind of union.

With respect to Palestinian realities, one could claim that there was a lack of primary motivation to establish a political party of broadest scope — that is, a parliamentary body set up by a general election — and therefore that it was not feasible to do so. At the beginning of the

1930s there was even a suspicion on the part of HH that joining a broad-based political party would move the center of gravity away from the settlement organizations, the Kibbutzim, which were considered the mainstay of political activity.

As a result of these contentions, the position of the Austrian HH was rejected, since the Austrians inherited from the national Marxist party a positive attitude to a united class party, and compared it with Mapai in Palestine.

HH's leadership not only objected to a comprehensive political union which lacked clear Marxist lines, but even stipulated for Marxist principles within the Palestinian reality. These principles were a more energetic "class struggle" within the Jewish Yishuv and the Zionist federation; organization of the Arab workers; and dissent from the Second International, which Mapai had joined. The class struggle in the sphere of labor relations and other aspects of societal life would bring the socialist revolution in Palestine closer.

Mapai's leadership, however, saw the role of the workers within the Jewish community as leading the combined efforts of all its members to widen the economic and demographic bases of the Jewish national homeland. Within this framework, it of course encouraged both immigration of pioneers and workers, and the labor economy, although it did not see this as tending to the socialist revolution but to the realization of Zionism above all.

International socialist questions, which were only of marginal interest to Mapai, were of key significance to HH. It was careful to phrase its positions in Palestine in such a manner as would be relevant to the international socialist revolution. We have already seen how this expressed itself in its Palestinian policies. Within the framework of global realities, HH did not support the Second International which was, it felt, a clear expression of social democracy and reformism, and it was also critical of the Comintern and its policies, especially with regard to the Middle East.

Marxism, for HH, was not only a justification for revolutionary socialism and the foundation of its objection to social democracy; Marxist formulations could also serve as a guide for solving the problem of nationalism in Palestine.

The communist interpretation of Marxism in the Palestinian reality gave priority to the existing proletariat, that is, the Arab one, and saw it as the forerunner of the revolution. Zionism was rendered invalid, as we have seen, both in and out of itself and as a means for spreading the revolution in the Middle East.

On the other hand, HH adopted Borochov's justification of Jewish

proletarian nationalism. The Jewish need for "conditions of production" and the need of the proletariat for a "field of work" validated
the Jewish settlement in Palestine, which had not done harm to the
Arab proletariat since the economic opportunities that it created
could serve only to help it.

In one respect, HH of the late twenties and early thirties accepted
the kind of Marxism which plays down the importance of the state *per
se* and, obviously, that of the national state as well. The state which is
a result of class relations is destined to disappear, or at least to become
weakened in the socialist revolution. In contrast, a state built on class
domination would arise as the force which would shape life in
Palestine — the solidarity of the Jewish and Arab proletariats.

These two basic positions had specific interpretations — HH established its stance with regard to labor relations in Palestine, which was
said to further Jewish-Arab solidarity and suggest a political program
for the future of Palestine.

In the field of labor relations, HH objected to Mapai's demand for
full Jewish labor in the agricultural settlements, and demanded partial
Arab labor as well. It also supported professional organization of Arab
laborers. The element of international class solidarity was stronger in
its view than the element of zeal for an exclusive national economy. It
believed that Jewish-Arab proletarian solidarity would make it possible to direct a developing Jewish economy in Palestine. According to
HH, the expansion of Jewish labor itself in the plantation was not to
be considered as a national enterprise which demanded national interclass cooperation, nor as preceding cooperation with the Arab proletariat or the class struggle within Jewish society.

XI

The question of HH's Marxism became of greater significance with
reference to its dealings with Mapai on the subject of union in
1939-1940. The ideology of the majority party, as well as its political
requirements, propelled it towards union with HH, for it believed that
ideological unity with respect to Zionism and socialism was sufficient
for forming a political union as well. Global and Palestinian political
realities only increased HH's political involvement, and in 1936 it
aligned itself with urban workers who had organized the "Socialist
League." It was clear that if HH and Mapai did not combine, there
would emerge a new left-leaning workers' party.

The debate on merging with Mapai made evident the importance
and meaning of Marxism for HH, as well as its disagreements with

Mapai on the subject. HH demanded insertion of the terms "Marxism" and "class struggle" in the joint political platform, not only as a political subject but also as a way of interpreting history. Mapai's leaders wished to preserve spiritual freedom and pluralism with regard to socialist viewpoints. They suspected any dogma which would endanger their Zionist loyalties or dictate their political behavior. Union among workers appeared to them to be implanted in the real political world and not in that of ideology. Complete and total union on both the ideological and political planes, and the possibility of transferring concepts from plane to plane, appeared to the vast majority of them to be at best doubtful. By contrast, there arose among HH a group of intellectuals who strove for unity based on doctrine and faith, action within the political sphere being possible only with overall loyalty to doctrine.

Berl Katzenelson, the spiritual mentor of Mapai, viewed HH's demand for a Marxist spiritual definition as the dogmatization of general and Jewish historical conceptions. Attempts to express Jewish history in Marxist terms were always suspect in that they led to abandonment of content which was not expressible in such terms.

Some of the Marxist formulations whose inclusion HH demanded within the platform were those of the "working class" and "class struggle" — two concepts without which there was no reason for the merger, according to HH. To this, Mapai responded with the answer given by the social democrats to the avant-gardists — that it was itself the representative of the working class and the class struggle in their respective interpretations within the Palestinian scene. Mapai returned to its unwavering stand that it is not the philosophical formulations of class struggle which are significant, but the unity of the workers and the practical political conclusions drawn from it.

HH interpreted Marxism as sanctioning the dictatorship of the proletariat. Commenting on this, Berl Katzenelson claimed that this concept was destructive to the workers' movement, but within Mapai Ben-Gurion was more tolerant of the idea, and it is obvious that the United Kibbutz (Kibbutz Meuhad) and Faction B (Siya Bet) inside Mapai did not reject it outright.

XII

The 1930s saw the political plane becoming more fateful and decisive than that of labor relations. At the beginning of the decade, HH thought it could solve the problem of relations among the different nationalities by extracting the political bone of contention *in toto*:

the socialist regime would cancel out the national state and the class subservience which it entails. The accepted formula at that time was a "bi-national socialist society."

The test of Zionist loyalty did not come about in the thirties, or in any other era, as a test of loyalty to this or that constitutional formula, but as one to the principle of maximum Jewish immigration and objection to any limitation of it. To this HH stayed loyal throughout all its generations, and even based it on Marxist principles.

Zionism remained valid only insofar as it fulfilled the needs of the masses of Jewish working people, as was stated at the start of the century. Thus the program for political agreement with the Arabs was presented not only as a basic socialistic solution but also as a means for realizing "greater Zionism." At the beginning of the 1940s, HH presented its political program as a striving for a bi-national state in Palestine — that is, a state which would differentiate between governmental relations and the relative proportions of its population. Equality of nations would manifest itself in government, administration, economy, culture, language, and religion.

This idea is not the only answer which Marxism offers for the question of nationality. In its consideration of the concept of a bi-national state, HH adopted one possible version of the Marxist tradition. It resembled the Austrian socialist school of thought, which demanded separation of national government from national autonomy. HH found it especially suitable for the situation in Palestine. Its nationalist foundation remained Borochovist and rested on the "forces of production" which the territory supplies; in the forties, however, HH published Otto Bauer's book on the national question.

XIII

In the late thirties and forties, HH's Marxism was expanded from the field of political and social realities to the spiritual field. In place of the romanticism of the individual and society, it demanded intellectual discipline and an intellectual framework which would not only be coherent and answer individual demands, but would also express reality, a theoretical framework which would allow action as well as thought. Eliezer Hacohen was the leader of this trend.

The social science inherent in Marxism came, according to him, to supplant religion and metaphysics, whose appeal extended beyond reality and man. Kantianism was rejected since it was founded on a universe created by the subject, thus becoming a screen between the subject and reality; and this was presented as being in the interest of the bourgeoisie, which sought to restrict the spirit of social change.

Marxism, on the other hand, appeared as a scientific system and a creator of reality. Only through Marxism was the philosophical goal of a comprehensive science of being realized. Marxist dialectics was considered a logic which grasped existence and was not merely a form-alistic logic; it was to serve in the struggle against the tendency towards specialization in the sciences. The early works of Marx, it was said, dealt with the psychology of the "concrete man"; this man became the model in HH education.

The 1940s were also a period of the publication of many relatively authorized translations of Marxist literature into Hebrew. Marx was retranslated, and the works of Kautsky, Luxembourg, Bauer, Bogdanov, and Plekhanov were published. In the fifties, the works of Lenin and Stalin were also rendered into Hebrew.

There was even a sharp disagreement between the far left and Berl Katzenelson of Mapai with regard to translation policies. The latter desired to publish selected Marxist writings, explaining them in the context of the times and avoiding dogmatism.

XIV

Marxism aimed at integrating HH and Zionism in the international revolutionary process, although it was not an effective guide to active appreciation of international socialism in the thirties and forties. HH avoided the Socialist International, in which it saw the expression of reformism. It rejected completely the idea of gradual transition from a capitalist to a socialist society, but felt itself close to the political socialistic trend of the Vienesse socialists, especially as represented by Max Adler, finding in it a socialist vision which did not limit itself to "formal" democratic processes. This close alignment with Max Adlers's policies did not nullify a rejection of his philosophical methods and his Kantian basis.

During the thirties, HH attempted to align itself with the leftist, non-communist branches of socialist movements in Europe, but quickly abandoned the idea, regarding them as too "sectarian."

Despite its striving to identify with the great process of world-wide socialist revolution, HH did not in the 1930s equate Marxism and socialism with the Soviet Union. It appreciated her "socialist con-structive effort," but in no way avoided criticizing other aspects of Soviet society and politics. Elimination of the opposition in the Soviet Union and the Moscow trials merited strong condemnation. The

USSR's joining the League of Nations in 1934 and entering on the political scene drew criticism from both sides. Trotskyites within HH saw this as abandonment of the world revolution; other trends criticized the Soviet Union's alienation from the democracies and both denounced the Ribbentrop-Molotov agreements of August 1939, but were careful not to reject entirely the "dictatorship of the proletariat" and the Soviet Union as its practical exponent.

Despite the condemnation prevalent in HH over the German-Soviet agreements, Marxist explanation of the Second World War created severe political problems. Until June 1941, HH supported the anti-fascist war but kept its reservations towards the western democracies. In April 1942, a conference was convened which rejected the Trotsky-ite trends and supported "national fronts" in the struggle against Fascism. Criticism of the Soviet Union abated towards the end of the 1940s owing to her role in the war against the Nazis, rescue of Jews, and support of the establishment of the State of Israel, which proved, as it were, that the Soviet Union was the historical interpretation of Marxism in the forties.

XV

The thirties and forties brought new interpretations of Zionist Marxism, even outside Leftist Poalei Zion and HH. Marxism became at that time a symbol of the active class struggle against capitalism and Fascism; countertrends such as reformism of the humanistic socialism of De Man were regarded as a surrender to Fascism. A certain actuality was ascribed to adherence to Marxism within the Palestinian reality as well. This was not a return to the Marxism of orthodox Poalei Zion, which dissociated itself from constructivism and did not believe in its socialist value. Rather, it was an effort to show that constructive institutions − kibbutzim and the Histadrut − were part and parcel of the struggling working class. Hence a renewed Marxism began to spread within the ranks of Mapai, the great workers' party which had inherited its principles from Ahdut Haavoda. It expressed itself in demands for "class independence" within Palestine and in a feeling of kinship with the world revolution being led by the Soviet Union.

Marxism declared a militant socialism and no compromising with the existing regimes. It was the symbol of the war against Fascism; within Palestinian reality, Zionist revisionists were seen to exemplify Fascism.

The demands for more equality among workers and for hegemony of the kibbutz movement were also presented in the name of the world class struggle between capitalism and socialism. This was in opposition to the policies of the leaders Ben- Gurion and Katzenelson, who sought the hegemony of the workers' party in the Zionist movement, as well as in the Jewish settlement in Palestine, although not by means of conquest of power or eliminating private enterprise.

Leftist groups who were close to Marxism arose in the United Kibbutz (Kibbutz Hameuhad) movement and in less well-to-do factions of the urban workers. In 1944 they split from Mapai.

In the mid-40s, the various factions of Marxist Zionism, the old as well as the new, became united, overcoming their historical differences of opinion. It was at this very time that they assumed that Marxism would become a common denominator even more relevant than "constructivism," "pioneering," and "class struggle" – concepts which had divided them ever since the Bolshevik Revolution.

The Soviet Union's war against the Nazis and her support of the creation of the State of Israel were understood as revolutionary socialism's recognition of Zionism; the Zionist struggle against the British was interpreted as anti-imperialist. The internal contradictions which arose in the Palestinian labor movement, and increased with the development of the economy and emergence of the political dominance of labor on the national scene were seen as a struggle between revolutionary socialism and reformism.

XVI

The fifties changed scholastic formulae into fateful political platforms; Borochov's formulae of 1905–6 became the topic for concrete political debate.

The right of nations to exist in the face of the world revolution, and the right to exist of the Jewish nation and its separate state, were made somehow dependent on the interpretation of theory. The right of Yugoslavia to differ with the Soviet Union, the right of Jews to emigrate to Israel, and the right of the Palestinian Jews to set up their own government, were all put to the test. The meaning of Zionism as a world-wide movement and the existence of an independent Jewish society in Palestine were subjects for discussion in the light of Marxism as the practical expression of world revolution.

In 1948, but a few months before the declaration of the establishment of the State of Israel, a large, united and professedly Marxist workers' party was formed (for the first time since 1919). Mapam fulfilled an important political role during the first years of the State of Israel by voicing opposition to the government's internal and foreign policies as delineated by Ben-Gurion and Mapai.

In the years 1948–52, the party became more and more leftist, and this expressed itself on the ideological plane by its acceptance of Marxist doctrine. The resolutions adopted at Mapam's Congress in May–June, 1951, were the culmination of the doctrine's influence on any major Zionist political party. This was the orthodox Marxist interpretation of the early part of the century transplanted into the historical context of the early fifties.

The conference declared that the "United Workers' party is based upon Borochov's theory of a Marxist solution to the Jewish people's national problem ... and upon the Marxist-Leninist theory as a universal outlook and a course to be taken by revolutionary workers throughout the world in their political struggles."

We may ask what the background was which equated realities with Marxist doctrine, and what meaning this doctrine had in 1951.

Marxism in 1948 did not depend upon analysis of capitalism and the existing Palestinian proletariat; it could not even rest, as Borochov's theory proposed, upon analysis of the development trends of the proletariat in the Diaspora, since this no longer existed.

The interpretation of Marxism, under those conditions, was the strategy of the world socialist revolution as it was understood against the background of international realities in 1948–52: the founding years of the State of Israel and the establishment of her internal and foreign policies.

Marxist ideology was intended to explain international reality. In those years, it appeared that there were insurmountable contradictions between declining capitalism and rising socialism, and these could not be solved in a peaceful manner, nor by agreement. Rather, they demanded universal and national class struggle. The Soviet Union stood at the center of the revolutionary struggle, and therefore revolutionary socialists should identify with her. Any workers' movement which was not revolutionary was accused of accepting the existing regime.

However, the struggle against regimes had an additional meaning for Zionism. The freedom of the Jewish people and its "territorial concentration" were part and parcel of the historical process. The support of the Soviet Union and the Eastern Bloc in the establishment of the State had an ideological significance; the sympathy and aid the revolutionary world gave to Zionism would only increase until there was complete reconciliation between the two, which would mean the immigration of Russian Jews to Israel and Israel's becoming a people's democracy. The kibbutz movement would emerge as the socio-economic leaders of the political socialist revolution.

Parallel to this political orientation, Marxist doctrine became increasingly deeper-rooted. It alone was thought to be "scientific-socialism" — the Leninist interpretation of the ideology of Marx and Engels was accepted as the true interpretation of the revolutionary period, and non-Marxist socialism was accused of actually abandoning the class mission of the worker, both in the Israeli and in international spheres.

This brand of Marxism, which was dependent upon the international political situation, began to break down after a short time. Political and doctrinal conflicts started to appear as parallel phenomena. The first rift was in the interpretation of political and national problems in Palestine. HH indeed abandoned its idea of a bi-national state after the establishment of the state of Israel, although it did consider restoration of the political unity of Palestine by the setting up of Jewish and Arab states which would be closely linked. This idea was not accepted by the Ahdut Haavoda faction of Mapam, and in any case was not feasible. More practicable was the reception of Arabs into Mapam. HH supported this, but AH found it to be a negation of the very essence of a Zionist party.

However, the great test of loyalty to Zionism and the necessity to choose between it and "world revolution" came in the field of international relations, on the occasions of the Prague trials (1952), in which Mordechai Oren, a leader of Mapam, was accused of being an imperialist spy, and of the doctors' trials in Moscow (1953).

The former showed that "dual loyalties" to Zionism and communism were incompatible. At the first stages, Mapam attempted to criticize the trials only from a Zionist and not from a general socialist viewpoint. The Prague trials challenged the ideological formula of "equality of value" between Zionism and socialism as accepted by Mapam. The more leftist factions of Mapam, led by Moshe Sneh, did not view it as an equality of value, but as the relation of a segment (Zionism) to a whole (world revolution) — the priorities here are obvious.

This controversy brought to the forefront the essence of the question of nationalities and the "theory of stages"; the definition of nationality as formulated by Borochov was greatly criticized by the extreme left, and it became necessary to adapt the doctrine of temporary national cooperation of the "theory of stages" to the circumstances of the fifties.

Mapam's far left faction, under Moshe Sneh, expressed its extremist attitudes in both the political and doctrinal spheres. Politically, Sneh protested against the right of Zionism, the State of Israel, or any other national movement to oppose world revolution led by the Soviet Union. Doctrinally, he protested against Borochovist theory, which since 1906 had legitimized the Marxist basis of Zionism, and had been accepted by HH since 1927. Mapam's extreme left demanded the acceptance of the Stalinist definition of nationality (territory, language, economy, characteristics) instead of the Borochovistic one, which recognized extraterritorial nations as well. Even though the extreme leftists were prepared to accept the Jewish anomaly as an exception, they refused to allow for the right of other nations to reject the Stalinist definition and the control of the Soviet center. The Yugoslav example was completely dismissed.

HH and its leader, Meir Yaari, considered Sneh's attitude as a symptom of Zionist liquidation and a sliding into anti-Zionist communism.

During the fifties, difficulties arose with respect to the "theory of stages." When it was initially formulated in the 1920s, it seemed that the national solution of the "ingathering of exiles" (Jewish territorial concentration) would precede the social world revolution. National cooperation was limited to the phase of integration and strengthening of the economy. During the fifties, however, it appeared that social revolution would precede the "ingathering." Yaari therefore defined the third stage of the "theory of stages," stating that immigration to Israel would continue, and not end with the social revolution. Zionism could therefore find legitimacy even within the socialist regime as the movement of the entire Jewish people, and not only by the right of self-determination of the Jews in Palestine.

Just as the first wave of Marxism, which began in 1904, exploded over the Comintern's objection to Zionism in the 1920s, so the second wave (essentially that of Hashomer Hatzair), which began in 1927, exploded over the political realities of the fifties.

During the mid-50s, revision of Mapam's adherence to Marxism-Leninism found expression in the theory of nationalities, and was later applied to socialist ideology as a whole. The Twentieth Congress of the communist party and criticism of Stalinism and of Soviet policy in the Middle East and Hungary — as well as the attitude towards Jews in the Soviet Union — all brought about a more thorough revision of the 1951 stand when Mapam held its Third Congress in 1958. Alignment with the "world movement of revolutionary workers," which was not necessarily to be led by the Soviet Union, replaced the ties with the Soviet Union herself.

The controversy appeared to be one of semantics; in the early fifties, Mapam had spoken of Marxism-Leninism as an indivisible whole. Now this unity dissolved and was not to be perceived as an indivisible entity. The Congress decided to "devote all their energies to adapting Marxist *and*Leninist principles — the theoretical basis of international revolutionary socialism — to the present conditions of our people and country, without being bound by dogmatic fetters."

These decisions of the Congress do not indicate the entire process of change. In fact there arose criticism of the whole theoretical structure of HH, that of the twenties and thirties. One section of Mapam demanded the abandonment of the idea of the "proletarian dictatorship," which was an explicit attribute of revolutionary socialism, and adopting instead the doctrine of many courses leading to socialism. Thus the concept which had been firmly implanted in HH in the later twenties and thirties had undergone a change. Activity within the framework of the existing regime was not restricted to one "phase," the pre-revolutionary one, and did not necessarily have to be replaced by the seizing of power of the second "phase." Economic and political activity within the existing regime could only further socialism.

The discarding of the idea of realizing socialism through revolution eliminated the reasons for the existence of a vanguard party. Socialist parliamentary activity demanded a broad-based party, or at least participation in a government coalition; indeed, Mapam began to become more and more involved in the Israeli political scene and finally joined an alignment with the labor party.

The old guard of Mapam, and its leader, Meir Yaari, still sought to fulfill Marxist ideas. In 1963, Yaari was prepared to abandon the Marxist notions of the "theory of pauperization" or the "theory of crises." The flourishing of capitalist economies after the Second World War disproved them. Despite this, however, he saw certain historical principles as being unchangeable. He wished to preserve the intellectual foundation which would maintain within Mapam a secular and "objective" grasp of history. This outlook would avoid the concept of Higher Power and, along with this, be free of scepticism with regard to possibilities for progress. Mapam might therefore remain loyal to "historical and dialectical materialism."

Mapam even ought to object to a capitalist regime because of its appropriating "surplus values," and the contradiction between it and technological progress.

Yaari still thus desired to maintain not only his objections to capitalism but also preserve the method of "class struggle," and even "dictatorship of the proletariat as a necessary phenomenon."

Only two manifestations of the shortcomings of Marxism were recognized openly — despite their devotion to Internationalism, members of Mapam began to claim that Marxism did not develop a theory of nationalism. In addition, Marxism's treatment of agrarian problems was thought to be lacking.

For HH, Marxism not only served as a guiding principle, but also supplied an intellectual pattern for a comprehensive ideology which was transmitted through kibbutz schools and youth movements. Relations between political attitudes and the intellectual world operated in both 'directions — conceptions consolidated attitudes and attitudes became conceptions.

Political reorientation during the sixties, which found expression in renunciation of close ties with the Soviet Union and rejection of the course of revolutionary dictatorship, also manifested itself in intellectual change. Several factors caused this: Mapam's senior generation found it necessary to examine the ideological hypotheses of the twenties and see whether they were to be blamed for the political misconceptions; the younger generation became indifferent and even antagonistic to Marxism. In a HH kibbutz poll, only a small percentage of the population declared itself to be Marxist and Borochovist.

A third reason for the renewed discussion of Marxist principles was the growing number of institutes of higher learning in the kibbutz movement which gave a more theoretical character to ideological discussions.

Despite the disappointment in Marxism as a political guide and the critical attitude of intellectuals, Mapam continued to adhere to Marxism as an ideological doctrine, believing that history and politics, without a systematic ideological outlook, would only lead to opportunism.

The intellectual change in Marxism took several courses, one of which was a call to return to the "original Marx." His interpreters were accused of distorting his teachings by rendering them dry, sterile, and repellant to the public. Other trends found fault with conservative Marxism, decrying the absence of philosophical anthropology and Kantian elements, which would add absolute values to historical relativism. Such elements would be epistemological or ethical; in any case, they would prevent subjection to real or imaginary historical processes.

Another criticism of the theoretical plane was that there did not develop a theory of nationalism analogous to the political theory. The lack of a Marxist nationalist theory brought about the domination of

Hungary and Czechoslovakia, according to this view, which also explained the relationship of the Soviet Union to Zionism.

In these examinations, HH and Mapam voiced criticism regarding the traditional hypotheses of Marxism, such as: recurring crises in capitalist society; the form revolution would take and the dictatorship of the proletariat; abolishment of private property through nationalization as the fundamental principles bringing about a total change which would ensure the creation of a better society. The Soviet Union was presented as an etatist society ruled by a bureautechnocracy, a regime which was held responsible for the outrages of Soviet policy.

HH remained faithful to its initial Marxist concept of the relationship between the "foundation" and the superstructure. It saw the basic flaw in Soviet society as the contradiction between a nationalized economy and one administered by the workers themselves. A society autonomously administering its own production could be free of the shortcomings warping the Soviet Union's internal and foreign policies.

SUMMARY

The widespread acceptance of Marxism by consecutive generations of Zionists is surprising for a number of reasons. The conditions for the development of capitalism and of the working class in Palestine were either entirely different from those prevalent in Russia and Galicia, or, at best, only partially similar. On the other hand, Marxism spread great confusion among Zionists, who accepted it only after longwinded polemics. Nevertheless, there are important values which Marxism imparted to Zionism, such as the territorial principle of nationalism, historical determinism, analysis of the Jewish economic structure, the possibility of harmony between Zionism and universal class war, and solidarity among the people living in Palestine.

Marxism was one of the factors that assembled and consolidated the workers as a separate body within the Zionist Movement — even though, as mentioned above, the tendency towards unity in the labor movement opposed doctrinaire Marxism. The negation of private property during the realization of Zionism was justified on either Zionist or on moral and not on Marxist grounds, but the influence of Marxism still remained powerful.

Marxism raised great difficulties for Zionism in that it placed strong emphasis on class distinctions among the Jewish people during the national effort and on the potential schism between Jewish loyalty and class or international proletarian loyalty. Marxist Zionists attempted to solve this conflict of loyalties by means of the theory of "division into stages." Borochov differentiated between the stage of building a capitalist economy in which there is a spontaneous partnership among the classes, and the stage of struggle for national and class emancipation led by the proletariat.

Hashomer Hatzair differentiated between the stage of national construction and the stage of revolution in which the national interclass partnership would come to an end. These "stages" were found unsuitable to political behavior and were accused of causing a division of loyalties.

One characteristic phenomenon of Zionist Marxism from 1920 was the identification of the majority of Zionist Marxists with the dictatorship of the proletariat, and the acceptance of the Bolshevik interpretation of Marxism over a reformist or orthodox one. Zionist Marxism was also generally associated with the avant-garde type of ideological party rather than with a wide-class party.

In addition, the constant attachment of Palestinian Marxism to the dictatorship of the proletariat and the Soviet Union linked its ideology to the changing political relations between Zionism and communism, relations which generally could be characterized as sharply antagonistic.

Zionist Marxism was more the theory of an intelligentsia which endeavoured to lead the Jewish labor class than a theory of the Jewish working class itself. This class as it existed in Eastern Europe, and in so far as it maintained a Jewish Marxist ideology, followed the lead of the Bund.

The Zionist Marxist intelligentsia did not succeed in directing the Jewish working class in Eastern Europe or in America and in bringing it to Palestine. Nevertheless Marxist ideology had become one of the motivations for building a national economy in Palestine and Israel and for establishing a Jewish working class there, as well as an impetus for workers' hegemony in the national life in general.

The weakness of Jewish capitalism in Palestine and the lack of a national state prevented the adoption of the conventional "class struggle" by the Jewish working class there even when this formula was used with connotations different from those in European Marxism.

Labor economy in Palestine was usually not judged by Marxist criteria — it was tested by its national, economic, and moral value, more than by its capacity to undermine capitalism.

The discrepancy between Marxism and the Jewish social reality in Palestine and the difficulties that arose, lead us to seek psychological motives for Marxism's acceptance. They can be found in the quest for concepts of social analysis and the wish to localize the social ideal in a materialist reality, in the orientation of the historical process and in the striving for a coherent ideological and political universe. Marxism's power was manifested in the historical status it gave the proletariat. In the case of Palestine, this was not an existing proletariat but one which developed voluntarily, due to the needs of the Palestinian economy and Zionist labor ideals. The concept of the national pioneer found its intellectual and social counterpart in the mission envisaged for the working class by Marxism. Recognition of this mission made it possible to demand the consolidation of the working class in Palestine and Israel. This class was, in fact, greatly variegated, comprising laborers and settlers, members of cooperatives and self-employed workers.

Marxism's intellectual impact can best be illustrated by the vacuum it has left in the intellectual and public spheres over the past few years, now that its influence has decreased.

Marxism, which had permeated Jewish society in Eastern Europe, faces today a completely different situation. The geographical distribution and class structure of the Jewish people have changed radically. Jewish unity, the trends in Jewish society and the place of Israel in the life of the Jewish people — cannot be formulated in the Borochovist-Marxist terms of the beginning of the century.

The social reality of Israel and its intellectual life pose new problems for Marxist Zionism. Some of these problems are common to all developed societies and some are peculiar to Israel.

Marxism is no longer considered a valid theory for the explanation of social reality. Concentration of capital, pauperization, social polarization, crisis and revolution are not relevant descriptions of the social process. Dictatorship of the proletariat cannot be adopted as a revolutionary strategy under the present class structure, pluralist society and democratic state. Obedience to the Soviet Union is rejected for both Zionist and socialist reasons.

From the intellectual point of view Marxism can no longer be considered as the only "scientific" method for the interpretation of social reality. The free and pluralistic intellectual life does not permit the dogmatism that was prevalent in Eastern and Central Europe at the beginning of the century. In spite of the collapse of the traditional Marxist Zionist theories during the 1960s and in spite of the radical change in world and Jewish situations one cannot claim that Marxism in Israel is intellectually dead. Of course, it is no longer considered a guide to the interpretation of history as a national or international class struggle. It has lost its appeal as a revolutionary strategy.

However, it still maintains its appeal as a comprehensive philosophy of Man and Society. It is considered of value as a theory which attempts to achieve the philosophical ideal of a free and rational individual in the economic and social reality. It is considered a critique of the market economy and the culture of consumption. In a modified form it can serve for an analysis of Israel's economy and society. The existence of the Kibbutz movement in Israel is a formidable factor which attributes significance to Marxism as an ideal of a socialist society.

Note: Since the documentation is mostly in Hebrew and Yiddish, it will be attached to the Hebrew version of this article.

MARXISM IN THE ARAB WORLD: THE CASES OF
THE EGYPTIAN AND SYRIAN REGIMES

SHIMON SHAMIR
Tel-Aviv University

An Egyptian journalist, when asked to explain why in his opinion Marxism would never prevail in the Arab world, replied, "It is quite simple: We believe that there is no God but Allah, and Mohammed is his prophet; while they believe that there *is* no God, and *Karl Marx* is his prophet." This statement, paradoxically, may reflect the compatibility between Marxism and Arabic-Islamic culture rather than the incompatibility.[1] But the point made by the journalist is nonetheless valid and resistance to Marxism in Arab-Muslim society has been quite pronounced from its first appearance in the area. There had been Marxists in the Arab world prior to World War II — Marxists who bore names like Arturo Schwartz and Henri Curiel — but they obviously belonged to marginal groups. Marxism has penetrated the predominantly Muslim, Arabic-speaking sector of local society only in the past three decades.

Today, Marxist concepts and ideas are expounded in the Arab world by persons who belong to one of three different categories. First, there are a number of individual Arab thinkers whose writings reflect a downright Marxist point of view. They are not the products of direct Soviet influence or of an education in Eastern European universities, but are mostly graduates of such universities as the LSE, the Sorbonne and Columbia and offshoots of various Western intellectual circles. Many of them no longer live in the Arab countries but are *émigrés* or political exiles; nevertheless, their works can be read in most Arab states. This category includes intellectuals like Ṣādiq Jalāl al-'Aẓm, who wrote among other things an interesting work on the criticism of religion, and "Mahmoud Hussein," the authors of *La Lutte des Classes en Egypte.*

The second category consists of various political movements of Marxist persuasion. They include the "old left" of the various Communist parties — some of them legal, some clandestine — and the new radical movements which have produced several guerrilla organizations, such as the Palestinian National Fronts of Ḥabash and Ḥawatmeh and the National Front for the Liberation of the Arab Gulf. In the major Arab states the political power and influence of these movements is quite limited. Their members are mainly middle class intellectuals and many of them still come from minority groups.

The third category includes Marxist intellectuals who have been operating within those political systems in the Arab world that term themselves "liberated" regimes — in countries like Algeria, Egypt, Syria, and Iraq. These intellectuals are sometimes given the opportunity to guide the indoctrination institutions or draft the official programs of their respective regimes and thus can effectively disseminate Marxist concepts.

This brief paper will deal only with the third category. Although it should be admitted that the first two groups may be quite significant intellectually or otherwise, the fact is that they exist mainly on the margins of Arab society. Since Marxism — at least for Marxists — is an applied science, the degree of its pervasiveness should be examined in terms of political power. In these terms, the fact that the third group has drawn close to the centers of various Arab power structures gives it greater significance.

Two regimes in particular deserve to be discussed — those of Nasserite Egypt and Ba'thist Syria. The semi-Marxist or pseudo-Marxist terminology appearing in the programs of these two regimes reflect the degree of penetration of Marxism into the mainstream of Arab political life.

The turning point in the attitude of the Egyptian regime toward Marxism took place following the dissolution of the union with Syria in 1961. In his *post mortem* to the union, President Nasser declared that the lesson to be learned from this failure was that the socio-political structure of the Egyptian Revolution needed reinforcement; that it was necessary to adopt a socio-political doctrine that could strengthen the power base of the regime and enable it to cope with challenges coming from hostile — predominantly bourgeois — groups of the kind that it had been compelled to face in Syria. In May 1962 President Nasser appeared before the Egyptian people and read to them a fairly long manifesto — the "Charter of National Action" — which was meant to be the answer to that need.

Basically, the ideas expounded in the Charter did not differ much from what is known in the Arab world as "Arab Socialism." On the economic level, it calls for the nationalization of considerable parts of the economy and the creation of a public sector. On the social level, it calls for the establishment of a system based on the "five forces of the working people" – namely the peasants, workers, intellectuals, "national capitalists" and soldiers. On the political level, these "forces" are urged to produce jointly a political organization, named the Arab Socialist Union, which would guide the revolution.

Essential to the tenets of Arab Socialism is the claim that it is an authentic Arab system – emanating directly from the heritage and the realities of the Arab people. Yet, scattered throughout the Charter are certain themes that can be identified as having been influenced by Marxism (evidently through the models of Yugoslavia and certain regimes of the Afro-Asian world). Going through the Charter, one finds sentences such as: "It is an indisputable fact that the political system in any state is but a direct reflection of the prevailing economic state of affairs, and an accurate expression of the interests controlling this economy." Or: "No citizen can be regarded as having political freedom unless he is free from exploitation in all its forms." The Charter explains that "the Socialist path paves the way for the inevitable development leading to the liberation of the people from the Feudalist and Capitalist systems," and refers to the Socialist solution as an "historical inevitability." It calls for the transfer of large industry and trade from private ownership to the public. And it lays down that "the suitable style for finding the right method leading to progress is scientific socialism," a term often taken as synonymous with Marxism.[2]

It should be noted that this selection of phrases and themes can be misleading. The Charter is basically a rather eclectic mixture, including elements which belong to different ideological systems, some of them definitely anti-Marxist. Nevertheless it was innovative in the sense that for the first time Marxist concepts were included in the formal program of the Nasserite regime.

For disseminating a doctrine which is partly based on Marxism, the regime needed to have among its ranks some genuine Marxists. Indeed, after the proclamation of the Charter, Egyptian Communists were gradually released from the prisons and detention camps in which they had been held. Following the self-dissolution of their Communist Party, in 1965, they were granted important positions in the cultural and educational institutions, the media and the indoctrination system of the regime's political organization (the Arab Socialist Union). Thus, such Marxists as Maḥmūd Amīn al-ʿĀlim, Fuʾād Mursi, Muḥammad al-Khafīf and Ismāʿīl Ṣabrī ʿAbdalla joined the Nasserite technocracy, and the last even attained ministerial level.[3]

As could perhaps be expected, the Marxists did not content themselves with the role of a channel for transferring ideas from the Nasserite regime to the public, but tried to have an impact on the regime itself. They refused to regard the Charter as a blueprint for a static social and political order and saw it as the first step in treading the path toward "genuine" Socialism. They considered themselves the *avant garde* of the Revolution, precipitating a dynamic process of transformation.

The many ambiguities and contradictions in the Charter allowed them a wide scope for debate with the non-Marxist élite of the Nasser regime. Among the typical issues debated was the interpretation of the Charter's slogan "the fusion of the differences between the classes": did it assume for society, as the Nasserites explained, a harmonious coexistence between classes based on national solidarity or, as the Marxists claimed, indicate a dynamic struggle gradually to liquidate those classes which had no real place within the category of "the working forces of the people"? Another question was the meaning of "Arab Socialism": did it refer to a qualitatively different brand of Socialism, as many Nasserites argued or, as the Marxists preferred it, only to an Arab road to Socialism which was none other than the universal message of Marxism?

These questions were disputed for a long time. Nasser himself preferred to maintain the ambiguity of the Charter — albeit without allowing the Marxist interpretations to gain hold. However, following Sadat's accession to power, the debate was finally settled. With the revival of more traditional and Islamic concepts, the rift with the Soviet Union and the new Western-oriented "Economic Openness," not much scope has been left for the Marxist interpretations of the regime's program. Indeed, at the end of 1972, an official committee of the ASU issued a ruling eliminating the Marxist versions. Since then, a good many Marxists have quietly been removed from their positions.[4]

No less interesting is the Syrian experience. Here the breakthrough was achieved by Syrian Marxists in September 1963 — some time after the *coup d'état* which had brought the Ba'th party to power.

The regime established by the coup d'état was identified with the Ba'th party, but the group which held effective power was a clique of young military officers, and not the intellectuals who had founded the Ba'th and still kept the key posts in the leadership of that movement. These officers faced several problems which they hoped they could alleviate by adopting a well-formulated revolutionary doctrine. First, they had a difficult and embarrassing confrontation with Egypt. Among other things, President Nasser ridiculed the Ba‘th regime for its pretensions to be based on a particular ideology while, to his mind, Ba'thism had no distinctive features. Therefore, the Syrian leaders wished not only to prove that their rule was rooted in an effective and meaningful doctrine, but also to seize the initiative and demonstrate that their ideology could be applied to other countries as well. Second, there was the problem of the competition between the military officers and the machinery of the Ba‘th party, including those who had led the party prior to the coup d'état. The officers sought to replace that machinery, or at least to reduce its power, by introducing new ideas and a more dynamic orientation.

Apparently for these reasons the military clique endorsed a group of Marxist intellectuals — including Elias Murquṣ, Yāsīn al-Ḥāfiẓ and George Ṭarabīshī[5] — most of whom were ex-Communists and some of whom had been affiliated with the Ba‘th party for some time but were antagonistic to the romantic and idealistic formulations of its founders ‘Aflaq and al-Bīṭār. These Marxists were now given an opportunity to play a major role in an ideological committee which was set up by the officers in power in order to reformulate the program of the party.

The outcome was a document entitled "Some Theoretical Points of Departure," most of which the Ba‘th party officially adopted, in the same year, through the resolutions of the Sixth National Congress. The Points of Departure go several steps further toward Marxism-Leninism than the formulations of the Egyptian Charter. As against the Nasserite concept of an alliance of "five forces," it declares that "the Revolution does not serve all the classes of society but only those who have a direct interest in it: the peasants, workers and revolutionary intellectuals"; omitted are the soldiers and, more significantly, the "national capitalists." Unlike the Charter, the Points of Departure make an explicit committment to class struggle: "The masses must face the question of the class struggle against the reactionary classes in a clear and decisive fashion — either we survive or reaction does; any compromise settlement is a deception.

The role of the *avant-garde* is laid down in these terms: "The revolutionary Socialist *avant-garde* is the instrument of the masses in bringing about a transformation of social and economic relations." Unlike the ASU, which is a popular mass organization, the Ba‘th is defined as a leading *avant-garde* corps. The Points of Departure ridicules "State Capitalism," which is a code phrase for the Nasserite system, and states that the economy should be directed only "by the toiling masses."

Many other themes in the Syrian document can be interpreted as a challenge to the Nasserite doctrine. It rejects Nasserite Arab Socialism with its claim to cultural distinctiveness and its overstress on Nationalism. It ignores religion completely, whereas Nasser accepted religion as one of the basic elements of Arab Socialism. In one of its sections the Syrian document declares pointedly that "knowledge of the laws governing the transformation of society and the course of history" should be gained and applied in a revolutionary regime.

It is interesting to note that Points of Departure, just like the Charter, does not endorse Marxism formally and the word itself is not mentioned in the document. One of the leading Marxists of this group later warned against the mechanical application of Marxist doctrines to the Arab case, as the Communists wanted. Instead he advocated "the Arabization of Marxism" — a more sophisticated adaptation to Arab realities and Arab needs.

The heyday of the Marxist intellectuals in Damascus was soon over. Once the new ruling clique was firmly entrenched in power, the intellectuals became expendable and, indeed, in the first half of 1964 they were ousted from the party and some of them even arrested or exiled.[6]

This, however, did not bring to an end Marxist influences on the Syrian political system. Such influences continued to manifest themselves mainly in two political groups: in the radical faction of the Ba'th (mostly military) leadership and in the Syrian Communist Party. The radical faction, led by Ṣalāḥ Jedīd, seized power in Syria in the February 1966 *putsch.* It removed the original nationalist Ba'th leadership and introduced a radical militant style, both in domestic and foreign policies. Following this *putsch,* ties with the Communists were strengthened, with the blessing of the Soviet Union. This was not an entirely new policy for the Ba'th, for this party had occasionally collaborated with the Syrian CP since 1955. However, under the radicals' rule, Communists were admitted into the Cabinet, were given various key positions in the state, and their leader, the veteran Khālid Bakdash, was allowed to return from exile.

The Syrian regime has thus gone much further toward the left than Egypt, yet the vision of the Syrian intellectual Marxists has not been realized and Syria has not really entered a continuous process of transformation guided by what they dubbed "the revolutionary doctrine." The Communists have remained a tolerated and closely-watched external force which was not allowed access to the centers of power. Their effort to form an alliance with the Ba'th left wing turned out to be counter-productive: it discredited the left wing and increased the suspicions of the rulers, who occasionally clamped down on the Communists and conducted arrests among them. The radical government itself was toppled in 1970 and replaced by that of Ḥāfiẓ al-Asad who has been more pragmatic and conciliatory toward the conservative and bourgeois elements in Syrian society. This type of government appears to have a greater capability of maintaining in Syria a stable and effective regime than its more radical predecessor.[7]

The cases of Egypt and Syria, to which those of such Arab countries as Algeria and Iraq could have been added, lead to the following conclusions. Arab societies do have today a small but not insignificant number of Marxists who are sufficiently close to the political centers to conduct a meaningful interaction with them. The ruling circles, predominantly nationalists with military backgrounds, occasionally seek the collaboration of Marxist intellectuals and Communists and take them into their service. They usually do this as a conciliatory gesture toward the Soviet Union, or as a maneuver in the internal struggle for power, or in a genuine effort to strengthen the ideological dimension of their social reforms and economic control. The Marxists, on their part, are usually motivated by the wish and hope to be able to influence the regime from within.

These expectations have been frustrated over and over again and in the third quarter of the century the Marxists have failed to set the political systems in which they functioned on a one-way course toward Marxism-Leninism. The Marxist intellectuals have not managed to gain the confidence of the ruling groups. Communists were absorbed into the political system either by disbanding their party and admitting their members into the regime's institutions on an individual and selective basis, or by integrating their party into a "National Front" which served to control the Communists rather than to give them a springboard to power. True, some Marxist concepts, in broad and vague forms, have penetrated the terminology of the prevailing regimes and a more serious impact has been made on some circles of intellectuals, students and activists in workers' organizations, but the influence of Marxism, on the whole, has been marginal and the Marxists have failed to create for themselves an effective power base.

The causes of this failure have been amply discussed by the observers of Arab contemporary history. To the extent that Marxism was at all a candidate for predominance in the major Arab states, its advent was hampered by a large number of factors. Soviet power politics in the region were definitely detrimental to the Marxist cause. Arab nationalism has remained the prevailing ideology and it often appeared as diametrically opposed to Marxism. Islam, as an all-encompassing system, has not left much scope for a rival system of truth, and the nature and structure of Arab society is hardly amenable to such a Western doctrine as Marxism.

The gap between the Arab-Islamic heritage and Marxism reveals itself also in the great difficulties Arab Marxists face in searching for adequately well-defined terms in the Arabic language to convey the European terminology. When Arab Marxists express themselves in Arabic — a language that uses the same term for science and for religious knowledge — the outcome is either almost incomprehensible or a very artificial text that alienates a good part of the educated public in the Arab world. Marxist writings in Arabic thus emphasize the alien origin of Marxism and manifest the wide gap separating the Marxists from the rest of their society.

NOTES

1. Cf. Bernard Lewis, "Communism and Islam," *Int. Aff.* Jánuary 1954.

2. See Nissim Rejwam, *Nasserist Ideology: Its Exponents and Critics,* Shiloah Center (Tel Aviv University), Jerusalem 1974. The full text of the Charter, in English translation, is given in the Appendix.

3. For tests of Egyptian Marxists, see Anouar Abdel-Malek (ed.), *La pensée politique arabe contemporaine,* Paris 1970.

4. See the author's "The Marxists in Egypt: The 'Licensed Infiltration' Doctrine in Practice," in M. Confino and S. Shamir (eds.), *The U.S.S.R. and the Middle East,* Shiloah Center and Russian Center (TAU), Jerusalem 1973, pp. 293–320.

5. For texts of Syrian Marxists, see Bassam Tibi (ed.), *Die arabische Linke,* Frankfurt 1964.

6. See Itamar Rabinovitch, *Syria Under the Ba'th, 1963–66: The Army Party Symbiosis,* Shiloah Center (TAU), Jerusalem 1972. Parts of the Points of Departure, in English translation, are given in Appendix F.

7. See Moshe Ma'oz, "Syria Under Hāfiz al-Asad: New Domestic and Foreign Policies," The Davis Institute (Hebrew University) *Jerusalem Papers* No. 15, Jerusalem 1975.

MARXISM IN THE ARAB WORLD

EMANUEL SIVAN
The Hebrew University of Jerusalem

Accepting the three-pronged typology of Arab Marxism, I intend to concentrate on the first two groups of Marxists – the Communists and the leftist fringe groups – and their role in the Arab world.

However, first I want to comment on the third group: those Arabs in the mainstream of society who are tinged with, or tainted by, Marxism. If one is to assess the situation in a brutal manner, one may say that the third category involves a "pseudo-Marxism." The masses or numbers of people adhering to the Marxist movement are not necessarily the criteria that should be taken as the measure of its influence. What is important in Marxism as an applied science – in the sense of *praxis* – is the way Marxist tools are utilized in the analysis and dissection of an existing society and even, though not necessarily, in the forging out of solutions for the future. It goes without saying that any work of destruction is easier than constructive work, but even destruction must occasionally be undertaken. And what is rather characteristic of the Egyptian, Syrian, and Algerian effort in this sphere is its very eclectic way of taking from Marxist doctrine those elements that support an ideology or a program already selected. Thus, goals already chosen are given a certain varnish of Marxist respectability.

Let us not forget that the Arab national movement has been incorporated, since Bandung, into the Third World of nonaligned nations. In that world, Marxist modes of speaking are an object of respectability and even of adulation, and the Arabs play this game. To some extent people educated in Eastern Europe play an influential role, but, the main sources of influence are indigenous. Because of this factor, one cannot seriously trust the elements of Marxist phraseology used by the three regimes – Egyptian, Syrian, and Algerian – as really Marxist. It is simply a way of behaving according to the *bon ton* of the moment, while never taking Marxist tools for social dissection. One might expect such manipulation of meaning and phrasing from a Nasser, from the leaders of the Ba'ath party, even from Ben Bella during the periods when he was toying with Marxism. But this is even truer as regards the self-styled leftists within the various parties – the Elias Morkos group in Syria, the Tali'a group in Egypt, and the Mohammed Harbi group of "Revolution Africaine" in Algeria. Even among these "leftists" there was never any genuine belief in Marxism in any of its extant versions. There was never any effort to use those Marxist tools in a creative manner.

But to return to the Communists, the card-carrying brand: Here the question is not so much whether, after more than fifty years of Communist presence in the Arab world, they have attained power and some participation in an Arab government. In Syria, for example, it is not a question of the amount of popular support nor even a question of the degree of Communist penetration beyond the intelligentsia into the "toiling masses" (proletariat and peasants). The principal question – or the chief accusation held against the Communists in their own frame of reference – would be that they also have never attempted to use Marxism as an element for understanding or having others understand the realities of the Arab world; they have never tried to propose solutions based upon this heuristic method. I am not certain that the explanation sometimes suggested, concerning the basic incompatibility of Islam and Communism, is really valid. One could even argue that since both concepts, Communism and Islam, are "holistic" ones – in a way even totalitarian in the sense of trying to mould the whole system of belief and behavior – passage from one to the other could be rather easy. The transition could be patterned after the well-known phenomenon of European intellectuals in the 'thirties who passed from Communism to Fascism, a shift that can perhaps be explained to a large extent from the basic similarity between these two systems.

The explanation of the basic incompatibility of the two systems, Communism and Islam, is even less valid when it is observed that the Communists never – or virtually never – tried to attack, at least in a frontal assault, the major role of Islam in Arab society, either as a source of belief or as a norm for behavior. Apart from a short period in 1921–1922 and most notably in Tunisia – when the Communist Party used atheistic propaganda – the Communists quickly learned that this was not the way to influence the Arab masses. Therefore they tried to forget and make others forget the question altogether; or alternatively, they tried to prove the compatibility of Islam and Communism, to show that this compatibility existed not only in theory, but also in actual life, in the Central Asian republics of the USSR.

This is once more proof of the major default of Communists and many other Marxists in the Arab world throughout the last fifty years. They never tried to attack the roots of the problems of the Arab world using their Marxist tools, although Marxist thought would have necessarily brought them to different attitudes vis-à-vis Islam. It is quite interesting to note that one cannot blame the Russian Communist Party, its rigidity, its way of conceiving hegemony over other national parties, for this failure. Until well into the 1950s and many even into the early 1960s, most Communist Parties were under the rule of the CP's of their European colonialist powers. As such they may perhaps have had more leeway. For those European parties (French, Italian, and British), the problems posed by the colonial parties were so marginal that no real effort was made, at least not on a regular basis, to try to instill into them a European-centered concept, which, of course, could not be applied to a colonial situation. Most of the faults thus really lie with the local Communists.

As for the second group, one could say that a new phenomenon has emerged in the last decade. The situation is no doubt in flux and one cannot make any predictions. But there certainly has been a new departure since the mid-sixties, a departure intensified, of course, by the 1967 War. This departure consists in the rise of a new generation of Arab Marxists, most of whom learned their lessons in Europe, though usually not from orthodox Marxists; sometimes from Trotskiists, at times from all kinds of maverick Marxists. True, many of these people live in exile, but quite a few of them also live and work in the Arab countries, especially in Beirut. There are at least two important intellectual reviews in the Arab states today, *Dirâsât Arabiya* and *Mawâqif,* which are to a large extent influenced by the views of this new generation of Marxists. Though the whole development lacks contact with the masses, at least this group, for the first time, makes a genuine effort to apply the Marxist system of analysis; *Marxist,* but not necessarily Leninist, although they utilize many Leninist elements. They surely do not employ the Stalinist system, which is a term of vituperation among them, nor do they regard post-Stalinist Russia as a model. This group is actually trying to use Marxist tools of analysis in order to understand their own society and to build up a strategy of revolution.

An example of this process is the fact that for the first time there is a frontal attack, and a very serious one, on the question of Islam as a major source of Arab nationalism. The attack is not so much on Islam itself as on Islamic history, as one of the two major elements in the definition of Arab nationalism, a definition always taken for granted both by the Communists and by those in the mainstream of Arab nationalism having recourse to Marxist phraseology. On the other hand, an attack is also mounted on Islam as a system of beliefs moulding behavior in many fields of life, as for example, on the sexual mores of even those Arabs who consider themselves to be liberated. These self-styled "revolutionary" and "liberated" Arab males are shown to behave in their households and towards their wives as the most extreme male chauvinists, and Islam-inspired chauvinists at that.

The question of mores, however, is overshadowed by the question of Islam as one of the major elements of Arab nationalism which imposes orientation in history: the need to assimilate the past, to make oneself worthy of one's history, to justify one's acts according to one's past. This need is one of the major spectres haunting Arab society today. And for the first time an effort is being made to build, with the help of Marxist tools, a future-orientated theory of which there are almost as many versions as there are Marxists. Still, this may well be a genuine form of Marxism. The past, they contend, is lacking in relevance for the world of today, or at the very least, the past has a marginal relevance simply because it is a product of previous eras. As such, it is the product of a well-defined system of social relations built upon a specific economic infrastructure and is not necessarily to be revered today. Many of this new group (such as Fucad Zakariyya, Salah Isa, Nadím al-Bítâr, and Sadek al-'Azm) clearly speak in terms of a total gap between present and past and therefore try to define Arab nationalism in a new way and the needs and goals of Arab society in an entirely different manner. This is a rather minor phenomenon for the moment, although as an intellectual development it is one of the most refreshing to date. For the first time Arab Marxists have undertaken to attempt a trenchant systematic criticism, on the one hand, of the major religious doctrines of Arab society and, on the other hand, the major norms of behavior of that society. This analysis is made not only with Marxist tools but with, what is perhaps more important, intellectual rigor and intellectual discipline, not in the eclectic and apologetic manner of yore. As with all intellectual argumentation, the criticism of al-'azm, Zakariyya, and others contains gaps. But at least it ushers in a process of authentic growth of a Marxist way of thinking, for the moment primarily in the area of destructive work, but perhaps one day in constructive fields as well.

PRACTICE AND THEORY – KANT, MARX, LUKÁCS

NATHAN ROTENSTREICH
The Hebrew University of Jerusalem

The subject matter of the present exploration is a critical assessment of the transformation of the concept of practice from Kant via Marx to Lukács. The reference to the correlated concept of theory emerges in that context because of the very meanings involved. In order to place the topic in its proper context, it is apposite to preface the investigation by a comment on the background of the concept of practice in so far as that concept can be traced to Greek philosophy and to the extent that the Greek legacy became an integral part of Western philosophy.

There are distinctions, insofar as nuances go, between Plato and Aristotle in their respective description of acts and activities; but what is common to both is the distinction between two areas of activity – *praxis* and *poiesis.* For reasons related to the specific subject matter of our investigation, it might be feasible to sum up briefly only the gist of the Aristotelian view. As to acts of *poiesis* or production and pro- ductivity it can be said that their end lies outside themselves; a bridge or a house produced is meant to serve ends beyond the produced structure. As against this direction of *poiesis, praxis,* or in Aristotle's sense, practical wisdom, refers to things that are good or bad with respect to man, and are done for his sake. In this sense *praxis* refers to desire or to choice. In a sense it can be said that for Aristotle the good deed is an end in itself, and thus it relates to *praxis* and not *poiesis.* Moreover, since the emphasis is laid on the position of being an end in itself, theory, which is an end in itself, becomes the good deed, or the good situation par excellence. It has to be observed parenthetically that in the course of the development of the philosophical analysis as well as of philosophical terminology the two terms, *praxis* and *poiesis,* somehow coalesced, or their distinction became blurred. Kant, for instance, maintains the distinction between practice and technicality, or else between practical and pragmatic – though pragmatic does not correspond to the poietic, but rather to the involvement in the world and its affairs.

It can be said at the outset of our analysis that, by and large, Kant comes back to the basic meaning of praxis or practice insofar as he relates that concept to the shaping of the will or to initiation of acts whose end lies in themselves. But within these broad contours of the Kantian position there are some rather significant innovations. For the sake of their analysis it is mandatory to look into the juxtaposition between theoretical propositions and practical ones. Theoretical propositions, says Kant, are propositions which refer to an object and determine that which is to be attributed to the object and that which is not to be attributed to it. As against this, practical propositions are those which assert an act through which, as a necessary condition of it, an object becomes possible.[1] Thus it can be said that theoretical propositions are of a descriptive character, while propositions referring to practical activity, like commandments or imperatives, refer to activities which make an object possible. Theoretical propositions refer to present objects, while practical propositions refer to an activity which is a ground and a grounding for the very prescence of an object. In this sense practical cognitions *(praktische Erkenntnisse)* contain imperatives, and these in turn are opposed to theoretical cognitions.[2] Clinging to that distinction it can be said that for Kant theory proper cannot be realized, since realization is a creation of reality, even when we assume or presuppose that the model for the reality precedes the to-be-realized reality. The fact that theory by definition cannot be realized, since it is of a descriptive character, is reinforced in Kant insofar as he tends to identify theory with critique: critique has at least as one of its components the merely negative attitude, namely that of making us aware of the limitations of our faculties or cognitive faculties. An awareness of limitations, or the negative component of theory, makes it impossible by definition or as an outcome of mapping out the different directions of approaching the world, to assume that theory can be realized.

Yet the most interesting and perhaps paradoxical point in Kant is that practice cannot be realized either. Practice proper is not only described as making objects possible, but practical principles are propositions which contain a general or universal determination of the will. It is pure reason which is practical, since it can contain a practical ground which is sufficient for the determination of the will; insofar as this is the case, there are practical laws.[3] Hence there is an exclusive relationship to the component of will, or else a continuity from reason to will. A different rendering of the same idea would be the establishment of the relationship between reason and freedom. "I say that freedom is the condition of the moral law and later assert that the moral law is the only condition under which reason can be known, I will only remind the reader that, though freedom is certainly the *ratio essendi* of the moral law, the latter is the *ratio cognoscendi* of freedom, for had not the moral law already been distinctly thought in our reason, we would never have been justified in assuming anything like freedom, even though it is not self-contradictory. But if there were no freedom, the moral law would never have been encountered in us."[4] This closed-circle structure characteristic of the relationship between reason and freedom, can be understood obviously as a closed-circle structure characteristic of reason and free will, or thus as will proper, or the intelligible will. The latter is sometimes distinguished by Kant from will as *Willkür* which connotes a capricious excitement, urge or choice *(Kür)*, unrelated and unmotivated by reason, or by practical reason at that. Since this interdependence between reason and will is characterized by the employment of the two terms *ratio essendi* and *ratio cognoscendi*, Kant's system can be viewed as containing this peculiar tendency of referring to practice as well, but not referring to action which is bound to take place in the empirical world, and thus embody a shift from the realm of intelligibility to that of experience.

One of the major manifestations of that contraction of the impact of practice on will, and not on action proper, is to be found in one aspect of Kant's doctrine which he himself described as motivating factor of the pure practical reason, the aspect translated into English as "incentives of pure practical reason." Moral law, according to the theory of motivation, should directly determine the will, and thus become the spirit of one's intention. Because of this position of the moral law, the famous distinction between legality and morality can be introduced. Morality occurs when the moral good appears not only in letter but also in spirit, while legality is present where the action conforms to the law but does not occur for the sake of it. Kant assumed that the moral law as such is *"eine Triebfeder,"* and this can be shown a priori. The positive expression of the presence of practical reason as the shaping factor or determining ground of our will is in the attitude of respect − insofar as the positive direction can be discerned − since respect is respect for the moral law and therefore of a kind of feeling produced by an intellectual cause. The negative concomitant of the determination solely produced by reason is the striking down of self-conceit in its different forms, like self-regard, benevolence toward oneself, or self-satisfaction. Broadly speaking, the determination by the moral law brings about the derogation of self-love and inclinations. There is in Kant a clear tendency to identify the level of inclinations and their power with self-love, or self-indulgence. Kant goes even further by suggesting the contradiction between humiliation, which is synonymous with lowering of the pretensions of moral self-esteem, and sensuous urges which have to be not only controlled by the respect for the moral law but replaced by that respect. The moral interest must be a pure non-sensuous interest of the practical reason alone. Summing up, we may say that the impact of practice is on will or on self-evaluation. It amounts to the subjugation of the will to the universality of the moral law. But because of the dichotomy between the sensuous and the pure, and because of the fundamental lack of a bridge between the level of intelligibility and that of sensuousness, practice is practical only insofar as the determination of the will goes. The question of the transmutation of the will into deeds is not solved in Kant by the emphasis laid on practice, and not even by the primacy or superiority attributed to practical reason. Practice does not create a totality of its own, though it does bring into prominence the inner enclosedness of the practical sphere in terms of the relation between the law and the will. But certainly not in terms of the relationship between these two, and empirical historical reality.

As a matter of fact, we find this dichotomy in its social and historical implication described by Kant himself in the fourth thesis of his essay "Idea for a Universal History." From the point of view of practical reason proper, universality ought to prevail and thus create a realm or a kingdom of ends, whereby all moral agents will be subject to the universal categorical imperative, and not motivated by self-love in its diverse expressions. But historically or empirically it is not so, because of the presence of antagonism between human beings. Antagonism is a manifestation of an opposition pertaining between human beings. It is the strength of that opposition that it awakens all the powers of man and brings them to conquer their inclination to laziness. The empirical human beings involved in antagonism are propelled by vainglory, by lust for power and avarice. Their motivation is to achieve a rank among fellow human beings, whom they cannot tolerate, but from whom they cannot withdraw. The steps from barbarism to culture, steps which consist in the social worth of man, are related to all these selfish urges and inclinations, and not to practice in the delineated sense of that term. The emergence of a society which is not driven by natural feelings but which composes a moral whole is a gradual process whose initiation lies in motivating factors which differ from the destiny to be achieved. Without these selfish pretensions all talents would remain hidden, unborn in an Arcadian shepherd's life, and men, good-natured as the sheep they herd, would hardly reach a higher worth than their beasts. Insofar as the distinction between intelligibility and experience amounts to the distinction between practical reason and nature, thanks are due to nature, since without the natural forces of competitive vanity or the insatiable desire to possess and to rule the excellent capacities of humanity would rest forever undeveloped and would sleep.[5] It is clear that for Kant there is a basic, though a transient, distinction between the impact of the moral law and the historical dynamic forces. Since history belongs to the realm of experience, it is not grounded in reason or in the moral will. It is grounded in natural factors of human activity and behavior. Those factors are urges of self-love, and thus they are factors diametrically opposed to the direction of practical reason and its commandments. Kant assumes that (a) the historical progress will eventually lead to the establishment of the realm of ends, and even that the turn for the better of the human race is already now in sight, but (b) he assumes that insofar as human beings can themselves accomplish anything, or insofar as anything can be expected of them, it can only be through their negative wisdom, namely in furthering their own ends.[6] Hence forces which differ from those grounded in practical reason serve practical reason with this, most significant, reservation, namely that there is a chasm between the intentions and the result. That chasm is rather significant since, according to Kant, as we have seen before, the very intention is an essential aspect of morality, and in case the intention lacks, morality is absent. Hence we may say that Kant wavered between two positions: according to one only legality can be the consummation of human history, since the intentions do not emanate from the practical reason, or else, in his second position, legality eventually establishes morality to the extent that the motivation and the moral law coincide in the human consciousness. It will be our next step to show Marx's position can be dovetailed with this Kantian philosophy of practice and the concomitant discrepancy between practice and history.[7]

II

To lodge Marx's position within the Kantian context, it has to be said in the first place that Marx replaces the Kantian dichotomy of reason and will on the one hand and inclinations and urges on the other, by a synthesis. That synthesis amounts to assigning a position in terms of human dignity to needs of the proletariat, or in categorical terms, there is a specific need which cannot be viewed as a need only and thus as belonging to the sensuous realm. The need of the proletariat is essentially or objectively related with the capacity for universal emancipation,[8] as Marx himself puts it. We can replace the notion of need and urge by the notion of interest, being aware of the fact that terminologically Kant relates interest to reason, assuming that reason as such has a certain direction, mainly a practical direction. Here again Marx transposes the notion of interest to historical reality, assuming that the interest of the proletariat is in its very essence related to value of human beings or to their dignity. Thus Marx, as against Kant, presents a view which can be described as an exoneration of interests and needs. Obviously at this point he is guided versus Kant's dichotomy by the Hegelian notion of synthesis. But it is not accidental that he sees that synthesis realized on the level of practice and not on the level of thought, since for him it is not enough that thought would strive to actualize itself. It is actuality which must itself strive toward thought.[9]

But it is precisely at this point that we have to ask the question: to what thought does Marx refer in the context? The conjecture presented here is that Marx refers to the idea of man as an end, or to the idea of dignity as worth against price as worth. This idea, in turn, is grounded in Kant's distinction presented in *Grundlegung der Metaphysik der Sitten,* and in his related writings. In those writings Kant distinguishes between price, dignity and what he calls affective price. Whatever has a price can be replaced by something else as its equivalent. As against this, there is dignity which is above all price and therefore admits of no equivalent. Affective price in turn does not relate to a need but to what Kant calls taste, which relates eventually to the mere purposeless play of our faculties.[10] Precisely Marx's criticism of the bourgeois society applies these Kantian distinctions, whereby the attribution of value to the world of things (*Verwertung der Sachenwelt*) comes along with the diminution of value from the world of men (*Entwertung der Menschenwelt*).[11] Labor does not produce commodities only. It produces itself and turns the laborers into a commodity. The essence of the laborer turns into a means of his existence or subsistence, defeating the categorical imperative which prohibits the turning of a person into a means only. In the context Marx's interpretation of needs and interests can be interpreted as follows: Certain interests are objectively of a moral position, since they represent the deformation of the moral world. Human beings, who are deprived of dignity as the irreplaceable value, or as juxtaposed to things, in expressing their interests and in attempting to overcome the obstacle in the process of the realization of their value and dignity, are lifted up to the moral level or, from the other end, the moral level inheres in their existence. There are interests which represent the notorious evil pertaining to the human situation. Hence interests grounded in the evil and aimed at its total replacement are on the one hand instrumental in the realization of the moral idea, but on the other hand are themselves imbued with a moral meaning. Marx was aware of the fact, and pointed this out in one of his smaller writings, that there is an affinity even etymologically, between *Wert* and *Würde* – both can be put in English as "worth."[12]

Along with the synthesis of practice and needs a reevaluation of the factors of history came about. Kant, as we have seen, refers to historical factors like vanity and greed. From the point of view of the day-to-day human existence, these factors can be viewed as spurious interests, a kind of luxury, originally beyond the scope of subsistence. Marx points to real interests, related to the very subsistence of human beings, but by the same token these interests are initially referring to the real value of human existence, to men in their dignity and not in their vanity. Marx rejects not only the notion of actualization on the level of reflection but also the notion of actualization beyond the scope of action and will, namely in the world beyond. This is virtually his criticism of Kant, since Kant was satisfied with the mere "good will," even when that will remains without results. Kant places the actualization, *die Verwirklichung* (Marx uses here the same term and he applies it to philosophy in general), of that good will, the harmony between the will and the needs and urges of the individuals in the realm of "the beyond."

Hence it can be said that Marx's criticism of theory has, to say the least, two targets, both conceptually and systematically. He criticizes in the abstract thinking reflection as such, or reflection as self-contained. He criticizes Hegel as a philosopher who conceived of reflection as the locus of realization. But he also criticizes a philosophical position which does not change the world, or he criticizes Kant whose moral philosophy remains a sort of theory only, without being realized in concrete historical existence. That lack of realization is essential for this particular ethical philosophy. To change the world is to bridge over the dichotomy between the moral law and interests. But at this point it has to be observed that only a certain type of theory can be assumed as realizable. A theory which would mean theory in Kant's sense, namely the sum total of descriptive propositions, cannot be realized, because description is a description of data through concepts, apart from the data. Only practice can be realized, or only practical reason can be realized, because practical reason supposedly creates the momentum for action. In Kant's sense it creates the momentum only insofar as the impact on the pure will goes, but does not percolate onto the level of day-to-day human needs. It is in this sense that Marx states his position that the practice of philosophy is itself theoretical, in spite of the psychological law according to which the theoretical mind, having become free in itself, turns into practical energy.[13] It turns into that energy only within the enclosed circle of the will, but not insofar as the shaping of action goes or, to put it from the opposite end, insofar as elevating action to the level of the moral law goes. What is meant here is the development of all human powers as such, and the development of those powers and the powers themselves are an end in itself. When Marx speaks of man producing his totality,[14] it means not only a variation on the theme of the *homo universalis,* but also a totality which comprises the different levels of human existence and most prominently the subsistence level and needs as well as the value level and dignity.

III

Coming back to our previous short historical survey, we may say that Marx attempts at a synthesis between *poiesis* and *praxis.* According to the classical distinction, *praxis* connotes acts performed for their own ends, while *poiesis* connotes deeds subservient to ends. One of the legacies of the classical distinction is to view poietic acts as embodies in products, like a house or a ship. Marx, in his philosophical as well as in his economic analyses, tries to show that man is placed in the realm of *poiesis,* namely that he is subservient to ends, because he is involved in the process of production which is meant to bring about commodities and makes man the creator into a commodity. The way to solve this predicament is by revolutionizing *poiesis* by *praxis* or, to put it differently, by placing *praxis* within the realm of *poiesis.* But this attempt is meant to achieve the elevation of *poiesis* in so far as human existence goes, and by no means the denigration of *praxis* to the, as it were, logic of *poiesis.*

Hegel criticized Kant that he rested with the distinction between existence and the "ought," and he interpreted the preservation of the dichotomy as an indication of the impotence of the spirit (*die Ohnmacht des Geistes*). To some extent Marx follows Hegel on this issue, mainly on the separation between the is and the ought. But unlike Hegel, and paradoxically more closely to the basic trend of Kant, Marx does not spiritualize existence, but shows that existence as it is in the sensuous features of itself is bound to lead to the overcoming of the initial dichotomy between praxis and historical existence. There is a polemical taint against Hegel. But the polemic against Hegel is meant to undercut the very position of the identity of subject and object, while the polemic against Kant is meant to take, as it were, *praxis* seriously, or to realize it in the realm of concrete existence; it is meant not to let the progress come only from the top, but to supplement the idea of progress by the historical processes and to reinforce the idea by a basic synthesis of the ethical imperative and the given urges. Those given urges in turn are not natural urges but historical ones, since the degradation of human dignity does not emerge within the scope of man's metabolic relation with nature, but within the scope of the self-created human history. To be sure, the most distinctive aspect of this consideration is that the center of gravity moves from urges of human individuals to a class, to a group of people whose common interest is objectively grounded in their situation within historical time and the historical process and society. The shift toward class is possible only when an accompanying shift occurs from the component of will and self-legislation, combining both will and reason, to interests. It is the function of consciousness to become aware of the interests and not to become aware of the moral imperative only. Just the same, the moral imperative is taken for granted, and the very terminology which Marx applies is a clear indication of this. When we move now from Marx to Lukács, we may preface our analysis by saying that to some extent Lukács out-Hegeled Marx, since the axis in his presentation is the identity of subject and object, and not the realization of practice, though to be sure, Lukács refers to that aspect too.[15]

IV

Before coming to a more detailed examination of the main direction of Lukács' interpretation of Marx, let us make a comment of a terminological character, related to the employment of the two terms "person" and "personality" on the one hand, and "subject" on the other. Person and personality had been used by Kant mainly in the moral context: he refers to personality as connoting the freedom and independence from the mechanism of nature, regarded as a capacity of a being to be subjected to pure practical laws, given by the personality's own reason. Person connotes a being as belonging to the world of the senses, being subjected to his own personality, and this is possible insofar as he belongs at the same time to the intelligible world.[16] It emerges from this text that personality is the moral agent proper, while person is a sort of partial realization of personality, since it points to existence in the realm of sensuous reality, but by the same token to the intelligible world. Sometimes the two terms, person and personality, coalesce or coincide, and we may make a distinction between persons and things, or persons and property – and in this sense Hegel in his *Philosophy of Right* carried over Kant's concept of person or personality. Marx is concerned with the position of the person or personality, not allowing for the Kantian distinction between belonging to the sensuous world versus belonging to the intelligible world.

Though the terminology is not clearly delineated, it can be said that the concept of subject has more of an epistemological or ontological meaning; it refers to the thinking subject who is, by the same token, the thought object. It is sometimes referred to as the I or as the ego, and as such connotes, again in Kant's sense, that which in thinking is always a subject and never a predicate. While person or personality refer to the moral law, the tendency is to endow the concept of subject with a meaning referring to thinking. *Pari passu* the concept of object points to the correlate of thinking in the sense that it refers to the manifold of intuition (*das Mannigfaltige der Anschauung*); thus there is no basic difference in the position of an object when we refer to the object of experience as the manifold unified, or the object to which understanding refers, since in the latter sense too the object is a correlate of understanding or thinking.

Coming now to Lukács and to the Hegelian undercurrent of his interpretation of Marx, one paramount fact emerges, namely that the basic categorial concepts are subject and object, and not person or personality. Lukács formulates his program as establishing the most vital interaction, namely the dialectical relation between subject and object in the historical process[17] or, negatively speaking, he does not make the principal theme the position of the person vis-à-vis the circumstances of his existence. The proletariat for Lukács is the identical subject-object of the historical process.[18] Hence it can be said that Lukács attempts to establish the identity between the subject and object in the Hegelian sense, but to accomplish this on the level of history which is Marx's main concern. Lukács tries therefore not only to realize pure will or practical reason on the level of existence or realization qua history. He attempts to realize reflection as an activity of the subject by employing Hegel's notion of identity. That identity realized in Hegel on the level of reflection has to be realized according to Lukács beyond reflection. From the negative point of view, one could be led astray and think that Lukács's criticism of what he calls contemplation is his criticism of a view of man detached from man's practical existence in the sense interpreted by Marx. Lukács points to the inverse relation pertaining between activity becoming less and less active in the process of progressive rationalization and mechanization, while becoming more and more contemplative. Contemplation tends to establish perfectly closed systems; probably pointing to the theory of relativity, Lukács says that it reduces space and time to a common denominator, while degrading time to the dimension of space.[19] It is clear that Lukács employs here a *pars pro toto* reasoning: after all, theory or contemplation as such do not necessarily lead to the theory of relativity and to the particular interpretation of time, an interpretation which is meaningful only within the scope of a certain theory or system. Theory, speculation, or contemplation – and these are by and large synonymous terms – can relate to different fields, and allow for the meaning of time in history which will differ from the meaning of time in physics. Hence there are two interwoven aspects in Lukács: contemplation qua reflection is understood by him as appearing insofar as it pertains to the nature of man under capitalism;[20] with the disappearance of capitalism contemplation will disappear as well. But if we understand contemplation in a broad sense as reflection and its various manifestations, reflection has to be presupposed vis-à-vis the particular analysis of capitalism and cannot disappear with the disappearance of capitalism. What can disappear is the degraded position of man qua person or personality, and not what Lukács calls the contemplative subject of knowledge, who is posed as being in contradiction to the given and empirical reality, once the contemplating subject of knowledge is understood as being self-generated and wholly inwardly turning from the given reality.[21] We see here again in Lukács an attempt to superimpose the structure of subject and object on the structure of man and reality and to argue that with the change of the interaction between man and reality the change in the position of subject and knowledge will occur.

But we have to reiterate here that a distinction has to be made between the position of the person and the position of the subject. A subject of knowledge cannot be realized in historical reality, unless the position of knowledge is undermined. What can be realized is man's position in his environment or in historical surroundings. Even when we view man versus environment as a particular but limited realization of subject and object, there is bound to emerge the surplus position of subject as well as of object, since both are categorial positions and cannot be identical with any of the segments of either subject or object. When Lukács refers to subject as a totality,[22] he has to imply that a totality is unrealizable in the historical world, since even when we assume that the subject is realized in history, he always remains a subject, and therefore he thinks about history or reflects about it. Thus the subject is involved in the infinite regression of the idea, the idea of idea, etc. in Spinoza's sense. To maintain the concept of subject and at the same time to maintain the primacy of realization is to combine the impossible, or else to speak the Hegelian language, which is applicable to the locus of reflection, in a Marxian context. But Marx's context does not suggest the movement from reflection to reality but the movement from the intelligible to the sensuous.

The perplexity pertaining to the wavering between the levels comes to the fore in the fact that Lukács refers to two totalities: "The totality of an object can only be posited if the positing subject is itself a totality; and if the subject wishes to understand itself, it must conceive of the object as a totality."[23] In Hegel's sense the totality of the subject and the object is one totality, since it is essentially the totality of the subject, or in the well-known Hegelian phrase, it is substance which has to be conceived rather as a subject. But Lukács refers here not only to the correlation between man and world but to the correlation between subject and object, while both have to be viewed not only as correlated but as identical, and yet not only as one all-embracing totality but as two totalities. Lukács does not make the distinction between concepts referring to material aspects of reality, material in the sense of *Inhalt*, and concepts referring to perspectives. Man and the historical process are material descriptions of segments of reality. Subject and object are categorial distinctions presenting perspectives, or loci, and not to material fragments of reality.

Lukács somehow blurs distinctions and commits a sort of categorial mistake: he speaks about history as a realm of human activity. Yet he tries to realize within history the Hegelian identity, that identity which Hegel tried to show as realizable only on the level of speculation, and not on the level of objective spirit. To be sure, Lukács retains the Marxian motif of the interest of the proletariat, but he does not direct that motif towards the synthesis between urges and the moral commandment of dignity. He directs it towards concretization and realization of speculation. Because of this synthesis, as it were, of Hegel and Marx, which replaces the presence of Kant in Marx, Lukács is bound to interpret, as we pointed out before, contemplation as being a passive attitude or as lacking activity. But obviously this is not the case, since phenomenologically speaking contemplation as an intentionality is an activity, though, to be sure, a different sort of activity than that of realization which takes place in history. The very application of the concept of subject and object makes Lukács' doctrine more contemplative than he meant it to be, because of his own description of the character of contemplation. This is bound to be so, and we witness here a sort of poetic justice of theory, since the sort of theory implied by Lukács centered around the concept of subject and object cannot be realized in the sense employed by Marx.

What is common to Lukács and Marx is their attack on abstraction. But it seems to be now textually warranted that the targets are different. Abstraction attacked by Marx is that of practice lodged on the level of reason only, i.e. the Kantian abstraction. Marx came along to show that this abstraction is unwarranted because it can be overcome through the synthesis of the historical deeds. The abstraction attacked by Lukács is that of Hegel which, as we well know, provides room for history but leaves society, civil society and state within the dichotomy of the abstract and empirical presented by Kant, in spite of Hegel's own criticism of Kant's abstraction. But Lukács attempts not to map out reality from the point of view of speculation and to show in Marx's sense that a part of that mapped out reality can contain the synthesis between morality and action. Lukács tries to show that abstraction as such and speculation as such can be abolished by realization, and total speculation and total reality will eventually become identical – on the level of reality, and not on the level of speculation. Lukács accepts from Marx the locus and from Hegel the substance qua subject, without realizing the irreconcilability of the two positions.[24]

NOTES

1. Immanuel Kant's *Logik,* ein Handbuch zu Vorlesungen (zuerst) herausgegeben von Gottlob Benjamin Jäsche, neu herausgegeben von Walter Kinkel, 3 Auflage (Felix Meiner, Leipzig, 1920), pp. 120–121.

2. *Ibid.,* p. 96.

3. *Kritik der praktischen Vernunft,* 9. Auflage, herausgegeben von Karl Vorländer, 1929 (Felix Meiner, Leipzig, 1922), p. 21. *Critique of Practical Reason,* translated with an introduction by Lewis White Beck (The Liberal Arts Press, New York, 1956), p. 17.

4. *Ibid.,* pp. 4ff., note transl. pp. 4ff. note

5. "Idea for a Universal History from a Cosmopolitan Point of View," translated by Lewis White Beck, in *Immanuel Kant on History,* edited with an introduction

by Lewis White Beck (The Library of Liberal Arts, The Bobbs Merrill Co., Indianapolis New York, 1963), pp. 15–16.

6. "The Contest of Faculties," in *Kant's Political Writings*, edited by Hans Reiss, translated by H. B. Nisbet (Cambridge University Press, Cambridge, 1970), pp. 189–190.

7. On the transformations of the concepts of theory and practice compare the present author's *Theory and Practice, an Essay on Human Intentionalities*, the Van Leer Jerusalem Foundation Series (Martinus Nijhoff, The Hague, forthcoming).

8. K. Marx, *Critique of Hegel's Philosophy of Right*, translated by Annette Jolin and Joseph O'Malley, edited with an introduction and notes by John O'Malley (Cambridge University Press, Cambridge, 1970), p. 141.

9. *Ibid.*, p. 139.

10. *Grundlegung der Metaphysik der Sitten* (Leipzig, 1897), pp. 60–61. *Foundations of the Metaphysics of Morals*, in *Immanuel Kant, Critique of Practical Reason and other Writings in Moral Philosophy*, translated and edited by Lewis White Beck Chicago, 1949, pp. 92–93, also *Metaphysik der Sitten*, 31. *Ibid.*, 11, and *Anthropologie in pragmatischer Hinsicht*, 87 (Kirchmann, Lepizig, 1870), p. 111.

11. *Ergänzugsband* vol. 1 (Berlin, 1968), pp. 511, 516.

12. "Randglossen zu A. Wagner's 'Lehrbuch der politischen Oekonomie,' " in Karl Marx/Friedrich Engels, *Werke*, vol. 19 (Berlin, 1962), pp. 372–373.

13. David McLellan, *Marx before Marxism* (Penguin Books, 1972), p. 89.

14. See for instance, David McLellan, *Marx's Grundrisse* (Paladin, 1973), p. 139.

15. Consult the present author's *Basic Problems of Marx's Philosophy* (The Bobbs-Merrill Co., Indianopolis/New York/Kansas City, 1965), as well as "Human Emancipation and Revolution," in *Interpretation*, Winter 1973, vol. 3/2, 3, pp. 205ff. *From Substance to Subject, Studies in Hegel* (Martinus Nijhoff, The Hague, 1974), pp. 106ff.

16. *Ibid.*, part 5, pp. 89, 101.

17. Georg Lukács, *History and Class Consciousness, Studies in Marxist Dialectics*, translated by Rodney Livingstone (Merlin Press, London, Book Club Edition, 1968), p. 3.

18. *Ibid.*, p. 199.

19. *Ibid.*, p. 89.

20. *Ibid.*, p. 97.

21. *Ibid.*, p. 124.

22. *Ibid.*, p. 39.

23. *Ibid.*, p. 28.

24. Consult: Richard J. Bernstein: *Praxis and Actions, Contemporary Philosophies of Human Activity* (University of Pennsylvania Press, Philadelphia, 1971).

CZECHOSLOVAK MARXISM IN THE REFORM PERIOD

GALIA GOLAN
The Hebrew University of Jerusalem

The Czechoslovak reform system, initiated tentatively in 1968, was the result of numerous sociopolitical-economic factors which broke the bonds on Marxist thinking in Czechoslovakia just as they opened the way to experimentation in the arts and other fields. Yet these very factors were themselves, in part, effected and determined by currents in Czechoslovak Marxist thinking and by a theoretical inquiry undertaken by Czechoslovak Marxists for some years before 1968. It is not the purpose of this paper, however, to examine the interrelation of theory and praxis in the Czechoslovak reform movement, nor, specifically, the role played by Czechoslovak intellectuals in bringing the reform regime to power and in determining its subsequent policies and decisions.[1] Rather, I will investigate here some of the key ideas and theoretical bases for the phenomenon known as "socialism with a human face."

The single most important — and infuential — theoretical work of this period in Czechoslovakia was that of the philosopher Karel Kosík, *Dialektika Konkrétního* (Dialectic of the Concrete) published by the Czechoslovak Academy of Sciences in 1963 (reprinted in 1965 and 1968).[2] Kosík's point of departure, as indeed he claimed *must* be the point of departure for all philosophy, was "the existence of man in the workd, the relationship of man to the universe."[3] In a work permeated with the humanistic emphasis of Marx's economic and philosophic writings (which Kosík argues are not qualitatively different from the later works), man is seen as a being, simultaneously in history and nature, each of which are but conditions of a concrete totality, i.e., reality. Yet man produces this reality, of which he is an integral part, just as he makes history.[4] "Reality is not an authentic reality *without* man, no more than it is (only) the reality of man. It is reality of nature as an absolute totality, independent not only of man's consciousness, but also of his existence, at the same time that it is reality of man who creates, in nature and as a part of it, a social and human reality, superior to nature and defining in history its place in the universe."[5] It is through work, not in the limited economic sense alone, that man realizes his humanity, through *praxis* that "man inscribes his meanings upon the world and fashions a meaningful structure of his universe."[6] Praxis is not practical activity juxtaposed to theory but is considered to be the determinant of human existence as an "elaboration of reality," i.e., it is that which unifies man with the world, matter and spirit, subject and object, product and producer, while providing that element which distinguishes man from animal.[7]

Through his concentration on man, Kosík returned one's thoughts to socialism as the liberation of man, as described in the early writings of Marx, with the claim that humane socialism had different roots from bureaucratic socialism.[8] This was the pointed meaning, at least for the Czechoslovak reader, of Kosík's exposition of the young Marx's theory of alienated man, slave to his daily concerns and object of socioeconomic manipulation.[9] Similarly, the Czechoslovak reader could easily find contemporary objects for Kosík's denunciation of the tendency of "materialist philosophy" (or "mechanistic materialism") to base artistic creation on the economy (which itself, Kosík declared, was created by man himself as a product of human praxis) and value it only as a witness to the socioeconomic conditions in which it was created — disregarding the independent creative quality of art.[10] And so too one could find many applications for Kosík's criticism of the use of "mystifiers" or "mystifications" (e.g. the deterministic or natural law theories of history) as false explanations of reality (or history).[11] In fact, he offered art and philosophy as "demystifiers" of reality, which itself was not readily accessible to the naive everyday consciousness.[12]

In addition to the ideas opened up by Kosík for discussion — particularly the idea of alienation and society's manipulation of the individual — the appearance of this book in 1963 had the added significance of projecting on the Czechoslovak scene many of the ideas of persons till then considered taboo by the regime, such as Gyorgy Lukacs and Herbert Marcuse.[13] At the same time it offered a theoretical basis for the intellectuals' demands for a change in cultural policy and criteria, while generating (as well as providing a theoretical framework for) a widespread discussion, albeit at this stage limited to small circles of intellectuals, as to the nature of Czechoslovak socialism in *all* spheres, be it the economy, welfare policies, or the body politic.

A few years after Kosík's important book, another theoretical work appeared which also sought to provide a basis for the examination of

socialism but from an entirely different point of view. This book was
in fact the report of an interdisciplinary team set up in 1965 by the
Czechoslovak Academy of Sciences, Institute of Philosophy, under the
direction of Radovan Richta, in conjunction with the Party, *Civilizace
na rozcestí* (Civilization at the Crossroads) (Czechoslovak Academy of
Sciences, Prague, 1966).[14] Investigating the Soviet-authorized problem of technological and scientific progress, the team argued that in
fact a new, post-industrial revolution was taking place *in the production base of society* which was to have a qualitative effect both on
production relations and on the whole superstructure of society. According to this theory, manual labor, even of the machine-watcher
type characteristic of the late (mechanized) industrial period, was
being (or to be) replaced by intellectual work and creativity suited to
the automated computer-based industries of the scientific-technical
era (with "the elimination of man from participation in immediate
production").[15] Struggling to remain within the confines of the "acceptable" discussion underway in the Soviet Union on this subject, the
authors often simplistically declared that socialist society under the
guidance of the Communist Party was the best possible environment
for this new revolution. Yet the theory was based to a large degree
upon a criticism of industrial society which even the authors frequently admitted applied to socialist as well as capitalist industrial society,
for example, alienation of man, his manipulation as a "means" rather
than his participation in guiding society, the dehumanizing division of
labor with its separation of intellect and labor, the devaluation of
esthetics and individual creativity and the emergence of bureaucracy.[16] Moreover, the socioeconomic-political changes recommended
for adaptation to the new situation (the scientific-technological revolution) involved drastic alteration of the present organization and
direction of socialist society, creating conditions – and problems –
quite different from those of contemporary socialist society and even
those envisaged for socialist society by the current socialist regimes.
For example, with the shift away from production work to intellectual work, the preparatory stage of production was to take precedence, with a commensurate shift from extensive (quantitative) criteria to intensive (qualitative) criteria in the economy. To achieve this,
however, there must be a change in education with the new emphasis
placed on culture and the all-over development of man as a creative
individual capable of grasping – and initiating – the rapid innovations
of science and technology. Such an education and capability, however,
would require the development not only of the creative facilities of
man but also of his capacity for independent thinking. This in return

would require freedom from arbitrary interference from directing centers (or managers), the wide dissemination of information — necessary for innovations — as well as a higher degree of individual participation in both the economic and the political sphere in order to overcome the tensions (created by man's feeling of "loneliness") which hinder motivation.[17]

> A *social climate* conducive to scientific progress possesses, alongside the economic factors (and resting on them), its socio-political and psychological background, too. Science calls for quite a different type of management, working regime, different standards and rules in society's everyday life, than those suited to industry, because it involves a much higher degree of inner subjectivity and responsibility, a greater measure of initiative and self-realization. There has to be much greater reliance on man, on his creative abilities and powers. In contrast to the hierarchy of the industrial system, science reaches a stage in its development where it demands fuller implementation of democratic principles.[18]

Two significant points raised (though not necessarily resolved) here were the nature of political power in such a society and the social structure of this society — both issues being linked. As classes are eliminated by socialist society, new differentiations appear that are determined by the *content* of one's work. Thus an emerging problem, even with the conversion of the working class to one scientifically and technically qualified, is the cleavage between the intellectual (i.e. "those performing exacting creative work") and the manual laborer (i.e. "those occupied in simple operative tasks").[19] This may lead to elitism, even of a political nature, for government in a technologically advanced society requires "professionalism," though during the transition stage (in which Czechoslovakia found itself in the 1960s) the opposite, vulgar egalitarianism and resistance to science could come to the fore as the weapon of the less-skilled (who as yet do not grasp the universal significance of scientific advance).[20] Since the era of scientific-technological innovation is one of constant change, a polarization may well take place even there between "conservative" and "progressive" attitudes, with the innovative dynamics producing a "stream of conflicts."[21] Frictions may well emerge between social groups — based on differences in their type of work — as well as a sharpening of the generational conflict "evoked by the widening gap set between modes of life in the course of two or three decades."[22] These conflicts are to be seen positively, however, as the very dynamics of society whose task it will be "*not* to resolve all social and human problems once for all, but [to] afford the means of resolving them through cooperative efforts, and ultimately, in fuller measure, through mutual development of people."[23]

The central value of this book was similar to that of Kosík's work (although it was much less sophisticated and profound, and indeed simplistic when compared with Kosík's book). It focused on man the creator and on his free self-realization as the cornerstone of socialist society. In a sense the Richta team worked deductively from society in the scientific era to the importance of the individual, while Kosík had taken the early Marx's alienated man as his starting point. Kosík himself was critical of the Richta work, however, seeing in the so-called "scientific-technological revolution" still another mystification, created by ideologists as a camouflage for social contradictions. He saw both modern science and technology as a "technical reason" capable of transforming reality into "a secured, surveyable, and manipulatable object," but this was not to be identified with reason in general, for then "everything non-technical, non-disposable, non-calculable, and non-manipulatable [would be] posed against it and against man as non-reason."[24] Thus, Kosík argued, both science and the socialization of the means of production were essential but not sufficient to socialism, the historical role of which was to transform these very elements into "concrete totality" constituting the liberation of man (from misery, exploitation, oppression, injustice, lies, mystification, unfreedom, indefinitive indignity, and humiliation).

In terms of the lay public, the Richta work had the added value of criticizing the modes of direction and management even in present socialist society while condoning, indeed elevating, the existence of social differences, contradictions, and conflicts of interests to the positive role of the very dynamics of society (although it did so, as Kosík said, within the protective camouflage of the scientific-technical revolution). This was in fact the undercurrent of a large part of Czechoslovak Marxist thinking in the 1960s, much of which focused on the very political questions, i.e., the nature of power in a differentiated yet socialist society, only inadequately answered by the Richta book. Both the Slovak legal scholar Michal Lakatoš and the Party theoretician—political scientist Zdenek Mlynár declared that the motive force even of socialist society was the conflict generated between conflicting interests.[26] The Stalinist approach, Lakatoš argued, ignored the "natural differences" among groups and individuals, viewing them as vestiges of capitalism. In fact, socialist society might be differentiated according to various relationships, such as the traditional Marxist class distinction, i.e., the relationship to the production process (in socialist society this could mean workers in the state sector, those in the cooperative sector, in the retail trades, etc.) or the relationship to the division of labor, i.e., workers in industry, agriculture, physical labor, mental labor, etc. Moreover, distinctions or differentiation could also be determined by the size of income, participation in the management of society, or ethnic origins or sex. In essence Lakatoš maintained that the traditional Marxist differentiation of society was inadequate to the socialist society, once ownership had been socialised and society was composed of a class of "non-owners." Indeed, he argued that in every society, including socialist society, there exists a "clash between the ruling and the ruled" so that even in socialist society, as both the Richta and Kosík analyses had implied, "those who govern can turn those ruled into a passive and apathetic nation that yields to any pressure exerted by the manipulators."[27]

Mlynář, too, rejected the identification of the interests of society as a whole with the particular interest of "various groups, strata, working collectives, and individuals." Recognizing the legitimacy of contradictions between particular interests, he called them nonantagonistic, although Lakatoš implied and the Slovak theoretician Ondrej Kopčok said that the "non-antagonistic contradiction between the Party and the masses [the rulers and the ruled] could easily assume antagonistic features."[28] Michal Suchý, of the Institute of Philosophy of the Czechoslovak Academy of Sciences, argued that, because of the defensive measures taken by the regime against antirevolutionaries and anti-Marxists in the first stages of socialism, a distortion had taken place in the superstructure which constituted efforts against "a contest of ideas" resulting in the hindrance of "the development of scientific thought." He argued that "once the principle is established that an exchange of views and mutual criticism are not allowed in a specific sphere (however limited it may be) rigidity of thought in this sphere . . . is inevitable."[29] Julius Strinka, another Slovak theoretician of significant stature and respect among theorists, approached the subject more concretely, when he maintained that a dialectical approach be applied to socialist society as well, since any society was constantly in motion, constantly producing the negation of itself. Therefore, he argued for an "integrated criticism," i.e., institutionalized rather than scattered, isolated criticism, to counter and correct integrated power in society — thus permitting the qualitative change even of socialist society, born of the dialectic. Strinka too maintained that this dialectic was based on the concept that "man is not exclusively determined by existing conditions (abstract laws of development) but also by his own projects, i.e. concrete social activity set in motion by man, with his particular motives, interests, and attitudes." Like Kosík,

Strinka called for a return to the concept of man as a "free, authoritative being" participating in and molding history. Thus the existing contradictions could be overcome, socialist society could develop with the dialectically necessary qualitative changes only "if those conditions, institutionalized forms and mechanisms are evolved in which the creative energy of the people as well as the people's activity in the critical and practical fields which helps to transform the present, will be able permanently to unfold to the highest possible degree."[30]

With these references to institutions and the relationship of rulers to the ruled and vice-versa, the issue of political organization and power were opened, for, as Mlynář said, "Provided that we do not want to explain the arbitrariness of power . . . simply by arbitrariness of power, we cannot take Stalin as the only factor determining the relationship of man and the power in the state."[31] Most theoreticians sought concrete ways of providing expression for the varied and even conflicting interests of society in the democratization of the political superstructure by means of reforms of the government and elected organs as well as the electoral system itself, and, more significantly in the role and nature of the Party, as well as in the social and economic organizations of society through some type of self-management and worker participation. Some went so far as to translate these ideas into a justification for an organized opposition such as an opposition party or an alternative to the existing "power."[32] However, such innovations were to remain with the framework of socialist society, for, as the theoreticians themselves explained, the issue was not socialism but the type of socialism (or as Kosík put it, which roots of socialism).[33] Rather, the specific proposals sought solutions which would go beyond the institutions of "bourgeois democracy," combining the urge for a more humane, individual-centered system with the general framework of a socialist, Communist-led society. These discussions, and indeed the myriad of political blueprints which were characteristic of the Prague Spring (some of which were even adopted by the Party in its Action Program and draft statutes), were however, more of the nature of probings in this direction rather than actual solutions.[34] Albeit seeking new forms they tended to remain within the realm of democratization, e.g., alteration of the National Front and social organizations, adjustment of the electoral system, renovation of the legal system and organs of government, change of the Party's role and modus operandi, and an expansion of individual freedom. This in itself was, nonetheless, sufficient to incur violent suppression by the Soviet Union and her orthodox allies who feared that such probings could but erode the power of the Party – which power (the "leading role of the Party") lay at the base of Moscow's approach to socialism.

For many, however, this "democratization" was not sufficient. The writer Ludvík Vaculík, for example, could not conceive of "power," even in a socialist society, submitting itself to a significant change. As he explained: "The first law of power is that it tries to maintain itself by reproducing itself more and more precisely. Secondly, it becomes more and more homogeneous, purging everything foreign to it until each part is a replica of the whole and all parts are mutually inter-changeable." Founding its own "constitutional dynasty," power, by its very nature, cannot but be a brake on change, creating a populace of humiliated servants — or collaborators — easily controllable and ignor-ant even of the possibility of change.[35] The philosopher Ivan Sviták called for a different approach altogether, which would extend even to the roots of power by means of "structural changes," for like Kosík and Richta (each within his own framework), he was concerned with the essential relationship of man to society, and like Vaculík, he con-sidered power ("totalitarian dictatorship") a closed, self-perpetuating system which institutionalizes itself.[36] Sviták distinguished between revolt ("a change of the ruling groups") and revolution ("structural social changes in class relations, in economic and political relations and in the structure of the power mechanisms"). Democratization remained within the category of revolt, i.e., providing no structural changes, while in fact what was necessary was democracy, i.e., an open socialist society, which could only be achieved through structural changes. His major target was "bureaucratism" which lay at the center of totalitarian dictatorship or "power apparatus," reducing human beings to mere tools.[37] Thus he urged, in fact, revolution in the institutions and structure of society to introduce human rights into "modern technocratically manipulated society," placing "back in the center of events the rights of man as against the dogma of ideol-ogy."[38]

Yet, for all his skepticism of the democratization process and the apparent radicalism of his call for "revolution," the essence of Sviták's proposals was the same as the political theorists' demands for demo-cratic socialism, i.e., socialist means of ownership as a means, not an end, combined with the basic democratic freedoms — and controls on power (particularly of the Party and its *apparat*) — familiar to tradi-tional democracies.[39] What was considered new, or revolutionary, by Sviták and many of the Czechoslovak thinkers, was this very com-bination which according to Sviták constituted a return to Marx's original intention: by socializing the means of production the civil liberties of bourgeois democracy were to be universalized, the basic humanism to be widened, not eliminated.[40] In the view of Sviták this humanistic, democratic essence of Marx's works was lost because of two phenomena: "the rise of the giant bureaucratic apparatus of . . . industrial societies," and the application of Marxism in a non-European semiliterate state which had undergone neither the Enlightenment nor the Renaissance and therefore had to transform Marx's views into "a bigoted orthodox faith in the unity of Church and State, which took the shape of a monopoly of power irreconcilable with European cultural tradition, with criticism, and with science."[41] Sviták was not the only one to imply that the distortion of Marxism lay in its adaptation to backward Russia, subsequently being exported in its new form as a model for others. He was the only one, however, to specifically call for a distinction between Lenin and Marx (not just Stalin and Marx), explicitly laying at Lenin's feet the responsibility for the monopolistic and dictatorial idea of the leading role of the party: "Marx defended the leading role of the *working class;* he defended its historical mission and its workers' activity, but he never imagined that this class itself might be dominated by a political party — and especially by the apparatus of this party. According to him the dictatorship of the proletariat was to be the *temporary* rule of the *majority* over the minority, not the *permanent* terror of a *minority* against the people."[42] In this Sviták blamed Lenin's concept of the party for the transformation of man as the subject of history to its manipulated object. The restoration of man as the subject of history then marks the first step towards overcoming his alienation in industrial albeit socialist society. What Sviták calls the contradiction between the "economic foundation of socialism" and individual freedom can be resolved by self-administration and "the transformation of the style of living along the lines of socialist humanism" (as distinct from the "materialist realism" of technocratic consumerism).[43] His criticism of democratization thus resembles Kosík's criticism of the theory of the "scientific-technological" revolution, i.e., the fear that the process will be only partial, relating only to the everyday false consciousness rather than the essence of man's dilemma in industrial society.

There were those in the Czechoslovak reform movement for whom Lenin represented a progressive rather than regressive appenditure to Marx. These were the Slovak Marxists who sought, as part of their concept of socialism, a role and meaning for nationalism. One of the major difficulties on this point was that Marx had specifically condemned Slovak nationalism as reactionary (primarily because of the Slovak national movement led by L'udovít Štúr against the 1848 Magyar revolution). It was the Slovak nationalist politician Gustáv

Husák who sought a Marxist reappraisal of Slovak nationalism by presenting the nationalism of the subject peoples of the Austro-Hungarian Empire as a progressive rather than conservative force. He claimed that within this context nationalism constituted a revolutionary program seeking revolutionary solutions to the political and social problems of the people (albeit within a national framework) against the conservative forces of feudalism and the oppression of smaller nations.[44] The Slovak Communist intellectual Vladimír Mináč argued that social emancipation of a nation could only be achieved when it had achieved equality of rights with other nations, but both Husák and Mináč argued that such equality for a smaller nation vis-à-vis a larger one could be protected only by means of separate, autonomous institutions (to safeguard against the "hegomonistic" tendencies of the stronger nation).[45] This could, however, be easily construed as narrow nationalism, indistinguishable from bourgeois nationalism, which ignored the universalist concepts of socialism. It was to Lenin, then, that the Slovaks had to look for their attempt to accomodate their nationalist sentiments with a socialist society. The national question could be settled in a socialist state only by Lenin's recognition of the right to self-determination, as the necessary first step on the way to the universal proletarian values.[46] The question as to exactly when this transformation from nationalism to internationalism was to take place within the socialist society was left unanswered. Indeed the Slovak nationalists sought first and foremost recognition of the very legitimacy of their nationalism and its realization in institutions providing this minimum stage of self-determination.

Some politicians and theorists saw the source of the national problem in the narrow, basically Stalinist approach which perceived the solution as merely a question of socioeconomic change, i.e., with the revolution the socioeconomic level and nature of relationships would eliminate the very basis for national distinctions. Others, however, saw it as an issue which could be solved only within the larger context of humanistic socialism in which man could realize himself in all his potential, with all his unique features or interests recognized and protected as a legitimate part of the whole — even as a source of dynamism of that whole. Nonetheless, the question of nationalism remained a practical-political one during the 1960s with almost no theoretical treatment offered by any serious Marxist thinker, although much attention was given to the Slovak question itself and the meaning of Slovak nationhood.[47] An exception to this was Karel Kosík with his probings into the nature of the Czech nation, for in his concept of "concrete totality" he had room for the "totality of national life" and the nation as a subject in history. This totality of national life is a question of values (or "political, cultural, spiritual synthesis") which, if based on truth, will provide the proper ("genuine") link between individual behavior and politics, science and public action, morality and culture, education and the everyday atmosphere.[48] Thus it was Kosík who looked to the heritage of the Czech nation, specifically the person of Jan Hus, for the idea of the unity of reason and conscience as the essential characteristic of humanity and the struggle of truth with the false consciousness of everyday "reality" and the mystifiers of history.[49]

This brings us to the question of Czech traditions and the degree to which these traditions influenced the development of Marxist thinking in Czechoslovakia as it emerged in the 1960s. The growing tendency amongst Marxists in the West and in Yugoslavia, for example, to concentrate on the humanism of Marx, the questions of alienation and bureaucratism, manipulation and individual freedom, is too widespread to be attributed to the characteristics or traditions of any one nation. Given the nature of modern society, even of modern socialist society, as well as the disillusionment with the Soviet model which for many is nothing more than a form of state capitalism, the development of such a trend in Marxist thinking was, indeed, natural and logical. Yet there are certain elements of the Czech tradition which do seem to have played a role – or at least were perceived by certain Czech Marxists as having played a role – in the development of Czechoslovakia's concept of socialist humanism (or humane socialism).

The core of Czech tradition is of course the heritage of Jan Hus, i.e., the democratic-liberal values which grew out of the Reformation, nurtured later by the Enlightenment. Rejecting the authoritarianism and dogmatism of the Church, the Hussite code respected the individual, who through his own use of reason was in need of no intermediary to bring him the truth. In this sense all men were not only equal but also free, for there were no inherent differences between them to justify the subservience of one man to another. This belief in the basic equality of man produced tolerance, which in turn generated a devotion to humanitarianism. The belief in the equality of men and the ability of each to use his own critical faculties of reason led to a respect for individualism, i.e., the right of each man to judge for himself independently of any institution or established authority. The Hussite watchword "Truth will prevail" (which became a slogan of the Prague Spring) basically meant that there is a truth and each man has the right to seek it; it is not a matter of an authority which dictates but rather truth which is more important than authority. On the basis of these ideals of equality, humanism, and the value of man there grew in time a tendency towards pacifism. This was essentially a preference for the use of reason as distinct from violence; it called for direct contact with the people and the use of persuasion rather than coercion, passive resistance instead of revolt, in the belief in the ultimate victory of truth and reason. It did not mean passivity, however, for Hus's ideas were permeated with the concept of participation and man's potential. At the same time the emphasis on reason brought respect for both education and discipline as distinct from arbitrary authority or blind anarchy. While the value of equality made for an anti-elitist tradition, from Hus through the Enlightenment which sparked the Czech national revival down to the philosopher-President of the First Republic, the intellectual was perceived as playing a leading role in the life of the nation. And this nation itself was traditionally seen as one among others, each a sovereign equal, each with something to contribute. The idea of having something to contribute was seen not only as the basis for a role in the community of nations but also as the very justification of the nation's existence. The ideas of education and discipline which developed during the Czechs' subjugation under the Austro-Hungarian Empire were indeed seen as means of ensuring that the nation be worthy of freedom; it was considered necessary constantly to renew or refresh the qualities being offered as a nation — the past being no guarantee of a nation's right to independent existence.

These traditions could but influence the Czech perception of socialism just as they influenced the pre-war democracy.[50] Thus early Czech socialists tended towards evolutionary democratic social-democracy rather than revolutionary-autocratic Bolshevism. Even in the 19th century, socialism in the Czech lands was disciplined, moderate, reformist. In the First Republic, Social Democrats and Communists alike emphasized social welfare and the distributive aspects of socialism. They advocated evolutionary, legal changes rather than revolution. The adaption of this policy by the Communists — be it because of political necessity[51] or because of their own inclinations as the inheritors of certain traditions — was the source of almost constant conflict with the Comintern. As a derivative of the Czech type of nationalism, the attitude of the Czech Communists was to seek a "Czech contribution" or a "Czech way" to socialism, without submerging themselves in a universalism which denied national sovereignty. And the Czech way they offered was nonviolent "revolution" through persuasion, reform, and parliamentary changes. Similarly, the Leninist concept of the Party with its paternalism and autocracy was not entirely acceptable, for the Czech worker was not an ignorant peasant — even once removed — but rather the educated recipient of the Hussite values of reason and persuasion. He would accept and value discipline but not blind obedience or authority. Indeed the early Czech Communists informed the Comintern (in response to criticism): "The Czech worker grew up in national struggle against the authority of the state and any authority at all . . . The path to the Czech worker does not lead through assertion of authority and discipline from the outside . . . he needs to be convinced and won over . . . The method of command will not win him."[52] For its part, the Comintern recognized that the "shortcomings" of the Czech Communists lay in "the tradition, training, and orientation of many of the members and an even greater proportion of the leaders."[53]

Without examining the degree to which the post-war Czech parliamentary way to socialism or the later imitation of Stalinism was or was not connected with these traditions, a straight line can almost be drawn from the traditions themselves and the Czechs' early concept of socialism, on the one hand, to the thinking of Czech Marxists in the 1960s, on the other hand. It is from this point of view that one can understand Sviták's complaint that Marx ("an earnest European, with deep roots in the European culture based on antiquity, Christianity, the Renaissance, and the Enlightenment") has been transformed, by his adaptation in a backward Asian country, into a bigoted faith irreconcilable with "European cultural tradition, with criticism and with science," suitable perhaps for the Russian working class but not for Czechoslovakia.[54] Kosík, too, spoke of the difference between a socialism developed from the starting point of democratic traditions in a democratic nation and the socialism constructed in a country void of democratic traditions.[55] Less consciously, perhaps, one may see the influence of the tradition in the preoccupation of Kosík, Sviták, and the other Marxist thinkers of this period with reason and truth, man's value as a free, thinking being, in opposition to authoritarianism and dogma; the demand for civil liberties and humanism, perceived, in fact, as a possible Czech contribution to socialism, thereby justifying the very existence of the country.[56] Even the politicians spoke in terms of molding a socialism suitable to the democratic, humanistic traditions of the country, and the Party's 1968 program sought a socialism suitable to Czechoslovakia — a Czechoslovak way.[57] Indeed the slow methodical effort of the reformers throughout the 1960s to bring about legal institutional change as distinct from sudden, emotional upheaval was characterisitic of Czech traditions. Just as a preoccupation with controls on power, legalistic institutional change and parliamentary democracy were more in keeping with the tradition than concentration on decentralized self-rule and the idea of the withering away of the state characteristic of Yugoslav reformism. This does not mean that without the 500-year-old Czech tradition of democracy and humanism the concept of socialism with a human face would not have emerged.[58] It would seem, however, that once freed of the Stalinist pattern and permitted open enquiry, Czech socialism may well have been predisposed to gravitate in this direction of Marxist thinking.

NOTES

1. These subjects are treated extensively in my books, *The Czechoslovak Reform Movement 1962–1968* (Cambridge University Press, 1971) and *Reform Rule in Czechoslovakia 1968–69* (Cambridge University Press, 1973), as well as in Vladimir Kusin, *The Intellectual Origins of the Prague Spring* (Cambridge University Press, 1971).

2. Published in a German edition *(Die Dialektik des Konkreten)* by Suhrkamp, 1967, and in a French edition *(La Dialectique du Concret)* by Maspero, 1970. For the sake of accessability, quotations will be cited from the French edition.

3. *La Dialectique du Concret* (Maspero, 1970), p. 147.

4. ". . . the first fundamental premise of history is that it is created by man," *ibid.,* p. 162.

5. *Ibid.,* p. 169.

6. *Ibid.,* pp. 146 and 164.

7. *Ibid.,* pp. 150–152.

8. Karel Kosík, "Epilogue," in Antonin Liehm, *Trois Générations* (Gallimard, 1970), pp. 321–322 and Karel Kosík, "Our Present Crisis" in *Literarni listy,* 9, 16 May 1968.

9. *La Dialectique du Concret, op. cit.,* pp. 46–62.

10. *Ibid.,* pp. 82–83; 85; 94–98.

11. *Ibid.,* pp. 155–165.

12. *Ibid.,* pp. 87–89.

13. An interview with Lukács published in *Literární noviny*, 18 January 1964, was itself a significant event, though Marcuse had to wait until 1968. For a direct application of the problem of man's alienation even in socialist society see Jindrich Fibich, in *Filosofia*, No. 6, November–December 1967.

14. Published in expanded form in English, translated by Marian Šlingova, the widow of Otto Šling, one of the Czechoslovak leaders of the Communist Party, tried and executed with Slánský in 1952, *Civilization at the Crossroads* (International Arts and Sciences Press, White Plains, 1969).

15. *Ibid.*, p. 28. See also pp. 32–37.

16. *Ibid.*, pp. 43; 110–111; 115; 118; 125–128; 178–179; 182. "Although people living in the changed conditions of socialist society are placed in a different relationship to their work (being now genuinely particles of the total social labour) and even if no socially useful and necessary activity, whatever its material guise, can be ignored in a community of labour, it is nonetheless obvious that, being stamped by its typical industrial limitations, much of this work reproduces its inner cleavage at a new level – man cannot realize himself in it directly as a creative, developing being, he finds in it no immediate source of satisfaction and enrichment, he does not live in it, but wins through it the means for a life that begins when the working day has ended, when the space for life has been more or less consumed by work and the reproduction of the capacity to work (i.e. standing on queues for food; bureaucracy, etc.)," *ibid.*, pp. 109–110.

17. *Ibid.*, pp. 205–206; 238–241.

18. *Ibid.*, p. 228.

19. *Ibid.*, p. 248.

20. *Ibid.*, pp. 240–241.

21. *Ibid.*, pp. 257–258.

22. *Ibid.*, p. 258.

23. *Ibid.*, pp. 258–259.

24. *Literární listy*, 16 May 1968.

25. Indeed in 1966 the Party even set up a committee to continue this aspect of the Richta team's work, under the direction of Zdeněk Mylnar.

26. Zdeněk Mlynář, "Problems of Political Leadership and the New Economic

Model," *World Marxist Review*, 12, 1965, pp. 58–64; idem; *Stát a člověk* (Svobodna slova, Praha, 1964). Michal Lakatoš, "On Certain Problems of the Management of our Political System," *Právny obzor*, 48 (1), 1965, pp. 26–36; idem, "Some Problems of Socialist Democracy from the viewpoint of the Citizens' Position in our Society," *Právny obzor*, 49 (3), 1966, pp. 213–227.

27. Lakatoš, *op. cit.;* Právny obzor, 49 (3), 1966, pp. 213–223.

28. *Pravda* (Bratislava), 8 July 1963.

29. Michal Suchý, "Freedom of Criticism and the Development of Marxist Theory," *Otázky marxistickej filosofie*, 19 (5), 1964, pp. 409–414.

30. Július Strinka, "Two Concepts of the Dialectics of Science," *Otázky marxistickej filosofie*, 18 (1), 1963, pp. 82–83.

31. Zdeněk Mlynář, *Stát a člověk, op. cit.*, p. 18.

32. E.g., Petr Pithart in *Literární listy*, 1 May 1968; Václav Havel in *Literární listy*, 4 April 1968; Václav Chytil in *Literární listy*, 20 June 1968, to name but a few.

33. Petr Pithart in *Literární listy*, 1 May 1968; Karel Kosík, in Liehm, *op. cit.*, p. 320.

34. A detailed discussion of these proposals is contained in my two books, see note 1.

35. *IV. Sjezd svazu československých spisovatelů* (Československy spisovatel, Praha, 1968), pp. 141–151.

36. Ivan Sviták in *Student*, 10 April 1968.

37. Ivan Sviták, *Lidsky smysl kultury* (Československy spisovatel, Praha, 1968), p. 28.

38. Ivan Sviták, *The Czechoslovak Experiment 1968–1969* (Columbia University Press, New York, 1971), p. 123 (lecture delivered in Yugoslavia, 6 July 1968).

39. Indeed a feature common to almost all of the Czech and Slovak theorists' demands in the 1960s was the concern that institutions, not just people, be changed, and that the reforms be institutionalized.

40. Ivan Sviták in *Student*, 22 May 1968.

41. *Ibid.*

42. *Ibid.*

43. Ivan Sviták, *The Czechoslovak Experiment 1968–1969, op. cit.,* pp. 124–125.

44. Gustáv Husák in *Nové slovo*, 6 June 1968; idem in *Kultúrny zivot,* 8 October 1965.

45. Vladimír Mináč in *Kulturny život,* 15, 22, 29 October 1965.

46. See Gustáv Husák, *op. cit.,* and Viktor Pavlenda in *Pravda* (Bratislava), 2 March 1968.

47. See for example, *Slovaci a ich narodony vyvin* (SAV, Bratislava, 1969) and *Historický časopis,* 4 (12), 1967, for two seminars on this issue.

48. Karel Kosík in *Leterární listy,* 7 November 1968 and 2 May 1968.

49. *IV. Sjezd svazu československých spisovatelů,* pp. 107–109; Karel Kosík in *Literární listy,* 1 March 1968.

50. During the period under the Habsburgs a strong Czech centralism and the concept of firm party discipline were also developed as factors in the nationalist struggle against Austria. These negative traits became part of the heritage of the First Republic as well.

51. The large, educated, and highly organized workers' movement in the Czech lands was pro-Republic and therefore more interested in workers' rights and benefits than in revolution to overthrow the new Republic.

52. Cited in Paul Zinner, *Communist Strategy and Tactics in Czechoslovakia 1918–1948* (Pall Mall, London, 1963), p. 39.

53. *Ibid.*

54. Ivan Sviták in *Student,* 22 May 1968.

55. Karel Kosík in Liehm, *op. cit.,* p. 325.

56. See p. 10 above. Sociologist Miroslav Jodl claimed that Czechoslovakia would "hold its own" only if it "succeeds in contributing to the establishment of a democratic, humanistic, and scientific socialism" (in *Literární noviny,* 7 January 1967). Dubcek too said that Czechoslovakia's democratic traditions could contribute both to the development of socialism and the making of socialism more attractive in the world (2 March 1968 speech to Kladno workers). Dubcek's

concept of the need for the Party constantly to reason and be worthy of its right
to rule was somehow reminiscent of the 19th-century view of Czech nationhood.

57. Action Program, 10 April 1968. See speeches by Josef Smrkovský in *Práce*, 20
March 1968; Alexander Dubcek, in *Rudé právo*, 23 February 1968; Josef Spaček in
Rude pravo, 11 April 1968.

58. Some Czech intellectuals, however, did say the Prague Spring was inevitable
because of this tradition (Alexander Kliment in *Literární listy*, 14 March 1968;
Václav Kotyk in *Predvoj*, 9 March 1968).

MARXISM: THE POLISH EXPERIENCE

Z.A. PELCZYNSKI
Pembroke College, Oxford

Reviewing the development of Marxist theory in the contemporary world, George Lichtheim wrote: "Intellectual paralysis has been total in the USSR and almost as complete in its satellites, with the significant exception of Poland."[1]

In this paper I wish to investigate Lichtheim's accurate but cryptic remark and to consider the reasons why Poland has not conformed to the general rule. Our concern is, of course, with the post-1945 period. But we must look very briefly at the earlier period, for Poland produced a few interesting, Marxist or *Marxisant* thinkers before World War I. Men such as Ludwik Krzywicki (1859–1941), Kazimierz Kelles-Krauz (1872–1905), and Stanisław Brzozowski (1878–1911), whose works and even names are largely unknown outside their country, were more than mere popularizers of Marxism. They accepted some of Marx's ideas, modified others, and rejected many more. They attempted to combine the ideas of other thinkers with those of Marx, believing that this would enrich Marxism. It was, I believe, Kelles-Krauz, who first used the term "open Marxism" in Poland. He wished the thought of Karl Marx to be accessible to new ideas and revised in the light of new developments. It is my contention that this "openness" has in fact marked the intellectual history of Polish Marxism except for a short spell of some five or six years (1950–1955). Its concomitants have been a lack of a tradition of orthodoxy and a pluralism of interpretations.

Interwar Poland produced only one significant Marxist thinker – Oskar Lange – and he, of course, was an economist. The thinking of sociologists such as Stefan Czarnowski, Kazimierz Dobrowolski, and Stanisław Ossowski showed strong traces of Marxian influence. But the influential Poznan sociological school of Florian Znaniecki was hostile to Marxism. Its method of empirical "grass root" social research was poles apart from grand sociological theories and problems of *Weltanschauung.* The philosophical climate of interwar Poland was even more hostile to Marxism. Its dominant analytical, formalist, and positivist tendency (represented by Łukasiewicz, Leśniewski, Kotarbiński, and Ajdukiewicz) rejected Marxism, together with most other traditional philosophical systems, as lacking the rigor, clarity, and logical consistency required of philosophy. In a negative way, however, this philosophical tendency contributed to the development of Marxism after the last war. It forced Marxism to the defensive and challenged it to prove its philosophical respectability in a free and rational debate. An "open," "revisionist" Marxism had a somewhat better chance of passing such a test than the set of dogmas known as "Marxism-Leninism-Stalinism."

As a political movement Polish Marxism also had the characteristics of pluralism and unorthodoxy. Apart from its reformist, social democratic form, represented by the Polish Socialist Party (PPS), there was a weaker revolutionary tradition which produced the Polish Communist Party (KPP) in 1919, and the Jewish Bund which politically stood somewhere in between. It is worth stressing the well-known fact that the first theoretician of the KPP – Rosa Luxemburg – was herself an unorthodox Marxist; although the KPP became Leninist after joining the Comintern, it took Stalin a long time to eradicate the "Luxemburgist tradition" (a loose label for various kinds of unorthodoxy). The KPP, although dominated by the intelligentsia, produced no original Marxist thinkers of Luxemburg's, Lukács's, or Gramsci's caliber. But it had a number of able ideologists and propagandists (such as Adolf Warski, Juliusz Brun-Bronowicz, and Jerzy Ryng), who had interesting and independent views on, for example, the strategy of the Communist revolution in Poland, the national question, and racism. The Stalinist straitjacket eventually made all deviations from the Soviet line impossible.

In a sense Stalin made an important negative contribution to the development of Marxism in Poland by his liquidation of the KPP's leading cadre during the Great Purge. Scores of highly intelligent men, who might have later become leaders of the "ideological front" in philosophy, sociology, and other humanistic disciplines, were wiped out. As a result in 1945 the Polish Worker's Party, although strongly entrenched in power, had only a handful of intellectuals who were able to battle on behalf of its ideology, and only one professional philosopher, Adam Schaff, who was a trained and avowed Marxist-Leninist. And even Schaff's background was unorthodox, since he had first graduated in philosophy at Lwow University (the birthplace of Polish analytical philosophy), and studied social sciences in Paris, before obtaining a doctorate in Marxism-Leninism from Moscow University. When the Marxist-Leninist offensive against other schools of thought began in 1950–1951, Schaff had acquired a number of able adjutants. But they were either very youthful (like Leszek Kołakowski, Helena Eilenstein, and Bronisław Baczko) or middle-aged converts who had been critics of Marxism-Leninism in the past (e.g. Julian Hochfel, Jósef Chalasiński, Tadeusz Kroński, and Bogdan Suchodolski). By 1956 all of them had deserted Schaff.

During the years 1944–1947, when Communism assumed power in Poland (at first shared with the Polish Socialist Party and other temporary allies), the simple propaganda of Marxism was the most pressing need of the Polish Workers' Party on "the ideological front." Conscious of the widespread popular and academic hostility to Marxism, the Party expounded and advocated it not as a narrow sectarian creed but as the culmination of a broad intellectual movement, originating in the Enlightenment and aiming at the emancipation of mankind from all sorts of mental and social shackles. Both the humanism of its social and political ideals and the scientific character of its sociological analysis were stressed in an attempt to win over at least those scientists and intellectuals who were not firmly committed to the right. The response of the leading intellectuals was encouraging. Although critical towards certain aspects of it, they seldom condemned and rejected Marxism *in toto* as pseudoscience and pseudophilosophy. Rather they expressed the highest regard for the intellectual heritage of Karl Marx and agreed that it could become a platform on which Marxists and non-Marxists would collaborate to develop humanities and social sciences and to solve many of the practical problems encountered in constructing a humane political, social, and economic system in postwar Poland.

Typical of this sympathetic response was a series of brilliant articles on Marxism published in 1947 and 1948 in *Myśl Współczesna* by the sociologist and social philosopher Stanisław Ossowski.[2] Politically an independent social democrat, and thoroughly versed in the writings of Marx, Engels, and Lenin, Ossowski pointed out that the obstacles to such cooperation were to be sought primarily in the Marxist camp.

> We can speak of a peculiar "unity of contradictions" in contemporary Marxist circles, especially those situated east of the Rhine. They fight for progress, for a revolutionary social program, they fight against prejudices, proclaim the dynamism of thought and the cult of scientific creativity, they believe in the unimpeded progress of science. Yet simultaneously, when any problem within the scope of Marx's doctrine comes under consideration, the

characteristic of many modern Marxist circles is neophobia, unwillingness to move outside the conceptual apparatus and the range of problems of the second half of the 19th century, as if — contrary to the proclaimed doctrine — they believed that in those fields there had been no change.

Ossowski argued that, by becoming the ideology of the socialist and communist movement, the doctrine of Marx assumed some features of a religion, in Durkheim's sense of the word; its primary function became the fostering of solidarity among its members, not the understanding and explaining of reality.

> The scientific function and the religious (in the Durkheimian sense) function of strengthening social links are not in agreement with each other. They require different psychic attitudes. A doctrine fulfills its "religious" function all the better when its immutability is strongly emphasized, when in the social group there is strong faith in the infallibility of authorities who are the guarantors of the doctrine, and when the obligation to believe all its contents is passionately felt. But these are just the attitudes which must be abandoned when a doctrine is to perform, in a milieu, a scientific function, which requires criticism, independence of thought and the conviction that every theory is only a stage in the further development of science.

Ossowski formulated a set of conditions on which the fruitfulness of a dialogue between Marxists and non-Marxists depended, and expressed the hope that the current political successes of the Marxist camp in the international arena would help it to overcome its intellectual conservatism, justified in the decades of weakness, isolation, and persecution, but now wholly outdated and inappropriate. Ossowski concluded one of his articles with this version of the future.

> It seems to me that in the Poland of today, where diverse intellectual crosscurrents exist, there are particularly favorable circumstances for the development of thought. In the postwar world Poland could aspire to playing the role of Holland in the time of Descartes and Spinoza, and Polish Marxism could fulfill a truly pioneering ambition. Then we would again certainly have the opportunity to affirm the truth that the dialectical method is alive and fertile when it is not reduced to conventional formulae and subjected to petrification.

Naturally Schaff and Hochfeld, who poth polemized with Ossowski's articles, indignantly rejected the "religious" aspect of Marxism and took exception to some other aspects of his criticism. But it was impossible for them to deny Ossowski's central thesis, i.e., that Marxism, to be scientific, had to be revised, developed, and enriched by the results of later social sciences, historiography, and philosophy.

It is worthwhile to be reminded of those polemics which took place almost thirty years ago, in a brief period of great intellectual freedom. For Ossowski's eloquent plea for "open Marxism," although soon stifled by the onset of Stalinism, did not remain without an echo. On the contrary, it was taken up after 1955 by a whole generation of young Polish Marxist intellectuals, and it became the inspiration of their dream of a Marxist renaissance that would follow after the dark ages of the Stalinist era.

Two characterizations of Stalinism, which appeared in Poland in 1956 and 1957, show the remarkable similarity of thought between them and Ossowski's articles of 1947–1948.

> Religion is the death of science. Over a long period of time religion also became the actual form of cultural life of many intellectual [Communist] circles – religion with all its accessories; the intrusion of revelation into the field of cognition, a system of magic and taboos, a priestly caste monopolizing the right to proclaim the truth, the ideology's endeavor to absorb totally all forms of human life (intellectual pursuits, art, customs, etc.). . . . As a result, an utter contempt for theory came to be voiced under the guise of declarations about its great worth. In fact, theory worked *ex post facto*, fashioning reasons for previously made decisions; it neither changed the world nor enlightened it. Forced to justify the most divergent moves, it necessarily became fuzzy; and the dialectic – an incisive tool for analyzing social phenomena in their full dynamics of evolution and internal conflict – was equated with ambiguity and lack of precision.[3]
>
> A result of this phenomenon [i.e. stifling of criticism] was the religious-ideological function, imposed on Marxist philosophy in the past historical period. . . . A philosophy which postulated the liberation of our knowledge of society from the blinkers of faith, the destruction of institutionalized social taboos, the unmasking of the social sense of symbols and social stereotypes, in the Stalinist epoch itself began to be used as an ideological muzzle, the justification of new taboos and the producer of new ideological symbolism. In this way Marxist philosophy became falsified. The social function of Marxist philosophy in its various manifestations became the negation of the system created by Marx.[4]

Let us now turn to a brief review of the achievements of Polish Marxism after 1956, beginning with the man whose influence left a lasting mark on Polish sociology. Julian Hochfeld played a prominent political role in the de-Stalinization movement of 1956–1957, pleading especially for greater independence for the country's parliament from party and government control. In the academic field he pioneered a return to empirical research on contemporary Polish society, which had fallen into complete disuse during Stalinism. His own views

on the character of Marxism did not differ fundamentally from Ossowski's but were stated in Weberian rather than Durkheimian terms.[5]
Marxism to Hochfeld was a theory of society which attempted to
explain the empirical world; as such it was objective, subject to verification, and, like all scientific theories, constantly perfectible in the
light of new facts. But it was also a *Weltanschauung* which gave meaning and direction to practical activity and inspired struggle for a just
society. This part of it was nonempirical. It belonged to the realm
of values rather than facts and was essentially subjective – a matter
of personal decision and commitment to an ideal. In sociology,
Marxism had to prove its scientific validity in competition with
other social theories, and where particular Marxist hypotheses
proved invalid they were to be revised or replaced by those drawn
from other sources.

Hochfeld advocated the development of a Marxist sociology of political relations, applicable both to capitalist and socialist societies. He
himself did not elaborate the subject very much further, but three of
his professorial assistants made important contributions in this field in
the late 1950s and 1960s. Wlodzimierz Wesołowski clarified the concept of class domination, which he distinguished from and related to
the concept of a system of rule. This enabled him to suggest a framework for the analysis of contemporary Western states which was both
Marxist and did justice to undeniable facts. He also explored the relationship between the Marxist concept of a ruling class and the Western
concept of power elite, showing that they supplemented rather than
contradicted each other. His third major interest has been the nature
of social stratification and conflict in socialist societies such as Poland.
Apart from conceptual clarification he conducted an ambitious empirical inquiry into the social stratification of select Polish cities.
Zygmunt Bauman's main concern was the concept of elite and its
applicability to the explanation of political phenomena in Western and
Eastern Europe. In a major historical study of the British working-
class movement he showed that the concept of elite could usefully
supplement the Marxist concept of class. But his attempt to investigate the elite character of the contemporary Polish Communist Party,
on both central and local levels, languished through the loss of official
party support. Jerzy J. Wiatr pioneered the empirical study of public
opinion and voting behavior in Poland, as well as the study of interest
groups. He also made an attempt to clarify the nature of the party
system in Poland, and to elaborate the Marxist theory of nation and
its relationship to the state. Perhaps more than any other Polish
sociologist, Wiatr specializes in the construction of bridges between

traditional Marxist-Leninist theory and the major trends in Western political sociology.

A number of other, even younger, Marxist sociologists have also made significant theoretical contributions along Hochfeldian lines since the late 1950s. But the great majority of Polish sociologists largely avoided wide theoretical issues and concentrated on empirical research of one kind or another. This is a task which they find academically more congenial since theoretical problems always carry the risk of offical party criticism for unorthodoxy.

In philosophy the risk has been less avoidable and the leading young Polish Marxist philosophers — Bronisław Braczko, Helena Eilenstein, and Leszek Kołakowski — have all incurred strong criticism and censure at one time or another. One way to escape scrutiny has been to write a study of a non-Marxist thinker and to analyze in the context of his theory problems of particular relevance to Marxism. Kołakowski's book on Spinoza and Baczko's on Rousseau are outstanding examples of this technique.[6] Kołakowski is also the author of some studies of medieval Christianity, the social and intellectual problems of which struck him as relevant to modern Polish society. In general the genre of sophisticated intellectual history, written from Marxist perspective, developed particularly well. Examples are Z. Ogonowski's studies of the Socinians and Locke, J. Szacki's book on the French counterrevolutionary thinkers, and Panasiuk's study of Marx and the Left Hegelians.

Kołakowski's philosophical contributions to Marxism are too numerous to enumerate fully. They include the clarification of its two aspects as a science and a world view,[7] the discussion of the function of both aspects, the problems of knowledge and truth, the nature of religion and morality, the relation of Marxism to contemporary philosophy, and many others. His finest writings probably were those on the subject of human personality, moral responsibility, and individual freedom. He was passionately concerned to show that historical determinism does not undermine individual freedom or moral responsibility for one's actions, and that pursuit of truth and other values takes precedence over political expediency. To formulate his position he turned to the young Marx where the concern for the individual and his well-being is not overlaid by the analysis of social processes and historical trends. But Kołakowski seems also to have drawn on Sartre's existentialism, which Sartre himself believes to be perfectly compatible with Marxism, indeed an "enclave" within Marxism.[8]

Many of Kołakowski's ideas were, at the time of publication, attacked by Adam Schaff in the name of preserving the distinctiveness

and integrity of the Marxist philosophical system. But Schaff came to
agree with Kołakowski on the need to develop a Marxist philosophy of
man in order to fill a gap which he felt was preventing Marxism from
fulfilling its world view function in contemporary society. He refused
any compromise with existentialism whose conception of the individual he saw rooted in indeterminism and therefore basically incompatible with Marxism.[9] But he found in the young Marx all that was
necessary to fill in gaps in traditional Marxism. Somewhat belatedly
(in relation to Western scholarship) Schaff perceived the importance
of the concept of alienation and attempted to bring it up to date. He
denied any incompatibility or significant difference between the
thought of the young and the mature Marx, arguing that the latter's
economic theories were inspired by and subservient to the socialist
humanism of the former.[10]

In his other works published after 1955 Schaff revised his earlier
interpretations (e.g. on the universal validity of the principle of contradiction and its relation to the Marxist dialectical logic) or constructed bridges between Marxism and other philosophical currents such as
semantics and the philosophy of language which he felt had been
wrongly ignored or dismissed as "idealism" by Marxist-Leninists in the
past. What is particularly interesting about Schaff is that he not only
accepted the idea of "open Marxism" in practice, but actually explicitly defended it.

> The Marxist system is an "open" one by its very nature. It is founded on the
> necessity of continually revising particular conclusions in the light of new
> facts and discoveries, on the continual creative development of its own
> theories. Marxism is always prepared to absorb new data, new discoveries,
> new achievements of theoretical thought, to generalize from them and, in
> case of need, to modify its existing propositions in the light of its generaliza-
> tions.[11]

The Polish tradition of "open Marxism" scored perhaps its greatest
triumph when the leading Polish Marxist-Leninist, the bastion of
orthodoxy and the scourge of all revisionisms, declared his adherence
to it in 1962.

So far I have been concerned to explain the peculiar character of
Polish Marxism mainly in terms of its long tradition of openness,
heterodoxy, and pluralism, and to indicate some of the ways in which
it has evolved and taken shape. Now a vital element in the analysis –
the political – which has been only incidentally treated, must be more
fully discussed. Since 1945 or at least 1949 the control of the
Communist party leadership over the country has been so strong that

without its consent or at least acquiescence, major intellectual developments would not have been possible. And Marxism-Leninism, as the avowed ideology of the Polish ruling party, has obviously been of particular concern to the leadership. In what way have the attitudes and policies of the party leadership contributed to the development of Polish postwar Marxism?

There was, as we saw, no problem during the period 1945–1948. The concern of the leadership was to strengthen the new regime by attracting to it all "progressive elements" in Polish society and creating a broad popular front under the party's leadership. Any kind of support for Marxism, however unorthodox, was welcome and an "open Marxism" was clearly more attractive to the non-Communist intellectuals and the intelligentsia than a dogmatic, sectarian, rigid doctrine of the Stalinist variety. All this changed after 1948 when the dominant political consideration of Stalin vis-à-vis Eastern Europe was its subordination to the Soviet Union, the consolidation of communist power in each country, and the mobilization of the Soviet bloc as a whole for the Cold War against the West. "Institutional Marxism," so well characterized by Kołakowski, was an appropriate instrument of what has come to be called "totalitarian" control.

> [Under Stalinism] the term "Marxism" did not designate a doctrine with a specific content. It meant a doctrine defined purely formally, its content being in every case supplied by the decrees of the Infallible Institution which, during a certain phase, was the Greatest Philologist, the Greatest Economist, the Greatest Philosopher, and the Greatest Historian in the World.
>
> In short, "Marxism" became a concept of institutional, rather than intellectual, content — which, by the way, happens to every doctrine connected with a church. Similarly, the word "Marxist" did not describe a man who believed in a specific world view whose content was defined. It referred to a man with a mental attitude characterized by a willingness to adopt institutionally approved opinions. From this point of view, the current content of Marxism did not matter. A man was a Marxist if he was always ready to accept as its content each recommendation of the Office.[12]

Kołakowski's brilliant critique of the fate of Marxism under Stalinism should not, however, obscure two basic facts: that Stalinism did not last long enough to do serious harm to the development of philosophy or the social sciences, and that it was very mild while it lasted. Nobody went to prison for opposing Marxism-Leninism in the past. Purged from the universities, the non-Marxist philosophers were given well-paid translation and editorial jobs in the Polish Academy of

Sciences. Their sociological colleagues even remained in the universities but had to teach the history of social thought instead of sociology. Nor were all unorthodox views wholly silenced. As late as 1952 Kotarbiński was able to defend himself in the militantly Marxist *Myśl Filozoficzna*, and a year later Ajdukiewicz could strongly rebut Schaff's criticism of his philosophy as "idealistic" in the same periodical. Soon after Stalin's death in 1953 the sociologist Józef Chałasiński engaged in a long polemic with Schaff in the academic quarterly *Nauka Polska*. It began with a dispute over the interpretation of Lenin's theory of the plebeian stream in culture, but during the subsequent two years Chałasiński developed it into a wide challenge to the official Marxist-Leninist interpretation of social phenomena. Meanwhile by 1955 the young Marxist cadre of the Central Committee's Institute of Social Sciences — the training ground of the watchdogs of institutional Marxism — were in open rebellion against some aspects of the party line. They demanded the reintroduction of the study of analytical philosophy, the resumption of empirical social research, and the importation of current Western philosophical and sociological literature. In other words, institutional Marxism, in its Polish variety, never wholly stifled independent thought or achieved the complete monopoly to which it pretended in the various fields of humanistic and social sciences. The former advocates of "open Marxism" crouched for a few years under the onslaught of Stalinist orthodoxy and then rose unscathed, with increased prestige, to resume quietly academic teaching and publishing. The new battle for "open Marxism," which began in 1955, was now fought within the Marxist camp itself, by young academics who rebelled against their elders, the leaders of the party's ideological front, who had used them as political tools and had made them glorify the man whom Khrushchev denounced as a murderer and megalomaniac in his secret speech to the XXth CPSU Congress.

This rebellion raised in an acute form the problem of the relation between Communist intellectuals and the party leaders. The problem was already discussed in the September 1956 issue of *Nowe Drogi*, in Kołakowski's article "Intellectuals and the Communist Movement." He summed up his conclusion in a few striking sentences.

> The Communist Party needs intellectuals not so that they can marvel at the wisdom of its decisions, but only so that its decisions will be wise. Intellectuals are necessary to Communism as people who are free in their thinking and superfluous as opportunists. Theoretical work cannot be useful to the revolutionary movement if it is controlled by anything besides scientific

stringency and the striving for true knowledge; it must therefore be free for the good of the movement.[13]

Kołakowski did not spell out in that article what institutional changes would be necessary to guarantee the freedom of interpreting Marxism and confronting practice with theory; he was merely concerned to establish the case for freedom in principle. But the political implications did not escape the Central Committee functionary Andrzej Werblan, who in the same issue of *Nowe Drogi* commented on Kołakowski's article.

Werblan agreed that serious mistakes had been committed by the party on the "ideological front." Instead of guiding and inspiring, the party had dictated to intellectuals views which should have been arrived at by free discussion in the intellectual milieux themselves. Party leaders had sometimes wrongly donned the mantle of theoreticians and ruled on matters which should have been left to the care of more competent men. Harmful barriers had been set up between Polish and Western intellectuals, and the former had found themselves disarmed by unnecessary ignorance in the ideological struggle against the capitalist world. On all these points Kołakowski was quite right and the party was now setting its house in order. But it was impossible to go as far as Kołakowski demanded. Unlimited intellectual freedom, even within the framework of Marxism, meant the freedom to criticize the party's leading bodies and to oppose their decisions. It amounted to a privilege of oppositionist activity within the party, incompatible with the principle of democratic centralism and the party's ban on factionalism. The party, through its leading bodies, was responsible for the successful construction of socialism in Poland, and it could not abrogate its responsibility to any other group. Hence Kołakowski's principal demand was un-Leninist, unrealistic, and harmful. This has remained the fullest statement of the official line of the party ever since.

For about two years after coming into power, the new party leadership under Gomułka tolerated a great deal of free discussion and scathing criticism of Stalinism. But it never conceded the point that the free development of Marxist philosophy and sociology demanded the dismantling of the system of control over the party's intellectual life which had been in existence before October 1956. The leadership was willing to restrict the scope and to change the methods of control, but no more. Gradually it saw itself forced to abandon its tolerant attitude. It found that among party intellectuals there were too few orthodox Marxists prepared to refute fundamental criticisms and check far-reaching theoretical innovations of a Marxist and non-Marxist nature, and that it could not dispense with discredited administrative measures. It became exasperated with the Marxist intellectual's obsession with the past and the unwillingness to accept changes and be grateful. It also came under pressure of the communist bloc, which condemned "open Marxism" and other political postulates as "revisionism", and declared it to be a form of bourgeois ideological penetration and a serious danger to socialism. With some reluctance Gomułka accepted the communist bloc thesis and ordered a purge of revisionist elements in the party. But the purge was quite mild and the leading revisionists such as Kołakowski remained in the party and continued to teach and to publish as long as they confined themselves to relatively abstract points of Marxist exegesis or to the critical interpretation, however independent, of non-Marxist philosophies and theories. Repression was reserved for gross breaches of party discipline and for particularly offensive criticisms of the working of the political system or particular policies.

One of the most severe cases was the treatment of the university assistants Kuroń and Modzelewski in 1965. For circulating an "open letter" to the Warsaw University party organization both men were tried and given short sentences of imprisonment. Their offence was preparing and distributing "works harmful to the interests of the Polish state." What was harmful in the letter was the application of some Marxist concepts to contemporary Polish reality. The authors argued that a sizeable share of the surplus value of nationalized industry was appropriated not by its producers, but by the central political bureaucracy in order to maintain their own power and privileges. They proposed transferring economic and political power to a system of democratically elected workers' councils.

In the same year Adam Schaff was censured at a special meeting of invited party intellectuals, presided over by a Politbureau member, for certain passages in his book *Marxism and the Human Individual.* The offensive passages referred to anti-Semitism and the enormous economic power of the central planning authorities as examples of continued "alienation" in a socialist society. In 1966 Kołakowski was at last expelled from the party for giving a critical talk to a student audience on the tenth anniversary of the Polish October. But a year later the Polish Scientific Publishers issued a collection of his philosophical essays under the title *Culture and Fetishes.* It was as if the party leadership was trying to differentiate between Kołakowski, the incorrigible party comrade, and the famous Marxist thinker and professor of philosophy. While the first had to be brought to heel, this did not affect the treatment of the second. Only after March 1968 was a total ban imposed on the publication of anything at all by Kołakowski.

By the mid-sixties the activities of party intellectuals had come under the close scrutiny of the security police, controlled by General Moczar and his so-called "Partisan" faction. Under the excuse of combatting "ideological diversion" of Western capitalist circles, incriminating material was being secretly collected against "revisionist" and "Zionist" elements in the party. In the wake of the Warsaw student disturbances in March 1968, a thorough purge of these elements — far more thorough than Gomułka seems to have intended — was conducted by the Moczar faction. Kołakowski, Baczko, Bauman, and others were illegally dismissed from their university posts for exerting harmful ideological influence on junior staff, research students, and undergraduates. At a subsequent Central Committee meeting Schaff himself was accused of ideological laxity and an overtolerant attitude towards revisionism, and, despite his protestations of innocence, was dismissed from the Central Committee. What is perhaps striking is not the brutality with which revisionism was suppressed, but the fact that it took almost ten years from the time Gomułka first declared it to be the main ideological danger to the party to complete the suppression.

Insofar as revisionism was a political movement among party intellectuals who had been involved in, and then reacted against, "the errors and distortions of the period of the cult of personality," it is probably right to consider it dead in today's Poland. The younger, post-Stalinist generation of Marxist philosophers and sociologists, brought up in the years of relatively "open Marxism," do not show much sign of a crusading spirit, yet they take "open Marxism" for granted as the only respectable intellectual position. But they do not assert it any more either; they get on with their narrowly philosophical work, with the history of ideas, or with empirical sociological research. Nor is there any pressure on them to abandon this position. Outside the party's ideological apparatus and a few survivers of the old Communist cadre one can find no more orthodox Marxist-Leninists in Poland.

The attitude of Gierek towards Marxist intellectuals (as it was of Gomułka) is one of pragmatism: as long as they observe party discipline and cause no political embarrassment, they can write and publish what they like. This is perhaps not a situation favorable to the production of great works, but it should ensure the continued development of Marxism as a living intellectual tradition, not the perpetuation of ossified dogmas, cut off from and irrelevant to the modern world, which comes to much the same thing as "intellectual paralysis."

NOTES

1. George Lichtheim, *Marxism: An Historical and Critical Study* (London, 1961), p. 394.

2. *Myśl Wspołczesna* ("Contemporary Thought"), December 1947, January 1948, and August 1948. Reprinted in Stanislaw Ossowski, *Dziela,* Volume 6, (Warsaw, 1970).

3. Leszek Kołakowski, *Marxism and Beyond* (London, 1969). From an essay on "Intellectuals and the Communist Movement," originally published in *Nowe Drogi,* September 1956.

4. Jerzy J. Wiatr and Zygmunt Bauman, "Marxism and Contemporary Sociology," *Myśl Filozoficzna,* No. 27, 1957.

5. These views can be found in a collection of essays under the title *Studies on the Marxian Theory of Society* (Warsaw, 1963).

6. Baczko's chief interest continued to be the Marxist analysis of other thinkers and the ideas underlying social political movements. Eilenstein was mostly concerned wity epistemological problems. Their and Kołakowski's ideas are discussed at length in Z.A. Jordan, *Philosophy and Ideology* (Dordrecht, 1963).

7. We can assume that with the gradual refinement of research techniques in the humanities, the concept of Marxism as a separate school of thought will in time become blurred and ultimately disappear altogether, just as there is no "Newtonism" in physics. . . . The greatest triumph of an eminent scholar comes when his achievements cease to define a separate school of thought, when they merge into the very tissue of scientific life and become an elemental part of it, losing their disparate existence. This process is obviously different and much slower in the humanities, but even there it is an essential part of progress.

With this situation Kołakowski contrasted the fate of Marxism as a philosophy of world view. Here no such assimilation and merging of original and distinctive perspectives or viewpoints was possible. But even

> "Marxism" in this sense does not denote a doctrine that must be accepted or rejected as a whole. It does not mean a universal system, but a vital philosophical inspiration affecting our whole outlook on the world, a constant stimulus to the social intelligence and the social memory of mankind.

Marxism and Beyond, op. cit., pp. 206–107.

8. Most of Kołakowski's essays on this subject can be found in *Marxism and Beyond.*

9. See *Marxism a egzystencjonalizm* (Warsaw, 1961), second edition translated into English, *A Philosophy of Man* (London, 1963).

10. See *Marksizm a jednostka ludzka* (Warsaw, 1965). (There are French and German translations.)

11. *A Philosophy of Man,* p. 220

12. *Marxism and Beyond,* p. 194.

13. *Marxism and Beyond,* p. 191.

THE CONCEPT OF THE ASIATIC MODE OF
PRODUCTION AND CONTEMPORARY MARXISM

MARIAN SAWER
Australian National University, Canberra

In 1963 George Lichtheim published an extremely interesting essay on the concept of the Asiatic mode of production. This essay consisted of an incisive account of the nature of the concept and of its place in the writings of Marx and Engels. It was written at a time when the concept was only just being "rediscovered" by Marxists. During the decade since the essay appeared Marxists have not only become familiar with Marx's concept, thanks to works such as that by Lichtheim, but have also been actively exploring the implications of the concept for contemporary Marxism. In this paper I shall be tracing the developments in Marxist historiography since 1964 associated with the rediscovery of the concept of the Asiatic mode of production.

THE UNILINEAR SCHEMA OF SOCIAL DEVELOPMENT

Before 1964 historical materialism was generally interpreted to mean that history consisted in a single sequence of universally occurring stages of social development, corresponding to different stages of the development of productive forces. The immanent logic of the development of material production was taken to be such that each stage of the succession would appear, unveil its inner contradictions, and give rise to the next, higher phase of economic production and social development. According to this law of social development the same pattern or sequence of stages would be found in the history of any given society.

This interpretation of historical materialism stems largely from two of Marx's more programmatic pieces of writing. The first of these is the *Communist Manifesto,* which like the *German Ideology* bears witness to the influence of Fourier's stadial analysis of human history. The second is the Preface to the *Contribution to the Critique of Political Economy.* In his Preface Marx wrote: "In broad outline, the

Asiatic, ancient, feudal and modern bourgeois modes of production may be designated as epochs marking progress in the economic development of society."[1] This passage has been the subject of some controversy, particularly in recent years,[2] but it has also served as the primary authority for the unilinear conception of human history.

Apart from these sources, the works of Engels, particularly in the period from the writing of the *Anti-Dühring,* contributed much towards the establishment of the unilinear schema as dogma. Statements such as the following assisted in the process: "Without the slavery of antiquity, no modern socialism."[3] Engels also believed, with Marx, that "to accomplish this [modern socialism] we need not only the proletariat, which carries out the revolution, but also a bourgeoisie in whose hands the productive forces of society have developed to such a stage that they permit the final elimination of all class distinctions . . . The bourgeoisie is consequently equally as necessary a precondition of the socialist revolution as the proletariat itself."[4] I.e., a full sequence of Western social stages was necessary for the eventual creation of socialism, and there were no alternative routes.

Engels was also largely responsible for the adoption into Marxist theory of Morgan's anthropological system. Morgan's system minimized the significance of external influences on the internal development of human societies, and hence reinforced the notion that social development progressed through a given sequence of necessary stages up to the socialist one, according to certain iron laws of its own.

The tendency to codify fixed laws of social development was linked with the more general tendency, also begun under the aegis of Engels, to transform Marxism into a "science of society." In its guise as a science of society, historical materialism was of great symbolic value to the European labor movement in the last quarter of the nineteenth century.[5] It was the ideological buttress of the socialist parties, insofar as it demonstrated the "objective necessity" of their cause; it had the further function, however, of assisting in the substitution of the party for the masses, as the repository of socialist consciousness. If historical materialism was a science it was more likely to be mastered by the scientists (i.e. the party theorists) than by the masses. The implication that was drawn was that the masses could never achieve class-consciousness spontaneously, even in the course of bitter class struggle; rather, they required the mediation of the party.

The diagram below represents the stage theory of "vulgar" or institutionalized historical materialism, and is largely derived from the Preface to the *Contribution to the Critique of Political Economy.*

THE UNILINEAR SCHEMA

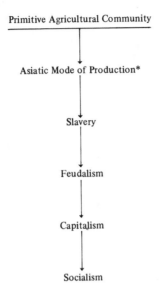

Primitive Agricultural Community

Asiatic Mode of Production*

Slavery

Feudalism

Capitalism

Socialism

* Frequently omitted

The difficulties incurred in trying to fit what Marx conceived of as a geographically specific mode of production, i.e., the Asiatic, into a universal schema of social development have been so formidable that they have frequently been resolved *modo tatarico*, as Wittfogel puts it, by simply cutting this socioeconomic formation out of the schema. It was quite logical for this to happen in Lenin's influential lecture on *The State*, published for the first time in 1929, as Lenin was following closely Engels' *Origin of the Family, Private Property and the State*. A more glaring example of deliberate extrusion may be found in the 1938 *History of the Communist Party of the Soviet Union, Short Course*, where the unilinear schema from Marx's Preface is reproduced exactly, with the single omission of the reference to the Asiatic mode of production.[6]

The concept of the Asiatic mode of production as an independent socioeconomic formation was virtually banned in the Soviet Union for a variety of political reasons which have been amply discussed elsewhere.[7] In 1933 the view then held by V. V. Struve (after some vacillations), that the ancient Eastern civilizations belonged to the slavery formation, was officially adopted, and is still influential today.

Struve has strongly supported the unilinear schema, and eliminates
Marx's notion of an endlessly self-perpetuating Asiatic mode of production by ascribing a slave stage to the ancient East, and a feudal
stage to the medieval East. Struve does admit that the slave stage in
the ancient East was marked by some peculiarities, such as the existence of rural communities, from which tribute was exacted, but he
describes this as a transient survival of the tribute paid to the military
aristocracy in patriarchal tribal societies.[8] The more important (because representing a higher stage of historical development) form of
exploitation in these societies, according to Struve, was the exploitation of slaves, in the nonagricultural sector, by the state (using the
revenue collected from the rural communities). Hence of the two
forms of exploitation present in the societies of the ancient East, the
slave form provided the "determining element" and the defining characteristic.[9] Struve does not here regard the distinction between private
slave-owners employing slaves chiefly for the purposes of primary production in a largely commodity-based economy, and the state employing artisans and domestic slaves out of its tax revenue from rural
communities in a predominantly natural economy as an important
distinction implying different modes of production. Furthermore
Struve completely overlooks the point that Marx believed the character of a socioeconomic formation to be determined by the mode of
production found in it which produces the bulk of the social surplus.
Because of the virtual disappearance of protagonists of the Asiatic
mode, Struve's past polemics on the subject of the ancient Eastern
civilizations were mainly directed against those who wished to extend
the concept of feudalism to these societies on the basis of the "attachment" of the peasants to the soil, thus neglecting the necessary sequence "slavery, feudalism" and replacing it with the sequence
"feudalism, slavery" as did the "bourgeois historians of the imperialist
epoch."[10] Such problems would clearly be avoided if one allowed the
possibility of an alternative formation which encompassed both the
attachment of the peasants to the soil, and state support of the nonagricultural sector. Struve, however, has been reluctant to concede the
existence of such an alternative path of historical development, or
indeed to concede any notion of historical plurality that might detract
from the concept of a "unitary world history."[11]

   The post-Stalinist textbook *Fundamentals of Marxism-Leninism*
(1961) faithfully preserves the five-stage Stalinist schema, despite the
assurance that: "Historical materialism does not impose preconceived
patterns on history and does not adapt the events of past and present
to fit its own conclusions."[12] The Kuusinen textbook outlines the

four socioeconomic formations which mankind passes through before achieving the transition stage to communism (i.e., socialism), and these exclude the Asiatic formation.[13]

Another method of dealing with the Asiatic mode of production in the context of the unilinear schema, more common since 1964, has been to dilute the concept of the Asiatic mode in such a way that it might appear to be a plausible analysis of a primitive universal stage of social development.

In 1964 the reopening of the discussion of the Asiatic mode of production in the Soviet Union was signaled by the publication of E. Varga's *Ocherki po problemam politekonomii kapitalizma* which contained an essay on the subject. Discussions were held in the (Academy of Sciences) Institute of Philosophy in December 1964, in the Institute of History on the 5th, 12th and 16th March, 1965, and in the Institute of the Peoples of Asia on the 27th and 28th of May, 1965. Meanwhile the French Marxists M. Godelier and J. Suret-Canale had prepared papers on the Asiatic mode of production for the Seventh International Congress of Anthropology and Ethnography held in Moscow, August 1964, and these papers, together with a reply from V. Struve, were published in the journal *Narody Azii i Afriki* at the beginning of 1965. Soviet scholars interested in employing the concept of a distinct Asiatic formation were able to discover from Godelier and Suret-Canale a definition of such a formation which was compatible with the traditional unilinear framework of Soviet historiography.[14] Thus: "The majority of the participants in the discussion, in its current stage, were of the opinion that by Marx's conception of the Asiatic mode of production one should understand not so much a specific particularity of the East (especially the particularity associated with the necessity for irrigation works) as those regularities *(zakonomernosti)* characteristic of nearly all early class societies, and which were retained over a prolonged period in many of the societies of Africa, Asia and pre-Columbian America."[15]

In the definition of the French Marxists and their Soviet followers, the Asiatic mode of production represented the original transition stage between classless and class society; the stage where the state had already come into being but private property did not yet exist. The stage was characterized by the existence of communal production and ownership at the village level, on the one hand, and by the appropriation of the surplus value by the state, and the existence of (state-directed) corvée labor on the other; economic classes did not yet exist, but there were elites associated with the state who performed religious, military and other public functions.

The broad definition of the Asiatic mode of production in general makes it more or less a substitute for Engels' somewhat problematic concept of "military democracy." Marx's concept was shorn of any of its geographical connotations, or its connotations of highly developed entrepreneurial and/or bureaucratic activity on the part of the state, and thus became far more plausible as a universal stage of development to be found in the history of any given society.

The universalizing of the concept of the Asiatic mode was exemplified in the work of Jean Chesneaux (with whom the Western pattern became more or less the exceptional case). Chesneaux wrote in 1964 that:

> The Asiatic mode of production for the very reason that it has been the most general form of evolution of primitive communist society, has established itself in very diverse regions, in societies on which both history and geography have imposed very different rhythms of development. Brutally destroyed in the Mediterranean by the Dorian invasion at the beginning of the first millenium BC, liquidated by the Spanish conquest in America in the sixteenth century, it nevertheless continued slowly to evolve in countries such as China, Egypt, India, and Black Africa.[16]

During the discussion at the Institute of the Peoples of Asia and Africa held on the 27th and 28th of May, 1965, Iu. M. Garushiants and M. A. Vitkin in particular were to support the universalist definition of the Asiatic mode of production provided by the French Marxists, thus avoiding the multilinear implications of the definition given by the first generation of Soviet scholars working on the subject, such as E. Varga and L. I. Madiar. Vitkin argued that: "the emphasis on the fundamental particularity of Asiatic history characteristic of nineteenth-century historiography underwent a sharp about-turn at the close of the century, so that the history of the East was assimilated to that of Europe. The particularity of the East was discovered to be only relative . . . because, as the latest information indicates, ancient Europe (Mycenae etc.) also experienced a stage similar to that which Marx described as characterizing the ancient East. The acceptable meaning of the Asiatic mode of production seems to be that it is the last stage of the primitive communal formation, the transition stage to class society."[17]

According to the new definition, the Asiatic formation had an internal dynamic provided by the fact that its elites would attempt to transform themselves into an economic class based on the private ownership of the means of production (e.g. ownership of slaves and land). The attribution of dynamic elements to the Asiatic formation was a necessary aspect of the attempt to fit it into a universal progression. However Marxists such as Parain, Chesneaux, Suret-Canale, Boiteau and Godelier in France were also, in eliminating the proposition concerning Asiatic stagnation, conscious of the need to make the hypothesis of an Asiatic mode of production acceptable to the national sensitivities of third world countries.[18] One Soviet Orientalist, who accepts the other elements of Marx's concept of the Asiatic mode of production, has gone so far as to say that "it is difficult to imagine that dialecticians such as Marx and Engels might be parties to the possibility of absolute stagnation in societies of the type under consideration."[19]

However, the manner in which the French Marxists and those following their formulation denied the proposition of Asiatic stagnation was itself guided by criteria drawn from Western experience. Thus according to Suret-Canale the persistence of collective property did not necessarily mean that the Asiatic formations represented an impasse: "their internal contradiction (collective property — class property) may be resolved by the dissolution of collective property and the appearance of private property."[20] I.e., the French Marxists preserved Marx's viewpoint, formed under the influence of the British political economists that the emergence of private property was the key to progress whether in West or East.

The broad interpretation of the Asiatic mode of production as the most primitive form of state exercised great appeal among French Marxists in that it enabled them to find a pigeonhole for the precolonial societies of Black Africa which had resisted classification under any of the other Marxist categories (and similarly it appealed to those Marxists concerned with other problem areas, such as pre-Columbian America and the Pacific).[21] The extension of the concept to such diverse areas naturally required considerable modification of some of the characteristics which Marx attributed to Asiatic society: Godelier, for example, talked of two forms of the Asiatic mode, that with and that without "great (public) works,"[22] the latter form being found in tropical Africa, where the functions giving rise to the state related to the control of trade, the protection of markets, etc. In the early euphoria resulting from the rediscovery of the concept Godelier also believed that it might provide the solution to the categorization of the nomadic pastoral societies[23] — i.e., the concept was on the way to becoming the portmanteau classification of all societies which had slipped under the net of the five-stage schema.

The elimination of the geographically specific features of the Asiatic mode has been one method of rendering the concept of universal applicability and making it compatible with the unilinear schema of development. An interesting attempt to retain the geographical specificity of the Asiatic mode, and its status as an independent formation, [24] while also upholding the authority of the unilinear schema, is to be found in the work of the Hungarian Sinologist Ferenc Tökei. Tökei argues that the Asiatic mode was essentially determined by conditions of internal and external isolation, which had prevented the universal laws of development from operating as they had done in Europe. However, according to Tökei, the existence of the (static) Asiatic formation by no means disproved the unilinear theory of the five stages: on the contrary, it bore indirect witness to the operation of such a universal law. He asserted that despite the isolation of, for example, China, which had retarded its development, tendencies towards a slave stage had appeared in the era of antiquity, and tendencies towards feudalism had appeared in the Middle Ages. The fact that these tendencies manifested themselves (even in a weak form) in such an isolated society as China confirmed for Tökei the universal validity of the five-stage schema. [25]

The attempt to make the concept of the Asiatic mode of production compatible with the unilinear theory of history, and the tendency to overextend the concept (to cover all societies which had resisted classification within the five-stage schema) are both typical of the initial phase of the de-Stalinisation of Marxist historiography. Marxist historians were eager to employ a concept, for which they now found there was ample authority in Marx, and which would serve to enrich the existing framework of Marxist historiography. But they were hesitant to explore the further implications of the concept, such as the implication that history was multilinear rather than unilinear, and that there existed other alternative modes of production not discussed by Marx because of his lack of information. Hence they loosened the concept of the Asiatic mode of production itself rather than loosening their approach to history in general, and attempted to "save" non-Western societies from the grip of the five-stage schema by introducing a sixth category to accommodate all the exceptions.

THE HEGELIANIZED VERSION OF THE UNILINEAR SCHEMA

The extreme difficulty of fitting every human society into the unilinear schema has given rise to yet another "saving device" within the unilinear view, that of treating it in a Hegelian way. According to Hegel, world history evolved through a certain sequence of necessary stages, but each stage was primarily embodied in only one nation or group of nations.

One reason why it seemed plausible to assert that the center of human progress shifted from area to area was primarily geographical — that different geographical factors became of decisive importance at different stages of socioeconomic development. The employment of this argument by Hegel, Mechnikov, Plekhanov and Wittfogel has been discussed elsewhere by the author.

Another argument concerns the hypostatization of a form of production in the society where it reaches its highest development. According to this argument, structures appropriate to a particular socioeconomic formation which also become associated with a period of national greatness, severely impede the development of structures appropriate to a later period.[26] Hence the next stage of human history tends to take place in a different arena, less cluttered with cherished institutional anachronisms.

The adoption of the "Hegelian" version of the unilinear schema, whereby different societies represent the different epochs of human development, makes the concept of necessary social laws governing the transition from one epoch to another even more difficult. There is a recurrence of the tension inherent in the Hegelian view of world history — i.e., world history consists in an organic process of development through various logically necessary stages, but within this process the leading role somehow passes from one society or group of societies to another.[27] The problem is to demonstrate the logical relationship between the stages when the subject of world history changes in such a manner. Nonetheless the concept of necessary laws governing the transition between epochs has remained a dogma within Soviet Marxism, even where the Hegelian notion of universal history has been most ardently embraced.[28]

One interesting attempt to grapple with the problem of the logical relationship between stages of history represented by different societies is to be found in the work of V. Gordon Childe. Childe was concerned with the logical relationship between the Asiatic and ancient formations, as progressive stages of universal history occurring in geographically distinct areas. He argued that the relationship between the Middle Eastern civilizations and Aegean civilization was a symbiotic one, the surpluses accumulated by the despotic states supporting the emergence of craft specialization in the West.[29] The secure Eastern markets meant that Bronze-Age civilization in the Aegean was able to reach "take off" point without the despotic or centralized control of the surplus which had launched the Eastern civilizations. And precisely the fact that the emergence of civilization in the Aegean had not depended on the leading economic role of the state meant that these societies had a greater potential for progress and change.

Childe's work has recently been utilized by the French Communist J.-J. Goblot in a series of three articles presenting the case for a universal history in which objective laws of development govern the transformations from one stage to another. One socioeconomic formation does not necessarily engender the next higher formation through the logic of its internal development, but it *does* produce the technical prerequisites of the next stage. Thus the "Asiatic" civilizations of the Near East and the Mediterranean provided the technical basis for the development of Greek antiquity (on Childe's evidence) and the Roman Empire provided the technical basis of Northern European feudalism. In both these cases the development of a new, higher mode of production depended on the fusion of a potentially more dynamic form of social organization, evolved within tribal societies external to the old civilization, with the technological achievements of the old civilization.[30]

The Soviet attempt to modify in a Hegelian fashion the rigid unilinear schema of history was officially promulgated by a Soviet spokesman at an international history conference in 1960. This modification did not extend to the overthrow of Stalin's five-stage schema which extruded the Asiatic formation. But according to the statement made in 1960, the Germanic and Slav peoples did not pass through an epoch of slavery, for the reason that at the period when they were forming themselves into states, the full contradictions of the slave-based mode of production had already emerged in the Roman and Byzantine empires respectively. The "fact" that the Roman and Byzantine empires represented the full working-out of slavery as a mode of production meant that the Germanic and Slav peoples on emerging from clan society, could move straight into an economic formation based on the comparatively more productive labor of dependent peasantry.[31]

In a similar vein, the statement observed that among the peoples incorporated in the Soviet Union were those who had been able to move straight from the feudal, or even the patriarchal stage of production, into the socialist one. This was due to the fact that the contradictions of world capitalism had already fully emerged and the socialist epoch had been ushered in by the time that these peoples emerged from their social isolation.[32]

The above forms of development may be summed up under the rubric of "the advantages of backwardness" − i.e., societies that develop late, or whose tempo of development has been slowed down by geographical and other factors, are able to benefit from the experience accumulated by other societies.

The development of societies on the periphery of the mainstream of history may also, however, be influenced by the *disadvantages* of backwardness. Thus the social development of the nations in propinquity to the Greek and Roman empires was distorted by the systematic removal of manpower and its absorption into the slave-based imperial systems,[33] and likewise the development of the societies on the periphery of Western Europe was later distorted by the effects of "colonialism."

As we have seen, the "Hegelian" version of the unilinear schema puts considerable stress on the external relations of human society, as compared with the schema previously discussed in which the inner logic of social development was the dominant factor.[34] In order that this emphasis on external relations should not seem to enhance the role of contingency too far, considerable effort has been devoted to creating a "universal periodization" which would systematically present the dominant influence in international relations in any given epoch. As a recent Soviet publication has expressed it, "without calculating the leading line of a given epoch or, in other words, without calculating the influence of the leading formation, every concrete analysis loses its point — the description of the facts remains, but it becomes impossible to ascertain their laws of motion."[35]

According to the kind of universal periodization described, the capitalist epoch of world history dates from the beginning of the seventeenth century, and the socialist epoch from 1917 . These dates are particularly important because the role of external influence becomes much more intense and generalized with the dawning of the capitalist era and the creation of the world market. Societies which are for the first time exposed systematically to external influence in these epochs are able to skip several stages of the five-stage schema. One aspect of Zhukov's periodization which would meet with less favor today (1974) is his suggestion that the revolutionary transformation from slavery to feudalism first took place in ancient China.[36] A recent Soviet article has strongly criticized Chinese historiography, particularly that appearing in the journal *Hung Ch'i,* for claiming that the Asiatic nations were in the vanguard of world history until the fifteenth century, and implying that the retardation of the East was only occasioned by the Western colonial powers. The Soviet author argues that on the contrary:

In the countries of the East, the Ch'in, Khazar, Mogul, Osmanli and other dynasties — supported by a centralised state apparatus — impeded the development of society; cultivated early feudal and pre-feudal forms of social relations; exhausted the strength of their peoples in predatory wars; destroyed the forces of production; and suppressed social thought. The feudal leadership of the absolute majority of Asiatic and African countries proved to be incapable of understanding the historical problems of the epoch — the preservation of the independence of their countries. They betrayed their peoples. It was not for no reason that the majority of Asiatic dynasties ended up as the marionettes of foreign capital.[37]

CHRONOLOGICAL AND LOGICAL PROBLEMS ASSOCIATED WITH THE PROGRESSIVE RANKING OF SOCIOECONOMIC FORMATIONS

As seen above, the "Hegelian" modification of the unilinear schema consists essentially in viewing the schema as the pattern of world history, rather than as the pattern inherent in the development of every society. Nonetheless the "Hegelian" version retains the standpoint that the transitions between the stages are of a logically necessary character. A different approach to Marx's schema, which has been attempted recently, has been to view it as an analytic ranking of socioeconomic formations, but not as a fixed chronological sequence in which the contradictions of one stage necessarily give rise to the next. This approach has been attempted by Eric Hobsbawm and J. J. Goblot. It is most obviously prompted by the fact that some societies (notably the Chinese) appear to pass through the "progressive epochs" of social history in the wrong order, or to pass through several periods of feudal disintegration,[38] or again not to pass through certain epochs at all.

The main problem involved in the interpretation of the unilinear schema as an analytic ranking consists in establishing the analytic criteria whereby socioeconomic formations are to be graded as more progressive, or in "crucial respects further removed from the primitive state of man."[39]

Hobsbawm's main criterion consists in the degree of "economic individualization" which exists in the given formation. Thus the most primitive socioeconomic formations are those which conserve to the greatest degree communal forms of property, while the most advanced are those which contain the most elements of free labor and capital.

However the difficulty of viewing Marx's schema as an analytic ranking according to this criterion is tacitly admitted by Hobsbawm himself when he states that "a reversion to feudalism from formations which, while *potentially* less progressive, are in actual fact more highly

developed — as from the Roman Empire to the tribal Teutonic King-
doms — has always been allowed for."[40] Here Hobsbawm is admitting
that the "ancient" formation is more highly developed than the feudal
formation, as it probably must be regarded by most Marxist indicators
such as the degree of division of labor, the level of commodity production and the productivity of labor in certain areas. Hobsbawm in the
passage cited is claiming that feudalism should be ranked higher than
"ancient society" because it has more potential for progress. However
this is less because the degree of economic individualization is higher
in the feudal formation (Hobsbawm's analytic criterion) than because
of the appearance of a particular urban structure within Western feudalism. Hobsbawm elsewhere attempts to bridge these viewpoints by
arguing that it was the degree of economic individualization in the
feudal countryside which made the system soluble, and enabled "free
labor" to be released to the cities, although even then he admits that
this was only one of at least three important factors which contributed to the rise of the West European cities.[41] Hobsbawm's ranking of feudalism above slavery really rests on the argument that the
slave stage contains contradictions which lead inevitably to its collapse
and not to the generation of higher structures within itself. The feudal
formation, while based on a fairly primitive economy, does appear to
Hobsbawm to have this potential, even if only in the unique circumstances of Western Europe.

Thus Hobsbawm retreats from an argument that the socioeconomic
formations represent an analytic ranking, without logically necessary
connections, to an argument that one formation (i.e., feudalism) is
more progressive than another because chronologically, and to some
extent logically, it has given rise to the stage of capitalism.

The problem of attempting to view the schema of Marx's preface as
an analytical ranking of socioeconomic formations is a general one
which extends beyond the work of Western Marxists such as Hobsbawm. It has been easier for Western Marxists, including Hobsbawm,
to view the schema fairly flexibly, and to argue that the precapitalist
formations are not of the same universal nature as capitalism and
socialism and hence are not governed by the same kind of universal
laws of transition. The earlier formations may be seen as governed by
specific historical and geographical circumstances, and technological
advances made in one stage may in fact be lost in the succeeding stage
owing to invasion or some other contingency such as the self-destroy-
ing tendencies of slave-based formations.[42]

However, Soviet Marxism has been far more committed to the line
that Marx's schema represents both a chronological and an analytic

summary of human progress, and that this progress is unidirectional. The criteria developed by Soviet Marxists to demonstrate that the five stages represent analytically more progressive stages of the development of production have been various. There has been a tendency to drop the criterion of development of division of labor, and hence of economic complexity, because of the complications already suggested with regard to the slave formation and feudalism. Other criteria associated with the degree of development of production which have been suggested are the materials used in production (ranging from stone and bronze to polymers); the sources of energy used in production (ranging from manpower and animal power through steam and electric power to nuclear and perhaps solar energy); and the forms taken by cooperation in labor, from the most simple forms resting on the simple aggregation of individual effort to the most articulated and complex forms of organization.[43]

Kachanovsky, in his work cited above, takes the level of development of productive forces as the best criterion of the progressiveness of a given epoch (i.e., in Marx's terms the degree to which man has mastered the forces of nature, plus the productivity of human labor).[44] According to Kachanovsky, however, two other criteria are of relatively high importance. The first of these is the degree of juridical emancipation of the worker. This criterion correlates fairly closely with Hobsbawm's economic individualization. The second is the role of class struggle in the economy. In the slave stage the role of class struggle in the economic process is posited as being insignificant, in the feudal stage much more important, and in the capitalist stage as being of preeminent importance in the realization of economic laws and the determination of economic life. This criterion is particularly tendentious and based on an extremely simplistic view of the class structure of the ancient world.

The difficulty of Kachanovsky's major criterion, the development of productive forces, is firstly that, as he himself admits, it is extremely difficult to establish a comparative analysis of levels of productivity in different socioeconomic formations. Secondly the criterion of the development of productive forces lends itself to any and every schema of history and not simply to the unilinear schema sometimes suggested by Marx. With Kachanovsky, for example, it is used to justify the exclusion of the Asiatic socioeconomic formation from Marxist historiography, because in Asiatic society the level of development of productive forces will correspond either to the level found in ancient society or to the level found in feudal society. The criterion of development of productive forces could, however, with equal justification be applied to some such schema as hunting/gathering, herding, subsistence farming, commodity production, industrial production and postindustrial production.

The judging of socioeconomic formations in terms of labor productivity leaves out of account the factor which Marx described as central to the description of any socioeconomic formation — i.e., the way in which the surplus is appropriated from the direct producers. The criterion of the way in which the surplus is appropriated would serve to distinguish sharply socioeconomic formations which by the criterion of basic labor productivity would be classed together (i.e., the Asiatic and feudal modes, although cooperation results in much higher productivity in some areas in the former mode of production).

THE MULTILINEAR SCHEMA OF HISTORY AS FOUND IN MARX

The publication of the *Grundrisse* has brought to light interesting new evidence on the question of how Marx perceived historical development. In the *Grundrisse* Marx described the development out of primitive communalism in terms of three major *alternative* forms determined by specific geographical, historical and ethnographic circumstances. The account of human history to be found in the *Grundrisse* is presented diagrammatically below:

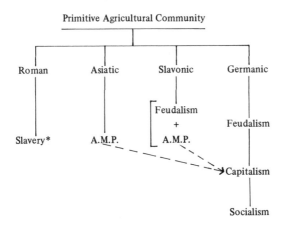

Legend

− − − Non-progressive, but can develop into capitalism under pressure
       from pre-existing capitalist systems.

*   Non-progressive and self-destructing.

As can be seen from the diagram, Marx believed that the multiplicity of forms of development which had existed in the precapitalist world would be brought to an end by the universalizing tendencies of capitalism. According to Marx the unifying force of the world market would ineluctably absorb all local particularities and prepare the way for the universal and uniform transition to socialism. "It [the bourgeoisie] compels all nations, on pain of extinction, to adopt the bourgeois mode of production; it compels them to introduce what it calls civilization into their midst, i.e., to become bourgeois themselves. In one word, it creates a world after its own image."[45] The transition from the multiplicity of forms in precapitalist society to the universal forms of capitalism and socialism is interpreted by the contemporary French Marxist Jean Suret-Canale as follows:

> With the appearance of class societies this diversity of forms which was due to geographical and historical circumstances, etc., moves onto a different plane, thanks to *class relations,* expressable in a more abstract and generalizable form. It is only with capitalism, given the very nature of the productive forces on which it rests, and the nature of the social relations which it engenders, that forces of production and their corresponding relations of production become henceforth, in their essence, entirely independent of the peculiarities of the geographical and historical *milieu. By its very nature,* capitalism, as well as being one of the great stages of human progress, also assumes a universal value, destroying or reducing to the status of residual survivals, the previous modes of production. *A fortiore* such universality appertains to socialism. But one cannot project this universality of the last two stages of social development onto the history which precedes them.[46]

One is left with the question of whether Marx did not exaggerate the universalizing force of capitalism, and whether there were not certain socioeconomic structures which despite the impact of Western capital were able to retain their homeostatic tendencies, and maintain their particularity into the new era.

VARIATIONS OF THE MULTILINEAR SCHEMA AS APPLIED TO PRECAPITALIST SOCIETIES

Even among those Marxists accepting the equation of multilinear development with precapitalist society, and unilinear development with postcapitalist society, many changes have been rung on the general theme. One such variation is that of Maurice Godelier, mentioned earlier in a slightly different context. Godelier combines the view that the Asiatic mode of production is an almost universally occurring transition stage (to class society) with the view that subsequent development is at least bilinear. As Godelier put it in 1964, given the specific circumstances, there might develop out of the Asiatic formation[47] *either* slave-owning and commodity production as in the Greco-Roman world *or* feudalism and natural economy, as in China.[48] The kind of feudalism which developed directly out of the Asiatic formation, rather than out of the ruins of a slavery-based formation, lacked the dynamic tendencies of Western feudalism, being still marked by many of the characteristics of the Asiatic epoch.[49] The following diagrams contrast the bilinear schema proposed by Godelier with the essentially bilinear schema suggested by Plekhanov and some of the participants in the first phase of the Soviet debate (1925–1931), such as Mad'iar and Lomakin. Whereas in the earlier schema the Asiatic mode of production was the *raison d'être* of the bilinearity, in Godelier's schema the existence of the Asiatic mode of production is incidental to it.

DIAGRAM I (Plekhanov, Mad'iar, Lomakin, *et al.*)

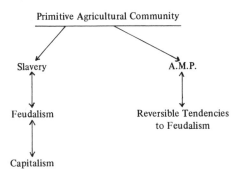

DIAGRAM II (Godelier)

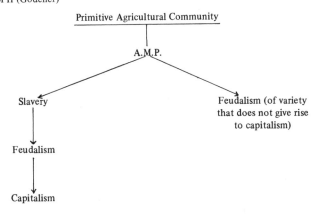

Note that the primary division into slavery and the A.M.P. corresponds to the two alternative accounts given in the *Anti-Dühring* of the genesis of state power.

More recently Godelier has tended to go beyond his bilinear schema:

> Numerous commentators . . . hesitate to follow Marx when he used the term "mode of production" apropos the Celts, Slavs, etc. They have suggested that Marx was treating primarily forms of property and not modes of production, and that he was using the latter term with a certain carelessness. This is to forget that for Marx relations of ownership only had a real existence in a definite process of production and that the older the forms of production, the more they assumed particular local forms, in contrast with the uniformity of the capitalist mode of production. There need be no constraint about multiplying the number of modes of production and even applying this notion to transitional forms between two distinct modes of production.[50]

In the same book Godelier writes that "all discussion of the Asiatic mode of production hence leads *further,* towards the establishment of a multilinear theory of the evolution of societies."[51] At the same time Godelier clings to his view that the Asiatic mode of production is a more or less universally occurring transition stage between classless and class societies.[52]

He also continues to argue that real progress does not occur in the Asiatic formation until it experiences the economic individuation achieved in Western societies.[53] Thus the Asiatic formation must be ranked logically below the classical and feudal formations. The Asiatic formation conserves the immediate unity of individual and community, at the village level, although historically the state supersedes the kinship community as the ultimate controller of the means of production. Within the Asiatic formation the direct producer is in a position of generalized dependence on the state and community, rather than in a position of personal dependence on slave owner or feudal lord.[54] However the position of the direct producer is not such that it can develop into the kind of personal freedom (but economic enslavement) represented by the free labor force of capitalism.

A more incisive attempt to reconcile the multilinear treatment of precapitalist society with the stadial conception of world history is to be found in a joint article by the Soviet historians L. S. Vasil'ev and I. A. Stuchevsky, entitled "Tri modeli vozniknoveniia i evoliutsii dokapitalisticheskikh obshchestv."[55] The burden of their argument is that the law of progressive development applies only to the following broad stages — primitive communal society (the primary formation of human history), precapitalist class society (the secondary formation), capitalist society, and socialism.[56] At a certain point of development each of these stages must be replaced by the next.[57] However, the variety of forms found within the precapitalist stage, or secondary formation, of human history are not governed or related by the same law of progression. According to Vasil'ev and Stuchevsky, precapitalist development assumes three alternative forms, the slave-holding, the feudal, and the Asiatic — the Asiatic form representing a fusion of slave-holding and feudal elements.[58] Wherever the primitive communal constitution is in the process of disintegration elements of either slavery or feudalism appear, but in the Asiatic formation these appear in conjunction with one another and hold each other in check. The lack of dynamism of the Asiatic formation is hence attributable to the "fact" that within it neither the contradictions of slavery nor of feudal society are able to emerge in a pure form.[59]

Where the Vasil'ev and Stuchevsky article is weakest is in its attempt to portray the Asiatic formation as merely representing a mixture of Western forms of exploitation.[60] Vasil'ev has since gone some distance towards remedying this weakness.

He has now taken more account of Marx's view that in precapitalist society, where surplus labor is not yet expropriated by purely economic means (as through the "free" exchange of the capitalist market), there occurs either "direct slavery, serfdom or political dependence."[61] I.e., that economic exploitation by the state, as in Asia, belongs to a different category than exploitation by private landowner or slaveholder and is not merely a fusion of the latter. Vasil'ev has, however, retained Marx's notion that stagnation was a structural characteristic of the Asiatic formation, and this marks his work off from those seriously concerned to develop the concept as the cornerstone of a new historiography.

Where the Vasil'ev and Stuchevsky article does move in the direction of the new Marxist historiography is in its suggestion that the old Marxist historiography has overlooked for too long that Marx and Engels regarded slavery and feudalism as *parallel* forms of development. As a consequence of this oversight the development of feudalism among the Germans and Slavs was treated as a result of the preceding technical and productive advances of classical antiquity.[62] The productive forces of feudalism were indeed, at least potentially, on a higher level than those of slavery, but this was not so much because the *tools* of production were of a more advanced nature, as because the direct producers had a higher stake in production, being semi-dependent rather than completely dependent.

The potential for development created by the use of semidependent labor did not depend on the contradictions of the slave relationship having been revealed; the emergence of feudal relations of production was determined by the particular development of the primitive community under given historical and geographical circumstances.[63] Thus the question of whether the primitive community would develop into feudalism or slavery was not related to the chronological period in which the transition to class society took place, or to the preexisting level of technological development, but to the nature of the prior development of the community.[64] This is an interesting rejection of the traditional Soviet view that societies which were isolated could not achieve feudalism without passing through a slave stage.

A different approach to the analysis of precapitalist societies, and one which opens up many of the problems associated with the new Marxist historiography of the non-Western world, is to be found in the work of the Soviet historian L. A. Sedov. Initially, at the discussion at the Institute of the Peoples of Asia in May 1965, Sedov put forward the view that there were three main types of preindustrial society: that based on agriculture without artificial irrigation; that based on agriculture with artificial irrigation; and that based on herding. These different productive bases gave rise to different socioeconomic structures which developed according to their own particular laws. Thus irrigation agriculture gave rise to a society dominated by a bureaucratic elite, while herding gave rise to a society dominated by a military aristocracy. Sedov's taxonomy at this period owed much to Wittfogel, particularly in relation to the status of stratified pastoral society as an autonomous socioeconomic formation.[65]

Sedov has since developed an even more interesting framework for the analysis of precapitalist societies. He has taken as his starting point Marx's comment that precapitalist economic formations are characterized by the appropriation of surplus value from the direct producers by means of extra-economic pressures (as contrasted with the capitalist formation where purely economic pressure is brought to bear).[66] He has then taken over some of the apparatus of the American structural-functionalists. He finds three different stages or moments of development to exist within the Asiatic mode of production (which is distinguished from European historical development by the dominant role of the state).[67] Like the French Marxists mentioned earlier, he is concerned to eliminate Marx's notion of the *semper idem* of the East from the concept of the Asiatic mode of production. The first of the stages identified by Sedov is that where the function of *integration* is dominant, i.e., the function of integrating the dispersed rural communities into a social whole by means of a state religion and associated theocratic structures. The second stage, according to Sedov, is that where the function of *pattern maintenance* is dominant. Here the state is modeled on the family and assumes the political form of the patriarchal bureaucratic monarchy.[68] The third stage in Sedov's typology is that where the function of *mobilization* is dominant, whether for military purposes, or to subserve ideological and economic competition with other states. In this stage the structures of the state are modeled on political or military organization. The concept of a "mobilization" stage (a concept which derives from David Apter) within the framework of a characteristically "Asiatic" political economy implicitly extends the chronological range of the Asiatic mode of production into the era of industrialization. As we will see later this step has been explicitly taken by certain non-Soviet Marxists.

Overall, Sedov is making the point that in precapitalist or noncapitalist formations the organizing principle of society may be the family, politics or religion. In these formations the economic subsystem is not separated out from the sociopolitical matrix in the distinctive fashion found in capitalism, and the priorities of social production do not stop short at "purely economic" desiderata such as the maximization of individual or social wealth. The function of pattern maintenance, for example, may actively militate against the accumulation of wealth.

The idea of kinship structure as the organizing principle of primitive society is to be found in the views expressed by Marx and Engels after they came under the influence of Morgan's anthropology. Marx and Engels adopted Morgan's proposition that the mode of production does not directly engender the forms of social organization found in primitive society but rather that the structure of the family, or kinship structure, develops according to its own specific structural laws. These include the progressive development of incest taboos etc. Such independently evolving kinship structures played a dominant role in organization of social life. Thus Engels wrote to Marx in 1882 that the amazing similarity between the Germans described by Tacitus and the American Redskins, despite their completely different modes of production, the American Indians lacking animal husbandry or agriculture, "just proves that at this stage the mode of production is less decisive than the degree to which the old blood bonds and the old mutual community of the sexes in the tribe have been dissolved."[69]

The emphasis on kinship structure to be found in contemporary

Marxist anthropologists reflects the influence of Lévi-Strauss and recent structuralist theory. Lévi-Strauss has said that in primitive societies the rules of kinship and marriage "have an operational value equal to that of economic phenomena in our own society."[70]

However, while modern structuralist theory incorporates the idea of the dominant role of kinship, it excludes other aspects of Morgan's anthropology which were accepted by Marx and Engels.[71] For example, there is a complete rejection of the kind of evolutionist anthropology found in Morgan, according to which social structures can be ranked on an evolutionary scale. Modern structuralists have concerned themselves with the way different societies have achieved the satisfactory communication of women, information and goods. Allowance is made for the fact that incompatibilities may arise between the subsystems of society, which may cause the breakdown of the existing system, but this process is not described in an evolutionary manner. Nor is the economic subsystem seen as the most dynamic element in society, the element liable to give rise to discontinuities in the rest of the system.

Most Marxists who have incorporated aspects of structuralist theory into their work would, however, argue that the development of the means of production does eventually assert its influence over the rest of society by giving rise to social tasks which cannot be fulfilled within the kinship structures.[72] New specialized structures then arise which express themselves as political relationships.

Marxists in general have also reserved the right to judge societies on an evolutionary scale in accordance with their capacity to control the external environment.[73] There are exceptions to this, for example among those influenced by the ecological school. Such anthropologists analyze societies on the basis of their *adaptation* to a certain environment, rather than on the basis of their assumed "mastery" over it, a mastery which is liable to give rise to imbalances in the ecological system.[74]

Certain problems connected with the incorporation of structuralist anthropology into Marxist theory remain unresolved. The most important of these is the relationship between the dominant role of kinship organization and ultimate determination by the development of material production. If the priorities incorporated in kinship organization (for example, the satisfactory regulation of the exchange of women) militate against investment in social production (i.e., wealth is squandered but an orderly allocation of women, as the scarce resource, takes place) how can the demands of production be seen as the ultimately determining factor? Godelier's approach to this question is to seek the reason why a certain stage of economic development should dictate the dominance of kinship relations or politico-religious relations within society.[75]

The usual reason given why kinship structures decay and are replaced by competing economic classes and a state structure is that an intensification of agriculture takes place, for population or other reasons. This brings about an increase in economic inequalities and a solidifying of economic classes. The state structure becomes necessary to deal with the increased quantum of social conflict generated by the economic differentiation now established. In this case economic imperatives have come to exercise both an ultimately determining and a dominant role in the structuring of society.

However, where communal ownership or possession continues to exist side by side with a territorially based state organization, as in the different types of Asiatic formation discussed by Sedov, economic imperatives do not assume this distinct and dominant role. In these cases the (as yet un-class-divided) society requires a strong centralized body to conduct certain large-scale public works or to deal with certain military exigencies. (The need to control trade and safeguard a central market seems to be part of a specifically African model, rather than to be an aspect of a universal "Asiatic" model *pace* the French Marxists.) In order to perform these tasks the state has to achieve the integration of the society under the umbrella of its common politico-religious authority. This authority assumes a dominant role in the society, and is the means by which the surplus is expropriated from the direct producers for redistribution to other sectors performing state functions. As mentioned earlier, the maximization of social wealth through, for example, technical innovation and the emergence of entrepreneurial groups may be actively discouraged in these societies, as in all precapitalist societies.

According to Sedov, the dominant pattern of state authority, and hence the structuring of all other social and economic relationships will depend on the particular crisis the society is going through in connection with its internal and external maintenance. Hence a multilinear pattern is manifested in the development of precapitalist societies.

THE DYNAMICS OF MODERNIZATION IN THE NON-WESTERN
WORLD: TOWARDS A NEW MARXIST HISTORIOGRAPHY

Although the multilinear perception of precapitalist society discovered in recent years in Marx's *Grundrisse* (and developed creatively by a number of Marxists with the help of conceptual tools borrowed from the social sciences) provides a more satisfactory framework of analysis than the unilinear schema previously attributed to Marx, it is still tied to value judgments which anchor it in the nineteenth century. While the concept of the absolute stagnation of the Asiatic formation has been eliminated, Marx's central thesis that progress towards industrialization is dependent on the dissolution of communal forms of economy in favor of private ownership has been retained. According to Marx's formulation in the *Grundrisse,* non-Western socioeconomic formations were incapable of developing towards industrialization without a fundamental structural change. On his view industrialization, the prerequisite of socialism, was itself made possible only by the development of the forms of individual property found in the West;[76] non-Western societies had to become Westernized before they could progress in the direction of socialism. Thus the multiplicity of forms of development in the precapitalist era had to give way to a uniformity in the capitalist and postcapitalist epochs.

One limited revision of Marx's *Grundrisse* schema, which is in line with Lenin's so-called "law of uneven development" is the argument that development may be multilinear up until the socialist stage; that the world market may still not have dissolved certain precapitalist economic formations by the time that they come under the influence of socialist systems. These socialist systems will still themselves have depended on the prior development of capitalism in Europe, but they will to some extent take the place of capitalism as the vehicle of change and as the model for industrialization and modernization. Thus the multiplicity of historical forms of development is only transcended with the achievement of socialism.

A more drastic revision of Marx's *Grundrisse* schema consists in the argument that the existence of alternative forms of historical development in, for example, Europe and Asia conditions alternative forms of the development of socialism. According to this argument the traditional economic role of the state in the Asiatic mode of production lends itself to a state-initiated industrialization process.[77] The traditional forms of village cooperation likewise present less obstacles to the development of a planned economy than the highly developed forms of private property found in Western Europe.

Thus the Asiatic formation may retain its distinctive structure and characteristics while undergoing the process of modernization and industrialization. The village communities retain their economic autarchy and continue to hand over their surplus value to the state. The state now uses part of this surplus value to subsidize industrialization, and the structure of state functionaries is supplemented by the managerial and technical cadres associated with industrialization. The symbolic attributes of the tutelary Asiatic state, embodied usually in a paternalistic "head of state," provide continuity into the modern age and modify the disruption engendered by the industrialization process.

According to the argument of Sencer Divitçioglu, whose economic model of the Asiatic mode of production will be reproduced below in a modified form, the basic dynamic of the Asiatic formation is provided by two classes, the state functionaries and the people. The traditional state functionaries have a class interest in preventing the development of a capitalist class and a capitalist system in the process of industrialization, as this would threaten their own position. [78] Nonetheless Divitçioglu points out that the "Asiatic" form of industrialization cannot give rise to popular socialism (i.e., the Marxist conception of socialism) as contrasted with tutelary socialism[79] until the class of functionaries is abolished and the state becomes identified with the people as a whole. One might add that even then the relationship between the individual and the collectivity is likely to differ from that in the West where individualism has played a larger historical role.

Divitçioglu's diagrams[80] firstly of the structure of the Asiatic mode of production in the preindustrial phase, and secondly of the structure as modified during contact with industrial countries and during the industrialization process are as follows:

DIAGRAM I

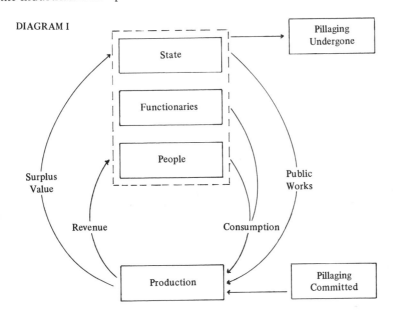

DIAGRAM II   (Reflecting the existence of some private enterprise, not all the surplus value is absorbed by the state.)

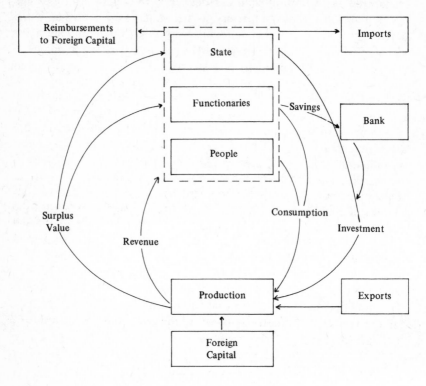

The idea illustrated in Divitçioglu's diagrams, that "Asiatic" society may retain its basic structure while undergoing industrialization, implies a complete rejection of Marx's thesis that the Asiatic form of political economy was incapable of generating anything approximating modern industrial development. According to Marx, the role of Western capital in *breaking down* the old structure of Asiatic society and providing the conditions for development in its own image was an essential element of the universal progress towards socialism.

Marx's perception of the dynamics of development in the non-Western world, together with some of the variations discussed in this essay, is illustrated in the diagrams on the following pages.

As can be seen, the first two diagrams are basically Europo-centric. Diagram I posits that the non-Western world would have developed capitalist and socialist stages independently, if it were not for the intervention of Western capitalism, which for some reason developed

DIAGRAM I The Stalinist Five Stage Unilinear Schema

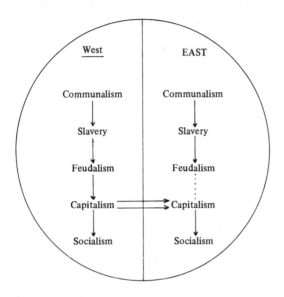

.... Buds or germs of capitalism which would have evolved independently into capitalism but for the impact of Western imperialism.

DIAGRAM II Marx's Grundrisse Multilinear Schema

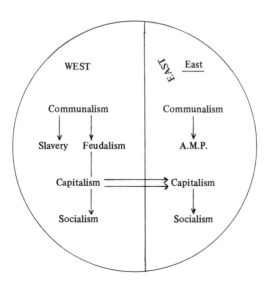

DIAGRAM III The Hegelian Version of the Unilinear Marxist Schema

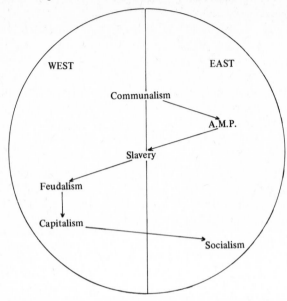

N.B, The geographical location of the centre of world history constantly shifts.

DIAGRAM IV A Non-Europo-centric Version of Diagram II

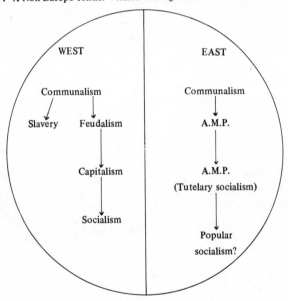

N.B. The Asiatic mode of production in this instance is conceived of as a dynamic structure
capable of sustaining modernization and industrialization.

faster than Eastern capitalism. *But* all the categories employed in this diagram are basically derived from the study of European history. Nonetheless Asian communist parties such as the Chinese, particularly through spokesmen such as Kuo Mo-jo, have been particularly anxious to validate Diagram I, by means of archaeological commissions etc.

Diagram II is, if anything, more Europo-centric than Diagram I. It posits an alternative non-Western form of historical development but this lacks any dynamic element. Only the universalizing force of the world market brings progress to the East, first in the form of capitalism, which through its own contradictions leads on to socialism.

Diagram III posits socialism as arriving first in the non-Western world, partly by reasons of the "advantages of backwardness." The fact that the preceding stages have reached their full flowering in the West means that the dialectical antithesis to capitalism tends to arise externally to the societies of Western Europe (i.e., the countries of the Third World represent the internal contradiction of capitalism, they are "proletarian countries"). This is the theory of the "retarding lead."

Diagram IV has the advantage of being less Europo-centric than Diagrams I and II, and on the other hand, not involving the logical problem of perceiving world history as a unitary organic process. According to Diagram IV modernization and industrialization can take place with less dislocation and violent structural change than was necessary in the transition between feudalism and capitalism in the West, or between capitalism and socialism. Diagram IV, with its basic structural continuity between the A.M.P. and tutelary socialism stages confirms Marx's belief that the structures of Asiatic society were extremely cohesive and resistant to change. On the other hand it contradicts Marx's notion that economic development or industrialization could not take place within the structures of Asiatic society.

The argument that certain social structures (for example the Asiatic) are basically more resilient than others in the context of rapid economic development does not entail the view that modernization would necessarily have been initiated in the "Asiatic" societies without the impact of Western capitalism and Western industrialization. Nor does it deny that the impact of Western capitalism on "Asiatic" societies may have been so strong as to foreclose the possibility of the kind of structural continuity sketched above. The implications of the concept of the Asiatic mode of production for contemporary Marxism lie in the realm of an enhanced understanding of the complexities of the historical process.

The functions of the model of an Asiatic mode of production in contemporary Marxist historiography have been to stimulate a new heuristic approach to Marxism as a theory of world history, and to strengthen the view that history is to be regarded as *prima facie* open, and not as a closed and unitary process governed by immutable general laws determining its movement towards a single goal.[81]

This does not mean a rejection of Marx's general view of societal dynamics, the view that social structures appropriate to one level of economic development are liable to become a fetter on further development and subject to revolutionary change. It *does* mean a rejection of Marx's Western European perspective, and a recognition that non-European forms of historical development may have their own dynamics, which, although overshadowed during the rapid industrial expansion of Western Europe in the nineteenth century, are now reasserting themselves in the form of self-proclaimed non-Western paths of development.

In the context of Europe itself the stress on the openness of history is linked with the idea that although the development of productive forces will invariably affect the forms of social organization, the achievement of the kind of socialist society which Marx foreshadowed will depend largely on subjective factors centering on social choice, social consciousness and social struggle. As these factors are deeply affected by the particular historical matrix in which they operate, the new approach assumes that the multiplicity of forms of social organization which Marx attributed to the precapitalist era will continue into the future. The spread of industrial technology through the operation of the world market is no longer depicted as necessarily giving rise to the spread of a single form of social organization. The assumption of unity has given way to an assumption of plurality, which expresses itself both in a more flexible historiography and in more flexible political and social policies.

NOTES

1. Marx, Preface to *A Contribution to the Critique of Political Economy* (Moscow Progress, 1970), p. 21.

2. See the section below entitled "Chronological and Logical Problems Presented by the Stadial Analysis of World History."

3. Engels, *Anti-Dühring* (Lawrence and Wishart, London, 1934), p. 203.

4. Engels, "Russia and the Social Revolution" (originally published as "Soziales

aus Russland," in *Der Volkstaat*, Leipzig, 21 April 1875), in *The Russian Menace to Europe,* edited by Paul W. Blackstock and Bert F. Hoselitz (Allen and Unwin, London, 1953), p. 205.

5. As recognized for example by Karl Kautsky in his *Der Weg zu Macht* (Buchhandlung Vorwärts, Berlin, 1909), *passim.*

6. *Short History of the C.P.S.U.* (Foreign Languages Publishing House, Moscow, 1939), p. 110.

7. See for example the author's Ph.D. thesis.

8. See Vassili Strouvé [Struve], "Comment Marx définissait les premières sociétés de classes," *Recherches internationales à la lumière du marxisme,* No. 57–58 (January–April 1967), pp. 93–94. This article, widely quoted by Soviet scholars, first appeared in *Sovetskaia Etnografiia,* No. 3, 1940.

9. *Ibid.,* p. 94.

10. *Ibid.,* p. 97.

11. Vassili Strouvé [Struve], "Le concept de M.P.A.: légitimité et limites" (first published in *Narody Azii i Afriki,* No. 1, 1965), *Recherches internationales à la lumière du marxisme,* No. 57–58 (January–April 1967), p. 238.

12. O. W. Kuusinen, editor, *Fundamentals of Marxism-Leninism* (Foreign Languages Publishing House, Moscow, 1961), p. 154.

13. *Ibid.,* pp. 154–164.

14. The P.C.F. had taken the initiative in reviving the concept some years previously. As early as 1958 Suret-Canale, a member of the Central Committee, had stated that it was impossible to apply the categories feudal or slave-owning to the societies of tropical Africa, and had suggested the use of the concept of the Asiatic mode of production (*L'Afrique noire occidentale et centrale, géographie, civilisations, histoire,* Editions sociales, Paris, 1958, p. 94). When the Central Committee set up the Centre d'études et de recherches marxistes (hereafter C.E.R.M.) in 1960 the question of the Asiatic mode was included in the program of the Oriental section, on the suggestion of Charles Parain. This section held working sessions on the Asiatic mode in 1962–1963, and the results began emerging in roneoed and published form in 1964 (the papers prepared for Moscow summarized the work done by Godelier and Suret-Canale at the Centre). See Jean Chesneaux, "Diskussiia o ranneklassovykh obshchestvakh na stranitsakh zhurnala 'La Pensée'," *Voprosy Istorii,* No. 9, 1967, pp. 192ff.; cf. L.V. Danilova: "At the present time, on the initiative of a group of French Marxist historians, J.

Suret-Canale, M. Godelier, J. Chesneaux, C. Parain, P. Boiteau *et al.*, the problem of the Asiatic mode of production has again become the subject of discussion." "Diskussiia po vazhnoi probleme," *Voprosy Filosofii,* No. 12, 1965, p. 150.

15. L. V. Danilova, "Diskussiia po vazhnoi probleme," *loc. cit.,* p. 156.

16. J. Chesneaux, "Le mode de production asiatique: quelques perspectives de recherche," *La Pensée,* No. 114 (January–February 1964), p. 53. See also J. Suret-Canale, "Problèmes théoriques de l'étude des premières sociétés de classes," *Recherches internationales à la lumière du marxisme,* No. 57–58 (January–April 1967), p. 14. For the application of the A.M.P. concept to the Minoan, Etruscan, Hittite and Mycenean civilizations see Charles Parain. Parain drew a parallel between the way the "barbarian" invasions brought about the fall of the Roman Empire and cleared the way for the development of a new "higher" mode of production, and the way in which the Dorian invasions brought about the fall of the Mediterranean empires and cleared the way for the development of the new, private slave-based mode of production. (Charles Parain, "Protohistoire méditerranéenne et mode de production asiatique," *La Pensée,* No. 127 (May–June 1966), pp. 24–43.)

17. M. A. Vitkin as reported by L. S. Vasil'ev, "Obshchee i osobennoe v istoricheskom razvitii stran Vostoka," *Narody Azii i Afriki,* No. 6, 1965, p. 97.

18. See Jean Chesneaux, "Diskussiia o ranneklassovykh obshchestvakh na stranitsakh zhurnala 'La Pensée'," *loc. cit.,* p. 194.

19. L. A. Sedov, "La société angkorienne et le problème du mode de production asiatique," *La Pensée,* No. 138 (March–April 1968), p. 72.

20. Jean Suret-Canale, "Problèmes théoriques de l'étude des premières sociétés de classes," *loc. cit.,* p. 14.

21. Apart from the bibliographical material published serially in *La Pensée* since 1964 by J. Chesneaux and M. Godelier, the bibliography attached to Iu. V. Kachanovsky; *Rabovladenie, feodalizm ili aziatskii sposob proizvodstva?* (Izd. "Nauka," Moscow, 1971) provides a consolidated index to recent literature on the subject.

22. M. Godelier, "La notion de 'mode de production asiatique' et les schémas marxistes d'évolution des sociétés" (first published in 1964), *Sur le 'mode de production asiatique,'* preface by Roger Garaudy (C.E.R.M., Editions sociales, Paris, 1969), p. 88.

23. *Ibid.,* p. 87. Chesneaux himself, although sympathetic towards extending the concept to Africa, America, etc., was to warn against such an enterprise; the

problematic area of early Mongol society was no more susceptible to analysis by the Asiatic concept than by the old five-stage schema. (J. Chesneaux, "Diskussiia o ranneklassovykh obshchestvakh na stranitsakh zhurnala 'La Pensée'," loc. cit., p. 194). Ernest Mandel has recently made a more far-reaching criticism of the tendency to extend the range of the concept beyond the agricultural societies of Asia and the Middle East. According to Mandel, "By thus expanding the scope of the idea of the Asiatic mode of production (just as the "dogmatic" Marxists who rejected this concept were forced to expand the scope of the idea of "feudalism") these writers [Godelier, Chesneaux, Suret-Canale, Boiteau] risk losing altogether the specific meaning of the idea." (E. Mandel, *The Formation of the Economic Thought of Karl Marx* (NLB, London, 1971), p. 125.) Cf. also I. Sachs, "Une nouvelle phase de la discussion sur les formations" (first published in *Nowe drogi*, March 1966), *Recherches internationales à la lumière du marxisme*, No. 57–58 (January–April 1967), pp. 301–302.

24. Tökei, like the French Marxists, conceptualizes the Asiatic formation as a transition stage from tribal to class society, but as having sufficient distinctive features to be regarded as an independent historical formation.

25. F. Tökei, *Sur le mode de production asiatique* (Akadémiai Kiadó, Budapest, 1966), p. 88. This line of argument may have been a ritualistic attempt by Tökei to come to terms with orthodoxy. It is inconsistent with much of the rest of his work which suggested a geographically determined multilinear pattern of development. For example, Tökei viewed the geographical configuration of the Japanese archipelago as serving the same function as the Germanic forests, in inhibiting centralization and giving rise to a feudal socioeconomic formation. (*Ibid.*, pp. 85–86.)

26. See A. Pannekoek, *Weltrevolution und Kommunistische Taktik* (Vienna, 1920), in *Pannekoek et les conseils ouvriers*, edited by S. Bricanier (EDI, Paris, 1969), p. 193. See also Antonio Gramsci on the comparative simplicity of making a socialist revolution in Russia, where capitalist civilization and cultural hegemony was weakly developed.

27. The need to discover the laws governing the development of universal history (i.e., the laws of transition from one stage to another) on the supra-societal level is stressed in V. N. Nikiforov, "K voprosu ob istoricheskoi osnove literaturnoi periodizatsii," *Narody Azii i Afriki*, No. 3, 1964, pp. 86–90.

28. See for example, Iu. V. Kachanovsky, *Rabovladenie, feodalizm ili asiatskii sposob proizvodstva?*, op.cit., pp. 245–263. Kachanovsky's book represents the most systematic Soviet effort so far to relate the concept of the Asiatic mode of production to Marxist historiography, even though this is done from the negative standpoint that the concept is fundamentally incompatible with Marxist historiography.

29. V. Gordon Childe, "The Bronze Age," *Past and Present*, No. 12 (November 1957), pp. 10–11.

30. J.-J. Goblot, "Pour une approche théorique des 'faits de civilisation'," *La Pensée*, Nos. 133, 134, 136 (1967): see especially Part III, *La Pensée*, No. 136, pp. 78–88.

31. Report made by E. M. Zhukov (Secretary to the Division of Historical Sciences of the Academy of Sciences, U.S.S.R.) to the Eleventh International Congress of Historical Sciences, Stockholm, 1960. "O periodizatsii vsemirnoi istorii," *Voprosy Istorii*, No. 8, 1960, p. 32. This line and its corollary discussed below had appeared widely among Soviet historians such as A. G. Prigozhin and B. D. Grekov since the thirties. The explanation of the absence of slavery among the Germans was elaborated by V. Struve in his article, "Marksovo opredelenie ranneklassovogo obshchestva," *Sovetskaia etnografiia*, No. 3. 1940. B. D. Grekov drew out the parallels between the interaction of the Slavs with East Rome and the interaction of the Germans with Rome itself. (*Kiev Rus*, translated from 1949 Russian edition by E. Sdobnikov (Foreign Languages Publishing House, Moscow, 1959), p. 37.) Grekov summed up the Slavic case as follows: "At the moment of their appearance the Slavs, and their eastern branch in particular, during the disintegration of their primitive communal system encountered a decaying slave-holding society. They were among the group of peoples who were able to regenerate moribund Europe with the aid of their community system. The new peoples possessed the potentialities of a more progressive system, the feudal system." (*Ibid.*, pp. 144–145.)

32. E. M. Zhukov, *loc. cit.*, p. 31.

33. Iu. V. Kachanovsky, *Rabovladenie, feodalizm ili aziatskii sposob proizvodstva?*, *op. cit.*, p. 103.

34. Marx himself appears to have considered such external (and contingent) relations to be of great importance. He lists the three possible results of conquest, for example, as: (a) the imposition of the mode of production of the conquering people; (b) the preservation of the old mode of production and the mere imposition of a tributary relationship; (c) the synthesis of the two modes of production. Which of these results would follow from conquest could not be established by any scientific law, although as seen, all of the alternatives are related to the modes of production in existence in the two parties (a negative determinism). Conquest of one people by another could not in itself give rise to a new mode of production as was argued by some theorists of feudalism, in particular. See the *Grundrisse*, Introduction, pp. 97–98.

35. Iu. V. Kachanovsky, *Rabovladenie, feodalizm ili aziatskii sposob proizvodstva?*, *op. cit.*, p. 106.

36. E. M. Zhukov, "O periodizatsii vsemirnoi istorii," *loc. cit.,* p. 25.

37. F. B. Beleliubsky, "Maoistskaia kontseptsiia vsemirnoi istorii i podlinnaia istoriia narodov Vostoka," *Narody Azii i Afriki,* No. 5, 1972, p. 64.

38. For example, the "refeudalisation" that took place in China between the collapse of the Han dynasty and the Sui reunification of 589 A.D.

39. Introduction to Marx, *Pre-Capitalist Economic Formations,* edited by Eric Hobsbawm (Lawrence and Wishart, London, 1964), p. 38.

40. *Ibid.,* p. 63.

41. *Ibid.,* pp. 46–47. The others were the development of urban crafts and the availability of money derived from usury and trade.

42. Although Hobsbawm does adhere sufficiently closely to the traditional view of historical materialism to argue that development of the forces of production must always ultimately result in the development of an even higher stage of social relations. What he is arguing against is the view that the formations laid down in Marx's schema are logically connected and must always follow one another. Hobsbawm does want to argue, however, that socialism develops logically out of capitalism, where one might well argue that the contradictions brought about by the development of productive forces within a capitalist system make the establishment of some new system of social relations necessary, but that only under very special circumstances will this result in a socialist system as Marx defined it.

43. See E. C. Welskopf, Einleitung, *Jahrbuch für Wirtschaftsgeschichte* (Berlin, 1967), Part IV, cited in Kachanovsky, *Rabovladenie, feodalizm ili aziatskii sposob proizvodstva?, op. cit.,* p. 86.

44. Kachanovsky, *Rabovladenie, feodalizm ili aziatskii sposob proizvodstva?, op. cit.,* pp. 84–89.

45. Marx and Engels, *The Communist Manifesto, MESW,* vol. 1, pp. 36–37. By 1858 Marx was more pessimistic about the rapidity with which the bourgeoisie would complete its universalizing functions. He wrote that: "The specific task of bourgeois society is the establishment of a world market, at least in outline, and of production based upon this world market . . . The difficult question for us is this: on the Continent the revolution is imminent and will immediately assume a socialist character. Is it not bound to be crushed in this little corner, considering that in a far greater territory the movement of bourgeois society is still in the ascendant? " (Marx to Engels, 8 October 1858, *MESC,* p. 111).

46. Jean Suret-Canale, "Problèmes théoriques de l'étude des premières sociétés

de classes," *loc. cit.,* pp. 8–9. Cf. J.-J. Goblot on the facticiously homologous character ascribed to the five stages of the Stalinist schema. Goblot, however, while arguing that the precapitalist stages are of a less universal nature than the capitalist stage, holds to the unilinear view of history according to which there is one main thread of development rather than alternative forms. J.-J. Goblot, "Pour une approche théorique des 'faits de civilisation'," Part III, *La Pensée,* No. 136, 1967, p. 69.

47. Defined, as previously noted as a transition stage where communal forms of property, still partly based on kinship relations, coexist with early forms of class exploitation; the latter expressed in terms of the appropriation by the state of surplus value and labor from the communities.

48. M. Godelier, "La notion de 'mode de production asiatique' et les schémas marxistes d'évolution des sociétés," *loc. cit.,* pp. 90–92.

49. *Ibid.,* p. 92.

50. M. Godelier (Editor), *Sur les sociétés précapitalistes: textes choisis de Marx, Engels, Lénine* (C.E.R.M., Editions sociales, Paris, 1970), introduction, p. 61, footnote 1.

51. *Ibid.,* p. 138.

52. *Ibid.,* p. 134.

53. *Ibid.,* p. 69.

54. *Ibid.,* p. 75.

55. L. S. Vasil'ev and I. A. Stuchevsky, "Tri modeli vozniknoveniia i evoliutsii dokapitalisticheskikh obshchestv," *Voprosy Istorii,* No. 5, 1966, pp. 77–90.

56. Cf. Marx to Zasulich, 8 March 1881, Third Draft: "The secondary formation comprises, as you must understand, the series of societies based on slavery and serfdom."

57. *Ibid.,* p. 89.

58. *Ibid.,* p. 85.

59. *Ibid.,* pp. 84–85.

60. This view is shared by Iu. I. Semenov, who argues that the nondifferentiation of these antagonistic relations of production in the Asiatic formation demon-

strates its immaturity. See Iu. I. Semenov, "Problema sotsial'no-ekonomicheskogo stroia drevnego Vostoka," *Narody Azii i Afriki*, No. 4, 1965, pp. 69–89; and also comments by Iu. A. Levada.

61. Marx, *Theories of Surplus Value*, Part III, p. 400.

62. L. S. Vasil'ev and I. A. Stuchevsky, "Tri modeli . . .," *loc. cit.*, pp. 81–82. For an example of the kind of treatment the authors are criticizing see Sid Douglas in *Marxism Today* (vol. 5, December 1961, p. 381) arguing that China must have passed through a slave stage because: "Primitive communism cannot accumulate enough wealth, even when it is affluent, to make a change to feudalism practicable."

63. L. S. Vasil'ev and I. A. Stuchevsky, "Tri modeli . . .," *loc. cit.*, p. 83.

64. *Ibid.*

65. Cf. the later Wittfogel's classification of preindustrial societies into (a) stratified pastoral societies; (b) hydraulic societies; (c) helotage-based, free peasant-based or slave-based nonfeudal societies; (d) feudal societies. (K. A. Wittfogel, *Oriental Despotism* (Columbia U.P., New Haven, 1957), p. 419.) Stratified pastoral societies have been notoriously difficult to fit into the five-stage unilinear schema. As we have seen, as soon as an additional mode of production (the Asiatic) was discovered, attempts were made to apply it to nomadic pastoral societies. However, the Asiatic concept was designed for bureaucratic agricultural societies, and is inapplicable to pastoral societies, which can perhaps best be viewed as Sedov has done, as yet another alternative mode of production determined by local circumstances. At least one passage from Marx could be adduced as authority for this view: "Among the nomadic pastoral peoples, the commune is indeed constantly united, the travelling society, the caravan, the horde, and the forms of supremacy and subordination develop out of the conditions of this mode of life." (Marx, *Grundrisse*, translated by M. Nicolaus (Penguin, Harmondsworth, 1973), p. 491.)

66. Marx, *Theories of Surplus Value*, Part III, p. 400; *Capital*, vol. 3, p. 791. Here Marx cites only the role of force in the appropriation of surplus value in precapitalist formations, but elsewhere he discusses the role of sacred authority.

67. See L. A. Sedov, "La société angkorienne et le problème du mode de production asiatique," *loc. cit.*, pp. 75–76. As Sedov wrote elsewhere: "It is quite obvious that one cannot compare these secondary class structures with feudalism of the European type, which in the course of further development could give rise to capitalism." The state retains its dominant role in the exploitation of the people and the distribution of the surplus produce in spite of the appearance of private property and elements of slavery and feudalism. Status is still determined

primarily by position in the service hierarchy. Hence "the changes and progress which took place in South-East Asia in the fourteenth and fifteenth centuries were only in the order of evolution within the framework of the 'Asiatic mode of production,' seen as that type of social structure within which stages can be distinguished distinct from the formations observed in Europe." (M. G. Kozlova, L. A. Sedov, V. A. Tiurin, "Tipy ranneklassovykh gosudarstv v Iugo-Vostochnoi Azii," *Problemy istorii dokapitalisticheskikh obshchestv*, Kniga 1, edited by L. V. Danilova *et al.* (Izd. 'Nauka,' Moscow, 1968), p. 545.)

68. Sedov discusses in detail the existence of stages one and two in Cambodian history of the Angkor and post-Angkor periods. Cf. M. Godelier: "To set forth a theory of the differentiated development of societies is therefore at the same time to set forth a scientific theory of kinship, of politics and of ideology. It means being ready to recognise that in certain conditions kinship *is* the economy – or that religion can function directly as the relations of production." (Preface to *Sur les sociétés précapitalistes*, edited by M. Godelier, *op. cit.*, p. 141.)

69. Engels to Marx, 8 December 1882, *Werke*, Vol. 35, p. 125. Engels has been subjected to Marxist "correction" on this point. He has been criticized for not consistently applying the principles of historical materialism to the organization of primitive society and for seeing the development of the family as an independently determining factor. "In reality, however, the forms of the family were also dependent on the conditions of production." See I. Sellnow, "Die Grundprinzipien einer Periodisierung der Urgeschichte," *Völkerforschung* (Akademie-Verlag, Berlin, 1954), p. 161.

70. Claude Lévi-Strauss, interview in *Témoignage Chrétien*, 8 April 1968, p. 18, quoted in Emmanual Terray, *Marxism and 'Primitive Societies,'* translated by M. Klopper (Monthly Review Press, New York, 1972), p. 139.

71. One aspect of Morgan's anthropology which is now rejected by both Marxists and non-Marxists is the idea of a universal transition from matrifocal to patrifocal forms of social organization.

72. Preface to *Sur les sociétés précapitalistes*, edited by M. Godelier, *op. cit.*, p. 140.

73. See E. J. Hobsbawm, "Karl Marx's Contribution to Historiography," in *Ideology in Social Science*, edited by R. Blackburn (Fontana, London, 1972), pp. 275–277.

74. See, for example, Marshall Sahlins, *Stone Age Economics* (Aldine-Atherton, Chicago, 1972).

75. M. Godelier, *Rationality and Irrationality in Economics*, translated by Brian Pearce (NLB, London, 1972), p. ix.

76. It has frequently been observed that for Marx industrialization was synonymous with capitalism and hence he tended to view history in terms of the creation
of the preconditions of capitalism – i.e., increasing individuation. As Marx himself
said: "What is called historical evolution depends in general on the fact that the
latest form regards earlier ones as stages in the development of itself and conceives
them always in a one-sided manner . . ." (Marx, *Contribution to the Critique of
Political Economy, op. cit.,* p. 211). Marx's own work, despite his recognition of
the existence of alternative historical paths, bore witness to the all-pervasive influence of the evolutionary paradigm in nineteenth-century social science. There was
a tension in his work between the idea that different forms of social organization
represented real alternatives and the idea that different forms of social organization merely represented different stages of a universal historical development.

77. See for example B. McFarlane and S. Cooper, "The Asiatic Mode of Production – An Economic Phoenix? ," *The Australian Quarterly,* Vol. 38 (3) (September
1966), pp. 27–43.

78. Sencer Divitçioglu, "Essai de modèles économiques à partir du M.P.A.,"
Recherches internationales à la lumière du marxisme, No. 57–58 (January–April
1967), pp. 288–289.

79. Divitçioglu himself uses the expression "tutelary state."

80. *Ibid.,* pp. 279, 286.

81. The openness of history is in principle a separate point from whether all of
history follows a European pattern, but the recognition of diverse patterns of
historical development has in fact coincided with and to some extent given rise to
the tendency to treat history as open.

THE STUDENT MOVEMENT:
MARXISM AS SYMBOLIC ACTION

EHUD SPRINZAK
The Hebrew University of Jerusalem

THE PHENOMENON OF RE-MARXIZATION AND
THE PROBLEM OF EXPLAINING IT

It is hardly deniable today, that one of the most significant cultural and intellectual phenomena of the nineteen-sixties has been the wide rediscovery in the West of Marxism as an alive philosophy, theory and ideology. Since Marxism had already been very influential among western intellectuals before the Second World War, it is, I think justified from the point of view of the sociology of knowledge to talk today about the phenomenon of *re-Marxization.*

The phenomenon of re-Marxization is remarkable, indeed, because it came as a total surprise to many intellectuals and social scientists who have spoken with great confidence since the early nineteen-fifties about the "end" or the "decline" of ideology. The term "end of ideology" itself may have been very poorly chosen, and there are very few people today who would like to use it.[1] But as Seymour Martin Lipset forcefully argued, not long ago,[2] very few Marxists and non-Marxists alike predicted or foresaw the new Marxist revivalism.

When we consider the phenomenon of re-Marxization in greater detail, I believe we can identify two central motives in it; a moral and humanistic motive, and a scientific and methodological one. The first motive has to do with a growing need for the ethical values embedded in the Marxist philosophy, especially in the early writings of Marx, rediscovered in recent years. The reason for this growing need would appear to be the impatience among many western intellectuals with the relativistic positivism, so typical of the modern social thinking of the first half of this century. The second motive concerns a growing need for Marxism as a source of fruitful guiding concepts in social research. The reason for this need, it would appear, stems greatly from the failure of the modern social sciences to cope properly with some of the deep social and political conflicts that emerged in the postwar era. It cannot be denied today that behind the postwar social sciences there prevailed a strong and naive belief in a linear progress that was leading "us," the survivors of the Second World War, towards no more wars, towards peaceful and democrafic decolonization of the Third World, and towards affluent and consensual western democracy. This belief contributed greatly to the rise of a "developmental" approach to the analysis of modern democracy and to the emergence of a wide use of the idea of modernization as a universal concept in the social sciences.[3]

However, with the rise of the deep conflicts in Indochina, Algeria and Cuba, with the shattering of the dreams about the introduction of the "Westminster-type democracy" into the new states of Africa, Asia and the Middle East, with the reemergence of the black problem in the United States and with the reappearance of problems involving minorities in other western countries, there emerged a need for a paradigm that was based very deeply on the notion of conflict in History. Marxism as a social theory has always had this feature and many western minds have consequently felt the need to turn to it as a point of departure in social and political research.

There exists however one major problem with the explanation of the phenomenon of re-Marxization. It concerns the fact that the rediscovery of Marxism occurred not only among aloof philosophers, moralists and social scientists. Re-Marxization appeared among tens of and, perhaps, hundreds of thousands of young students in the West who became, at least for a short time, devoted adherents of Marxism as a political ideology. It is true that the Marxist and Communist parties, particularly in France and Italy, had not disappeared from the political map of Europe and were able to attract even during the so-called "decline of ideology" years, millions of voters. But almost no one really expected a Marxist revivalism outside the old communist strongholds and certainly not in the "ivory towers" of the western académe. Moreover, one of the basic reasons for the decline of the prestige of Marxism as a political doctrine and ideology was the great disillusionment with its soviet version of bureaucratic Stalinism and its failure to fulfill the political promise of the Marxist dream — the free society. To expect a political re-Marxization of young, open-minded and independent students so short a time after 1956, the year that witnessed the brutal crushing of the Hungarian revolution and was marked by Khrushchev's revelations regarding the Stalinist terror, was therefore hard indeed. This is then a cultural and behavioral phenomenon that observers and social scientists should not only observe and take notice of, but also try to explain. The purpose of this paper is to make some contribution to this problem of explanation.

MARXISM AS A SYSTEM OF SYMBOLS OF PROTEST

Briefly stated, my argument is that in addition to our understanding of Marxism as a profound moral philosophy and as an important source of fruitful and critical concepts for the modern social sciences, and in addition to its being a source for official ideologies and state doctrines, we should also understand it as a rich source for symbols of protest against the liberal democracy. Every ideology, according to this argument, may be viewed as what Clifford Geertz calls "a cultural system of symbols"[4] and Marxism may rightly be looked at as a cultural system of symbols implying protest.

Political protest, according to this argument, is not an ordinary social condition and it does not imply a static pattern of behavior. It is a special type of political behavior that presupposes very intense feeling. It sometimes expresses itself in a dynamic process of radicalization vis-à-vis the prevailing regime. This radicalization may, under certain circumstances, take the form of a process of delegitimation and when it is very intense it tends to develop from an early *crisis of confidence* in the regime into a *conflict of legitimacy* within it. The conflict of legitimacy is, for the protest movement, a different existential stage in which the protesters require new and powerful symbols that unequivocally convey an attitude of mistrust and illegitimacy towards the regime. When such an existential stage of radicalization develops, the protesters are not craving simply for any available system of symbols of protest, but for the most prestigious system of this kind that is available in the existing milieu of ideologies. Marxism — for all its shortcomings — has remained in the modern world the most prestigious system of this type. Marxism, according to our proposition, does and always did imply an attitude of illegitimacy opposite to the political arrangements of the liberal democracy. It always maintained that in principle the parliamentary democracy, the multiparty system, the free competition of political elites on the votes of the electorate were devices invented by the bourgeoisie in order to secure its hegemony. In principle these were illegitimate political arrangements. There has consequently developed a habitual tradition to turn to Marxism, to talk about the revolution, to adore the proletariat, to make a class analysis of society and to think dialectically, because these symbols are associated with a deep attitude of illegitimacy vis-à-vis the liberal democracy. When one is in an acute stage of protest, when one feels

very strongly that not only does he disagree with the prevailing policies but that something very basic is wrong with the political system
under which he lives, then one is likely to turn to militant Marxism
because it best expresses one's protest.

Before I proceed to some examples, it is important to clarify what
would be suggested here by way of maintaining what would not: (a) I
do not want to sound too simplistic and reductionist by delimiting my
view of Marxism to its sole description as a cultural system of symbols
of protest. It is just one aspect of Marxism that attention will be
drawn to, a behavioral one, the seeing of Marxization as a symbolic
action; (b) (and even more important) I do not intend to maintain
that there is only one single model of symbolic re-Marxization. Each
political community has its own cultural tradition, which in turn determines the pattern of the symbolic re-Marxization. It is necessary to
understand this phenomenon in the social and cultural context in
which it happens.

In order to demonstrate both the case and the second point, I
shall bring three examples that were examined in some detail: the
case of the American New Left, the case of the French student protest
movement, and the case of "Siah" (Israel New Left).

THE RE-MARXIZATION OF THE AMERICAN NEW LEFT

American observers who are reminded of the S.D.S. (Students for a
Democratic Society), or S.N.C.C. (Students Non-Violent Coordination
Committee), the core organizations of the American New Left —
usually remember the young rebels who took over the University of
Columbia in 1968, entered into a bloody confrontation with the Chicago police at the Democratic Convention of Summer 1968, the student organizations which gave birth to the Weatherman organization
in 1969 and to the famous Black Panthers at about the same period.
These observers usually have in mind the image of young revolutionaries who speak and use a very militant version of political Marxism,
seeing as their heroes Third World revolutionary Marxists like Che
Guevera, Ho Chi Minn and Chairman Mao. It is therefore a little
surprising to note that in its early history the American New Left was
a *liberal democratic* movement. A close examination of the symbolic
language of the *Port Huron Statement,* the original Manifesto of the
S.D.S., shows clearly that, although it is a critical document, it was
written very much in a liberal spirit and a democratic symbolic language, with little Marxist inference. It is true that from its inception,
the S.D.S. severely criticized the American Democratic and Republi-

can parties. It accused them of becoming equally conservative and of denying to American citizens the possibility of choosing between real ideological alternatives regarding problems of great concern, such as the Cold War, the proliferation of nuclear armaments, relations with the Third World, racial discrimination, and domestic economic policies. It accused the national parties of sustaining an "organized political stalemate."[5] However, the conclusion of this critique was not a class analysis of the American society, a call for antidemocratic revolution nor a quest for a political system guided by one revolutionary party representing the true interests of the "proletariat." Rather, it projected a liberal democratic system of "Two genuine parties, centered around issues and essential values . . . 'with' sufficient party disagreement to dramatize major issues, yet sufficient party overlap to guarantee stable transition from administration to administration."[6] Indeed, the S.D.S. saw itself as a spearhead of a "New Left" concentrated in the American campus. Yet this New Left was very peaceful and nonviolent. Commenting on Marx, Tom Hayden, the cofounder of the S.D.S. in his letter to the New Left, maintained that although "Marx, the humanist, has much to tell us . . . his conceptual tools are outmoded and his final vision implausible."[7] He was equally unhappy with the "nonideological" thinking of revolutionary leaders of the rising nations, as for example, that of Che Guevera.[8]

Not only did the S.D.S. of the early sixties reject the traditional solutions of the Marxist left of the prewar era, but it also refused to grant membership to members of Communist and, in general, "totalitarian" organizations. Section 2 of Article III (membership) of the S.D.S. constitution declared:

> S.D.S. is an organization of democrats. It is civil libertarian in its treatment of those with whom it disagrees, but clear in its opposition to any totalitarian principle as a basis for government or social organization. Advocates or apologists for such a principle are not eligible for membership.[9]

Between 1962 and 1965, the American New Left had undergone a process of radicalization. The details of this process cannot be traced here. They have to do with the growing confrontation in the South between the radicals of the civil rights movement and the local authorities in Mississippi and Alabama, and with the failure of the Administration of John F. Kennedy to provide support and defense to those radicals.[10] This radicalization was greatly intensified with the beginning, in February 1965, of the massive bombing of North Vietnam. The S.D.S. soon took the lead in the antiwar activities and its main activists were now ready to enter into a total conflict of legitimacy with the American system of government. It was at this time that the political re-Marxization of the organization began.

In its 1965 national convention, the S.D.S. dropped from its constitution the "exclusionist" clause which had denied eligibility for membership to "advocates or apologists" of "totalitarian principle."[11] Members of the Maoist Progressive Labor Party (PLP) were now eligible for S.D.S. membership. They streamed in *en masse,* accepting formally the libertarian non-organizational idea of "participatory democracy" but intending informally to take over control of the S.D.S. Many of the S.D.S. veterans were aware of the PLP's intentions and its demand to put students in the service of the American "working class" and they fiercely resisted these changes. They could not, however, resist the growing pressure from the local branches of their loose organization[12] to implement these ideas nor could they reject the illegitimizing power of the Marxian categories. Convinced that the system which allowed racial discrimination, poverty, and now, massive bombing to take place, was structurally corrupt, the veteran S.D.S. members searched independently for a new, symbolic frame of reference that would express their sense of illegitimacy toward the regime without succumbing to the growing pressures of the PLP.

Early in 1967, an influential group within the S.D.S. published a paper, entitled "Towards a Theory of Social Change in America,"[13] in which a theory of the "new working class" was formulated. Gregory Calvert, the president of S.D.S., elaborated on this new theory in a major policy speech at Princeton University. It was now suggested that students were *themselves* part of a "new working class" created and exploited by "this super-technological capitalism."[14] The former symbol of "corporate liberalism" was replaced by "corporate capitalism" ("American corporate capitalism is an incredibly brutal and dehumanizing system whether at home or abroad"). The system was now challenged not by radical democrats, but by the working class heading towards revolution. The gist of the new theory was that modern society has created a new proletariat composed of middle class and professional workers. This "new working class" was presented as *a class* not because of its peculiar relation to the means of production — a unifying relation depriving it of a decent means of living — but because of conditions of "unfreedom"[15] in society, conditions affecting deprived minorities, high-salaried, middle-class professionals, and students living in "factory-like multiversities."

Had Karl Marx ever heard Calvert's speech and his claim to be a Marxist he would have probably screamed aloud what it is told he once said, "I am not a Marxist." For indeed, the new theory and especially its conceptualization of a "new working class" which would bring on the inevitable revolution had almost no analytical relation with classical Marxism nor any considerable empirical support whatsoever. How could one seriously create a *class* out of such diverse groups and believe earnestly that such a class could carry out a revolution? The Marxian conceptual tools that the S.D.S. developed remained, as Tom Hayden noted in 1962, highly "outmoded" for diagnosing the American social, economic and political realities as well as the position of students in this world. *But in 1967 and 1968 the New Left did not need an analytically valid and reliable social theory. It needed a cultural system of symbols expressing a deep mood of illegitimacy towards the regime.* In the late nineteen-sixties, Marxism as a cultural system had come to provide the most prestigious symbols of this kind. When, in the summer of 1969, the S.D.S. split into three factions – each representing a different tactical and strategic perspective – they all had one thing in common: they presented their case in a militant Marxist language directed at what they considered a totally discredited and illegitimate political system.

THE CASE OF FRENCH STUDENTS
THE RE-MARXIZATION OF THE UNEF

A first look at France does not provide us with the same picture at all. The reason for this is that Marxism in France and the Marxist subculture remained relatively strong even in the hard season of the so-called "decline of ideology" period. The French extreme left, dominated by the Communist Party, remained very much Marxist and alive. Thus, the phenomenon of re-Marxization did not have to take place in France because France was not *de-Marxized* in the first place. It can also be said that the open conflict of legitimacy that is known to be built into the French political system and is expressed by the attitude of the French extreme left toward the regime did not decline significantly in the fifties, and consequently did not have to be revitalized in the sixties.

However, upon a closer examination, the picture is not so simple. What is revealed upon such an observation is that the process that developed in France during the nineteen-sixties was like that in the United States; a process of delegitimization of the establishment. But the establishment that was delegitimized in France was not so much the regime itself as the cultural and political antiregime, the Communist Party. What occurred in France was that within the French Left, there emerged a deep *gauchist* conflict of legitimacy expressed in a rejection of the official line of the party regarding its peaceful and reformist approach to internal and international politics. This process was to a great extent – though not exclusively – carried by small student groups (called *groupuscules*), of Trotskyite and Maoist leanings, which were not publicized sufficiently at the time.[16] Part of this process, which was about to produce the explosion of May 1968, could not literally be called symbolic Marxization because it took place within the French Marxist culture. But it had many behavioral characteristics of the same type. However, another part of this process had obvious characteristics of symbolic re-Marxization in it. The process referred to is the re-Marxization of the UNEF, the National Union of French Students.

The UNEF has long been a very active national student union. Since 1946 it even tried to associate itself with other labor organizations in France by defining in its *Charter of Grenoble* a student as "an intellectual worker."[17] However, it never developed a distinct student Marxist ideology and system of Marxist symbols even in those periods in the fifties when it was under the domination of communist and other leftist groups. It always stuck to democratic and legitimist symbolics of moderate syndicalism even when it entered into serious confrontations with the regime regarding student rights and demands. A typical statement by George Danton, the President of UNEF in 1958, at the beginning of the internal conflicts regarding the war in Algeria, may illustrate the case. It shows clearly UNEF's acceptance of the legitimacy of the present regime and its basic framework:

> ... if the UNEF must protest, it must also remain in a framework which is its own, namely the syndicalist framework. This is why we refused to associate ourselves with the political demonstrations organized by the political movements. ... But, if we have to remain calm, we also have to show in an unequivocal manner an attachment to the republican institutions and to the democratic liberties which are guaranteed by those institutions. Those liberties being themselves the only guarantees for the expression of a culture which is given to us by our university. ... In a democratic regime free syndicalism is one of the most confident guardians of the institutions. . .[18]

However, from 1959–1962 the UNEF had undergone an unprecedented experience. It became closely involved in the home phase of the Algerian War of Independence. This phase included massive demonstrations and protests against the War, violent confrontations with the police with the rightist OAS, and a sharp disagreement with the equivocal position of the Communist party towards the FLN. Certain leaders of the UNEF even took direct part in illegal underground activities.[19] Following that, the UNEF underwent a process similar to the one the American S.D.S. had undergone. It radicalized, coming under the ideological domination of its Sorbonne branch. What the young radicals, members of FGEL (Fédération des Groupes d'Etudes de Lettres) which dominated the UNEF, now needed, was not simply a social theory capable of explaining objectively their social life as students in France. Like the S.D.S. of 1966 and 1967, they looked for a cultural system of symbols capable of expressing their experience of intense protest, their sense of being radicals and revolutionaries. The most prestigious system of such symbols was of course the Marxist system. However, it had to be a special Marxist theory capable of providing a major role to the bourgeois students in the coming revolution in France. Such a theory was then composed and can be found in two long articles by Marc Kravetz and Antoine Griset – the leading theoreticians of FGEL – which appeared in *Les Temps Modernes* in February 1964 and in April and May 1965.[20] Within the UNEF this approach earned its proponents the title "La gauche syndicale."

The fundamental question before the young theoreticians was how to direct the thousands of students mobilized for direct political action into a struggle not only against the university's repressive structures, but also against the so-called French "neo-capitalist" society.

Had it not been for the last three years, FGEL's leaders, acting in the very dogmatic environment of French Marxism, might have had little choice but to accept the position of the Communist Party, which basically rejected the revolutionary role of students except insofar as they were members of the "revolutionary party" representing the French proletariat. But, after the war, in which the Algerian students played an important role, and after the Cuban revolution, which had been led by middle-class intellectuals and students, they saw the possibility of a different solution. They argued that the socialist revolutions in the colonial world, in which moral revolt created a *conscience révolutionaire* even in bourgeois students, proved that such a possibility existed even for French students.[21] The experience of the students in 1960–1962 demonstrated to them that, provided a real issue was found, a massive *prise de conscience* could take place and the French students could be mobilized to revolutionary action without having begun with a revolutionary (i.e., proletarian) consciousness.

The whole analysis of FGEL regarding the orientation of the UNEF and the French students thus became Marxist, by projecting the National Union as heading towards a socialist revolution. The UNEF could now compete equally with other student Marxist groups, Trotskyites, Maoists, Castroists, etc., that were developing quickly in the Latin Quarter of Paris.

It is true that FGEL's control of the UNEF did not last long and that it soon became just another grouplet struggling for the hegemony of the union. The significant fact remains however that since the period of its ideological domination, no non-Marxist grouplet could expect to win over the control of the national bureau.

When, in June of 1968, in the aftermath of the student explosion, a group representing many of the revolting students in the various French universities approved the "Charter of Nanterre," they phrased the first article in this language:

> Article I. The student movement is not only a response to police repression, nor is it a reaction to the inadequacies of education or to the difficulties involving job openings. It rejects the university which prevents it from penetrating the conflictual nature of social relations. Starting from questioning the university, the student movement aligns itself as rejecting a given type of society. It conceives its true dimensions by associating itself with the struggle of the workers against capitalist society.[22]

THE CASE OF SIAH (ISRAEL NEW LEFT)

In the perspective of the student protest movement of the nineteen-sixties, Israel's role was hardly significant because of its lack of protest movements at its universities, as had been seen in the West. There were various reasons for this inactivity. However, in the context of our argument, this is exactly the importance of the Israeli case. Israel is a country where significant symbolic re-Marxization did not take place. In the social sciences, as Max Weber once noted, we must study not only the cases that occurred, but also the cases that did not occur but could possibly have occurred. The story of Siah is then a case in point.

Siah is one of two Israeli leftist groups that became very active in promoting extraparliamentary politics in the aftermath of the Six Day War.[23] The other group is the Israeli Socialist Organization (better known as "Mazpen"). Since Mazpen may very well be seen as an Israeli leftist *groupuscule* that developed like some of the French grouplets within the Marxist milieu, its analysis is irrelevant in the present context. Siah emerged in the campuses in Jerusalem and Tel Aviv after the Six Day War. It was characterized by a strong resistance to the continuation of what it saw as the annexationist policy of the Israeli government. It also avowedly demanded the recognition of the rights of self-determination for the Palestinians. From its birth in

1968, Siah was clearly a protest group. Its members participated in many protests, demonstrations and other direct activities that took place between 1968 and 1972, and the very fact that its name was chosen in 1969 speaks for itself.[24]

The most significant point about Siah, in our comparative perspec- tive, is however, that unlike the protest movements that development in France and in the United States, the protest movement that developed in Israel never got very far. Unlike France, and the United States, Israel has never had anything close to Algeria, a Civil Rights struggle, or Vietnam. As a result *a serious process of radicalization leading to an intense conflict of legitimacy with the regime never took place.* Thus, when we examine the theoretical texts of Siah, its pamphlets, and when we interview its activists, we do not find a symbolic re-Marxiza- tion — that is — a forceful attempt to read the social context in Marxist terms at all cost. We do find among Siah activists a growing theoretical interest in Marxism as a philosophy and social theory. The two main branches of Siah in Tel Aviv and Jerusalem have, almost since their inception, established seminars for the study of the classics of Marxism and Marxist Zionism. However, as for the use of the Marxian categories for the description of the existing social relations in Israel, the Arab-Israel conflict and the future developments in the Middle East, it is found that most of Siah's activists are extremely cautious, critical and empirical. With very few exceptions, even most of the ex-communists among Siah's activists appear skeptical in this respect. They do not speak in slogans, they do not force the Israeli complex reality and the Israel-Arab conflict into a one-dimensional explanation of class contradictions and oil policies of the international imperialism. They also do not expect a *deus ex machina* proletarian Arab-Israel revolution to solve the conflict. All the Marxist symbolic activity that is so typical of a conflict of legitimacy with the regime is totally alien to Siah.

For various reasons which have to do with internal disagreements, among its activists, Siah never formulated a broad ideological state- ment. It only agreed publicly on one programmatic chapter, a chapter regarding the Arab-Israel conflict. In that one-page chapter approved by the Third National Convention of Siah in 1972, the group states that "Israel-Palestine is the territorial base for the realization of the self-determination of two nations . . . " the Jewish and the Palestinian. Siah severely criticizes the

> state of occupation characterized by *de facto* annexation, colonial settle-
> ment, accompanied by systematic expropriation of the Arab population,

increasing exploitation of cheap Arab labor in the Israeli economy, enrichment out of war profits and widening of the social and ethnic gap, militari-
zation of education and culture, growing aggression towards the democratic
liberties of oppositional elements, secular and clerical nationalism and
dangerous erosion in the personal values of the Israeli individual.[25]

This is indeed a serious criticism but, as we can see, it is not made
within a Marxist framework. Siah as a cohesive group never did enter
into a *conflict of legitimacy* with the regime. The most that could be
said about Siah is that at the height of its dissenting activities (which
have declined recently) it developed a serious *crisis of confidence* in
the regime. This crisis — as reflected in the deliberations of Siah's members — reminds one very much of the style and the manner of the
American New Left of 1963—1964. But while the American New Left
radicalized further, Siah, as a group, never did.

The main conclusion that is to be drawn from the example of Siah
in the comparative perspective presented here, is not that the Israelis
are more pragmatic and rational than the American and the French
radicals. The conclusion and the main argument of this paper is that
under certain circumstances of intense radicalization and deep crisis, a
process of symbolic re-Marxization is highly probable and it is happen-
ing not as a consequence of a theoretical need but of an emotional
one. The pressure of the emotional attitude of protest and total denunciation of the powers that be creates then a situation of a conflict
of legitimacy, and the result is an intense search for new and appropriate systems of symbols. A process of this nature took place in the
nineteen-sixties in the United States and in France. It did not develop
in Israel.

NOTES

1. The literature that has developed around the debate about the "end of ideology" is vast. Most helpful and representative of it is Ch. I. Waxman (editor), *The
End of Ideology Debate* (Funk and Wagnall, New York, 1968).

2. S. M. Lipset "Ideology and No End — The Controversy till Now," *Encounter*,
December 1972.

3. For an analytical critique of the "developmental pradigm of democracy" see
E. Sprinzak, *Democracy and Illegitimacy: A Study of the American and the
French Student Protest Movement and some Theoretical Implications*, unpub-
lished doctoral dissertation, Yale University, 1972, Chapter 1.

4. C. Geertz, "Ideology as a Cultural System," in D. Apter (editor), *Ideology and Discontent* (The Free Press of Glencoe, New York, 1964).

5. "SDS: Port Huron Statement," in M. Teodori (editor), *The New Left: A Documentary History* (Bobs-Merrill, New York, 1969), p. 167.

6. "The Port Huron Statement," SDS pamphlet, New York, 1964, pp. 46–47. (This section does not appear in Teodori's selection.)

7. Th. Hayden, "A Letter to the New (Young) Left," in M. Cohen and D. Hale (editors), *The New Student Left* (Beacon Press, Boston, 1968), p. 3.

8. *Ibid.*

9. *SDS Constitution,* 1963, Mimeographed pamphlet.

10. Those developments are described and analyzed in E. Sprinzak, *op. cit.,* Chapters 4, 5. See also J.P. O'Brien, *The Development of a New Left in the United States 1960–1965,* unpublished doctoral dissertation, University of Wisconsin, 1971, Chapters 3–9.

11. On the issue of nonexclusionism within SDS and the New Left cf. A. Haber, "Nonexclusionism: The New Left and the Democratic Left," in Teodori, *op. cit.,* pp. 218–228.

12. For an analysis of the struggles within SDS cf. A. Kopkind, "The Real SDS Stands Up," in H. Jacobs (editor), *Weatherman* (Ramparts Press, Inc., 1970).

13. D. Gilbert, R. Gottlieb and G. Tenny, "Towards a Theory of Social Change," in *New Left Notes,* January 23, 1967.

14. G. Calvert, "In White America: Radical Consciousness and Social Change," in Teodori, *op. cit.,* p. 416.

15. *Ibid.* p. 415.

16. For an analysis of the process of delegitimation of the *groupuscules* see E. Sprinzak, *op. cit.,* Chapter 6. Also R. Johnson, *The French Communist Party Versus the Students* (Yale University Press, New Haven, 1972), Chapters 4–6.

17. For a good analysis of the UNEF see A. Belden-Fields, *Student Politics in France* (Basic Books, New York, 1970), Chapters 2–4.

18. G. Danton, "All the Syndicates Stand up for the Defense of the Liberties," *L'Etudiant de France,* no. 6, April–May–June 1958, p. 1 (my translation).

19. Cf. A. Belden-Fields, *op. cit.*, pp. 38–39.

20. M. Kravetz "Naissance d'un Syndicalisme Etudiant," *Les Temps Modernes,* February 1964; Antoine Griset and Marc Kravetz "De l'Algérie à la réforme Fouchet: Critique du Syndicalisme Etudiant (I–II)," *Les Temps Modernes,* April 1965, May 1965.

21. Griset and Kravetz *op. cit.* (II), pp. 2070–71.

22. "Convention Nationale des Universités de France, Chartre" in A. Schnapp, Vidal-Naquet (editors), *Journal de la Commune Etudiante* (Editions du Seuil, Paris, 1964), p. 737.

23. For general information and analysis of the post-1967 extraparliamentary politics in Israel, see E. Sprinzak, *The Emergence of Politics of Delegitimacy in Israel 1967–1972,* mimeographed (Levy Eshkol Institute, The Hebrew University of Jerusalem, 1974.) (Hebrew).

24. E. Sprinzak, *op. cit.*, Chapter 5.

25. *Siah's Highlights* (pamphlet), 15 July 1972.

MARXISM IN LATIN AMERICA

HUGH THOMAS
Reading University

The most substantial contribution of Latin America to the mainstream of European ideology sometimes seems to have been the provision of red shirts for Garibaldi's volunteers in Uruguayan wars: hence, ultimately, the black, brown, blue and other shirts worn by European fascists. There is an element of poetic justice in this: Latin America, a politically stable, and, except for certain freak areas, an economically stable continent until the 1920s, has provided the world with much more material than ideas. Coffee and bananas, gold and silver, copper and tin, oil and sugar: the history of Latin America is the history of commodities, not of ideas. On the other hand, it has often received ideas, if only by imitation. Though there may not be a Latin American Marxism, there have been, and there are, many Latin American Marxists.

Marx and Engels were ignorant of Latin America. Marx has admittedly some superficial and contemptuous passages about Bolivar and about the Third Empire's intervention in Mexico. Engels knew nothing, however, about the South American Indian civilization when he wrote *The Origins of the Family, Private Property and the State;* and Marx's son-in-law, Lafargue, a Cuban, showed little interest in the island where he was born.

The first movements of social protest in Latin America were anarchist rather than Marxist. Anarchism came to the continent through the Spanish workers who, in far greater numbers than ever before, even during the height of the Empire, flocked to South America in the last quarter of the 19th century and the first quarter of this century. Wages were far higher in Havana, or Buenos Aires, or Montevideo than they were in Spain, and there was also the possibility of moving up into the shopkeeper class. In Spain too anarchism was the dominant movement of working-class protest and the Latin American workers' movement depended on the mother country, even though formal links between the Spanish government and the new republics were tenuous, and though there was not much cultural interchange either. Latin American workers anxious to challenge the system assumed that anarchism (or anarchosyndicatism after 1910) was the best, perhaps the only way.

It is not necessary to explore very far to find the reason for this anarchist affiliation. It was purely imitative. In Spain itself, explanations include: the politicization of rural banditry, the federalist tradition in the petty bourgeoisie, and the desertion of the land by the Church.

What needs some explanation is why the Spanish social democratic movement, self-avowedly Marxist up till at least 1919, had no Latin American colonies, so to speak. The fact was that that movement was relatively small until after World War I (200,000 perhaps to the anarchists, 700,000 or so in 1919). It was concentrated in Castile, particularly Madrid; whereas most emigrants to the New Word came from Galicia, the Basque country and Catalonia.

There were one or two self-styled followers of Marx before 1914 in South America: but when the minuscule Socialist Labor party of Puerto Rico was formed in 1899, and came out "frankly in favor of the international program of Karl Marx," one of its subsequent leaders, Santiago Iglesias, was right in saying that the members "had not seriously considered these principles, nor had they read and studied these ideals. In those days, Socialism was, for the workers of Puerto Rico, a doctrine much like the doctrine of emancipation preached by Jesus Christ . . . it was an intuitive idealization of justice and well-being. It meant more bread for the hungry, higher wages, and fewer hours of work. It meant civil, social (and) human liberation."[1] There was, however, an Argentinian socialist, Juan Just, who translated Marx into Spanish before 1914, and who was the center of a small group of socialists who later became Bernsteinists.

These things changed as elsewhere with World War I and the Russian Revolution. In the years after 1917 a number of small communist groups branched off from the anarchists and became reorganized by the Comintern as, for example, the Communist party of the Argentine (1920), Mexico (1919), Uruguay (1921), Chile (1921), Brazil (1921) and Cuba (1925). None of these parties had more than 2,000 members before 1929. All were faction ridden. Most had a large percentage of new immigrants among their members (Italian, Spanish and East European immigrants flowed without restriction into South America in the 1920s). Thus it was entirely typical that, at the founding meeting of the Cuban Communist party, the Mexican Comintern representative, Flores Magón, had to have an interpreter present to translate into Yiddish; that the *eminence grise* of that party in the early years was a Polish Jewish immigrant, Fabio Grobart (still a member of Castro's Central Committee of the Communist party in the 1970s); and that the powerful secretary general of the Argentine party, Codovila, should be an Italian immigrant. (It might perhaps be appropriate to underline the very mixed origin of modern Latin America: the continent may be Spanish or Portuguese in culture and politics, but, in addition to the substantial Indian or Negro minorities, Italians, Germans, modern Spanish, Central Europeans and Chinese make a substantial contribution. This side of things was expressed vividly in the Chilean elections of 1970 when the successful candidate Salvador Allende was seen to have a German mother — he was Allende y Goossens —, his defeated conservative opponent was Alessandri, grandson of an Italian, the Christian democrat Tomic was a first-generation Croat; while his predecessor, Dr. Frei, was Swiss in origin.)

Perhaps this is a good moment to mention the gifted Peruvian Marxist, Mariateguí (1895–1930) whose *Siete Ensayos de Interpretación de la Realidad Peruana* (1926) is often regarded as the most original Marxist contribution in South America. Mariateguí was cultivated, travelled and of a sceptical temperament.

During the depression, the anarchists were largely ousted by communists in most countries as Latin America's chief revolutionary group. Leadership passed in many countries to young intellectuals, rather than workers' leaders. (The details of the eclipse of the anarchists are obscure and would benefit from a careful study.) Also significant was the almost complete absence of any social democrat movement. There were many people who, in Latin America, shared the aims of European social democratic parties and the English Labor party, to seek humane social change through democratic means. But they were not organized. I suspect this reflects not only the internal political circumstances of the continent, in which military dictatorships concentrated the mind of their opponents on the simple necessity to overthrow tyrants, and leave the character of the subsequent regime to be decided later, but also the external political (and economic) circumstances of ever greater U.S. influence. If the U.S.A. had developed a democratic labor movement, no doubt South American countries could have done so also. As it was, however, the main parties of South America in those countries which were democratic, had more in common with the Republican or Democratic parties than with any European models. Here one sees again a certain cultural imitativeness. (The U.S.A. had had, of course, an influence in South America for many years; in most countries the very constitutions were a reflection of that of the U.S. For example, everywhere the President was the head of government and nowhere did he have to attend meetings of his legislature.) Another influence was Mexico, where a social revolution had followed the armed revolution and civil war of the 1912–1919 years. Social reformers could look to the achievements and experiments of the Mexicans including their disassociation from "U.S. imperialism" to suggest a colorless but effective type of social engineering which could surely be copied. Hence the preoccupation with agrarian reform in most Latin American countries to this day, regardless of the size and the character of the landholding concerned.

The depression hit Latin America hard, particularly Argentina, Cuba, Chile, Bolivia, Uruguay, which by means of intensive capital investment (including substantial and usually dominant foreign investment) in a single product (beet, sugar, copper, wool, oil) had made substantial economic advances in the preceding generation. The average wage in Cuba in the 1920s, for example, probably the richest Latin American country, was about half that in the U.S. or two-thirds that of Britain. But, in the 1930s, the collapse of international commerce made it economically unprofitable even to grind cane, dig up copper or tin. Unemployment was severe. Communist parties thrived in the underused sugar mills, tin and copper mines, ports and railways. So did, for the first time, parties self-confessedly Marxist and revolutionary, which sprang up in the universities and which neither sought nor gained Moscow's approval. All these parties played quite an important part in the political history of the middle and late 1930s. In many countries the communists emerged as the leading influence in the trade unions, however small their actual numbers. In the late 1930s the Good Neighbor policy of Roosevelt (basically a scheme to avoid the U.S. military intervention in the affairs of Latin America and Caribbean states which has characterized the last 30 years) on the one hand, and the Popular Front policy of the Comintern on the other, had the effect of making communist parties in Latin America almost respectable, giving them in some countries an acknowledged role in the trade union movement, and in some (Chile, Cuba) even allowing communists briefly to enter coalition governments. This collaborationist period was in some ways creative. Thus in Cuba, between 1938 and 1944, the Communist party played a prominent part in working out the democratic constitution of 1940, framing a new social code which decisively tipped the balance of economic power towards the unions. They also helped in preparing the ground for the gradual re-Cubanization (though not nationalization) of the sugar industry. This interesting period lasted throughout World War II and up till about 1947. It had manifestations virtually everywhere in Latin America. After 1947, the cold war made such collaboration impossible. The communist parties everywhere drew in on themselves, their membership dropped and became secret and, although usually not persecuted, they were not to be found in any prominent position in public life, though of course leaders remained and party members were to be found in such professions as teachers, university professors or railway workers. An exception was Mexico, where the Communist party, partly through the international fame of such painters as Siqueiros, Orozco, and Rivera (all of whom were more or less communists for a time, the first of them being even secretary general of the party) enjoyed a privileged position among intellectuals, the more secure since it had no chance whatever of making headway against the ruling Institutional Revolutionary party (P.R.I.). In return, there were a great many people, particularly intellectuals, who regarded themselves as Marxists though not communists. If the matter is pursued, it would probably turn out that all such people were what Popper describes as "vulgar Marxists": that is, they were men (and women) who accepted the social implications of Marx's writings, believed that economics was the determining drive of history (particularly of the attitude of the U.S. to the continent) and had a general respect for a conspiracy theory of politics; if all the facts were known, all political parties would be shown to be the instruments or executives of economic interests. But such people would not regard politicians as the *blind* instruments of economic forces; nor would they necessarily accept the view that historical change in the direction of proletarian revolution was inevitable. They would not necessarily distrust social engineering. This pragmatic Marxism spilled over in most countries from the universities into the arts; and many painters or poets regarded themselves as Marxists without having ever really read a word of Marx. Still, it is what people call themselves that is important; the Bulgarians think of themselves as Slavs, the Egyptians as Arabs; and the world accepts these designations. So too, it has accepted the claim of Neruda or Nicolas Guittén to be Marxists.

In some countries these "Marxists" or "Marxisantes" had a political grouping of sorts. The most notable example was Chile where a Socialist party had grown up which was definitely "Marxist" and "revolutionary" but distanced itself, on the issue of Russian direction, from the communist party as such. In addition, there were a number of South American political parties which like Democratic Action (Venezuela), APRA (Peru) and even the Autenticos of Ortodoxos

(Cuba) had some elements of Marxism within them. What do I mean by that? I think that I meant to suggest that one or two leaders of the parties concerned (Betancourt in Venezuela) had once been communists, still sometimes used Marxist jargon and, perhaps more specifically, regarded it as a matter of urgency not only to overthrow military tyrants but also to carry out with effect some measure of social reform. (Haya de la Torre, the founder of the influential APRA was a "Marxist" in his youth.) The trouble was partly that if one troubled to read Marx even superficially, it would be obvious that what he predicted was not relevant to a still largely agricultural continent; and that even where the proportion of workers in agriculture was falling below 50%, the persons concerned were going not into industry, but more often than not into service of some sort – the tertiary sector which Marx neglected.

In the 1950s South American Marxism would not have needed much more historical definition than I have already given it. It is true that the cold war had already made of the U.S. once again the monster of the north rather than the good neighbor that it had been in the early 1940s. Political leaders who had come forward as radicals in the thirties had now, with power, become conservative democrats whom the population explosion and the communications revolution of the 1950s were passing by.

Though American political power was operated much less explicitly in the 1950s than, say, in the 1920s, and economic interests were changing, U.S. cultural influence was ever more aggressive through such things as the Spanish editions of *Life, Time,* or *Readers Digest.* A more important factor was that many countries were economically stagnant in the 1950s, particularly after the end of the Korean war: international demand for minerals was less acute, other and artificial sources of supply were opening up, while population growth was making the actual living conditions probably less promising in the 1950s than in the 1940s, though immensely better than in the 1930s. Still, South America is one area of the world where the theory of greater misery seemed to be valid.

Two or three political events of considerable importance locally lacked much continental resonance; thus the Bolivian revolution of 1952 which destroyed the big landowners and tin miners remained a Bolivian affair par excellence. The crushing of the Guatemalan revolutionary government in 1954 by a section of the army, helped by the CIA, passed without much protest, though those present (who included Guevara, the Argentinian "Marxist" who later joined Castro) drew the conclusion that no program of social reform would be allowed to go unchallenged by the U.S.A. On the other hand, the overthrow of the Venezuelan dictatorship in 1958 and the emergence of Betancrant's democratic regime seemed to suggest a general democratic movement as possible in the Caribbean (Figueres in Costa Rica, Múnoz Marin in Puerto Rico, even Bosch in the Dominican Republic were the other leading figures in this development). What changed all this was the decisive alteration in the political situation brought about by the Cuban revolution.

Castro, a middle-class liberal with largely urban petty bourgeois followers, made a successful challenge to Batista's corrupt tyranny. This challenge was less a civil war than an armed political campaign, with much attention paid to liberal opinion in the U.S. as well as in Cuba, carried out by armed men who set themselves up in hilly country. The Cuban communists held off, but some of the "Marxists" of the country (many of them previously grouped in the Orthodox movement) supported Castro from the start. Once he had captured power in Havana, Castro came under the influence of the self-confessed "Marxist" Guevara, and Raúl Castro, his brother, who had been a member of the communist youth movement. Both men urged the leader to use the old Cuban Communist party to carry out the proposed nationalist revolution. As a result, after many intricate dealings and quarrels, in a few years Castro emerged as "maximum leader" of a Cuban communist party, which, though it included the older communists, was actually dominated by Castro's friends who themselves proclaimed themselves Marxist-Leninists. Castro even explained in one famous speech that he had always been a Marxist and had got as far as page 262 of *Das Kapital* at his university; he hoped one day to finish it. Actually, there is little of the Marxist in Castro. He has a strong social conscience and a contempt for bourgeois institutions. But otherwise he seems a traditional South American caudillo or military leader, more honest and hard working than most, and much more occupied by practical questions of agricultural management than any Marxist. It is true that one prominent old communist, Carlos Rafael Rodríguez, "a good Marxist" it is said (by which I understand to mean an educated economist), has been of great use to the Castroist regime. In addition, the nation has been culturally Marxistized and education is certainly "Marxist-Leninist" by which I mean that appeals to what Marx or Engels said are often made in textbooks and there is a general economic-conspiratorial attitude in history. But even that is qualified by heroic nationalism — a glorification of the heroes of Cuba's two wars of independence against Spain and of all fighters against the various dictators of the 20th century, not only communists such as

Mella, Martinez, Villena or Pablo de la Torrenti Brau; but also radicals
such as Chiba, Guiteras or Echevarria (a Christian democratic leader
killed under Batista). Nevertheless Cuba's communist regime is plainly
South America's most obviously important contribution to Marxism
in practice. If we compare it with other Marxist countries, there are
the following points of difference:

1. the now united party of old communists and Castroists is smaller in
   numbers than other parties in, say, Eastern Europe;
2. the regime has abandoned its early attempt at industrialization
   and, possibly under Russian direction, has concentrated on good
   agricultural crops, particularly sugar;
3. as concomitants of this, much play has been made of the desir-
   ability of reversing the international trend towards concentrating
   populations in capitals: it is doubtful whether this has actually been
   achieved, though no doubt the imbalance in the availability of education and health in town and country has been reversed;
4. as a result of the virtual lack of manufactured goods, the government has had a prolonged experiment with moral incentives as reward for work and has even gone far to proclaim the virtues of
   poverty and a moneyless economy. Guevara, the Marxist of 1960,
   became the advocate of the New Man in 1965 before going off to
   be killed in Bolivia in 1969, trying to start a continent-wide civil
   war against the U.S. and her friends. This approach has been modified in the last year or so, more consumer goods are available,
   higher wages are being paid and the continential guerrilla has been
   dropped. The economy is in better shape in 1974 than it was in
   1970, due to the rise in the international price of sugar, from which
   Cuba has however been unable to benefit fully because of her already existing commercial agreement with Russia;
5. the army has played a greater part in the Cuban regime than in any
   other communist country. As the only effective and reliable national institution it seems to have a stranglehold over agriculture. The
   Central Committee of the Communist Party formed in 1965, and not
   changed since except by "death or disgrace," had some 70% senior
   army officers as members. This is an institutional reflection of the
   militaristic flavor of the regime; Castro and his politicians appear
   customarily in uniform and nationalistic propaganda emphasizes the
   constant need to be on the watch against the U.S. invader. (Actually there has been no such danger for 12 years and very few Cuban
   soldiers have had any combat experience although they had dabbled
   in it in Bolivia, Congo, Zanzibar and even on the Golan Heights, it
   seems);

6. the personal position of Castro as "maximum leader" has been of comparable significance to Cuba as that of Mao, Stalin or Tito: we have not yet attained the institutional stage of the revolution (Castro is still under 50). Like Stalin and the others mentioned, and like all charismatic leaders of the century, he has imposed much of his own style on his country and its ideology. This takes the form of an appearance at least of improvization and spontaneity; Castro still arives 2 or 3 hours late for appointments, he still seems to move around from house to house, he still seems to have no settled home life;

7. there have been one or two other semiinstitutional innovations, the most important being the so-called Committees for the Defence of the Revolution (CDRS), partly neighborhood snooping committees, partly means of participation of the masses in government.

The impact of Cuba on South American Marxism was first of all and most important to give encouragement to all who think that if so apparently strong a regime as Batista, so close to the U.S., could be overthrown then there could be hope for any armed rebellion. Castro's political skill in "holding out" against the U.S. for 15 years is also naturally admired in a continent where the *macho* virtues of courage and manliness are prized. (There are many right-wing South Americans also who seem to admire Castro's success against such conventional Russian-type communists as Aníbal Escalante actually supported by Russia.) So the immediate consequence was a shot in the arm for the idea of the "armed struggle" as a means of gaining power. Rather reluctantly, the old communist parties of the continent, composed (just as the Cuban party had been) of leaders active in the "struggle" since the 1930s and therefore middle-aged men in general, gave these ideas their blessing to begin with. Violent left-wing movements, with Marxist phraseology and mainly middle-class membership, were founded almost everywhere (for details see Richard Gott, *Guerilla Movements in Latin America*).

These movements of the early 1960s were different from Castro's before he came to power in two ways; *first,* they made deliberately revolutionary appeals, whereas Castro had appealed to a broad consensus of liberal opinion in fighting a dictatorship. Admittedly that approach was difficult for revolutionaries such as those operating in Venezuela — which had a near civil war in the early 1960s — who were fighting against a fairly elected popular Democratic Action government with considerable peasant support; *secondly,* they were more genuine rural guerillas than Castro and his friends had been. For Castro was always a politician in the Sierra Maestra operating at several levels of which the guerilla was only one, and, except for some battles in 1958, not the most important one; the guerillas in Peru, Guatemala, Colombia, Venezuela, Argentina of the 1960s were of people convinced of the validity of, and even in some cases, of the purifying effect of war. On the other hand, almost everywhere guerilla operations had some local characteristics: thus Douglas Bravo, the Venezuelan guerilla leader in Falcón province (still active there I believe), was a member of a family which had for many years been fighting the local Montagues. Further, most "rural" guerilleros were actually townspeople seeing in their commitment to the underdeveloped countryside a means of purification. (cf. the Kibbutz?). Agrarian reform played a major part in their programs.

One additional point to explain the attractiveness of the "armed struggle" in Latin America in the 1960s: It is not always realized that Latin America has been far and away the most peaceful of the continents over the last five centuries. It took part only very marginally in the two world wars (a Brazilian unit fought at Monte Cassino), there have been only two major wars between the republics (the Pacific war of the 1880s, the Chaco war of the 1930s), and, of civil conflicts, only the Colombian troubles of the 1950s, the Mexican Revolution, the Cuban Independence Wars of the 1870s and 1890s, and the Wars of Independence 1810–1825 have killed not more than a few thousand at most. (The Cuban war between Castro and Batista probably killed less than 2,000).

Meanwhile, once the orthodox communist parties of the republics observed that, as they had suspected, the new armed struggles were not being very quickly successful, they went back to their traditional posture of cautious parliamentarianism, an attitude much approved of by the Soviet Union. Hence the many difficulties between the Castro government, the communist parties, the revolutionaries and Russia. Several interesting theoretical arguments followed, in which a French Marxist, Debray, made an interesting contribution to his book on the theory of guerilla warfare *Revolution in the Revolution* – a sequel to Guevara's textbook of guerilla warfare published in 1960. In the middle of the crisis, Guevara was killed in Bolivia leading his Cuban soldiers. The dramatic circumstances of that event obscured the failure of the expedition. Guevara became a cult/hero overshadowing Castro. He seemed to stand for a variety of Marxism which was, first, less material than that offered by Russia and implicitly accepted by Castro; second, more militant; third, more immediately likely to lead to the final stage of communism rather than remain permanently fixed in the dictatorship of the proletariat. The basic text for Guevarism is his essay,

Socialism and the New Man, which had as large a success in Europe as in Latin America. This "Guevarism" was further enhanced by Castro's endorsement of the Russian humiliation of Czechoslovakia, by the persecution of the poet Padilla (both in 1968), and rather tortuous further quarrels between Castro and the surviving Latin American guerilla movements.

Allende's election to the presidency in Chile in 1970 and his over-throw in 1973 were the most recent crucial events in the history of Latin American Marxism. The Chilean Socialist Party was Marxist, not social-democratic; but its leader came to power at the head of a coali-tion of forces of which the socialists were only one, admittedly im-portant, group. Allende had also behind him radicals who bore a marked resemblance to the French party of that name – they split very easily and formed a part of almost every recent government; the orthodox communists; some breakaway left-wing Christian democrats; and, unimportant electorally but significant politically, a group of revolutionaries called the MIR – the Left Revolutionary Movement, composed chiefly of students or ex-students who had grown up in the 1960s in the standard guerilla tradition (some ex-communists too). Allende, an experienced parliamentarian, announced that he, unlike Castro, was determined to follow a peaceful road to socialism. Now here we enter a very contemporary situation since Chile is now an important side issue in European politics. But despite his past, Allende clearly defined socialism by conventional Marxist or communist terms – "I have reached this office in order to bring about the economic and social transformation of Chile . . . our objective is total, scientific, Marxist socialism," Allende to Regis Debray, *Conversations with Allende* (London, 1971), p. 118. He was interested in getting his goal, it seems to me, by democratic means (cf. Gotlwald); but he made it no secret that, when a socialist regime was in power, it would abolish the bourgeois parliament and courts. The free press and television services were certain to go too; this was to be accompanied by wide-scale nationalization and expropriations of both industry and agriculture. All this was indeed begun. Since 50% of the population were against this policy, a political crisis was inevitable. Allende, having destroyed the democratic consensus, was forced to bring the army into politics. This Trojan horse ultimately destroyed him, at a moment when his numerous democratic opponents were, as he knew, powerless to do so.

The tragic *denouement* of Allende's regime, and the severe military repression that has followed, should not disguise the fact that Allende's democratic road was probably leading to totalitarian social-ism, not to a prolongation of democratic socialism. To the end Allende and many of his followers believed that that form of government was the only one to ensure the social change in Chile that they thought desirable. But social change had been begun many years before and, so far as social conscience is concerned, there is not much to make one think that Allende and his team felt more strongly than their Christian Democratic successors: they differed from them about tactics, not morals.

At the time of Allende's overthrow, there was controversy in England as elsewhere and, in a letter to the *Times*, I wrote to suggest that despite the fable of a democratic road to socialism, Allende's overthrow signaled a defeat not for democratic socialism but for Marxist socialism. That still seems to be self-evident, though it is not an interpretation which finds favor among even the majority of English democratic socialists; whom I conclude are either more ignorant or less democratic than they pretend.

Perhaps it would be desirable to summarize the present situation. One Marxist regime, Cuba, survives, though still isolated. Communist parties exist in all the other republics, some open and active though not very effective (as in Venezuela), most clandestine. The clandestinity has been the consequence of the imposition of military regimes in most countries, that is itself caused largely by the apparent threat of revolutionary Marxist groups. (Democracy in Brazil was overthrown in 1964 because President Goalart welcomed Guevara there, the democracy in Peru in 1967 because President Belaunde seemed ineffective. The military regime in Peru has some pretensions to a socialist nationalist approach in the style of Nasser.) At the moment, there are only three working democracies in this subcontinent: Venezuela, whose stability seems quite assured because of its oil resources; Columbia, whose old-fashioned parliamentary politics must be regarded as vulnerable; and Costa Rica. Mexico is formally a democracy but the same party has been in power for 30 years and the countryside has given birth in the years since 1968 (date of a famous clash between students and army just before the Olympic Games) to a major insurrectional movement. Argentina, despite Perón, seems at the mercy of desperate guerilla groups, some of them proclaiming themselves to be Marxists, though Marx himself would be assuredly shocked by these gangsters who use his name. In Uruguay, a feeble democracy was also debilitated by the Tupamaru kidnappers who thereby let in the army. All these guerilla groups have in common three things: a revolutionary message; considerable vagueness about, or ignorance of, ideology; and a belief that the existing social structure is so bad it justifies violence. On the other hand, some work done by me on political gangsterism in

Cuba in the late 1940s and early 1950s has made me somewhat skeptical of the profundity of social consciences among some of these radically named parties of the 1970s in Argentina and elsewhere; if you drive around in a large car filled with machine gunners raiding banks and kidnapping Americans and killing policemen, you have to do more than call yourself the Marxist Liberation Front to satisfy the world that you know much of the dialectic. Some are sustained in the struggle by a sense of historic inevitability, others by the gloomy truth that, practically speaking, Latin America has become polarized and more desperate over the last ten years in consequence of guerilla activity. The counterinsurgency courses offered by the U.S. at Panama, the fright of the national bourgeoisies in consequence of the Cuban revolution, have unhappily made authoritarianism more effective and the possibility of democratic compromise less likely.

This broad conspectus of the present situation ignores one group, the MAS (the Movement towards Socialism) of Venezuela, composed partly of ex-guerillas, partly of ex-orthodox communists. This seems to be the most interesting of existing Marxist parties if only because the leaders (José Vicente Rangel, Pompeyo Marquez, Toedoro Petkoff) are all men who have been through the "armed struggle" and have seen its futility. They contested the last presidential election in Venezuela in 1973 and alone of the parties avoided the traditional Venezuelan political party's demand for the nationalization of the oil companies. It is possible that this group will be a considerable force in the next few years, particularly, of course, if the ruling Democratic Action Party fails to make realistic progress in the redistribution of resources.

NOTE

1. Quoted in: Luis Aguitor, *Marxism in Latin America,* 1968, p. 76.

APPENDIX

GEORGE LICHTHEIM – IN MEMORIAM

SHLOMO AVINERI
The Hebrew University of Jerusalem

George Lichtheim was born in 1912 in Berlin, and spent a few years as a child in Constantinople, where his father, Richard Lichtheim, was at that time representing the Zionist Organization in the capital of the declining Ottoman Empire. Like many of his colleagues in the early Zionist movement, Richard Lichtheim came from a highly assimilated Jewish-German family, and his conversion to Zionism was rooted in the universalist ethos of 19th-century Central European liberalism. These seemingly conflicting convictions of his father – a universalism embedded in an historical awareness of the meaning of particularism – were central to the ideas that were to emerge in George's own writings.

It was the richness of the Central European intellectual Jewish tradition that formed the spiritual background of George Lichtheim's early years. Despite the Zionist background at home, George came in his student days in the 1920/30s under the influence of the dissident Marxist ideas of the German *Sozialistische Arbeiter-Partei:* his favorite political authors were Karl Korsch and Franz Borkenau. After the Nazis came to power he spent a brief period in London and then, between 1934 and 1945, he lived in Jerusalem, where he worked for the *Palestine Post.* When the war was over, he was sent to cover the Nuremberg Trials for the *Post,* traveled widely in Europe and subsequently settled in London.

His Jerusalem years were far from easy: though they were intellectually perhaps the most stimulating years of his life, he felt basically out of place. The company he kept in Jerusalem was as exciting as it was unique: he was involved in a literary-cultural circle that included, among others, the historian of Jewish mysticism and messianism Gershom Scholem, the historian of science Shmuel Sambursky, the

Egyptologist H. J. Polotsky and many other Jerusalem luminaries. It was the cream of the German-Jewish intellectual elite that found its way in those years to Jerusalem and they adopted George despite his much younger age. Nonetheless he felt constricted in Jerusalem, the immiment Arab-Jewish conflict depressed him, and despite his deep feeling for Israel he ultimately felt at home in Hampstead much more than in Zion.

I have dwelt at some length on this unusual background of Lichtheim because he was an unusual person, not easy to fit into neat categories, often perplexing and sometimes extremely irritating. He could be simultaneously conversant in a number of cultures — but belonged to none. German by education, he felt abhorrence at Germany and in his later years had little sympathy for the philistinism of the *Bundesrepublik;* Jewish by background, he felt that Zionism, despite all of its historical justification in the age of nationalism, was too parochial for his truly catholic intellect; English by adoption, he felt that Britain too was going down the drain and that he himself was upholding the ideas of English liberalism much more than the English society in whose midst he was living. The perpetual pilgrim, the committed yet alienated intellectual, the Wandering Jew, Lichtheim always remained a free-lancer, living by his wit, unattached and unaffiliated, a rarity in the second half of the 20th century — the private scholar. Despite occasional short spells at a few universities, he rejected the many offers that came his way from various universities and research institutes. The consequent necessity of living by his pen sometimes affected the quality of his writing: but by and large his ability to sustain over a relatively long period of time the steady stream of informed, intelligent, sparkling and witty writing still stands out as an unusual achievement, almost without parallel in our present age.

For George Lichtheim straddled the gap between high-class journalism and academic writing in a unique way, being much more the 19th-century *littérateur* in the style of de Tocqueville, Mill (and Marx) than a 20th-century academic geared to the distinction between "journalism" and "research"; I am sure that had he chosen to write about this arbitrary dichotomy, he would have come up with a typically iconoclastic piece that would have shattered many a sacred cow in the groves of academe. He was not, however, himself totally immune to the value judgement inherent in the distinction: for many years he sheltered his journalistic pieces behind the pseudonym of "G. L. Arnold," and only with the publication and success of his *Marxism* did he drop this defensive device and sign all his writings (except, of course, the necessarily anonymous contributions to the *TLS*) with his true name. It was as if he did feel reconciled to his self again only with the publication of a "serious" study.

I still consider *Marxism* to be his major work, despite his many important later writings. Published in 1961, it was this book more than any other that reestablished the academic respectability of dealing with Marxism as an intellectual and historical phenomenon, rescuing it from the jejeune apologetics of orthodox Marxists as well as the no less arid polemics of its Cold War opponents. Here was a work that could integrate Marx's intellectual achievement into the fabric of Western philosophy and culture while at the same time pointing out its historical limitations. This ability to see the enormous importance of Marxism as well as see through it was perhaps connected with Lichtheim's own ambivalent attitude to bourgeois society itself: nobody could be a more typical product of the High Culture of the European bourgeoisie, and one facet of this upbringing was the critical faculty that led him to embrace socialism as part of this heritage. Yet despite all this attachment to the social vision of Marx (if not to his analysis), one would be hard pressed to classify Lichtheim, the author of *Marxism,* as a "Marxist" in any of the many accepted senses of the term. The world which Marx envisaged moving towards socialism was itself shattered beyond repair in 1914, 1917, 1933, and 1939. For Lichtheim the bourgeois world was dead, but it did not die the way that Marx had forecast for it; with its violent death under the impact of world war, bolshevism, fascism and modern techological horror, the dream that was nascent in this bourgeois world – the dream of Marx – was also affected, probably mortally affected.

Hence Lichtheim's growing pessimism, not only on a personal level, which led to his suicide in London in 1973 – but also on a general cultural level. Hence his distaste for the various bastardizations of Marxism, be it at the hands of New Left students, whose ignorance of history he saw as a New Barbarism masquerading as an intellectual vision, or at the hands of Third World dictators for whose antics he had as much patience as Marx had in his days for the mixture of petty tyranny, chauvinism and quasi-social rhetorics symbolized by the *Bas Empire* of Napoleon III. Hence also his quest for path-breaking attempts to apply the traditional categories leading from Kant through Hegel to Marx to contemporary reality: his Introduction to a new English reprint of Baillie's translation of Hegel's *Phenomenology* has a whiff of this; and his great admiration for Habermas and his attempt to bridge some of the traditional epistemological dichotomies between "theory" and "practice," i.e. between philosophical cognition and sociohistorical action, has also to be seen in this context.

In a world of academic overspecialization sometimes devoid of intellectual commitment and political enthusiasm sometimes innocent of knowledge, George Lichtheim was an oasis. He may not have left disciples. But he left all of us impoverished by his tragic decision to depart from this world which he made so much more intelligible to so many of us.